D0680097

# Psychology

## A Complete GCSE Course

Ⓛ

The Lutterworth Press

The Lutterworth Press
P.O. Box 60
Cambridge
CB1 2NT

**website:** www.lutterworth.com
**e-mail:** publishing@lutterworth.com


British Library Cataloguing in Publication Data:
A catalogue record is available from the British Library


ISBN 0 7188 3002 4

Copyright © Geoffrey Shoesmith, 2003

Printed in the United Kingdom by
Athenaeum Press

To Sharon, Hannah and Esther

# Foreword

It would be more accurate to call this book Two Complete Psychology Courses because the lessons inside cover both of the two GCSE Psychology specifications available in England, Northern Ireland and Wales, published by the AQA and the OCR examination boards. Some lessons are common to both specifications but others are dedicated to one board or the other, so it is important to follow the lessons for one or the other if you intend taking the GCSE exam. The Introduction tells you which lessons are to be followed for each board.

The book can be used by students in college or school, or by home-based students. There is a separate introduction for each of these. The Introduction also guides you to tutor support if you want to study from home.

If you are a general reader who just wants to learn about the basic principles of psychology and not take any exams then you can work through the lessons as you please. There is a separate Introduction for the general reader too.

Finally, teachers will find a separate Introduction that explains how this book can be used in the classroom and lecture theatre.

I do hope you enjoy using the book and wish you every success if you are taking the exam.

Geoffrey Shoesmith

# Contents

# HOW TO USE THIS BOOK

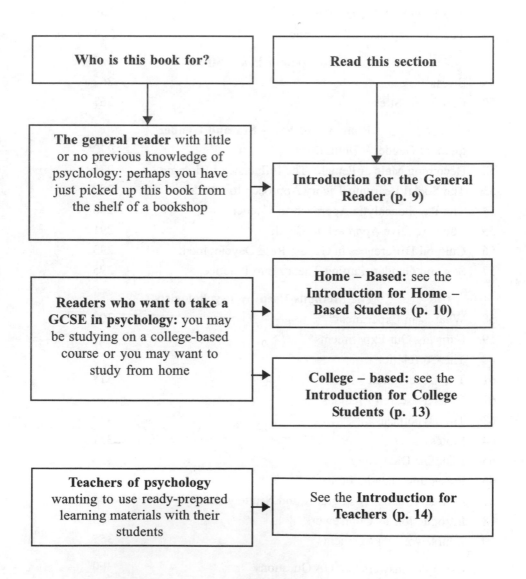

| Who is this book for? | Read this section |

**The general reader** with little or no previous knowledge of psychology: perhaps you have just picked up this book from the shelf of a bookshop → **Introduction for the General Reader (p. 9)**

**Readers who want to take a GCSE in psychology:** you may be studying on a college-based course or you may want to study from home →

**Home – Based:** see the **Introduction for Home – Based Students (p. 10)**

**College – based:** see the **Introduction for College Students (p. 13)**

**Teachers of psychology** wanting to use ready-prepared learning materials with their students → See the **Introduction for Teachers (p. 14)**

# Introduction for the General Reader

## What is in this book?

Topics that most psychologists will cover in their first course. Psychology aims to describe and understand behaviour and experience, so most psychologists start out with a broad base of topics that cover a wide range in much the same way as a doctor starts by studying how the body works. As you can see, the book is arranged in the form of lessons, just like a college course would be. They cover:

- **Social Psychology**
- **Learning**
- **Anti-Social Behaviour**
- **Child Development**
- **Prejudice**
- **Memory**
- **Perception**
- **Biological Aspects of Behaviour**
- **The Methods Used by Psychologists**

Not all psychology topics are covered. For example, Mental Illness is not included; this would normally be studied after a good understanding of normal behaviour has been achieved.

## How Do I Use the Book?

As a general reader, you have the luxury of being able to pick and choose lessons as you wish. Very occasionally, a lesson requires that you have read an earlier one; if this is the case then it will say so at the beginning of the lesson, so that you can go back and cover what is required. Apart from this, lessons tend to be free-standing, but they were written as a series of groups and we think that you will enjoy and understand them more if you simply start at the beginning and work through them.

## What are all the boxes and empty spaces in the text for?

Read the section "How To Use The Lessons" later in this Introduction – you will benefit most from this book by following the advice there. Like GCSE students, you will also benefit from making notes on the topics as you go through them.

## What are the "Exam Style Questions" for?

These are for use by readers who wish to practise for the GCSE exams. You don't need to do any of these unless you want to. Buying this book does not entitle you to tutorial support but if you would like to consider becoming a GCSE student then you may like to read the "Introduction for Home Based Students" (situated later on in the Introduction), where further details are given and the option of buying tutorial support is described.

Good luck with your study of psychology!

# Introduction for Home-Based Students

## I have just bought this book and I want to do the GCSE course – what do I do now?

### Right at the beginning of your study you need to:
- Arrange for support from a psychology tutor
- Plan your course up to the exam
- Read about how to use the lesson material
- Start your lessons and
- Arrange to enter the exam.

### Arrange for Tutor Support

If you have not yet obtained support from a tutor then you must do so. The coursework in the GCSE is compulsory and accounts for 20% of the GCSE mark. It must be supervised by a tutor who will advise on whether or not the exam board will accept the ethics of what you intend to do in the study – remember you are dealing with other human beings when you carry out a study. There are two main ways you can arrange support:

1.  **Home Based Study Ltd** is responsible for writing these materials and can offer tuition by post or by email. You can get further details of this service by visiting www.homebasedstudy.com or phoning 01924 527822 or writing to Home Based Study, 7 Ingham Close, Mirfield, West Yorkshire, WF14 9NP.

2.  **Your local Further Education College**
    Many local further education colleges provide an evening class in GCSE psychology and, if this suits you, then you can enrol each September: these materials can be used with your course. If you prefer to work from home, the same college may be able to provide tutor support (the college will probably make a charge for this service depending on the college policy and your personal circumstances). You should be able to find the address and phone number in your telephone directory or yellow pages.

3.  **Do other organisations offer home study psychology courses?**
    Yes. They are: National Extension College in Cambridge (visit www.nec.ac.uk or write to them at Purbeck Road, Cambridge, CB2 2HN, telephone 01223 400 200), and Oxford Open Learning in Oxford (visit www.ool.co.uk or write to them at 4, King's Meadow, Oxford OX2 0DP, telephone 01865 798 022). They will want you to use their own learning materials of course, but you should find this book useful as an additional source of knowledge for their courses.

**Your tutor will**
- Answer queries about use of the materials, the psychology topics, the assignments, the exam, or other aspects of study
- Supervise your coursework and help you obtain the best result you can
- Advise you on entering the exam.
- Mark your assignments and make suggestions about improving your studies

## Which Specification and Lessons should I Follow?

Two exam boards offer GCSE Psychology:

- AQA (the Assessment and Qualifications Alliance) specification GCSE 3181
- OCR (Oxford, Cambridge and RSA Examinations) specification GCSE 1989.

The exam is only available in England, Wales and Northern Ireland and you need to sit the exam on a day specified by the exam board. It is not available in Scotland or anywhere outside Britain.

Only the AQA offer the facility to sit the exam if you are not registered for it at a college or school. You can take the exam at one of their "Open Centres" in London, Manchester or Liverpool. The AQA will send you further details of these and we strongly encourage you to buy a copy of the specification as well – no matter which one you decide to follow. You can enter the exam for either board at a local school or college but only if the school or college agrees to let you do so – and few do so make enquiries as early as possible. In reality, home-based students tend to take the AQA exam so this Introduction will assume that you will do so.

You can get further details and specifications from the addresses below:
AQA Publications Dept. at Stag Hill House, Guilford, Surrey GU2 7XJ Tel: 01483 302302 or Alden House, 39 Heald Grove, Rusholme, Manchester M14 4NA Tel: 0161 953 1170 or visit www.aqa.og.uk OCR Publications at 1 Hills Road, Cambridge CB1 2EU Tel: 01223 553998 or visit www.ocr.org.uk

When you have decided on a specification, look at the section "Lessons Covering the AQA Specification". These will help you to plan further.

## Plan Your Course Up to the Exam

It is important that you comply with the exam board's calendar of administration procedures. Moreover, you may not be able to sit the exam and gain your GCSE unless you meet the board's deadlines. To save having to wait an extra year, therefore, you need to plan over a long period. The section "Lessons Covering the AQA Specification", later in the Introduction, suggests planning over a period of 35 weeks – most college courses last for about this time. Read these suggestions and make a plan for yourself.

## How to Use the Lesson Materials

See the general section "How to Use the Lessons" for guidance on the best way to study with this book – you will find out what to do with the blank boxes, exam-style questions, Feedback sections and other important aspects of the materials.

## Start Your Lessons

You can dip into the lessons anytime you want – even before you have planned your course or arranged for a tutor, but once you have finished your planning you should start on the lesson you have planned first and work according to your timetable.

## Exam Centre

You need to register for the exam at an official centre, by the December or January before the June exam. There are two ways of accessing exam centres:

1.  Your local Further Education college may accept "Private Entries" and supervise you for the exam at the college for a fee. The college may only accommodate **one** of the two exam boards (OCR or AQA). If so you will have to choose the specification that matches this board, and follow only the lessons that cover it (see "Lessons Covering The AQA Specification" or "Lessons Covering the OCR Specification" in this Introduction).
2.  You can enter for the AQA exam at one of three "Open" centres; they are in London, Liverpool and Manchester. The AQA will give you further details if you telephone them on 0161 953 1180 or write to them at AQA, Devas Street, Manchester M15 6EX

Your tutor should agree all your exam arrangements before you go ahead.

## Revision

**Past Exam Questions** from the previous specification can be bought from the boards (addresses above), however, bear in mind that the exam for the new specification will be different. Only use the past questions from the board whose exam you are taking. Each board has published Specimen Exam Papers to guide students on what the new papers will be like. Past papers from actual new exams will be available after the June 2003 exam onwards. You should attempt past and/ or specimen papers as part of your revision programme, and you should have the paper marked in order to gain feedback on your performance and advice on improvement.

## Do I need another textbook?

No. This book covers all aspects of the GCSE courses. If you do purchase a second text book, however, then check that it covers your chosen specification (AQA or OCR) before you buy it.

Good luck with your study of psychology!

# Introduction for College Students

Your teacher may be using this book as the basis for the course, or you may have bought it to supplement your college lessons. Whatever the role of the book, it covers all the topics necessary for success in either the AQA or the OCR exams **and** coursework. It is not necessary to work through all the lessons for either exam, and details of which lessons should be covered for each exam are given in the sections "Lessons Covering the AQA Specification" or "Lessons Covering the OCR Specification". Your teacher will confirm which exam board you are using.

## The Basis for the Course
- The teacher will guide you on the sequence of lessons to follow and this may depend on whether you are learning at your own pace or working with a group of other students.
- Follow the teacher's instructions about the use of materials. You can read about how to use each lesson in the section "How to Use the Lessons" – it is important that you follow these instructions about self-assessment and using the exam-style questions.

### To Supplement Your Lessons
- You can use the table "Lessons Covering the OCR Specification" or "Lessons Covering the AQA Specification" to identify which lesson in the book matches the part of the specification you are covering in the classroom.
- You may find your college teacher is willing to mark your answers to the Exam Style Assessments.

## Coursework
Use the last two lessons in the book to support your approach to the coursework. Read them when your tutor introduces the coursework and as you do your coursework.

## Research Methods
Remember that the Research Methods section will help you to both answer questions in the exam and prepare for your coursework.

Good luck with your study of psychology!

# Introduction for Teachers

## What do these materials cover?

Both the AQA and the OCR specifications for GCSE Psychology:

- AQA 3181 GCSE Psychology
- OCR 1989 GCSE Psychology

All aspects of the specifications are covered including psychology content, research methods and coursework. There are self-assessment questions, exercises, and exam-style questions for both boards. These are designed for the student to attempt and compare with example answers, and for you to mark.

## How can they be used?

You can use them in a number of ways.

- To provide the content of lessons – either of the whole course or single lessons you choose to cover
- As open learning materials for workshops
- As individual learning programmes for self-paced learning or students learning at home

You may not photocopy these materials (except within the rules of the copyright licensing agreement), but instead must ensure that students have individual copies. You may, of course, ask students to write their answers on separate paper so the books can be re-used.

## Which Lessons should be covered?

The tables "Lessons Covering the AQA Specification" and "Lessons Covering the OCR Specification" in this Introduction show which lessons need to be covered for each section and sub-section of the respective specifications. There is a suggested one-year, week-by-week programme of study for each specification, in the section "Planning your week-by-week programme of study" later in this Introduction. Lessons are titled to make sense to the reader, rather than according to specifications; with the exception of the exam-style questions and suggested answers, which are titled according to the sections and sub-sections of the specifications. You can alter the programme to cover two years if this meets your students' needs better.

### Rationale for the AQA sequence

For the first two weeks students follow social psychology for two lessons per week. In the third week they start Research Methods (lesson 58), which they study alongside social psychology. This means they are studying two topics at once for nine weeks, up to the coursework. This should not be difficult as students can do a Social Psychology lesson on one day of the week and the Research Methods lesson on another day of the week.

After six weeks, students change from Social Psychology to the Learning sub-section of Cognitive Psychology. This is because later topics need the knowledge gained from studying Social Learning Theory in the Learning sub-section. They will return to the final part of Social Psychology six weeks after the coursework.

Students start with two lessons per week as a "gentle" introduction, but build to three lessons per week after the coursework period. This pace can be altered and students may wish to increase to three lessons per week earlier, or to go onto another topic while they are doing the coursework. Some lessons are longer than others.

The period before the coursework allows the student to sample three areas of psychology that should provide them with ample opportunity for coursework ideas. Memory, Cognitive Development and Sex and Gender tend to be rich in opportunities for designing studies, so students may prefer to look at one or more of these before deciding on coursework.

During the revision period, students should revise according to the specification sequence rather than according to the above sequence. This is because the exam is set according to the specification sequence and it is better for the students to see it the same way as the examiner.

**Rationale for the OCR sequence**

Students start by studying two topics at once – Social Influence and Research Methods. This should not cause any problems because, they can study one topic on one day of the week and the other topic on another. This continues until the twelfth week by which time they have completed the Research Methods lessons and covered two other topics – Phobias and Aggression. They then complete Attachment before starting their coursework. Three lessons per week are completed during the last three weeks before revision.

The period before the coursework allows the student to sample four areas of psychology that should provide them with ample opportunity for coursework ideas. Memory, Cognitive Development and Sex and Gender tend to be rich in opportunities for designing studies, so students may prefer to look at one or more of these before committing themselves to a study for coursework.

## How should each lesson be used?

Read through the section "How to Use the Lessons" to understand fully what the boxes and empty spaces, self-assessment, Feedback and Exam-Style Questions are all about. Your students will benefit from following these instructions carefully as well as from taking brief outline notes of each lesson. Lesson are of different lengths.

## Can my students access other psychology tutorial support?

Yes. Home Based Study Ltd., who were responsible for this book, also supply home study tutor support and this can be used by your students – including for the coursework. See the sub-heading "Arrange for Tutor Support" in the section "Introduction for Home Based Students" in this Introduction.

## Specimen and Past Exam Papers

You can obtain these from the exam boards and ask your students to complete them as part of the revision process – as you would do normally. The Exam Style Questions and the answers supplied in this book are only indicative of the type of questions the student may find on the paper; they are not actual questions from papers.

# How to use the lessons

## Self-Assessment: What are all the boxes and empty spaces in the text for?

This is not just a textbook but also a series of lessons, designed to help you understand by asking questions and providing answers to check your understanding.

> **Question boxes**
>
> As you go through the book, you will come across boxes with double borders like this:

Some contain quizzes and exercises. To help your understanding and to help you see whether or not you have understood, you should attempt to carry out the exercises or answer the questions on a separate sheet of paper.

If there are "correct" answers to the question then these will be given in the Feedback section at the end of the lesson. If you are asked to reflect on your own experience and make a note of it, there will be no answer but there may be an example of the sort of thing you may have written – generally after the box.

Some answers to questions are given immediately after the box. This is because the answer forms part of the "flow" of the text. In this case you should avoid looking at it. To improve your understanding it is important that you write down answers when asked. Psychologists' knowledge about memory shows that writing down the answers is more useful than thinking about questions.

## Cover Boxes

Of course, being human, it is difficult to stop the eye from "casually" glancing down at the answer, so we suggest that you use a piece of paper to cover the area below any box as you work through the lessons – only reveal the next lines when you are satisfied you have tried to answer.

## What are the Exam-Style Questions and How Do I Use Them?

These are for readers who are taking the GCSE exam. They are not real exam questions but are meant to replicate the sort of questions asked in an exam. At the end of each sub-section is a group based on the OCR exam board's style and another on AQA's. Suggested answers for each paper begin on page 360.

When you have completed all the lessons you have to cover in any sub-section you should attempt the exam-style questions. You can check your answers against those given, and see if yours are similar. After comparing your answers with the book's, show them to your tutor with any points you don't understand.

## Taking Notes

It is always useful to make brief notes as you read through the lessons, just as you would if you were in a lecture. These should be written in such a way as to form an outline record of the main points in the lesson, so you may find it useful to use the headings and sub-headings in each lesson as a structure for your notes.

# Planning your Programme of Study – AQA

## Lessons Covering the AQA Specification

This table shows which lessons you need to complete to cover the AQA specification. There are 61 lessons altogether, which includes Research Methods and preparation for the coursework.

| Specification Section | Sub-Section | Lessons |
|---|---|---|
| Cognitive Psychology | 10.1 Perception | 42-47 |
| | 10.2 Learning | 10-12 14-15 |
| | 10.3 Memory | 36-41 |
| Social Psychology | 11.1 Forming Impressions of Other People | 8,9 |
| | 11.2 Prejudice and Discrimination | 33-35 |
| | 11.3 Social Influence | 1-6 |
| Developmental Psychology | 12.1 Attachment and Separation | 22-25 |
| | 12.2 Cognitive Development | 27, 28 |
| | 12.3 Sex and Gender | 51-54, 57 |
| Pro- and Anti-Social Behaviour | 13.1 The Development of Moral Behaviour | 29-32 |
| | 13.2 Pro-social behaviour | 20, 21 |
| | 13.3 Anti-social behaviour | 16-19 |
| Research Methods | 14.1 Methods of investigation | |
| | 14.2 Methods of control | 58-63, 65-67 |
| | 14.3 Ethical considerations | 64 |
| Coursework | 17/18/19 | 68, 69 |

**Planning your week-by-week programme of study – AQA Specification**
This scheme of work:

* is designed to cover the AQA specification over a period of 35 weeks
* includes 5 weeks revision
* includes 6 weeks spent on coursework (a similar proportion of the course as the coursework marks are worth) timed to be handed to the tutor with adequate space to mark and re-draft before the board deadline if necessary
* covers the sections in a sequence which should engage and interest students rather than merely follow the sequence of the specification
* starts with two lessons per week, leads into six weeks of coursework then increases to three lessons per week.

If the scheme is started at the beginning of September then the coursework can be marked and if necessary re-drafted, in adequate time to meet the exam board's deadline. It can be adapted as necessary to suit holidays and individual needs in consultation with the tutor.

| Week | Lesson – assignment follows emboldened number | Assessment Assignment |
|------|-----------------------------------------------|----------------------|
| 1 | 1, 2 | |
| 2 | 3, 4 | |
| 3 | 5, 58 | |
| 4 | 6, 59 | |
| 5 | 8, 60 | |
| 6 | **9**, 61 | Social Influence |
| 7 | 10, 62 | |
| 8 | 11, 63 | |
| 9 | 12, 64 | Phobias |
| 10 | 14, 65 | |
| 11 | **15**, 66 | Learning |
| 12 | **67**, 68 | Research Methods |
| 13 | 69, Coursework | |
| 14 | Coursework | |
| 15 | Coursework | |
| 16 | Coursework | |
| 17 | Coursework | |
| 18 | Coursework | Coursework Deadline |
| 19 | 16, 17, 18 | |
| 20 | **19**, 29, **21** | Aggression, Pro-Social Behaviour |
| 21 | 22, 23, 24 | |
| 22 | **25**, 27, 28 | Attachment; Cognitive Development |
| 23 | 29, 30, 31 | |
| 24 | **32**, 33, 34 | Moral Development |
| 25 | **35**, 36, 37 | Prejudice |
| 26 | 38, 39, 40 | |
| 27 | **41**, 42, 43 | Memory |
| 28 | 44, 45, 46 | |
| 29 | **47**, 51, 52 | Perception |
| 30 | 53, 54, **57** | Sex and Gender |
| 31 | Revision | |
| 32 | Revision | |
| 33 | Revision | |
| 34 | Revision | |
| 35 | Revision | |

## Exam

The AQA exam has one paper of two hours accounting for 80% of the GCSE marks. There are four questions of equal marks, one on each of the first four sections – Research Methods questions are integrated into the first four sections. Each question is divided into shorter questions worth 1 to 6 marks. The remaining 20% of the marks come from the coursework.

# Planning your Programme of Study – OCR

## Lessons Covering the OCR Specification

This table shows which lessons you need to complete to cover the OCR specification. There are 52 lessons altogether, which includes Research Methods and preparation for the coursework.

| Section | Sub-Section | Lessons |
|---|---|---|
| 5.1.1 Methodology | | 58-63, 65-67 |
| 5.1.2 Ethics | | 64 |
| 5.1.3 Applications | { Integrated throughout | |
| 5.1.4 Cultural Diversity | { course | |
| 5.2.1 Social Psychology | Social Influence | 3, 4 |
| | Environment and Behaviour | 7 |
| 5.2.2 Behavioural Psychology | Phobias | 10-13 |
| | Aggression | 15, 16, 17 |
| 5.2.3 Developmental Psychology | Attachment | 22-26 |
| | Cognitive Development | 27, 28 |
| 5.3.1 Individual differentiation | Aspects of Morality | 29, 30, 32 |
| | Attitudes of Prejudice | 33, 34, 35 |
| 5.3.2 Cognitive Psychology | Memory | 36-37, 40-41 |
| | Perception | 43-46, 48 |
| 5.3.3 Bio-psychology | Stress | 49, 50 |
| | Sex and Gender | 51-56 |
| 7.2, 7.3 Coursework | | 68, 69 |

**Planning your week-by-week programme of study – OCR Specification**
This scheme of work:
- is designed to cover the OCR specification over a period of 35 weeks
- includes 5 weeks revision
- includes 6 weeks spent on coursework (a similar proportion of the course as the coursework marks are worth) timed to be handed to the tutor with adequate space to mark and re-draft before the board deadline if necessary
- covers the sections in a sequence which follows the specification.

If the scheme is started at the beginning of September it should provide for the coursework to be marked by the teacher and re-drafted if necessary by the student in adequate time to meet the exam board's deadline. It can be adapted as necessary to suit holidays and individual needs in consultation with the tutor.

| Week | Lesson – assignment follows emboldened number | Assessment Assignment |
|------|-----------------------------------------------|------------------------|
| 1 | 3, 58 | |
| 2 | 4, 59 | |
| 3 | **7**, 60 | Social Influence |
| 4 | 10, 61 | |
| 5 | 11, 62 | |
| 6 | 12, 63 | |
| 7 | 13, 64 | |
| 8 | **15**, 65 | Phobias |
| 9 | 16, 66 | |
| 10 | **17, 67** | Aggression, Research Methods |
| 11 | 22, 68 | |
| 12 | 23, 69 | |
| 13 | 24, 25 | |
| 14 | **26**, Coursework | Attachment |
| 15 | Coursework | |
| 16 | Coursework | |
| 17 | Coursework | |
| 18 | Coursework | |
| 19 | Coursework | |
| 20 | 27, 28 | Cognitive Development |
| 21 | 29, 30 | |
| 22 | **32**, 33 | Moral Development |
| 23 | 34, **35** | Prejudice |
| 24 | 36, 37 | |
| 256 | 40, **41** | Memory |
| 26 | 43, 44 | |
| 27 | 45, 46 | |
| 28 | **48**, 49, **50** | Perception, Stress |
| 29 | 51, 52, 53 | |
| 30 | 54, 55, **56** | Sex and Gender |
| 31 | Revision | |
| 32 | Revision | |
| 33 | Revision | |
| 34 | Revision | |
| 35 | Revision | |

## Exam

There are two exam papers, each of 1 hour 15 minutes and each accounting for 40% of the marks. The first paper covers the Social Psychology, Behavioural Psychology and Developmental Psychology sections. The second paper covers the Individual Differentiation, Cognitive Psychology and Bio-psychology sections. The remaining 20% of the marks come from the coursework.

# Lesson 1
# How Others Affect Us

## 1. Who are you looking at?

Much of our behaviour takes place in the presence of other people and it is affected by their presence. Think about this for a moment: what do you do on your own that you do not do if someone else is present? Also, are there things you would do with others that you would not do when alone? This lesson focuses on two aspects of the influence of other people:

- the effect on our performance of working with other people
- the effect on our performance of someone watching what we are doing.

There are, of course, other effects caused by other people's presence: in particular, we may feel self-conscious or anxious when others watch us.

**"Facilitation"** is the idea that something is made to happen more easily, so **social facilitation** is the idea that something happens more easily because of the presence of others. Psychologists' studies show that the presence of others sometimes improves performance, but also that it sometimes has the opposite effect: this is **social inhibition.** This lesson examines the evidence for both of these effects.

## 2. The coaction effect

An early psychology study by Triplett showed how a task tends to be done better if someone is competing against us. He asked people to turn a fishing reel as fast as they could: it was attached to a simple device that measured the rate at which it was turned. He found that people turned the reel faster when someone was doing the same thing in competition next to them.

Allport, however, found that competition was not necessary for an effect to take place. In fact, even when he instructed people specifically **not** to compete with each other he found that performance increased when someone else was doing the same task. This increase in performance when a task is performed alongside someone else is referred to as the **coaction** effect.

Even more surprisingly Dashiell found that just telling people others are performing the same task elsewhere is enough to cause an increase in performance.

> What does the coaction effect suggest about studying alone?

It suggests that studying with a friend will increase your level of performance as a student: this may mean a better understanding of the subject and a better performance in any exam you take.

## 3. Audience effects

An "audience" here refers to anyone watching what you are doing, or anyone who **could be** watching what you are doing. An audience consists of one or more people.

> Can you recall carrying out a task watched by others? How did you feel?

Answers to this question can vary a lot. Some people are not at all bothered about doing anything whilst being watched. Others may say that it depends on what the task is, or who is watching. You may feel that you will perform better in some circumstances if someone is watching you, and that you will perform worse in other circumstances. You may feel more comfortable if friends watch you rather than strangers.

Psychology studies have measured the effect of audiences on a person's performance of different types of task. In particular the work of **Zajonc** has shown clear patterns that follow our "common sense" hunches of what the outcome should be. You may like to guess the effects of an audience on a person's performance by placing the words "increases" or "decreases" in the following table, before the text gives the correct answers?

The factors you have to consider are whether the task is simple or complex, and whether it is well practised (i.e. the person is already skilled in performing the task) or not.

|              | Not well-practised | Well-practised |
| ------------ | ------------------ | -------------- |
| Simple task  |                    |                |
| Complex task |                    |                |

Zajonc's findings were:
**i.    The complexity of the task**
- performance of simple tasks improved with an audience
- performance of complex tasks worsened with an audience
**ii.   The novelty of the task**
- performance of well-practised tasks increased with an audience
- performance of novel tasks decreased with an audience.

> If you have not already completed the table, do so now using the information above.

|              | Not well-practised | Well-practised |
| ------------ | ------------------ | -------------- |
| Simple task  | Decreases          | Increases      |
| Complex task | Decreases          | Increases      |

Zajonc also suggested that tasks can be seen in terms of whether they demand **dominant responses** or not. Dominant responses are the ones that are most likely to occur, and for most people they will be the result of a simple task that requires well practised skills. What constitutes "well-practised" will differ from person to person of course.

## 4. Summary

After looking at these studies we can draw some simple conclusions about the effects of others on performance.

- The presence of other people performing the same task generally causes an increase in performance
- The thought that other people are performing the same task causes an increase in performance
- An audience will improve performance on a simple, well-practised task
- An audience will worsen performance on a complex, novel task

## 5. Evaluation

### Are studies "real life"?

If another person is present and performing the same task it seems fair to question whether this coaction performer is not also an audience because they have the opportunity to watch. This suggests that the psychology studies we have considered have not been able to reproduce "real life" situations because real life situations consist of more complex arrangements than mere coaction or audience.

Another criticism of the unreality of these investigations is the task itself. Many consist of motor tasks that few people actually perform in real life. How many people, for example, turn fishing reels as quickly as possible? Other tasks consisted of crossing out letters in text, and similar "laboratory" occupations. Some even measured insects' performances instead of human ones (they resulted in the same findings).

## Social Loafing

Not only are "real life" situations usually more complex than the laboratory studies, but other studies have also shown that audiences do not always have the predicted effect. Some researchers, like Latané, have found an effect called **social loafing**. This occurs when a group of people cooperate on a task – unlike the situations described up to now in which only one person or a couple work together. In this case, individuals tend to work **less** hard because they believe that others will complete the task and their individual performance will not be monitored. Again, the tasks investigated tended to be laboratory type activities like shouting as loud as possible or playing tug-of-war, but they did reflect real activity to some extent (there may be times when we do have to shout as loud as possible).

## 6. Applications

- Open plan offices are good examples of the way in which knowledge of the effects of others can be applied to everyday life. Large areas where many people work may have a distracting effect; for example a surgeon would need to concentrate in a private area. For many jobs, however, the co-action effects and beneficial audience effects make open-plan offices more suitable.
- The notion of teamwork is important to many organisations. Employees are encouraged to work as a team because firms think this leads to better work. This may be because social loafing is discouraged in the team setting.

## 7. Explanations

Why are our performances affected by others in these ways?

i.   **Conformity** (yielding to the pressure of the group). The coaction effect may
     be the result of the individual conforming to the group norm (accepted
     behaviour) of higher performance, though this does not explain why the
     performance level of the group tends to be higher than that of the individual.
     Studies in the workplace have show that new workers joining an established
     group of workers tend to work at whatever pace the established group has
     already set.

ii.  **Arousal** The audience has the effect of increasing our arousal level. This
     means that our body is aroused as well as our mind. We breath deeper, sweat
     more, increase our blood pressure and so on. A little extra arousal can be a
     good thing for our performance, (it increases it), but a lot can be a bad thing
     because we become over aroused to the point where our anxiety interferes
     with the task and our performance falls. This is a finding first outlined by
     Yerkes and Dodson and is often referred to as the Yerkes-Dodson law.

If the task is simple then arousal increases to a beneficial point but if the task is
complex then this adds to the arousal which goes beyond a beneficial point and
performance falls because of the associated anxiety. In graph form it looks like
Fig 1

As arousal increases from point A to point B, so performance improves from
0 to 1. When arousal goes up to point C, then performance improves even more to
2. Performance reaches its peak of 3 at point D. However, if arousal goes up as
far as point E, then it is too much for the person concerned and performance
starts to fall to point 2. If arousal gets as far as point F, then performance falls
even further to 1.

Fig. 1

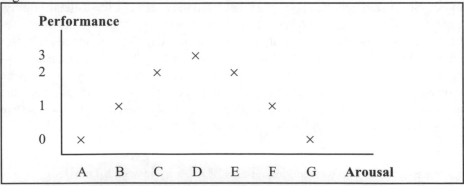

**The Yerkes Dodson Law**

**Quick Quiz**

i. When two people are doing the same task together their performance will tend to be_____than when they are doing it alone. This is known as the _____effect. (2 marks)

ii. Generally, the effect of people watching someone performing dominant response will be to_____performance. This is known as the_____effect (2 marks)

iii. Give one piece of advice to a student which results from the findings in 1. and 2. (1 mark)

iv. A criticism of the studies upon which these findings are based is that_____

_____(1 mark)

v. Social loafing suggests that people tend to work harder in a group because they assume that the others will not work as hard. True or false? (1 mark)

vi. A possible explanation for coaction effects is_____(1 mark)

vii. A possible explanation for audience effects is_____(1 mark)

viii. Social facilitation refers to_____

_____

_____(1 mark)

## Feedback

**Quick Quiz – Answers**

(i) better, coaction

(ii) improve, audience

(iii) (e.g.) work alongside others – as long as they really are working!

(iv) (e.g.) they are often not "real life"

(v) false

(vi) conformity

(vii) arousal

(viii) the idea that something is made to happen more easily by the presence of others.

# Lesson 2
# Why Bystanders Don't Help

## 1. Has this happened to you?

Read the following accounts of two newspaper articles; as you read, ask yourself if you can remember being in a situation in public when you felt you should intervene.

---

### Youths assault three girls while train passengers just watch

Passengers returning to Liverpool from a Sunday outing to the seaside resort of Southport ignored the cries of three teenage girls as they were held down and indecently assaulted by a gang of boys aged 10 to 16 in a railway carriage on 1st May. The passengers did nothing to help the girls and were reported by the girls to have just looked the other way.

The girls escaped from the train after their ordeal at an early station and reported the incident to railway staff who alerted police at the next station but the gang escaped before the police arrived at the train. The railway spokesperson reported her shock that the passengers did not even trigger the communication cord alarm let alone attempt to intervene

Other reports of passengers ignoring victims of crime on trains have been made including a 20 year old man who suffered head injuries when a gang attacked him after protesting that they had taken a bag of crisps from his brother.

---

### Man dies chasing burglars

A 48-year-old Warwickshire man died when he was attacked by two burglars he saw running from a house. The men were running with electrical goods and the burglar alarm was sounding when Malcolm Albrighton intervened and chased them. The burglars turned on him and beat him to the ground. He suffered head injuries and was taken to hospital but did not recover.

Police praised his actions as those of a good citizen prepared to fight crime and promised to do everything they could to bring his killers to justice.

---

Both of the above articles were reported in the *Daily Telegraph* of 3rd May, 1994.

If you have been in a similar situation did you intervene? Did you regret your decision? If you have not been in a similar situation do you think you would have intervened on the train, had you been there? When people do intervene it is referred to as **bystander intervention**; when they do not, it is referred to as **bystander apathy**. Bystander apathy is an old term that is still used quite often but gives the wrong impression because we now recognise that it is not really "apathy" that prevents people from intervening. As you will read below, other factors prevent intervention but lack of intervention gives the impression that people are apathetic

> Take a few minutes to consider why the passengers on the train did not intervene and jot down your ideas.

The trouble with newspaper articles is that they are not well-structured and controlled psychology studies. Newspapers sensationalise incidents to stretch the reader's emotions and sell more papers, so it is dangerous to rely on articles such as this as evidence. Soon after the article appeared in national newspapers some of the passengers from the train managed to get their side of the story into some newspapers. They explained how they had seen the young people together as a group and that there had been no sexual assault, just embarrassing behaviour which they had come to expect from groups of young people.

Even if this particular story is not reliable evidence, there is no doubt that these situations do occur, after which people regret not intervening or feel guilty and inadequate that they felt they could not do so. Psychology evidence tells us, however, that failing to intervene is a normal human response under particular circumstances, and this lesson will examine this intervention response and the circumstances under which it occurs.

In the previous lesson, evidence for **social loafing** was outlined and this is perhaps a first step in understanding how people's behaviour is influenced by the presence of others. In a sense, when someone "loafs" like this, they are deciding not to intervene in a situation they could contribute to.

## 2. The Kitty Genovese case

This is probably the most famous case of bystander behaviour in modern psychology texts, mostly because of its chilling story and sobering implications.

Kitty Genovese was attacked and stabbed on the way home to her New York apartment one night in 1964. The attack lasted more than thirty minutes and during this time the attacker left her twice, thus making three separate attacks on her.

She called out after the first attack and the assailant left. He returned and attacked her again as she stumbled round the side of the apartment building. Again, she screamed and he drove off in his car. She managed to get into her apartment building but lay at the bottom of the stairs to her apartment. The attacker returned for a third attack and this time stabbed her to death.

On each occasion that Ms Genovese called out, neighbours turned on their lights (it was the early hours of the morning), opened their apartment windows and called out. From what they could hear (she screamed "He stabbed me" and "I'm dying") and see, it was obvious that she needed help, but the important feature of this case is that nobody went to her assistance **or even telephoned the police**.

Thirty-eight people later admitted to witnessing the event without taking any action. It seems natural to condemn the witnesses for being irresponsible and uncaring but could thirty-eight people be so odd, or is this the response that anyone would have under the same circumstances? This was the question that Latané and Darley set out to answer. The witnesses later told newspaper reporters their conscious reasons for not intervening, these included being afraid, not wanting to get involved or thinking that it was just a "lovers' tiff".

> You may like to pause here to compare your answers to the question about why you thought the train passengers did not respond to the incident with the answers given by the Kitty Genovese witnesses, and with your answer to the opening question in this lesson about your response to any similar experience you have had.

If this case gives the impression that we are all unhelpful and selfish then we only have to look at the newspaper article at the beginning of this lesson which describes the passer-by "having a go", to recognise that passers-by do intervene sometimes.

One of the significant differences between the Kitty Genovese case and the "have a go" case, is the fact the there were thirty eight "passers-by" in the former case but only **one** in the latter. Latané and Darley later found the **number** of passers-by was an important variable in determining whether or not people would intervene; as the studies described below show.

## 3. Psychological studies of the effects of bystander behaviour
### i. Latané and Darley's "smoke" studies: defining the situation as an emergency.
The researchers asked participants to complete questionnaires in a room with one, two, three or no other people. Whilst the questionnaire was being completed, "smoke" (in reality, steam) was made to appear through the ventilation system. When participants were alone, many of them (75%) reported the smoke and they tended to do this very quickly. When they were with other people, however, participants took much longer to report the smoke and fewer of them did so. Latané and Darley believed that the participants failed to see the situation as an emergency because nobody else was reacting to it as an emergency. One of the factors that govern bystander intervention, then, is defining the situation as an emergency.

**Test your understanding**
Jot down answers to the questions in the double bordered boxes. Suggested answers can be found in the **Feedback** section at the end of the lesson. Check your answers as you go along.

> **1.** What is the relationship between the bystanders' reactions and the likelihood of a person intervening shown by the Latané and Darley smoke studies?
> **2.** What do the smoke studies show about the Kitty Genovese case?

### ii. Latané and Rodin's "falling" studies: pluralistic ignorance
In this series of studies Latané and Rodin set up a similar situation to the "smoke"

studies, but this time arranged for the "secretary" in the adjoining room to fake a fall, cry out and moan. The researchers then measured the time taken for the participants to go to see what the trouble was. Participants were interviewed after the event and many of them reported that they had taken their cue for action from the other participants. If the other person remained calm and did not react to the sounds, then they felt that there could not really be a problem and this tended to inhibit them from action. This was referred to as **pluralistic ignorance.**

From this and other reports we conclude that one of the variables which determines whether or not bystanders intervene, is **the way in which they define the situation**: they have to "see" it as an emergency before taking action and one of the ways in which they define the situation as an emergency is to take cues from the reactions of others. In England, not making a fool of oneself is a norm of behaviour, so there is a learned tendency to **not** react to disturbances – the lack of response from others is taken as confirmation that one's own lack of response is the appropriate way to behave and so the cycle of behaviour turns full circle and bystanders fail to intervene.

> **3.** How does Latané and Rodin's idea about "defining the situation" explain the behaviour of the train passengers in the newspaper article?

### iii. Latané and Darley's "intercom" studies: diffusion of responsibility and the number of other bystanders

The researchers asked participants to discuss problems by sitting in cubicles and using linked intercoms (to "save embarrassment"). Of course, there were no real discussions because the participants were unknowingly listening to recordings of discussions, whilst waiting their "turn" to "contribute". Some participants were led to believe there were only two people in the discussion, some three and so on. During the discussion, one of the discussants mentioned that he had trouble with "seizures" and later made noises suggesting an epileptic fit: the researchers were interested in how long it would take for the participant to come out of the cubicle to find the "victim", or in other words, to intervene.

> From your knowledge of previous studies, which situation is more likely to lead to the participant intervening: one in which there are five discussants or one in which there are two?

As we may expect, the smaller the number of discussants, the more likely the participants were to intervene. Darley and Latané pointed to the idea of **Diffusion of responsibility** in these situations. The larger the number of bystanders, the less likely the individual is to accept responsibility and act, because they expect someone else to take responsibility.

## 4. Further work

More studies of bystander behaviour are outlined in the lesson "Pro-Social Behaviour and Bystander Intervention".

## 5. Practical applications of bystander intervention studies

A number of situations can be helped by our knowledge of why people **fail** to intervene. Here are some examples:

- **Police training.** It can be useful for police officers to know that bystanders may not automatically come to their aid in emergency situations. This allows them to expect to call for other officers to help.
- **Accidents.** If you are at the scene of an accident, it is often not useful to shout "someone call an ambulance" because the likelihood is that other passers-by will assume that someone else will call it, some of the other factors discussed in this section will prevent intervention too. Instead, point at somebody and say, "Will **you** call an ambulance?"
- **Fires.** Even large fires can go unreported to the fire brigade. Again, many of the factors discussed in this section will be relevant. At one time, fire brigades made appeals asking people to not assume that someone else had called them, because everyone thinks that way. They emphasised that they would prefer to be called by many people than by no one at all.

## Feedback

**Test your understanding: suggested answers**

1. If the other bystanders do not react as if it were an emergency, then a person will not define the situation as an emergency.
2. The lack of contact by the witnesses with the police is only what psychologists would expect in such a situation. Each witness saw thirty-seven others not react so each one failed to define the situation as an emergency. It is more likely that the police would have been called if only **one** person had witnessed the attack.
3. Any individual passenger would look to the other passengers for signs that they saw an event, which required intervention. As nobody else was responding as though intervention was required, each passenger failed to define the situation as an emergency – pluralistic ignorance occurred.

# Lesson 3
# Conformity

## 1. All together now!

### UFO Cult Suicides – 39 Dead

Thirty-nine members of a cult were found dead, believed to have taken their own lives in a mass suicide, in San Diego, California yesterday.

The cult was linked with the Hale-Bopp comet by the belief that they would be delivered to eternal life after death if they committed suicide at the right moment and linked up with the comet's tail, it was revealed. The cult known as the Heaven's Gate had its own web site and left details of the suicide in videotaped announcements. Police found the bodies of the 21 women and 18 men in a wealthy suburb near San Diego. The cult used purple shawls in triangular shapes to cover parts of their bodies and all of them were found in the same position. Their deaths were believed to have been the result of an overdose of sleeping tablets.

The group had prepared themselves well for their "departure" with suitcases and notes about the drugs they had taken; these were mixed with alcohol.

They had also left official papers to allow themselves to be identified easily and had written details of their mission which had been posted on the Internet.

27th March, 1997

Read the article above, taken from the daily newspapers of 27th March, 1997

Most of us would be shocked that so many people would take their own lives together like this. But this is not the first time that it has happened and it is not the largest group of people to have done it. In November, 1978, almost 900 members of a group in Guyana, led by the Reverend Jim Jones, committed suicide together by taking poison.

The Heaven's gate sect, mentioned in the newspaper article, believed that committing suicide at a specific time would return them to the planet from which everybody originated, and that this was desirable. We know this from the records left by the sect. One of the features of the life of the group before the mass suicide, was the acceptance of one way of behaving. All aspects of behaviour were regulated by the sect, as well as the clothes they wore and even shaving. The suicides, and other behaviour, can be seen as extreme examples of conformity.

A **definition of conformity** is "**Yielding to group pressure**". In other words, doing what the rest of the group expects us to do.

Psychology research shows that accepted ways of behaving are established whenever people are in groups.

## 2. Conformity

It may seem a big jump to go from wearing the right clothes to committing suicide, but the same processes are at work.

**Other definitions of conformity.** One definition of conformity has already been given – "Yielding to group pressure". In the case of suicide it may seem that the pressure must have been very strong, but psychologists there are different types of conformity and when we consider some of these then it is possible to see how such extreme behaviours can result.

### i. Compliance

Compliance involves acceding to a request: Milgram asked passengers on the New York subway to give up their seats without any explanation and found that about half of them did so. If we comply with social norms we do so without agreeing that this is the "best" way to behave but we keep our belief to ourselves, usually for the sake of remaining a member of the group, but sometimes to avoid disturbance – as may have been the case with Milgram's obliging subway passengers.

> Construct a short definition of "Compliance" from paragraph (i) above.
> There is a suggested answer in the Feedback section

### ii. Identification

If we identify with a person or a group we are much more likely to adopt the norms they establish; we are more likely to comply with their requests and to conform to their pressure. Identification involves linking ourselves in some way with another person or group: seeing them as important to us and worthy of being imitated. We are more likely to identify with people we see as powerful or as successful in solving problems we have. Identification is a step further towards conformity than compliance is, because we are starting to become someone who is more likely to follow the lead of the group. Gang members show this identification with some outward sign like a symbol on their clothes, a hairstyle or "private" language.

> Construct a short definition of "Identification" from paragraph (ii) above.
> There is a suggested answer in the Feedback section

### iii. Internalisation

This is the point at which the beliefs, values, opinions and behaviours of another person or group become our own. We internalise them and they become part of us. We conform truly at this point because there is now no difference between the group's belief's and our own. We are not grudgingly following others' examples, nor are we copying their behaviour whilst maintaining private thoughts that contradict the group's. We have taken the group's beliefs and made them our own.

To return to the example of the mass suicides, it is at this point that we may understand how large numbers of people come to believe that death is the best thing. They have internalised the notion that death on earth would allow them to be carried by a comet to a distant planet where they would find eternal life. It seems as right as staying quiet during religious services or shouting at a football match.

> Construct a short definition of "Internalisation" from paragraph (iii) above. There is a suggested answer in the Feedback section.

## 3. Studies of Conformity

Three studies of conformity follow. Read them carefully; after the descriptions you will be asked to decide which one best illustrates compliance, which best illustrates identification and which best illustrates internalisation.

### i. Sherif's study of the Autokinetic Effect

Sherif made use of a visual illusion called **the autokinetic effect**. "Kinetic" means moving. "Auto" refers to self; so autokinetic refers to "self-movement" and describes the effect resulting from the fact that the eye is never still – it constantly "shivers" to scan the visual field. Consequently, if we look at a spot of light in a darkened room the light appears to move as a result of this activity: the apparent movement is the autokinetic effect.

Sherif asked people to estimate the distance moved by the light and he found a wide variation of estimates. He than allowed the participants to hear each other's estimates in a group situation and found that the estimates were much closer to each other. Finally, he asked them to re-estimate individually. The second individual estimates were much closer to the group norms.

### ii. Asch's study of line length

This is probably the best-known series of conformity studies. More than one study was carried out in the early 1950s. Participants were asked to compare a standard line on a piece of card with three other lines of different lengths on another card; they had to say which of the three was the same length as the standard line. Only one line was the same and Asch established that it was clear which one was the same.

Participants were asked to make this judgement under unusual circumstances. They were put with about eight other judges who knew what the study was about and who had been asked to make specific mistakes in their judgements. The participant did not know that the other judges were actually confederates of Asch. Also, the participant was always the last in the group or the last but one to be asked for his judgement, so he always heard the other judgements before he gave his own.

Have you predicted what happened? The participants often gave the same answer as the confederates. The outcome was not quite as straightforward, however. On average, the participants gave the incorrect answer about one time out of three. One participant in four never gave incorrect answers; of the remainder, 47% gave 1 to 7 incorrect answers, 28% gave 8 or more incorrect answers and 5% gave incorrect answers every time.

Later, the participants gave the following reasons:
a)  some did not want to "upset" the experiment
b)  some doubted their vision and thought their eyesight was mistaken
c)  some did not realise they had made any mistakes
d)  some did not want to "look a fool" or be different.

### iii. Abrams' study of psychology students

Abrams repeated Sherif's autokinetic effect study using psychology students who did not know the study. He told one group of students that the other people in the study with them were also psychology students and he told another group that the other people in their group were history students. He found that the agreement that he expected in judgements of movement of the light only occurred in the group who thought that the others were psychology students, not in the group who thought the others were history students. This suggests that they only conformed when they thought that the group was one to which they belonged.

> In the table below write the name of the study that you think best illustrates the type of conformity shown. The answer is given in the Feedback section.

| Type of Conformity | Name of Study |
|---|---|
| Compliance | |
| Identification | |
| Internalisation | |

## 4. Factors Affecting Conformity

### i) The existence of an ally.

Asch found that if one of the confederates agreed with the participant's judgement then the participant was less likely to conform – no matter how big the group was. The explanation for this could include the idea that the group norm is undermined; as soon as two people agree they form their own group, so a new group norm within the original group is formed. Also, another group member agreeing with a dissenter would provide emotional support and improve the confidence of the dissenter. The reasons for conforming, given above, would be removed: it would not be the participant who was upsetting the experiment, the accuracy of their vision is confirmed to some extent, they would see that the others may be making a mistake, and finally, they would not look different as someone else was saying the same thing.

### ii) The size of the majority.

If there were two confederates in Asch's study then conformity was greater than if there was only one to disagree with. If there were three confederates then the conformity rate increased, so it looks like the bigger the majority, the bigger the conformity. However, the increase stopped at this point and four or more confederates did not have any effect on the rate of conformity. An explanation for this could be that, again, only a small number of people are required to form the sub-group and additional members do not make the group any more of a group beyond a certain point.

### iii) Privacy.

If participants were allowed to give their answers in private, then conformity dropped, though there was still some. Presumably this reveals that a large portion of the conformity in this study is the result of compliance, where private thoughts are not in line with publicly expressed opinions. This could be explained again by reference to Asch's findings in the debriefing; participants would not be "upsetting" the experiment as others could not be influenced by their "incorrect" view and they would not appear different from the other members of the group because the other members would not know their decision.

---

**Delete the inappropriate word to summarise the factors affecting conformity.**

Correct answers are given in the feedback section

We are less likely to conform to the group when there is a (small/large) number of people in the group who agree with each other, when (one other/no one else) agrees with us and when we have to give our opinion in (public/private).

---

## 5. Evaluation of Conformity Studies

How good are these studies of conformity? Can we draw any conclusions about our own conformity and that of others from the studies? They can be criticised on the grounds that they were "laboratory" studies and not real life – yet there was some element of reality in them all. Judging the number of beans in a bottle **is** the sort of thing we may try at a fair though facing a group of eight others who have all been pre-trained to misjudge lines is more unusual.

The Asch studies were carried out in the USA in the 1950s when the McCarthy congressional hearings were emphasising the importance of the American way of life; the participants were male engineering students. Does this represent the majority of United Kingdom residents in the second millennium? Larsen repeated the Asch study in 1974 and found much less conformity. Would we find none now? Yet most people seem to experience conformity. Many smokers cite a desire to fit in with their friends as the reason for stating.

Ethical problems arise with the studies, which use deception to gain information. Some parts of the Asch study put pressure on the participants and they clearly felt stressed to greater or lesser extents. Should we be doing this to people and is the information gained from such stress valid information?

**Possible cultural differences** Some cultures place much more emphasis on group norms than others. The group is far more important in Japanese culture than it is in most European cultures, for example. A lifetime's commitment to one's employer was the accepted attitude of most workers (though this has changed slightly in the previous decade with economic changes). Japanese commitment to the group includes the family, school or college and other informal groups like music or dance groups. The former eastern bloc countries like Russia also encouraged adherence to group norms much more than, say, the USA. In America, individual freedom and self-sufficiency is more important. The US Bill of Right enshrines this cultural norm.

The work of Asch and other psychologists is very much approached from a western European and American viewpoint. Conformity is seen as a "weakness" and there does seem to be an implication that we should investigate it to discourage it. From the viewpoint of some cultures, however, conformity is an admirable quality to be encouraged. This also means that the findings of the research would probably be different if it had been carried out in countries with more commitment to the group.

## 6. Pro-Social Behaviour and Conformity

Pro-social behaviour is defined as behaviour that benefits society in some way. Conformity benefits society; it allows the group to function smoothly and with less effort on the part of the leader. The cost may be individual liberty, embarrassment on the part of the individual and so on.

## Feedback

**DEFINITIONS:**

**Compliance:** agreeing to do something or act in a particular way but without changing our "private" thoughts that the behaviour we are performing is not what we would want to do normally.

**Identification:** thinking of a person or group as worth emulating then acting as they do.

**Internalisation:** "absorbing" the group's culture-norms, values, beliefs, language and so on. These things now become a part of the person and there is no difference between their private thoughts and their public statements and behaviours.

**Which study best illustrates which type of conformity?**

| Type of Conformity | Name of Study |
|---|---|
| Compliance | Asch's study of line length |
| Identification | Abrams' study of groups |
| Internalisation | Sherif's study of the autokinetic effect |

Although some of Asch's participants said they thought the answers they gave were correct most of them were aware they were giving wrong answers and were making comments like they did not want to upset the experiment.

Abrams' participants wanted to identify with other psychology students and were not really expecting to agree with historians.

Sherif's participants did not know what the "reality" of the situation was and seemed to have believed the group answers to be the real ones – they internalised this version of reality and it became part of their world.

You may disagree with some elements of these arguments but on the whole these are the **best** "fits".

**Delete the inappropriate words**

We are less likely to conform to the group when there is a **small** number of people in the group who agree with each other, when **one other** agrees with us and when we have to give our opinion in **private**.

# Lesson 4
# Obedience

## 1. Do as you're told!

Strangely enough, most people **do** do as they are told, and psychologists' studies reveal just how far people will go to do as they are told.

**Definition**

Obedience is **responding as instructed to a direct order**. Sometimes, this involves doing something that the responder would not normally do or that the responder sees as unacceptable. Obedience is not the same as conformity. Conformity does not have the element of instruction – being told to do something directly; it is just the situation in which people act as others act.

## 2. Studies of Obedience

**Milgram's Studies**

These are probably some of the most often quoted studies in psychology. In 1963 Milgram advertised in a local newspaper for male participants in a study at Yale University (one of America's most famous and prestigious) and offered a small payment (which is quite normal). The people who responded to the advertisement were told that the study was looking at the effectiveness of punishment on learning, and that they were to work with another participant. The other participant was really a confederate of the researchers so he knew what was really happening.

At the beginning the pair drew lots to see who would be the "learner" and who would be the "teacher" in the study. The lottery was fixed so that the real participant always became the teacher. The participant watched as the learner was strapped into a machine which appeared to give electric shocks: at this point the learner mentioned that he had a weak heart and then he was placed in another area, partitioned from the teacher, at a control box which appeared to deliver the shocks.

The teacher was instructed to deliver shocks every time the learner gave a wrong answer to a question. The control box was designed so that the switches were marked from low voltages (15 volts) to high ones (450 volts). At 350v the switches were clearly marked "danger, severe shock". The shocks had to start off at low levels and increase by 15v every time the learner made a mistake. As the "shocks" increased a recording was played to give the impression that the learner was being shocked, calling out a little at first, shouting louder as the voltage increased, asking to stop, screaming, then eventually falling silent at 315 volts. Despite the appearance of death, participants continued to administer shocks up to the full 450 volts.

---

1. How do you feel Milgram treated his participants? Note any ways you consider that he mistreated them.
2. Why do you think Milgram advertised for males for the study?

The participants displayed varying levels of distress during the session, some of them were overcome with distress. The researchers gave them encouragement to continue if they started to "flag". They used phrases such as "The experiment requires that you continue", and carried on as though all was acceptable.

*65% of the participants administered shocks up to the full level of 450 volts.* Some of them were doing so even though the "learner" had been silent before that point – they possibly thought they were delivering shocks to dead man!

This study showed that people would obey; in fact the participants obeyed much more than anyone at the time thought they would. It was often referred to when war atrocities were examined. Massacres, attempted genocides, the killing of innocent civilians and the tortures administered to people during a number of wars, were explained in terms of obedience to commands. Trials of war crimes after the Second World War often heard the defendant claiming to have been "only following orders".

> **Varying Levels of Obedience**
> Before moving on, make some predictions about the effects that certain factors may have on obedience. Look at the situations below and write "increase" or "decrease" next to each one to predict which way you think each factor will affect obedience:
> 1.  If someone else says "I'll take full responsibility for the consequences"
> 2.  If the "study" appears to be conducted by ordinary people who are not university researchers.
> 3.  If the researcher does not wear a laboratory coat
> 4.  If the "learner" is in the same room as the "teacher"
> You can compare your answers to the findings in the following section: the corrupt answers are given in the Feedback section.

### Factors affecting obedience

But what of the occasions when people did not obey in Milgram's studies? In later studies Milgram found that levels of obedience varied according to certain factors:

**i. Responsibility**. If the participant was asked to instruct someone else to give the shock then obedience increased. If the participant was asked to hold the "learner's" hand on the device to receive the shock the level of obedience fell. If the researcher assured the participant that he (the researcher) would take all responsibility for the consequences then the obedience level rose. It was concluded that being able to psychologically "off-load" the responsibility would make obedience more likely. This echoes the war trial plea "I was only following orders".

**ii. Status of the experiment**. Milgram repeated the study in an office block in a run-down area of the town and found that the rate of obedience fell. It was concluded that the connection with Yale University gave prestige to the "study" and that prestige was a factor that affected obedience. The parallel with the armed forces is that a member of the ranks is more likely to follow an order from a General than from a Corporal.

**iii. Presence of an authority figure**. Participants were more likely to obey a researcher in a laboratory coat than one who was not. As the university gave prestige to the "study" so the white coat seems to give prestige to the authority figure.

    **iv. Proximity of the victim**. If the "learner" was in the same room as the "teacher" then the level of obedience fell. Presumably this can be extended to include the idea that if someone is closer to the consequences of his or her own actions then obedience to an undesirable order is less likely.

**Hofling's Study**

This took place in a real hospital with real nurses as the subject of the study. Doctors have the legal responsibility for patients in their care in hospital, so it is for them to make decisions about the treatment, though nurses are often the ones to carry out the decisions. The authority relationships between doctors and nurses are often, therefore, interesting social situations. A young, inexperienced doctor may often turn to an experienced nurse for advice before making a decision and hospital doctors who are undergoing training are often the butt of nurses' jokes about their competence.

    In the Hofling study a nurse was telephoned by a researcher claiming to be Dr Smith who asked the nurse to administer 20 milligrams of "Astroten" (not a real drug) to a particular patient and promised to come over in ten minutes to sign the authorisation for the drug. Nurses are not allowed to take instructions over the telephone in this way but 21 out of 22 nurses who were studied complied. They found the drug along with the others but the label clearly stated that the maximum daily dosage was 20 milligrams. Again, the 21 nurses all prepared the 20mg dose and would have administered it, but an accomplice of the researchers observed the nurses and stopped them at this point to explain the true situation to them.

> **Would you have obeyed the instruction if you had been the nurse?**

Another 22 nurses were told about a situation in which a doctor phones, asking them to administer the drug and promising to come over in ten minutes. They were asked if they would administer the drug and all of them said "no".

    Role expectations seem to be the clearest reason for obedience in this case. It is the role of the doctor to give orders about treatment and it is the role of the nurse to carry out instructions. The doctor's authority is made legitimate by the hospital system and so it is much more likely that nurses will obey him. The "lab. coat effect" was also noted, it is more likely that even patients would obey "doctor's orders" even though doctors have no *legitimate* power over them (i.c. power given to them by the organisation).

## 3. The ethics of obedience studies

Remember that "ethics" refers to "**A consideration of what is acceptable or right behaviour in pursuit of a . . . scientific goal**"

> **Were Milgram's and Hofling's studies ethical? If you think not, give some idea of what you consider was unethical about them.**

If you have already studied the **Methods of Investigation** section then you may like to compare what you learned in it with what you wrote in the box above, before continuing. Have any of the ethical principles listed in that section been broken in the studies? Did you manage to identify them in your answer?

Psychologists would be concerned about the following features of those studies:

1.  **Consent**. The participants in the studies ("teachers" in Milgram's, nurses in Hofling's) did not give consent to be studied. Even if Milgram's participants signed a consent form before becoming a "teacher" that would have related to a study which did not really exist, not the study in which they were really taking part. It is also established practice to advise participants that they can **withdraw** from studies whenever they wish, rather than to intimidate them into continuing.

2.  **Conduct**. The participants in Milgram's studies were put into a situation in which there was a high possibility of stress; indeed one of them was reported to have had "seizures" and many of them acted in a distressed way. Indeed the physical well being of some participants could have been jeopardised by heart trouble or other disorders. The researchers in Hofling's study were interfering with the professional conduct of the nurses. They were also undermining their sense of self-esteem by "tricking" them into realising how less competent they were than they may have thought – there are more compassionate ways of helping people to uncover their weaknesses than this.

3.  **Choice of method**. Considering the level of deception and stress would it not have been possible to study **real** obedience situations that would not have been created by the researchers, and so remove the ethical consequences? The armed forces, health organisations, police and other organisations have highly structured systems that should have provided opportunities for study.

Milgram did follow these criticisms with a survey of his participants and reported that all of them agreed that the level of deception was acceptable for the situation and that the knowledge gained justified the deception and stress. None of the participants reported any long-term effects from the study though many reported a type of depression from discovering their own potential for obedience. It must also be remembered that ethical considerations were not as commonly considered in 1963 as they are now.

> **Can you think of one positive point and one negative point about the two studies? Try it before reading the next section.**

## 4. Evaluation of obedience studies

As well as the ethical dilemmas presented above, the studies have some practical aspects that need to be evaluated.

**i. Artificial**. The Milgram studies were conducted in laboratory type conditions and we must ask if this tells us much about real-life situations. We obey in a variety of real-life situations that are far more subtle than instructions to give people electric shocks and it would be interesting to see what factors operate in everyday obedience. The sort of situation Milgram investigated would be more suited to a military context.

Hofling's study was carried out in a real-life situation and so has far more **ecological validity** (see the Methods of Investigation section).

ii. **Sample**. The participants in Milgram's study were all male. Do the findings transfer to females? The participants in Hofling's study were all likely to have been female. Would the findings transfer to males? In Milgram's study the participants were self-selecting. This is because they became participants only by electing to respond to a newspaper advertisement (selecting themselves). They may also have a "typical volunteer personality" – not all the newspaper readers responded so perhaps it takes this personality type to do so. Finally, they probably all had a similar income since they were willing to spend some hours working for a given amount of money. In Hofling's study we may even ask if all nurses have a common personality type. It has to be said that Hofling's study was conducted in 22 different hospitals but they all had similar rules.

iii. **The Times They Are A Changin'.** The Milgram studies were published in 1963, Hofling's in 1966. It is likely that attitudes towards obedience change from society to society and from time to time. It is also likely that there was a higher level of obedience in general in the early 1960s when these studies were carried out. The title of this section is the name of a song written by Bob Dylan who was labelled a "protest singer" (among other things) at that time. The idea of protest against the establishment and authority was becoming popular during that time, but most people were not protesters. Today, expressing opinions against authority and power figures (e.g. against the Royal Family) is quite commonplace but in the early 1960s it was still a novelty. It may be that studies like Milgram's and Hofling's carried out today would not find such high levels of obedience to authority.

iv. **Landmarks**. There is little doubt that these studies opened the eyes of psychologists and others to the level of obedience which humans may be capable of, and they acted as landmarks in our progress towards an understanding of the influence of social influence.

v. **Cultural Differences** As with conformity, we have to remember that some societies have higher levels of obedience as a norm and the findings from research are not necessarily applicable to all societies.

## Feedback
**Varying Levels of Obedience**
1. Increase   2. Decrease 3. Decrease 4. Decrease

# Lesson 5
# What Influences Us?

## Sources of Social Influence
## 1. Group Norms

> Consider two different groups, like a criminal gang and a church mothers' group. Can you suggest a behaviour that may be accepted by one group but not the other?

There must be many answers to this question; perhaps swearing would be an example, or smoking. Theft or other illegal activity is likely to be accepted by the criminals but not by the mothers' group. Working without a wage, for a charity, may be acceptable to a church mothers' group and not for a criminal gang.

These accepted ways of behaving are referred to as **group norms**. "Group" here can mean a variety of things; two or more people who meet face to face can be seen as a group. People can be members of groups that are much bigger and which could not meet in one place – for example a world-wide religious group like Jews. You may like to reflect for a moment on all the groups that you feel you are a member of (including that of "student") and see if you can identify particular norms that apply to those groups (ways of behaviour accepted by the majority) particularly those which are not necessarily adopted by other groups. Try putting some in the table below – a couple of suggestions have been made to start you off.

| Group | Norm |
|---|---|
| Father | Encouraging good behaviour in children |
| Theatre-goer | Keeping silent in the auditorium |
|  |  |
|  |  |
|  |  |

Psychology studies show how group norms form from standards often set by the majority. An early study of this process was carried out by Jenness who asked people to estimate the number of beans in a bottle. When people did it without any other information there was a wide variation in the estimates – some people estimated a large number and some estimated a small number. However, Jenness found that if he allowed people to discuss the estimates in a group, then give a second estimate, the variation reduced considerably and most people estimated a similar number.

---

**Coursework Suggestion**

You may like to ask one group of people to estimate the number of beans or sweets in a jar without any other information then compare it with the estimates made by another group who are allowed to see each other's estimates before making their own (perhaps by merely asking people to write them down and pass on the sheet of paper). Which group has the widest variation?

---

In another lesson you read about how Sherif made use of a visual illusion called **the autokinetic effect**. Sherif asked people to estimate the distance moved by the light and found a wide variation. He then allowed the participants to hear each other's estimates in a group situation and found that the estimates were much closer to each other. Finally, he asked them to re-estimate individually. The second individual estimates were much closer to the group norms.

These two studies illustrate how a group norm often develops from the majority view but the norm can influence our behaviour for different reasons:

### i. Informational Influence

Unless you are used to counting beans (which is unlikely), then how **can** you estimate the number? The situation is ambiguous: there could be hundreds, thousands or perhaps a million in jar! In ambiguous situations we tend to follow the way others behave. We may watch others to see what cutlery they use to eat a course of a meal, whether to tip hotel staff, how to get into the queue for a snooker table in a pub, how to address a bishop. The norm may give us the information we need to have about the situation, so seeing that most other people have previously guessed the number of beans to be in the hundreds rather than the millions, at least gives us a guideline to follow.

### ii. Normative Influence

This involves looking for the often unspoken rules in a group situation in order to know what is expected, so that we can fit in with the expected behaviour patterns and be accepted by the group. It can involve drinking the "right" drink, wearing the "right" clothes, listening to the group's preferred music or something more serious like committing crimes or taking drugs.

## 2. Internal Filters

Psychologists suggest that we unwittingly filter out certain information from our surroundings and allow other information in. This is the same as a coffee filter letting the water through but not the coffee grounds. Here, we allow some aspects of what is happening around us to influence our behaviour, but not other aspects. How do we decide what to "let in" and what to "keep out"?

**Scripts** may be one answer to this question. Scripts are schemas – like a plan of how we understand something. According to Schank and Abelson, writing in 1977, we have schemas about events; they are well-known patterns of actions and interactions.

For example, eating at McDonalds is probably one of the world's best known scripts. Generally, we enter McDonalds and expect the counter to be at the far end of the space. We expect to approach the counter, not for the assistants to approach us and show us to a table. We expect the assistant to greet us and ask us for out order. We expect to choose from a limited range of dishes that will be pictured above the counter. The assistant will take our money before putting the food on a tray. The food will be on mostly disposable containers. We, not the assistant, will carry the tray away and look for an empty table. After eating we may take the disposable containers and put them in a litter bin rather than expect an assistant to clear it away.

This script is more or less universal. The same procedure is followed at McDonalds in Paris or in Moscow. (There are slight variations – for example, in the Wall Street branch in New York, an assistant will show you to a table whilst someone plays a grand piano!). The script is different from the one used for eating in a hotel restaurant, where a waiter will greet you on entry and show you to a table, asking if you want a smoking or non-smoking area and so on.

Scripts, like stereotypes, make social interactions easier because they are prepared, "off the shelf", like a take away meal they need no work beforehand. They have drawbacks of course. They may not be an accurate perception of all social situations; they may not always be appropriate for all situations in which they are used (it is quite a surprise to be allocated a table in the Wall Street McDonalds and causes some little confusion to the customer inexperienced in eating there). On the whole, though, Schank and Abelson suggest that scripts are a fundamental mechanism in social interactions and help to regulate them.

Although scripts like this are internal (i.e. "inside" the mind of the person) they may be shared with others – everyone follows roughly the same script in McDonalds. We internalise scripts created by groups but tailor them to suit ourselves – our past experiences, our personalities, our expectations and so on.

There are other internal filters apart from scripts that cause us to be influenced by factors in our social environment. For example, our career aspirations may cause us to pay more attention to people who we see as important in our career; we may adopt some of the behaviours and interests of our line manager for example. Different personalities will be more sensitive to some social factors, or we may be attracted to someone and so pay more attention to him or her.

## 3. External Filters

External filters perform the same function as internal filters. They "filter out" some social factors and "let through" some others. The difference is that external filters are social mechanisms outside the mind of the person and outside the control of the person. They may include the media, peer groups, social institutions like school or church.

**The media** is a good example of the external filter. Some information is passed on by the media but some is not. Newspapers, television, radio and magazines select some information to pass on and some to withhold. In one famous case an international publisher withheld publication of a book about China because the book contained derogatory allegations about the way the country was run. The publisher also owned a company that was trying to obtain the licence to broadcast satellite programmes to China, so it was in the financial interests of the publisher to filter out the negative information about China from the books it sold in case it caused them to lose the profitable contract for satellite programmes.

Often, the media's use of filters will be unconscious and subtle however. A newspaper may prefer to publish a story about a soap star's failed marriage rather than about another soap star's successful marriage for example. The readers gain the impression that soap stars' marriages are unsound and their attitudes towards soap stars are influenced by this filtering process.

---

**Quick Quiz**

1. What is a group norm? (1 mark)
2. Identify one piece of research that supports the notion of group norms (1 mark)
3. Is a script an example of an internal filter or an external one? (1 mark)
4. What is a script in terms of social psychology? (1 mark)
5. Why are the media seen as filters in the process of social influence? (1 mark)

---

## Feedback

### Answers to Quick Quiz

1. Ways of behaving that a particular group finds acceptable.
2. e.g. Sherif's autokinetic effect study; e.g. Jenness' study of estimates of the number of beans in a jar.
3. An internal one
4. e.g. an expectation that a social situation will develop in a particular way.
5. e.g. because they only allow certain pieces of information to be presented to us and this information may influence the way we behave or think.

# Lesson 6
# Losing Our Sense of Self: Deindividuation

## 1. What is Deindividuation?

Deindividuation is the idea that we lose our sense of "self" or our personal identity in some circumstances – usually when we are part of a group of people. Because we lose our sense of self we may do things that we would not normally do: we are not the same person. The idea of deindividuation was originally suggested by Festinger and is often used as one way of explaining the behaviour of crowds when they become rowdy or even violent.

**Definition**: deindividuation is a process in which we lose our sense of self and gain the impression that we are part of a larger identity – the group.

Writers like Diener suggest that we are constantly monitoring our own behaviour and adjusting it, but this process stops when we become deindividuated. Instead of concentrating on our self, the focus of our attention becomes the outside world. Usually, we are also monitoring the reactions of others to our behaviour but this stops too; events that we find interesting draw our attention and we become more involved in these events and care less about what others think of us.

---

**Reflect for a moment on these ideas**
- Are they right in your experience? Do you find yourself constantly judging your own behaviour – perhaps just below the conscious level?
- Do you find yourself thinking about what others think about you? Again, perhaps not consciously? Do you even worry about what others think of you – feel that you are perhaps in some way not matching up to what others expect of you?

---

## 2. How can Deindividuation explain conformity and obedience?

---

Try answering the above question for yourself before reading on.
   Write an explanation for conformity and a separate one for obedience. Then compare your ideas to those following this box.

---

### Deindividuation and Conformity

If we conform, we do so in groups. Deindividuation would suggest that we lose our sense of self and become part of the group so we are far more likely to do the things that we see as what the group would do or want its individual members to do. Group members wear similar clothes because they "become" what the clothes symbolise.

- **Criticism** The participants in Asch's study of conformity (judging the length of lines) were interviewed after the group sessions and some of them expressed the view that they had been aware of making a wrong judgment. Others said they didn't want to seem the odd one out. To some extent, then, they **were** monitoring their own behaviour and they **were** conscious of what others thought of them

### Deindividuation and Obedience

Again, we lose our sense of self and stop monitoring our own behaviour. We no longer worry about what people will think so if we are asked to do something that we would not normally do we go ahead. We may do things that we would normally think of as outrageous because we are not taking into account how others will criticise us for it. Also, we are not judging our behaviour against our normal rules for living so there is nothing to stop us from carrying out an act we would previously have seen as unacceptable.

- **Criticism** Some of Milgram's participants refused to administer some of the punishments; this must mean that they **were** monitoring their own behaviour and that they did not lose their sense of self. However, participants who went up to the full voltage were later able to tell Milgram that they felt they were handing over responsibility for their own behaviour to those in authority (Milgram himself) – the idea of deindividuation does involve this merging of the self with a "larger", more important identity.

## 3. What is the evidence for Deindividuation?

### Zimbardo's Deindividuation Study

Zimbardo set up a "learning study" similar to Milgram's but using all female participants. Participants had to administer apparent electric shocks if the "learner" made a mistake. As in Milgram's study, the equipment did not really deliver electric shocks and the "learner" was a confederate of the experimenter, but the participants did not know these facts.

In one condition the participants wore their own clothes and were in a brightly lit room. In the other condition they wore hoods and gowns and the room was dimly lit.

> Can you predict in which condition more shocks were given?

More shocks were given and to a higher level in the *hooded/dimly lit* condition than in the *own clothes/well lit* condition. This would fit in with the idea of deindividuation because in the hooded condition the participants become anonymous and lose their sense of identity.

- Critics of Zimbardo's study pointed out that the hoods and gowns worn by his participants were very similar to the uniform worn by the Ku Klux Klan in the USA. The Ku Klux Klan is a group of white supremacists known for their cruelty to ethnic minorities and critics suggested that wearing these hoods and gowns would simply act as a "prompt" (technically known as a "demand characteristic") for the participants to behave more cruelly.

- To investigate this effect Zimbardo repeated the study using hospital gowns and facemasks worn in the operating theatre during surgery. He found that the effect was smaller but still apparent – the participants did administer more shocks with the gowns and masks on, but not as many as when they were wearing the previous hoods and gowns.

## 4. What factors affect deindividuation?

Looking at the work of Milgram, Asch, and Zimbardo we can see the following factors:

- **Individual Differences** Not everyone will react in the same way. In Asch's study of line length some people did conform and some didn't. It seems that some could have been more deindividuated and some less so. In the interviews later, some people said they were not aware of making a mistake whilst others said they were conscious of making the mistake but didn't want to spoil the study. The ones who were not aware of making the mistake could have been monitoring their own behaviour and the reactions of others less than the ones were aware that they were making mistakes.
- **The Complexity of the Groups** Asch found that if a participant had at least one other person in the group making the same "mistake", then the participant would be less likely to conform. Deindividuation involves giving up the self to the group but in this case there is more than one group (the mass of confederates forms one group and the supporting confederate plus the participant forms the other group) so the participant has a choice of groups in which to invest his sense of identity. By investing in one group the participant conforms but by investing in the other group the participant keeps the self intact.
- **Level of Anonymity** In Zimbardo's study, more shocks were given when the participants were more anonymous. With hoods and gowns or masks and gowns a participant would have had the notion that neither the "learner" nor the other participants could know her identity.
- **Other Social Factors** The use of hospital gowns and masks led to less shocks than the use of Ku Klux Klan style hoods and gowns. Both sets of costumes would lead to very similar amounts of physical covering so the roles played by doctors and the roles played by white supremacists have also affected the level of behaviour of the participants and it could be that this was because the roles played by the people who normally wear these clothes lead to different levels of anonymity (we usually know the identity of the surgeon but not the Ku Klux Klan member). In the long run, there could be many other factors that affect the extent to which we deindividuate.

---

**Quick Quiz**
1. What do we lose during deindividuation?        (1 mark)
2. When we are more anonymous are we more likely to deindividuate? (1 mark)
3. What do we stop monitoring during deindividuation? (1 mark)
4. To what do we pay more attention during deindividuation? (1 mark)

5. Who studied deindividuation using female participants in hospital gowns? (1 mark)

6. In which condition did Zimbardo's participants give more shocks: the "own clothes" condition or the "hospital gown/mask" condition? (1 mark)

7. Name four factors that affect deindividuation (4 marks)

**Total 10 marks**

## Feedback

**Answers to Quick Quiz**

1. Our sense of self (1 mark)
2. Yes (1 mark)
3. Our own behaviour (1 mark)
4. External events (1 mark)
5. Zimbardo (1 mark)
6. In the "hospital gown/mask" condition (1 mark)
7. Individual differences; complexity of the groups; level of anonymity; other social factors. (1 mark for each correct answer = 4 marks)

**Total = 10 marks**

# Lesson 7
# Environment and Behaviour

## 1. Personal Space

If somebody comes too close it can make you feel uncomfortable. You may have experienced this particularly if the person who gets too close is a stranger.

In lifts, for example, we often have to stand much closer to strangers than we would normally do. On buses and trains, in queues and other places where we are expected to stand close to others, we may experience this discomfort. On the other hand we may be perfectly content to sit very close to someone we love – in fact we are likely to seek out such intimate proximity.

### How close is too close? Hall's Proxemics

Hall suggested that we tend to have four zones of personal space around us, which correspond to four levels of intimacy. If someone enters a zone that is not appropriate for them then we will experience a feeling of discomfort.

i)   **Intimate Distance** – between 0 and ½ m. Only our loved ones or family would normally be allowed in this space. There are exceptions – like contact sports when we come into close contact in a rugby scrum or dancing – but we would usually move away from someone who invaded this space.

ii)  **Personal Distance** – ½ m to 1½ m. People we are familiar with when we are having conversations with them would normally be in this zone

iii) **Social Distance** – 1½m to 3½m. Shop assistants or other strangers we are dealing with would be in this zone.

iv)  **Public Distance** – Over 3½m When relating to a group in public – e.g. in a lecture or aerobics class we normally stand at least this distance away: the far point depends on circumstances like how far our voice will travel.

### Cultural Differences

Hall pointed out that there are cultural differences in the sizes of body zones. He suggested that this is particularly noticeable in the Personal and Social distances of different cultures. North American and north European cultures in particular had much bigger zones than Arab and Mediterranean cultures, for example. He described the amusing sight of an Arab and an American trying to converse – the American continually backing away and the Arab continually approaching.

Differences like this are often subconscious and can easily lead to misunderstandings between people who only know that they feel uncomfortable with each other but do not understand why – in fact, one is insulted by the other's withdrawal and the other is feeling hemmed in.

### Other variations in personal space

A variety of factors other than cultural differences affect the size of our personal space:

- **Individual differences** like age, sex, social class, personality – even criminality can make a difference – criminals prefer larger spaces.
- **Situational factors**: we will allow people into our personal space in situations like lifts, contact sports and dancing, as mentioned above – but this does not mean to say that we necessarily feel less discomfort.
- **Status**: this has some interesting variations. Generally speaking, it seems that we will maintain a larger space between ourselves and people we perceive as having a higher status but we may feel a smaller space is acceptable between ourselves and people of a lower status – the boss can pat you on the back but *you* cannot pat the boss on the back!

**Study of personal space**

Felipe and Sommer observed the reactions of female students who had their personal space invaded in a library. The outcome of this study is not a surprise but the researchers' contribution is that the procedure was carried out in a systematic, scientific way so that we are not merely speculating.

The researchers targeted lone female students in the library. They defined "lone" carefully. They then carried out one of two procedures. In the experimental condition, a female researcher sat next to the "target" and brought her chair very close (again, "close" was carefully defined). The reaction of the target was noted and tended to be one of the following:

i) She moved away within a very short time

ii) She erected barriers using books, coats etc.

iii) She asked the researcher to give her space

iv) She used non-verbal communication (e.g. turning away) to signal her disapproval

In the control condition the researcher adopted a normal distance from the subject (again, carefully defined) and the reactions of the subject were noted. There tended to be no evidence of ii) to iv), and targets moved away considerably later than in i), in fact in the sort of time we might expect somebody to leave a library normally.

**Evaluation of personal space study**

Although there are ethical reservations about this study (it would be considered unacceptable to intimidate and harass people in this way) it does show, in a structured way, the existence of personal space.

---

**Consider Personal Space**

It would **not** be appropriate for you to try out studies like Felipe and Sommer's but you may like to interview your friends about any experiences they remember of having their personal space invaded. How many have had this experience? Can they put a figure on how close they feel strangers can come without making them feel uncomfortable?

---

# 2. Territoriality

Territory is different from personal space. A territory is an area that a person claims ownership of. Unlike personal space it cannot normally be moved around (though cars and other vehicles may be considered territories under some circumstances). It does have the effect of keeping people away from us, reducing crowding and establishing privacy but it has similarities with non-human animals' territories.

**Functions of territories**

In other animals, a territory is useful for survival because:

- it provides an area in which food can be located – it is obviously advantageous for a cat to keep other cats out of its area so that it does not have to share the mice it will find in its territory (or Kit-e-Kat!)
- it provides an area in which the cat can mate with other cats – the same argument applies to reproduction as applies to food; the cat can exclude competitors for its mate's sexual services
- it provides resources for a home – cats can use a variety of materials for nests – from discarded jumpers to long grass.

To some extent you may think that the above three functions are served in humans by territory too, but as our behaviour is more sophisticated so we would expect the functions of territories to more sophisticated for humans. We could suggest that human territory provides:

- Privacy – a place to which we can retreat
- A sense of control over our lives – a feeling of self-esteem
- A feeling of security
- An opportunity to express ourselves in decorations and furnishings
- The ability to organise ourselves – knowing what is kept where

**Characteristics of Territories**

Territories are

- **physical areas** – e.g. a person's home or a family member's bedroom in that home, or even a part of a shared bedroom ("That's my shelf!")
- **marked** – homes may be marked out as a family's territory, e.g. fences, hedges and gates may mark out the house, a style of decoration may mark out a room or furniture may be regarded as a boundary in a shared bedroom. The lack of this ability to mark out a home may be an important factor in the failure of some blocks of flats to offer a feeling of privacy and security – see "Defensible Space" below. Cats, of course, mark out their territories by urinating at its boundaries.
- **owned** – it is necessary for the person to be able to say "This is mine". Sometimes this may be through outright legal ownership or it may be a rented property, or it may just be an agreement between two sisters sharing a bedroom.
- **defended** – being able to lock doors and gates or shut others out in some other way may be very important.

> This may be a good point to consider whether this makes you think we are just like other animals.

**Types of Territories**

Altman and Chemers considered there to be three distinct types of territories:

i) **Primary Territory** This is an area we consider to be our own or to be largely controlled by ourselves. A home, bedroom, garden, desk in an office, locker or similar space.

ii) **Secondary Territory** This is a space that only you and a restricted few others can use for short periods and/or in turns. Your seat in a classroom, your table in a restaurant, even your favourite seat in the pub or snack bar may be considered "yours" but only for the moment.

iii) **Public Territory** This is available to everyone and is only yours while you use it. Your seat on a bus can be used by anyone when you are not sitting in it. Your space on the pavement is only yours for a moment. Your place in a queue: you can keep your place in a queue by asking someone to "stand in" for you in some cultures, but if you leave it, someone can take it.

---

**What Type of Space Is It?**
Consider the following spaces. What types of space do you think they are? Suggested answers are in the Feedback section at the end of the lesson but these things are sometimes debatable!
1. Your seat in a family car (if you are not the driver)
2. Your seat in your own car (you are the driver)
3. Your seat at the family table
4. Your seat in the college library
5. Your seat at the cinema

---

## 3. Territory and Crime – Defensible Space

Accommodation in large tower blocks of flats is relatively new in the United Kingdom; it only became a common feature of city landscapes from the 1960s. Crime and vandalism became key issues in many of the high-rise blocks.

Town planners and local authority housing departments asked why this should be. It did not seem to be overcrowding (referred to as "crowding" by psychologists). Many of the people in the new tower blocks had moved from overcrowded areas to the blocks, and there were many examples from other European countries of much more densely populated apartments.

One suggestion that planners have taken seriously results from our study of territoriality. It is the notion of Defensible Space. The term sounds like something from a war movie and is a little misleading; a term more like "belonging space" would be more accurate because it refers to an area which:

- **has clear boundaries**
- **can be watched over by people who think of it as "theirs"**
- **may have markings which indicate that it "belongs" to somebody**

All these features would be interpreted by an intruder as meaning that the space is not public – even though the public may have access to it.

For example, someone's front garden fits all these characteristics. The public may intrude on it under certain circumstances – to deliver leaflets perhaps but the intruders will feel they are being watched, and understand that they are being allowed to enter the area but that it is expected that they will leave when their business is complete. It is not a public area like a park but a secondary territory belonging to someone else.

Planners who have built these features into large-scale public housing have had success in deterring crime and keeping vandalism to a low level. The criminal walking into non-defensible areas feels no more sense of intrusion than he or she does when walking into a park. Passers-by would not be expected to notice the intruder in a large housing development with no defensible space any more than they would be expected to notice a member of the public walking through the park.

Flats gathered round a common courtyard, walls and fences marking out small areas and no large open spaces around the developments are features that create defensible space in housing. A large, high-rise block of flats with a repetitive pattern of windows placed in the middle of an empty space often cleared from a previously poor housing area and surrounded by derelict and/or industrial buildings is indefensible and public.

### Newman's study of housing

After examining two New York housing designs, Newman found the big differences in their crime rates and vandalism corresponded with big differences in their design. The Van Dyke "project" (a word used in America for "estate") fitted the image of the high-rise "public" building surrounded by open space. The Brownsville project was much lower rise (six storeys compared to the fourteen storeys of the Van Dyke) and had entrances which were shared between only a few families and which could be seen from the flats of all the families that used them.

Research like this supports the idea that humans, like other animals, have a tendency to regard different spaces in different ways. Both the potential intruder and the resident regard defensible space in the same way.

---

**Is your space defensible?**
Think for a moment about the place you live.
- What is your primary area?
- Is the space around your primary area defensible: does it have the three characteristics listed in the bullet points above? If not, would they be easy to establish?

---

## 4. Privacy

Privacy involves controlling the access that other people have to you. If you are able to exclude people from your company then you are in control of your privacy. Some people seem to put a high value on privacy and others are not so concerned.

To control privacy we need to be able to control access to our Primary Territory. A lock on the door may be needed, or simply closing the door may be sufficient to signal to others that they should not enter. Similarly, we may simply ask people to give us privacy or use non-verbal communication to let others know that we want to have privacy – for example, we may simply ignore someone's remarks or use a "grunt" to signal that we do not want to interact.

Sometimes, however, we may feel that our privacy is invaded in other ways: by noise or smells for example. Our mail being opened may be regarded as invasion of privacy as may someone listening to our telephone conversations or watching us in the street. If we think that our privacy can be invaded in a public place like the street then privacy must extend beyond our primary territory and become more a matter for our "psychological space" than for our physical space.

**Altman** suggests that we have a balance of privacy that may change. Too much privacy gives us feelings of being isolated but too little may lead to a sense of crowding.

## Feedback
### What Type of Space Is It?
1.  Secondary. It is not open to the public to use but you may share it with others. It is likely that you always sit in the same seat in the family car but it may be taken by another passenger sometimes – without your permission.
2.  Primary. It is your car; you control it.
3.  Secondary. It is likely that you always occupy the same seat at the table but it is possible that a guest may have it too.
4.  Public. It is only yours while you sit in it. You do not own it.
5.  Public. It is only yours while you sit in it. You do not own it.

# Lesson 8
# Forming Impressions of Other People

## 1. Who are you?

One of the country's most notorious shoplifters has a court order banning her from entering Marks and Spencer stores. Her favourite routine was to steal an item of expensive clothing from the store, make a small mark or cut in an inconspicuous place on the clothing, and then take it back to the store to demand "her" money back. The assistant would ask to see the receipt but the shoplifter knew that by dressing expensively and acting in an annoyed manner she could "fluster" the assistant into accepting the clothing and returning the money. The assistant would accept the impression the shoplifter gave of being a customer of high standing.

As well as telling us a lot about the "real" person we are inside, psychology can tell us a lot about these "surface" impressions that we often give out, usually without conscious intention. It can also tell us a lot about the way in which we form impressions of other people on the basis of a few pieces of information; this is referred to as impression formation.

## 2. Studies of Impression Formation: sources of bias and distortion

### The work of Asch: central traits and peripheral traits

Asch gave a list of personality characteristics to two groups of participants as follows:

| Group A | Group B |
| --- | --- |
| Intelligent | Intelligent |
| Skilful | Skilful |
| Industrious | Industrious |
| Warm | Cold |
| Determined | Determined |
| Practical | Practical |
| Cautious | Cautious |

As can be seen, the only difference between the two lists was the use of the word "warm" with Group A, which was changed to "Cold" for group B

Each group was told that the list described a fictitious person. After looking at the list, each group was asked to complete a further description of the person by choosing characteristics from a second list; this time both groups received the same list of characteristics.

When Asch examined the choices from the second list he found that the participants from the "warm" group had chosen quite different characteristics when compared to the participants from the "cold" group. The "warm" group had chosen words like

humorous,

popular,

generous and

sociable.

These give a positive impression of the person. The "cold" group had chosen completely different words that gave a more negative impression of the person.

From this study, Asch concluded that the warm/cold characteristics had altered the impression of the whole person.

Asch tried other words to see what effect they would have on the impression formed of the person. One of the pair of words he investigated was "polite/blunt" but surprisingly, he found no consistent difference between the words chosen from the second list by the two groups. From this, Asch concluded that some words were more "powerful" than others in forming impressions of others. The more powerful words he termed "**central traits**": the less powerful he termed "**peripheral traits**".

### The work of Kelley

In a similar study Kelley gave a curriculum vitae of a new lecturer to a class of students before the lecturer arrived. As well as listing his teaching experience, the curriculum vitae included a brief description of the person himself. One half of the students were given a description that included the phrase "rather warm person" and the other half were given the description "rather cold person". As could be expected from Asch's study, the "warm" group gave a more positive description of the lecturer afterwards and the "cold" group gave a negative one. Also, many more of the "warm" group took part in a discussion after the lecture, than did the "cold" group.

Once again, we can conclude that the use of the warm/cold dimension had altered the view of the whole person gained by the students. In general, psychologists refer to the **halo effect** when one positive characteristic in a person "distorts" our view and leads us to see a wider range of positive things about the person. The same thing can happen in reverse, of course, with a single negative trait leading us to see mainly negative things in a person and to ignore any positive traits or explain them away as chance or uncharacteristic.

Central and peripheral traits and the halo effect are examples of **Implicit Personality Theories** which psychologists suggest we all employ. These are unconscious theories about what people are like which are based on a small amount of information about the person. As well as the examples given above, studies show that we use aspects of people like their names to give us a quick and easy picture of what they are like. Is a name like Peregrine, Tarquin or Sebastian likely to conjure up an image of a coal miner, for example, or does Sharon or Lisette sound like the sort of name the royal family may give to the next heir to the throne?

---

Consider the studies carried out by Kelley and Asch. Which one would you say is more representative of a "real life" situation?

---

**Evaluation of the Asch and Kelley studies**

Neither study is truly naturalistic; both of them consisted of "contrived" situations but Kelley's study did have a "real" person for the participants to form an impression of whilst Asch's person was completely fictitious. The participants in Kelley's study experienced other behaviours and characteristics which people normally come across when they meet a person; they were, therefore, able to form an impression in a more realistic setting. How often would we have to "meet" or observe someone without any experience of what they look like, speak like or dress like?

**The work of Luchins: First Impressions Last – the Primacy and Recency Effects**

The phrase "First Impressions Last" can have more than one meaning. A question about the meaning will be posed at the end of this section.

Studies of memory suggest that we tend to remember the first items in a list and the last items – more so than the items in the middle. This tends to be repeated in the impressions we gain of people: the first impressions we form tend to be remembered more than later ones. Also, the impression we gained of someone the last time we met them tends to stick with us too.

Luchins read out a description of the behaviour of an imaginary character, "Jim". Half of Jim's behaviour suggested that he was introverted (withdrawn, quiet and shy) whilst the other half suggested that he was extroverted (outgoing, noisy and gregarious). The participants then had to rate Jim on a scale of extroversion-introversion, which meant resolving an apparent contradiction. The descriptions were presented as follows:

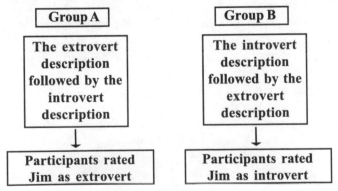

Luchins' results showed that Group A participants tended to rate Jim as an extrovert and Group B rated him as an introvert. The fact that participants were able to focus on one set of information and exclude the other half is interesting in itself but this study confirms the idea that first impressions are the most important, that they last longer than others.

Studies have also shown that when participants are manipulated into concentrating attention on later information about a person, they are more likely to remember that later impression – this is referred to as the **recency effect**.

> **Why is the phrase "first impressions last" a relevant one for psychologists?**
> An example of a suggested answer is in the feedback section at the end of the lesson.

### Evaluation of the Luchins study

While Luchins' study did suffer from the same drawbacks as Asch and Kelley – i.e. the situation is unrealistic – Luchins' work is consistent with the findings from the study of Memory in cognitive psychology, and when two ideas support each other in this way it makes them more credible.

## 3. Applications to everyday situations

The order in which we obtain information about a person is, therefore, a **source of bias or distortion** of the person. We only perceive a portion of all the aspects of the person and so our picture of him or her is distorted. If we know this to be true then there may be times when we need to take this fact into account.

"Making a good impression" is a common idea but our studies suggest that if we wish to do so then it is important that we focus on the first impression we give.

> Can you think of any situations in which you may want to give a good first impression? Some suggestions follow.

### Job interviews

These last for a very short time – often only minutes – and most people recognise the importance of the way they dress, sit and speak during a job interview. Similarly, an employer who is keen to recruit the right person for the job will be careful about the first impression given by the company. This often starts with the way the advertisement for the job is set out, the way the information about the job is sent to the enquirer and the way the applicant is treated by the company.

### Job aspects

Some jobs depend on first impressions for success. Salespeople, politicians and receptionists are examples of people who depend on their impressions for gaining the confidence of their clients. Salespeople, in particular, often have only a very short time to inspire confidence in the product or service, and this often depends more on giving a good impression of themselves than on the product or service.

### Other occasions

There are many situations we all find ourselves in which require us to present a particular first impression. Dealing with "authority" like courts often requires a conscious manipulation of our first impression. This may be a decision to ensure we look "respectable" or it may even be that we "dress down" so the court does not think we can afford to pay more! Some social situations are best met with a particular impression – going out with someone for the first time is often the situation which will "make or break" a relationship for example.

**Fill in the missing words in this exercise**
Answers appear in the Feedback section at the end of the lesson.
1. Asch manipulated the words_____and_____between two groups
and found that they had an effect on the overall_____of the fictitious
character. (3 marks)
2. Kelley found that students who had previously been given the impression
that a new teacher was "a rather warm person" were_____likely to take
part in a discussion during the lesson. (1 mark)
3. The words "polite" and "blunt" were not as effective in Asch's study
and so were concluded to be_____traits rather than _____traits.
(2 marks)
4. If we compare the study done by Kelley with the one done by Asch it
seems that the one done by_____ is more similar to real life. (1 mark)
5. When one positive characteristic in a person causes us to perceive a
mainly positive impression of him or her, we refer to this as
the_____. (1 mark)
6. We tend to be more influenced by the first and last impressions gained
of a person. Psychologists refer to these as the_____and
_____effects. (2 marks)
**Total possible marks = 10**

## Feedback

### First Impressions last

The phrase "first impressions last" is a relevant one for psychologists because
studies show that the first impressions that we create are likely to last longer in
people's minds than any impressions we give later.

### Fill in the missing words

1. Asch manipulated the words **warm** and **cold** between two groups and found
   that they had an effect on the overall **impression** of the fictitious character.
   (3 marks)
2. Kelley found that students who had previously been given the impression that
   a new teacher was "a rather warm person" were **more** likely to take part in a
   discussion during the lesson. (1 mark)
3. The words "polite" and "blunt" were not as effective in Asch's study and so
   were concluded to be **peripheral** traits rather than **central** traits. (2 marks)
4. If we compare the study done by Kelley with the one done by Asch it seems
   that the one done by **Kelley** is more similar to real life. (1 mark)
5. When one positive characteristic in a person causes us to perceive a mainly positive
   impression of him or her, we refer to this as the **halo effect**. (1 mark)
6. We tend to be more influenced by the first and last impressions gained of a person.
   Psychologists refer to these as the **primacy** and **recency** effects. (2 marks)

**Total possible marks = 10**

# Lesson 9
# You People Are All The Same! – Stereotypes

---

**The Surgeon Riddle**
**Try solving this riddle. The answer appears in the text if it defeats you.**
A young man is rushed to hospital after a road accident. He is taken to the operating theatre immediately for an emergency operation but the surgeon takes one look at the patient and says "I cannot operate on this man, he's my son". The strange thing is that the surgeon is **not** the patient's father. What could explain this?

---

## 1. Categorisation

If we had to "start from scratch" every time we met somebody it would probably be difficult to go about a lot of our business. It is easier to think of someone as a *Daily Mirror* reader or *Times* reader, as a Jaguar driver or Ford driver, or as a librarian or disc jockey rather than start examining all the individual personality characteristics of each person.

**Snap judgements of people – Applications to everyday situations**

When we meet people we often make a **snap judgement** of them. In making snap judgements we put them into categories on the basis of one or two characteristics.

---

What sort of characteristics would you suggest that we use to judge people?

---

**Clothes** – it seems to go without saying that we judge people by the clothes they wear. Studies have shown that passers-by are far more likely to help a well-dressed motorist with his car than to help a scruffily dressed one.

**Physical appearance** – a study by Piliavin showed that research assistants with a birthmark covering half their face were substantially less likely to be helped by other people than were assistants with no birth mark.

**Disability** – a phrase well known by people with noticeable physical disabilities is "Does he take sugar?". Disabled people point out how often they are assumed to be incapable of anything, including making decisions about whether they want sugar in their tea.

**Age** – the phrase "ageism" entered our vocabulary sometime in the 1970s and it is a useful word to remind us that we have fixed ideas about older people and younger people. A group of young males standing outside a shop is far more likely to be suspected of being up to no good than is a group of elderly females.

## 2. Stereotyping

This topic is also discussed as part of the Sex and Gender lessons and the Prejudice lessons.

A stereotype is "a fixed, often simplistic generalisation about a particular group or class of people." (Cardwell, 1996). Stereotyping involves creating these **over-simplifications,** which are more often coloured with a negative rather than a positive association. Stereotyping is a way of making a snap judgement and assigning someone to a category. If we stereotype somebody we assign them to one of the stereotypes we hold then make the assumption that the person has all the other characteristics of the group. The example of the teenagers, above, illustrates this.

### Positive and negative stereotypes

Most stereotypes probably tend to convey a negative impression. Positive examples would include judges (the phrase "sober as a judge" would suggest this is a stereotype with a very respectable set of characteristics), overweight people (who are often seen as "jolly") and television newsreaders (usually seen as highly dependable, respectable and impartial). Negative stereotypes seem far more common, however.

### Sex-role stereotypes (Gender-role stereotypes)

In a series of studies by Williams and Best carried out in over thirty countries, students were asked to say whether the following characteristics were more likely to be associated with men or with women: only 20 characteristics are listed here but in the original study over 300 were used. This would make a good study for coursework.

| Stingy | | Gentle | | Pleasure-Seeking | | Cautious | |
|--------|--|--------|--|------------------|--|----------|--|
| Reckless | | Suggestible | | Capable | | Understanding | |
| Greedy | | Stern | | Complicated | | Fickle | |
| Sophisticated | | Conceited | | Hard-headed | | Self-Pitying | |
| Complaining | | Active | | Disorderly | | Prudish | |

In the space next to each characteristic write "M" for male or "F" for female according to whether you think the characteristic is more often associated with males or females.

As you are reading about sex-role stereotyping it may be that you can "see through" the question and find it difficult to carry out this task because it may be rather obvious what we would expect the outcome to be. If you do find it difficult to complete, you could:

i.   try asking a friend to put M or F in the boxes or

ii.  you could think of it in terms of how often these characteristics are shown as associated with male or female characters on the television or in a novel you are reading now.

Williams and Best found that the same characteristics tended to be associated with males and females across the thirty countries. These were:

| Male – associated characteristics | Female – associated characteristics |
|---|---|
| Stingy | Sophisticated |
| Reckless | Complaining |
| Greedy | Gentle |
| Stern | Suggestible |
| Conceited | Complicated |
| Active | Cautious |
| Pleasure-Seeking | Understanding |
| Capable | Fickle |
| Hard-headed | Self-Pitying |
| Disorderly | Prudish |

Were yours similar?

The outcome of Williams and Best's study suggests that there are stereotypes of females and males and it may be that your responses have fallen in line with this.

**Evaluation**

- The Williams and Best study did show some clear-cut stereotypes held, but the method used was very far from real life – it had little ecological validity. In real life, we are not asked to fill in questionnaires about the people we live and work with.

To take this study a little further we could examine the quality of the stereotype as follows.

Here is the list again but this time in a different order and with a second box next to the characteristic; Try putting "P" for positive or "N" for negative in the first box after each characteristic.

| Stingy | | | Gentle | | | Pleasure-Seeking | | | Cautious | |
|---|---|---|---|---|---|---|---|---|---|---|
| Reckless | | | Suggestible | | | Capable | | | Understanding | |
| Greedy | | | Stern | | | Complicated | | | Fickle | |
| Sophisticated | | | Conceited | | | Hard-headed | | | Self-Pitying | |
| Complaining | | | Active | | | Disorderly | | | Prudish | |

After you have completed this, put the sex you assigned to the characteristic in the second box – you will have to look back at the first table of course. This will give 20 pairs of letters as follows:

| **PF** | **Positive Female** | **NF** | **Negative Female** |
|---|---|---|---|
| **PM** | **Positive Male** | **NM** | **Negative Male** |

Finally, count up the number of each pair that appears in your second table and put the results in the table below

| | **Female** | **Male** |
|---|---|---|
| **Positive** | | |
| **Negative** | | |

Do you find that there are more positive or negative female characteristics? Are there more positive or negative male ones? What do you think this tells us about sex-role stereotypes of male and female? Of course, it may be that you found no difference, and we only examined twenty characteristics.

Many writers point to the negative consequences for women and girls of sex-role stereotypes. Until recently, many children's books and radio and television programmes designed for children, seemed to portray girls as passive, dependent and unintelligent whilst boys were shown as decisive, active, strong and in control. Some people argue that having to live up to a stereotype of "decisive, active, strong and in control" can also be difficult for boys. Some publishers (e.g. Red House) now specialise in children's books which avoid the above stereotypes and which promote positive characteristics in both sexes.

> Think back to the books you read as a child. Think about some of the main characters. Can you remember how the girls behaved and how the boys behaved? Was there a difference like the one described above?

> The next time you watch a television drama, note the way in which the male and female characters are portrayed. Do they fall in line with the above stereotypes? Do some programmes portray males and females equally?

Did you solve the Surgeon riddle at the beginning of this lesson? The answer is that the surgeon was the patient's mother. Our stereotype of surgeons tends to be that they are male. Ask some friends if they can solve the riddle.

### Racial Stereotypes

Researchers have found that stereotypes exist of different races, cultures or ethnic groups. Although the terms race, culture and ethnic groups have different meanings, we shall take them to mean roughly the same thing at the moment.

The most famous study of racial stereotyping was published by Katz and Braly in 1933 when they reported the results of a questionnaire completed by students at Princeton University in the USA. They found that students held clear, negative stereotypes – few students expressed any difficulty in responding to the questionnaire. Most students at that time would have been white Americans and the pictures of other ethnic groups included Jews as shrewd and mercenary, Japanese as shrewd and sly, Negroes as lazy and happy-go-lucky and Americans as industrious and intelligent.

Not surprisingly, racial stereotypes always seem to favour the race of the holder and denigrate other races. It is probably true to say that every ethnic group has racial stereotypes of other groups; some psychologists argue that it is a "natural" aspect of human behaviour, which can be seen to benefit each group because it helps in the long-run to identify with one's own ethnic group and so find protection and promote the safety and success of the group. There is no evidence for this view, however, and many writers argue that it is merely a way of justifying racist attitudes and behaviours.

### Evaluation

- The Katz and Braly studies were done in the 1930s and it can be argued that cultures have changed since then and we are much less likely to hold these stereotypes.

Later studies done in 1951 and 1967 found changes in the stereotypes and the extent to which they are held. In general, stereotypes in the later study tended to be more positive but the belief that particular ethnic groups held particular characteristics still existed.

- Just because participants in a study will trot out stereotypes when asked does not mean to say that people go around acting on them. People do not necessarily behave as though the stereotypes are true.

**Are stereotypes "bad things"?**

Stereotypes do stop us seeing the "real" person and the majority do promote harmful images, but there are times when we need to make "snap" judgements – we cannot make a full evaluation of everybody we meet – and stereotypes can be useful then.

**References**

Cardwell, M (1996) **The Complete A-Z Psychology Handbook** Hodder and Stoughton.

# AQA Exam Style Questions: Social Influence

- **Answer all questions**
- **There is no time limit to this assignment**
- **When completed you may compare your answers with the example answers at the end of the book**
- **If you have tutorial support you should send a copy of your answers to your tutor to receive further feedback, comments and guidance**

A small town in England is well known for its glass products. At one of the factories, tourists are encouraged to visit and watch the glass blowers make their jugs, vases, and other glassware. Coach tours bring the tourists who walk round the factory in groups, four or five times per day accompanied by a factory guide. After the tour, the tourists may buy glassware in the factory shop.

   The production manager counts the number of products made every hour as part of the normal collection of information, but one day a comparison is made between production per hour and the presence of tourists. The data are shown in Table 1.

| Time | 10:00 a.m. | 11:00 a.m. | 12:00 a.m. | 2:00 p.m. | 3:00 p.m. | 4:00 p.m. | 5:00 p.m. |
|---|---|---|---|---|---|---|---|
| No of glassware items produced | 493 | 568 | 544 | 571 | 523 | 502 | 489 |
| Tourists present? | ✗ | ✔ | ✔ | ✔ | ✔ | ✗ | ✗ |

**Table 1**

**Key**

✔ = tourists present

✗ = no tourists present

a) Describe the results of the study. (2 marks)

b) The figures show one of the effects of the presence of others. What do psychologists call the effect shown in the results of this particular study? (1 mark)

c) As well as the presence of tourists, other factors could have caused the effects shown in the data. State **one** other factor that could have caused the effect shown. (1 mark)

**d)** You are walking through the town centre when you notice a young man flat on the pavement on the other side of the road. Nobody is stopping to help the young man. Using your knowledge of psychology, say what is likely to happen unless you take action yourself. (1 mark)

**e)** What is **deindividuation**? (1 mark)

**f)** Briefly describe a study that has investigated **deindividuation** (3 marks)

**g)** Make one criticism of the study you described in f) above. (1 mark)

**h)** What do psychologists mean by the term "obedience"? (1 mark)

**i)** Identify a factor that has been shown to affect obedience. Use evidence from a psychological study to support your answer. (4 marks)

**j)** Identify **one** source of social influence and explain how it can have an effect on our behaviour
**Source** (1 mark)

**Explanation** (4 marks)

**Total possible marks = 20**

When completed you should compare your answers with the example answers at the end of the book. If you have tutorial support you should send a copy of your answers to the tutor for feedback, comments and further guidance.

# OCR Exam Style Questions: Social Influence and Environment and Behaviour

- Answer all questions
- There is no time limit to this assignment
- When completed you may compare your answers with the example answers at the end of the book
- If you have tutorial support you should send a copy of your answers to your tutor to receive further feedback, comments and guidance

**Source A Social Psychology**
**Social Influence Environment and Behaviour**

One of the best-known studies in social psychology is the conformity study carried out by Asch. A "stooge" participant was asked to join a group of other students (who all knew what was going to happen and that the stooge was really the only person being studied). They all gave the wrong answers to questions about the length of some lines and the stooge tended to give the same wrong answers in many cases. The researchers concluded that the stooge had conformed to an expected way of behaving. Some critics were concerned about the ethics of humiliating the stooge.

1. According to the source, what did the researchers conclude? (1 mark)

2. Suggest **two** reasons why people might think that Asch's study of conformity was unethical. (4 marks)

3. When Asch interviewed the participants later, he built up a short list of reasons given by the participants for why they had conformed. State **two** of these reasons. (2 marks)

4. Give a definition of conformity. (2 marks)

5. Psychologists suggest that there are different **types** of conformity: **Compliance**, **Normative Conformity** and **Informational Conformity**. Choose **one** of these types and describe it. (3 marks)

6. Outline **two** factors that have been shown to affect conformity. (4 marks)

7. Suggest how an individual might establish his or her own territory in daily life. (4 marks)

**Total possible marks = 20**
When completed you should compare your answers with the example answers at the end of the book. If you have tutorial support you should send a copy of your answers to the tutor for feedback, comments and further guidance.

# Lesson 10
# Teaching Old Dogs New Tricks –
# Classical Conditioning

## 1. What is Learning?

**Learning** is defined as *any relatively permanent change in behaviour resulting from experience*. This means that we are talking about most of our behaviour and not just the learning behaviour we take part in when we intend to learn something – like learning about psychology as you are doing now, or attending school to learn about history. Talking, walking, relating to people, answering the phone – all of these would be regarded as learned behaviours.

Some psychologists argue that some of our behaviour is inherited and is specific to humans – if you have covered the lessons on Maternal Deprivation for example, (in the lessons on Attachment and Separation) you may see that some people would argue that bonding between baby and adult is not learned but is "built in" to adults and babies.

Despite this debate, the principles of learning can be used to explain many behaviours and to change them. Bad habits, fears, childhood misbehaviour (and adult misbehaviour too!) can all be changed by therapists using the principles we shall look at. In this lesson we shall examine the principles of **Classical Conditioning**, which are some of the earliest ideas about learning.

> **Can you remember?**
> **The definition of learning without looking back at it above?**
> (*Hint: it starts "A relatively.............."*) Check your answer with the one above.

## 2. Classical Conditioning

In the late 1920s a Russian physiologist, Ivan Pavlov, was investigating the digestive system of dogs. Dogs start to salivate at the sight of food (so do humans and other animals); this is a reflex action so it is not controlled consciously. It is like the eyelid blinking when a puff of air is blown into the eye. It is useful because the saliva helps to break down and digest the food that usually follows.

Pavlov was measuring saliva output from dogs and noticed that the dog was salivating when it saw the technician who brought its food, not when it saw the food itself. This is more important than it may seem at first. Salivating is a biological response which is triggered by biological causes but here, Pavlov pointed out, was a biological reaction to a technician!

Pavlov suggested that the dog associated the technician with the food and reasoned that if this were true then it should be possible to get the dog to associate other things with the food. To test the hypothesis of association, Pavlov rang a bell when the food was next brought to the dog and repeated this a number of times. Then he rang the bell without bringing food and noticed that the dog did, indeed, salivate at the sound of the bell. Pavlov had now made two important points:

1. Reflex actions like blinking and salivating are usually produced in response to specific events in the environment like dust in the eye or the sight or smell of food, but animals can associate these reflex actions with other objects or events – other stimuli in the environment.

2. It is possible to manipulate the reflex actions to respond to stimuli that we choose.

We can present this sequence, discovered by Pavlov, as a diagram.

| | Stimulus presented | Leads to | Response |
|---|---|---|---|
| Step 1 | Unconditional Stimulus (UCS) (food) | ⟶ | Unconditional Response (UCR) (salivating) |
| Step 2 | UCS + Conditional Stimulus (CS) (the food + the bell) | ⟶ | UCR (salivating) |
| Step 3 | Repeat | ⟶ | Repeat |
| Step 4 | Conditional Stimulus (CS) (the bell) | ⟶ | Conditional Response (CR) (salivating) |

What does this mean?

**Step 1** When food is presented to a dog it acts as a stimulus and automatically causes the response of salivating. Both the stimulus and the response are unconditional because they do not depend on anything – there are no conditions attached to them working. So **UCS leads to UCR**

**Step 2** Pavlov rang a bell at the same time as presenting the dog with food. The bell is the conditional stimulus because it will only work on condition that it is associated with food. Hence the food is still an unconditional stimulus and the bell is a conditional stimulus (UCS + CS). The dog is salivating again but at this stage it is still doing so because of the food so the response is still an unconditional response to the food (UCR). So **UCS + CS leads to UCR**

**Step 3** Pavlov repeated Step 2 a number of times so that the dog could associate the bell with the food.

**Step 4** The bell is now presented alone but the dog salivates. It is salivating in response to the bell instead of the food so the response is a conditional one; it only appears on condition that the bell has been associated with food in the past. So now the conditional stimulus (CS) produces a conditional response (CR). This response is also referred to as a "condition**ed**" response by some writers who see it as "conditioned into" the dog. So **CS leads to CR**

The dog has now learned to salivate when the bell is rung. Notice that this does not imply that the dog "understands" in the way that we understand that there is someone at the door when the doorbell rings. The word "learned" here simply means that the dog salivates when the bell is rung. It is "a relatively permanent change in behaviour as the result of experience".

## 3. Further Principles of Conditioning

**Extinction** If Pavlov continued to ring the bell without presenting food, the dog would continue to salivate each time but after a number of presentations the dog would cease to salivate. The association would have died out. This is referred to as "extinction" because the association has been extinguished. The conditioning could be re-established by repeating the first procedure.

**Spontaneous Recovery** Although a response may seem to have "disappeared", psychologists have found that if we leave the animal for some time after extinction then re-present the apparently extinguished stimulus a weak response **will** often recur spontaneously.

**Generalisation** Whilst the dog would respond to the bell it would also respond to similar bells and to buzzers. The dog has generalised the sound of the bell to other, similar sounds. People who have a fear of spiders may also fear similar "creepy crawlies", flies and moths: this is the process of generalisation.

**Discrimination** It is possible to enable the dog to discriminate between one bell and another, simply by sounding both bells at different times and presenting the food with one bell but not the other. The association then becomes specific to one bell and the animal discriminates between that bell and other, similar sounds.

> **Check your understanding of the further principles by completing the following:**
> (answers are in the Feedback section)
> "If an animal responds to a stimulus but not to a similar one, then it has learned to _____ between the two. If the opposite happens, whereby the animal will respond to a stimulus and to ones that are similar, the animal is said to be_____ Extinction can be brought about by_____ _____."

### Can Humans be classically conditioned?

Certainly! Look at two pieces of evidence. The first one is from a laboratory study like Pavlov's dog. The second is the sort of evidence you may observe yourself.

> **Worse than the cold shoulder!**
> What happens when you plunge your arm into a bucket of iced water? Apart from the obvious, the surface of your skin contracts. This is called "vasoconstriction" and results from the small blood vessels near the surface of the arm constricting to preserve the heat in the arm. Menzies (1937) plunged the arms of (consenting) participants into buckets of iced water and sounded a buzzer at the same time. He measured the constriction in the blood vessels. He repeated this several times. Can you work out what he did next and what he found? Make a note, then check your answer the Feedback section below.

**Sick of Pesto**

When S was pregnant she went through a period of feeling nauseous and vomiting. This is accepted as reasonably normal in pregnant women and often seems to happen in the mornings (morning sickness). One day S cooked pasta with a pesto sauce; pesto is a pungent sauce made from pine kernels, olive oil and basil – with a distinctive aroma. As she sat down to eat, she experienced a strong bout of nausea and had to go and vomit. From that day for the next ten years she felt nauseous at the smell of pesto sauce. Vomiting to the aroma of pesto had become a conditioned response – only one exposure was needed, no repeating occurred. Can you construct a diagram of this?

## Feedback

**Check your understanding of the further principles:**

"If an animal responds to a stimulus but not to a similar one, then it has learned to **discriminate** between the two. If the opposite happens, whereby the animal will respond to a stimulus and to ones that are similar, the animal is said to be **generalising**. Extinction can be brought about by **presenting the conditional stimulus repeatedly without presenting the unconditional stimulus**.

**Worse than the cold shoulder!**

- He sounded the bell without plunging the arm into icy water·
- He found that the arms produced vasoconstriction without the icy water – they had become conditioned to vasoconstriction at the sound of the buzzer.

**Sick of Pesto**

UCS (morning sickness) → UCR (vomiting).

UCS + CS (pesto sauce) → UCR (vomiting)

CS (pesto sauce) → CR (vomiting)

# Lesson 11
# Training Rats and Children – Operant Conditioning

## 1. The Basic Principles of Operant Conditioning

This type of conditioning differs from classical conditioning in a number of ways, but it also shares some features.

### Thorndike's cats

E. L Thorndike put a cat into a box from which it could escape if it operated a latch. The cat explored the box at first and after some time it operated the latch by accident. Thorndike timed how long it took the cat to escape, then put it back in (well he was a psychologist!). He timed the cat again and noted that it took less time to escape. This was repeated and on each occasion the cat took less time to escape until eventually it would escape as soon as it was put into the box.

Thorndike reasoned that the cat found the experience of escaping from the box rewarding and so proposed his **Law of Effect,** which is that behaviour which has a rewarding consequence is more likely to be repeated and behaviour which has an unpleasant consequence is less likely to be repeated. Notice that there is no claim made about the cat "thinking"; it simply repeats behaviour which has a rewarding consequence.

### Skinner's Boxes

B.F. Skinner designed boxes which could investigate the learning processes of animals, like rats and pigeons. The boxes contained a mechanism which could deliver a pellet of food onto a tray, and other equipment like a lever, lights or displays of different words and symbols.

When a rat is first placed in such a box it soon starts to explore it and eventually will press the lever as part of this exploring behaviour, like the cat in Thorndike's studies. Skinner was very particular about avoiding the idea that we investigate any mental processes and insisted that we should concentrate on the behaviour, not the thinking so he would ask us to be careful about the idea of the rat "exploring" the box; if you explore something you are implying that you are looking for something or have a purpose or a goal to achieve. Because of this he would refer to the "exploring behaviour" and focus on the rat moving around the box rather than the rat's intention to discover what is in its environment (exploring).

He waited for the rat to press the lever by chance. When it did so he delivered a food pellet using the food mechanism. Eventually, it was not necessary to watch the rat because the lever was connected to the food mechanism and it automatically delivered food when the lever was pressed. Quite soon the rat would be pressing the lever continually and obtaining the food pellet. Bearing in mind Skinner's ideas about concentrating on behaviour rather than thought processes he concluded that the consequences of the rat's behaviour had strengthened the behaviour.

In this example we can see the main principle of **operant conditioning**. The operant is the person or animal (collectively known as the organism) and the principle starts from the idea that the behaviour is initiated by the organism, and the conditioning results from the consequences of the organism's behaviour.

Scratching in the corner ———— No consequences

Climbing up the side ———— No consequences

Pressing the lever ———— Food pellet ———— Repeat

Sniffing at the lever ———— No consequences

The diagram above illustrates how the rat displays a range of different behaviours but that only one produces consequences which cause the rat to repeat the behaviour. Being in the box tends to affect the range of behaviours produced by the rat in the first place and Skinner placed importance on the things that preceded the organism's behaviours too. In this case, the box is a **stimulus** to each of the behaviours possible and the behaviours are all possible **responses**. The above diagram can be turned into:

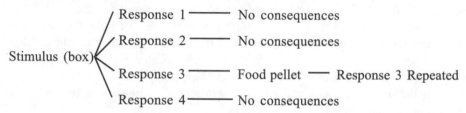

For Skinner, then, learning is a question of **strengthening the association between a stimulus and a response.** This is also referred to as **reinforcing** the behaviour.

### Skinner's behaviour shaping

Skinner now had a rat which would press the lever when it was put in the box. He found that he could "shape" such simple behaviours into much more complex ones. For example, he could alter the mechanism so that it did not deliver a food pellet on every press of the lever but on, say, every fifth press. The rat would press away and eat the food after the fifth press. This could be extended to ten or fifty presses quite easily. He could also change the mechanism so that it only delivered food when the light was on. At first the rat would press the lever no matter whether the light was on or not but after some time *extinction* occurred and the rat would cease pressing the lever. Because of the random nature of the rat's behaviour, however, their would be times when the rat would press the lever when the light was on, so the mechanism would deliver the food pellet. This association was strengthened so the rat would tend to repeat this behaviour and receive more food pellets, and this stimulus – response link was strengthened. So the rat's behaviour was shaped into a more complex pattern of only pressing the lever when the light was on.

It should be possible to teach pigeons to play Ping-Pong (table tennis) using behaviour shaping. Skinner used the process of **successive approximation** to train pigeons to do various tasks. He is featured on films demonstrating in a matter of a couple of minutes how to teach a pigeon to turn circles. A pigeon is placed on a table and given a food pellet reward when it turns a little. This is repeated a couple of times and the pigeon soon adopts this behaviour of turning a little.

The pigeon is then given a food pellet only when it turns **more** than previously and it soon displays this behaviour and is given the food pellet. Skinner then waits until the turning is much more extensive before giving a food pellet and eventually the pigeon turns **full circle** and is only given the pellet when it does so. The complex behaviour (turning full circle) is achieved in small steps. Each step becomes successively closer to the behaviour the researcher wants to achieve, and this is why it is referred to as **successive**. Also, each step is **approximately** what is required but not exactly what is required; hence, "successive approximation."

> Can you suggest how this process of behaviour shaping can be extended to teach the pigeon to play Ping-Pong?

We could give a food pellet to the pigeon if it turns towards the ball when it is placed on the table. We could then wait for the pigeon to approach the ball before we give it a pellet so that after a few repeats of this it should approach the ball when it is put on the table. In the next step we wait until the pigeon touches the ball before we deliver the pellet and then only give the pellet if the pigeon pecks the ball hard enough to knock it over the net. Two pigeons learning this behaviour could be left to their own devices to knock the ball back and forth!

## 3. Types of Reinforcement

**Positive reinforcement** is the strengthening of the association between a stimulus and a response using an experience that the animal finds pleasurable. There are different ways to do this. The different ways are also known as **Schedules of Reinforcement**

i.   **Continuous reinforcement** involves giving the animal a reward every time it produces the desired behaviour. It is normally used when the animal is learning a new response. This schedule causes the animal to respond at a low rate (press the lever few times per minute) and the response soon dies out if the reinforcement is removed.

ii.  **Fixed – ratio reinforcement** rewards the animal after a given number of responses – say after every fifth time it presses the lever. This causes a high rate of response (the more the animal presses the lever, the more rewards it receives) and the response is not extinguished as quickly as in continuous reinforcement (the animal does not receive rewards after each lever press, so continues to press "in case" it receives one at a later press).

iii. **Variable – ratio reinforcement** is similar to fixed ratio but the number of responses required for a reward is not the same each time; the first reward may be given after five responses the second after two, then ten and so on. The response rate is very high (because the reward arrives after an unpredictable number of responses) and is very slow to extinguish (because there is always a chance that it will come after just one more lever press).

iv. **Fixed interval** reinforcement is based on time instead of the number of responses. If a response is given during a particular period – say five minutes – then the reward is given at the end of the period, if the response has not been made during this period then no reward is given. The rate of response is low for this schedule and extinction occurs quite quickly.

v. **Variable interval** is another averaging type of schedule and involves giving a reward after an average amount of time, as long as a response has been given during the period. The average may be five minutes but in the first occasion it may be 2.5 minutes and the second occasion may be 7.5 minutes – which averages to 5 minutes. The response rate is very high and extinction is very slow for this schedule – the animal will keep on responding a long time after the researcher has ceased rewarding responses.

> Complete the following table to summarise the types of response rate and extinction rate linked with each schedule

| Schedule | Response Rate | Extinction Rate |
|---|---|---|
| Continuous | Low | Fast |
| Fixed Ratio | | |
| Variable Ratio | | |
| Fixed Interval | | |
| Variable Interval | | |

## 4. Punishment and Negative Reinforcement

These are two different things and they should not be confused. Most people are familiar with the idea of punishment but not negative reinforcement.

**Punishment**

If a piece of behaviour is followed by a negative experience then this acts as a punishment. If a child is rude and is scolded for acting this way then it has been punished. Punishment makes it **less** likely that a piece of behaviour will be repeated. There are arguments about just how effective punishment is in shaping behaviour. Skinner argued that it is not very effective and that a much better idea is to reward an animal for behaviour that you **do** want, rather than punish it for behaviour you do **not** want. A child punished for behaving one way is not necessarily aware of how it **should** behave, and so its behaviour does not necessarily improve even if it does not repeat the punished behaviour.

**Negative reinforcement**, on the other hand, starts with continuously subjecting an animal to an experience it finds unpleasant **before it has produced any behaviour**, and waiting for it to produce the desired behaviour; when it does display this desired behaviour then the unpleasant experience is removed.

For example, in the past, rats have been placed in cages with metal floors which have discharged a constant, mild electric shock. When the rat pressed the lever the shock was turned off. This reinforces the lever pressing (makes it more likely that it will occur) and is an example of negative reinforcement. Notice that the negative experience comes **before** the behaviour and that the behaviour is **desirable**. When it comes to punishment the opposite is true: the negative experience comes **after** the behaviour and the behaviour is **undesirable**.

---

**Negative Reinforcement or Punishment?**

Are the following descriptions examples of punishment or negative reinforcement?

1. A pet dog barks at the approaching postal worker. Its owner shouts at it and puts it into the kitchen.
2. A barking dog is put into the kitchen and left there until it quietens down, then its owner releases it.
   This next one is a particularly difficult problem to untangle. Is the following a description of negative reinforcement or of punishment?
3. A child has behaved noisily and rudely in the classroom all morning. The child has been asked to work quietly and be polite. Eventually, the teacher puts the child into the corridor until it becomes quiet and asks politely to be readmitted. When this happens the child is readmitted.

Answers are in the Feedback section

---

## 5. Primary and Secondary Reinforcement

Reinforcement is the experience which makes it more likely that a particular behaviour will be repeated. Sometimes the experience is obvious; a chocolate drop given to a dog after it has rolled onto its back in response to the sound "roll over", will act as reinforcement. On other occasions, items which have become associated with the reinforcer become reinforcement in themselves. For example, the rustle of the packet from which the chocolate drop is taken may be associated with the chocolate drop and the dog may perform a piece of behaviour just for the sound alone.

Skinner found that the click of the tray which delivered the food pellet to the pigeon was often enough to cause the pigeon to repeat the behaviour. These associated items are called **Secondary Reinforcers**, so the original item is called a **Primary Reinforcer**.

The chocolate drop is a primary reinforcer. The rustle of the bag is the secondary reinforcer. An example of secondary reinforcers in human behaviour is the payslip. People whose salaries are paid directly into their bank accounts receive from their employer a form that tells them how much has been paid into the account. Employees often look forward to receiving the payslip as if it were the pay itself.

If the secondary reinforcer is presented for a period of time, extinction occurs and the animal will cease to perform the behaviour unless the primary reinforcer is reintroduced. The dog will roll over for the sound of the bag for a time but will eventually give up unless the chocolate drop is occasionally presented.

---

**Quick Quiz**

Complete this quiz to consolidate your understanding of Operant Conditioning

1. State Thorndike's Law of Effect (without looking back)
2. What is the following statement a definition of? *"This process strengthens the association between a stimulus and a response"*

3. According to Skinner, what makes a behaviour more likely to be repeated?

4. What precedes a response in learned behaviour according to Skinner?

5. Would Skinner want to investigate the idea that the rat is looking for a way of getting food?

6. Which process involves achieving a desired behaviour in an animal by taking small steps which come closer to the final aim each time?

7. How is **continuous reinforcement** achieved?

8. Name one other type of reinforcement schedule.

9. In the process of **punishment**, which comes first, the undesired behaviour or the negative experience?

10. In the process of **negative reinforcement**, which comes first, the desired behaviour or the negative experience?

## Feedback

### Schedules of Reinforcement

| Schedule | Response Rate | Extinction Rate |
|---|---|---|
| Continuous | Low | Fast |
| Fixed Ratio | High | Slow |
| Variable Ratio | Very high | Very slow |
| Fixed Interval | Low | Fast |
| Variable Interval | Very high | Very slow |

### Negative Reinforcement or Punishment?

1.  Punishment
2.  Negative Reinforcement
3.  This has elements of both. The child is put in the corridor **after** it has behaved badly, which seems like punishment, but it is subjected to an unpleasant experience (being out in the corridor **is** an unpleasant experience for children) until it produces the desired behaviour (quiet and polite). The balance of the situation points more towards this being a negative reinforcement because if it were just punishment, no other behaviour would be demanded.

### Quick Quiz Answers

1.  Behaviour which has a rewarding consequence is more likely to be repeated
2.  Reinforcement
3.  Its consequences
4.  A stimulus
5.  Probably not. He investigated the behaviour rather than mental processes like "looking for . . . (food)".
6.  Behaviour Shaping. (Successive Approximation would also answer the question correctly)
7.  The animal is given a reward after each display of the desired behaviour.
8.  Fixed ratio; variable ratio; fixed interval; variable interval
9.  The undesired behaviour
10. The negative experience

# Lesson 12
# Similarities and Differences between Classical and Operant Conditioning

## 1. Comparing Classical and Operant Conditioning

Complete the following table as you read through the five corresponding sections below. Use pencil so that you can make any changes you consider to be necessary after you have checked your responses with the suggested answers given in the Feedback section. A suggestion has already been made in the first area to start you off.

| | Classical | Operant |
|---|---|---|
| **i. Difference in Reinforcement Procedures** | Presenting the Conditional Stimulus (e.g. the bell) with the unconditional stimulus (e.g. the food) | |
| **ii. Difference in Origin of Behaviour** | | |
| **iii. Similarity of Intent** | | |
| **iv. Similarity in assumptions about mental processes** | | |
| **v. Similarity in the meaning of Reinforcement** | | |

### i. Difference in Reinforcement Procedures

Reinforcement is the process in which the association between the stimulus and the response is strengthened. In classical conditioning reinforcement occurs when the unconditional stimulus is presented with the conditional stimulus (e.g. the food is presented with the bell): the response starts off as a reaction to the unconditional stimulus (e.g. salivating in response to the food) but eventually becomes a reaction to the conditional stimulus (e.g. salivating in response to the bell)

In operant conditioning, on the other hand, reinforcement occurs as the consequence of the animal's response to a stimulus (e.g. pressing a lever causes a food pellet to be dispensed): it makes the response more likely to occur next time the stimulus is presented.

### ii. Difference in Origin of Behaviour

In classical conditioning, the behaviour to be reinforced starts off as a reflex to another stimulus; for example, salivating starts off as an uncontrollable, unconscious response to the sight of food. In operant conditioning, on the other hand, the behaviour starts as a random reaction to the stimulus. There is no particular reason for a rat to press a lever, but left to its own devices a rat tends to sniff, rub against, nibble and eventually press the lever.

### iii. Similarity of Intent

Although the principles of conditioning have been outlined in terms of researchers like Pavlov and Skinner manipulating the behaviour of animals, these principles have been taken to be the ones which underlie all learning. Although Skinner intended the pigeon to turn full circle, he also used the same principles to explain why pigeons return to the same area of a neighbourhood (because they have previously found food there and so had the behaviour of flying to the area reinforced).

### iv. Similarity in assumptions about mental processes

One of the most controversial ideas in conditioning is that we do not have to pay any attention at all to thoughts, wishes, hopes, desires or any other mental processes. All we use to explain behaviour is the link between stimulus and response. A pigeon pecks at a ping-pong ball not because it wants to play ping-pong, but because this behaviour has been reinforced. An adult screams and hides under the table during a thunderstorm because this behaviour has been associated with thunder. This argument is true for both classical and operant conditioning.

### v. Similarity in the meaning of reinforcement

Although the procedure for reinforcement is different for the two types of conditioning, the end product is the same; reinforcement is the strengthening of the association between the stimulus and the response.

## Feedback

**Some suggested answers to the table**

|  | Classical | Operant |
|---|---|---|
| **i. Difference in Reinforcement Procedures** | The Conditional Stimulus is presented with the unconditional stimulus (e.g. the food). | The operant's behaviour has consequences which are reinforcing. |
| **ii. Difference in the Origin of Behaviour** | The behaviour is already "built in" to the organism a reflex reaction like salivating or sneezing. | The behaviour comes from – "random" activity of the organism like moving around or pressing a lever. It can also be "encouraged" by the environment – e.g. the existence of the lever is likely to lead to it being pressed. |
| **iii. Similarity of Intent** | Learning may be the result of an unintentional experience or it may result from a third party like a researcher or clinical psychologist manipulating the learning intentionally. ||
| **iv. Similarity in assumptions about** | There is no need to make any assumption that the organism (human or other animal) is making any **mental processes** conscious decision about its behaviour. ||
| **v. Similarity in the meaning of Reinforcement** | Reinforcement is the strengthening of an association between a stimulus and a response in both types of conditioning. ||

# Lesson 13
# Phobias

## 1. Incy Wincy Phobia!

Are you afraid of spiders? Many people are. The fear is regarded as irrational because there is no reason to be afraid of them. They cannot really do us any harm (*very* few bite or are poisonous) and they are easily overwhelmed by our superior physical strength (to be subtle). Is there something else you fear irrationally? Being in enclosed spaces or in open spaces are also common sources of irrational fear and there are many others ranging from darkness to daylight, water to thunder, school to cats. Irrational fears like this are called phobias and psychologists regard them as learned behaviours.

**Definition of phobias:** psychologists define phobias as "a . . . disorder in which there is a strong and persistent fear of objects or situations which is not justified by any danger they pose". (Stratton and Hayes, 1992)

**Common Phobias: here are some of the more common phobias.**

| Feared object or situation | Name |
| --- | --- |
| Confined spaces | Claustrophobia |
| Open spaces | Agoraphobia |
| Heights | Acrophobia |
| Spiders | Arachnophobia |
| School | Scholionaphobia (usually just called school phobia) |
| Strangers | Xenophobia |

There are many more phobias and from another viewpoint, virtually any object or situation causes fear in someone, somewhere. Water is an everyday object and while we would all be afraid of the sight of floodwater hurtling towards us, some people's fear of it extends to just water in a glass.

**Understanding Phobias**

Because we understand the principles of learning we can understand why phobias come into existence, and because we understand this we can use the same principles of learning to "unlearn" a phobia. Most phobias should be amenable to change by these principles. By the end of this section on learning you should be able to suggest ways of removing any phobia.

## 2. Using Classical Conditioning to Understand Phobias

You will remember that classical conditioning involves linking (or associating) a reflex reaction to an object of some sort. Pavlov, for example, was able to link the reflex of salivating to the sound of a buzzer. Some psychologists consider that phobias may be the result of associating a high level of fear with a relatively harmless stimulus. For example, a reflex reaction for a young child observing one of his parents screaming, is to feel fear. If the child associates a spider with the fear then he will experience fear when he is presented with a spider. See if you can complete the diagram below to explain this sequence. The answer is shown immediately below so be careful not to let your eyes wander to it.

| | Stimulus presented | Leads to | Response |
|---|---|---|---|
| Step 1 | UCS (parent screaming) | → | UCR (____) |
| Step 2 | UCS +CS | | |
| | (_____ + ____) | → | UCR (____) |
| Step 3 | Repeat? | | |
| Step 4 | CS (____) | → | CR (____) |

Check the answer now to see if you were correct.

**Explaining phobias**

| | Stimulus presented | Leads to | Response |
|---|---|---|---|
| Step 1 | UCS (parent screaming) | → | UCR (fear) |
| Step 2 | UCS +CS | | |
| | (parent screaming + spider) | → | UCR (fear) |
| Step 3 | Repeat? | → | Repeat |
| Step 4 | CS (spider) | → | CR (fear) |

In Step1 we can see the sight of a parent screaming causes the reaction of fear in the child. You may feel that this is questionable but it seems a reasonable assumption. The parent screaming represents an unconditional stimulus (UCS) and the child experiencing fear as a result, is the unconditional response (UCR).

In Step 2, we see a situation in which child and parent are together, perhaps in the kitchen, a mouse appears, and the parent screams. This means that everything is the same as in Step 1 except for the mouse being included in the situation. The child is still responding to the parent's scream with fear but now the sight of the parent screaming is paired with the sight of the mouse. The mouse is seen as the conditional stimulus (CS) – it will produce fear **on the condition** that it is paired with the unconditional stimulus. Fear is experienced in the presence of the mouse.

In Step 3 we may assume that the previous step happens more than once. The child experiences fear again because the parent has screamed and this happens again in the presence of a mouse. The association becomes consolidated and the conditional stimulus (CS) – the mouse – produces a conditional response (CR). Sometimes, the single experience is enough to consolidate the association and so the word "repeat" is followed by a question mark in the diagram above.

In Step 4, the mouse has now become associated with fear on its own. The child does not need the experience of seeing the parent scream for the fear response to occur.

Now use the table below to plot the sequence for a person who develops a fear of flying. A suggested answer is in the feedback section.

| | Stimulus presented | Leads to | Response |
|---|---|---|---|
| Step 1 | UCS (_____) | → | UCR (_____) |
| Step 2 | UCS +CS | | |
| | (_____+_____) | → | UCR (_____) |
| Step 3 | Repeat? | | |
| Step 4 | CS (_____) | → | CR (_____) |

**The case of Little Albert**

A famous case in which classical conditioning was involved in phobias is the one involving Little Albert. This study was carried out by Watson and Rayner in 1920 and raises some obvious ethical questions about whether or not they should have used an 11-month-old baby in a study such as this.

Watson and Rayner found that Albert would behave in a frightened way if they made a loud noise by banging a metal bar with a hammer. They gave him a range of things to play with including building blocks, wool, masks and a white rat. Albert showed no fear behaviour towards the rat or the other objects.

The researchers chose to associate the white rat with fear so they waited until Albert reached out for the rat and then they banged the metal with the hammer – producing the fear response. They repeated this over a period of time until, like Pavlov's dog's reaction to the buzzer, Albert showed the fear response to the rat. They had succeeded in conditioning Albert to be afraid of the rat.

Watson and Rayner also showed how Albert would produce the fear reaction to other, similar objects, like a white rabbit or Santa's beard. This showed **Generalisation** – Albert had learned to generalise his fear to similar objects.

## 3. Using Operant Conditioning to Understand Phobias

You will remember that operant conditioning involves reinforcing a behaviour, making it more likely that it will be repeated. Strictly speaking, we have to concentrate on **behaviours** concerned with fears rather than the experience of fear itself, if we are to understand phobias from this point of view.

In this approach we ask, "What is reinforcing the phobic person's behaviour?" For example, consider the range of responses that a person may give to a mouse:

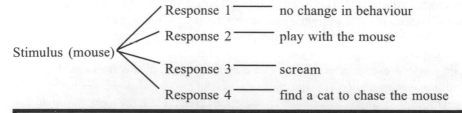

Stimulus (mouse) — Response 1 —— no change in behaviour
Response 2 —— play with the mouse
Response 3 —— scream
Response 4 —— find a cat to chase the mouse

Of course, you will be able to think of other responses. Using your knowledge of operant conditioning, can you work out what happens next?

The next step would be that one of the responses would be reinforced. To explain the response of screaming, we could very easily imagine that a person receives the attention of others if he or she screams. The phobic would find the attention a positive experience and so is more likely to repeat the behaviour next time the stimulus is presented (next time a mouse is seen).

In terms of the diagram, the situation would be:

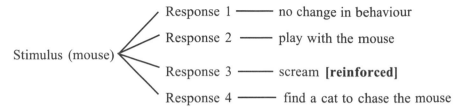

Stimulus (mouse)

Response 1 —— no change in behaviour

Response 2 —— play with the mouse

Response 3 —— scream **[reinforced]**

Response 4 —— find a cat to chase the mouse

## 4. Limitations of Classical and Operant Conditioning Explanations

Both of the explanations we have examined so far share certain limitations.

- They both assume that it is not important to understand what the phobic person is **experiencing or thinking**. The only important thing is the person's behaviour. This seems to belittle and dehumanise people, saying that their experiences, feelings and motives are not important, and that we can explain their behaviour in the same way that we explain the behaviour of a dog.
- If we accept these explanations then we can only treat the person by treating the phobic behaviour and this involves manipulating the person.

## 5. Alternative explanations of Phobias

Other explanations of phobias focus on the mind rather than behaviour.

i. **Psychodynamic explanation** This focuses on the unconscious mind. It is based on the ideas of Freud and the model of the mind that he proposed. In this approach there is no single explanation for all phobias. Each person has a different reason for an irrational fear. His case study of Little Hans can illustrate this approach.

---

### Freud's case study of Little Hans

Freud was approached by the father of five-year-old Hans. The father said that Hans was afraid of being bitten by horses, especially those wearing blinkers and having white marking round the mouth. In those days (1909), horses were an important means of transport for people and goods so a fear of horses caused many problems – Hans refused to go out for example.

Freud eventually told the father that Hans's fear of horses was really a fear of the father himself. The father wore spectacles and had a moustache and this was symbolised in the horse by the blinkers and white markings. Hans's fear of being bitten was actually a fear of being castrated by the father, according to Freud.

Freud advised the father to do nothing because he thought that the fear was simply part of the Oedipus complex, an unconscious process in which boys fall in love with their mothers, wish to possess them sexually, see their fathers as rivals for their mother's love and so fear that their fathers will recognise this and castrate them.

The boy was unable to express his fear of his father consciously because it was an unconscious fear so instead he displaced the fear of his father onto a fear of horses. Freud advised that the boy would resolve his complex and his fear of his father would leave him when he did so.

ii. **Cognitive explanation** This also focuses on the mind. The approach is based on the idea that phobias are the result of faulty thinking, irrational assumptions or maladaptive thoughts. Aeroplanes, for example, are feared because the might plunge from the sky. In fact, planes are exceptionally safe and cases of them crashing are statistically rare; we are safer in a plane than crossing the road. Psychologists like Ellis found that helping people to make their irrational thoughts explicit, and helping them to challenge the thoughts and then replace them with rational ones, would remove phobias.

## 6. Applying classical conditioning techniques to treat phobias

i. **Systematic Desensitisation** aims to sever the link that has associated a reflex response with an inappropriate stimulus, by using the principle of **extinction** which was outlined in the lesson on classical conditioning. In the case of spiders for example, an association has been reinforced somehow between an object (the spider) and a response which is appropriate in another situation (e.g. one's parent screaming and acting afraid). The finding on extinction was simply that if the conditional stimulus (CS) is presented without the unconditional stimulus (UCS) often enough, then the association just dies out. For example, if the bell is rung often enough without the food being presented, then the dog will cease to salivate.

If the spider is presented often enough to the fearful person without the fear response being invoked, then the association should eventually die out and the reaction no longer be associated with the spider. To do this, the person must be helped to relax when a spider is presented. This is usually achieved by introducing the spider in small stages. For example, a matchbox may be brought to the far corner of the room and the phobic person told that there is a spider in the matchbox; he or she is then helped to relax using a variety of techniques like berthing exercises, or even tranquillisers.

The box is brought closer and the spider revealed in small steps until eventually the spider is right next to the person who is helped to relax at every step. Eventually the person should be able to hold the spider without any adverse effects. Airline companies run one-day courses for people who are afraid of flying. These involve a modified version of this principle and culminate in the phobic people taking a short flight around the local area. They are generally very successful.

ii. **Flooding** also works on the principle of extinction but involves completely immersing the phobic person, in the object of his fears. For example, a person who is afraid of spiders would be put into a room full of spiders. After some time the person has not experienced any ill effects from the spiders and has probably lost the energy to continue with the fear reaction (screaming and trying to escape) so has "relaxed" automatically. The association has been broken down again and extinction has occurred.

Some researchers have carried out practices like this literally; Wolpe, for example, forced a girl who was afraid of cars into the back of a car and drove around for four hours until the fear was gone. There are obvious problems related to whether or not psychologists (or anyone else) should be doing this sort of thing to people. A "gentler" version of flooding is **Implosion Therapy**, which is similar but involves asking the person to *imagine* the therapy is happening (e.g. imagine a rat is nibbling at your toes and scurrying across your face).

---

**Which is Which?**

Read through the three imaginary studies of therapy below. Each one is an example of a different sort. Say what type of therapy you think each one is. The answers are in the Feedback section.

1. Elsie suffers from agoraphobia, a fear of being in open spaces. She has not left her house for sixteen years. The last time she tried was when she set off to attend her neighbour's daughter's wedding: she vomited half way up the garden path. Her therapist suggests that the treatment should start with her sitting in a chair in the hall and looking out of the open front door for half an hour a day. After this, she will be putting the chair at the front door to look out.

2. Anthony is afraid of water. He takes ages to climb gingerly into the shallow end of the swimming pool and never moves away from the edge. His father takes him to the pool one day and throws him into the deep end (**not** a method seriously recommended by psychologists!)

---

## Feedback

The sequence for a person who develops a fear of flying

|  | Stimulus presented | Leads to | Response |
|---|---|---|---|
| **Step 1** | UCS Sight of others in distress | → | UCR (fear) |
| **Step 2** | UCS +CS | | |
|  | (Sight of others in distress + sight | | |
|  | of plane in TV pictures of crash) | → | UCR (fear) |
| **Step 3** | **Repeat?** | | |
| **Step 4** | CS (sight of plane) | → | CR (fear) |

Strictly speaking, this links the *sight* of a plane with fear rather than linking *flying* with fear, but we could expect the thought of flying to include the phobic person visualising (i.e. producing a mental picture of) a plane.

**Which is Which?**

1. Desensitisation 2. Flooding

**References**

Stratton, P and Hayes, N (1993), *A Student's Dictionary of Psychology* (2nd ed) Edward Arnold.

# Lesson 14
# Applying Conditioning
# to Human Behaviour

Practising psychologists earn their living by applying the principles of psychology to situations in which people need help to improve their lives in one way or another. In this lesson we shall study some of the techniques, based on the principles arising from the study of conditioning. We have already described techniques used to treat phobias and the lesson on phobias should also be thought of as part of the study of attempts to apply conditioning procedures to human behaviour.

The aversion therapy, behaviour modification and token economy techniques described here, are ones that may be used typically by clinical psychologists working in places like a general hospital or local doctor's surgery. Behaviour modification is also often used by educational psychologists working with individual children in schools.

Programmed learning is also described below and this can be used in any teaching situation which requires a student to learn something. In the past it has proved popular as a method of teaching certain topics in the armed forces, perhaps because it is a very ordered and well defined set of procedures – perhaps typical of much of life in the services.

## 1. Applying Classical Conditioning Procedures to Change Behaviour

As you will remember, classical conditioning is the linking of a reflex response to a new stimulus.

**Aversion Therapy** uses this linking principle. If someone has an unwanted behaviour, like gambling or drinking too much alcohol, then associating this behaviour with an unpleasant experience will cause the person to avoid the behaviour.

This technique has been developed with the use of emetics which are substances that make us vomit. The emetic is administered at the same time as a picture of a glass of alcohol or the sight of a bottle of whiskey or some other item that is associated with alcohol. The person vomits. This may need to be repeated. Eventually, the person starts to experience the physical reactions associated with vomiting (sweating, retching, feeling faint etc.) when he or she sees anything that represents alcohol. They may actually vomit at the sight of the alcohol. The next time the person sees the alcohol he or she will quickly avoid further contact, leaving the room or declining the offer of the drink; people treated in this way should also avoid seeking out alcohol.

## 2. Applying Operant Conditioning

### Behaviour Modification

This involves techniques of behaviour shaping and reinforcement, and as the name implies, changing (modifying) behaviour. Like aversion therapy, described above, it pays no attention at all to any thoughts, intentions, motives or emotions experienced by the person whose behaviour is being modified. The process focuses on **maladaptive** behaviour – behaviour which is not appropriate or which is unwanted. The aim is to turn maladaptive behaviour into **adaptive** behaviour – behaviour that **is** wanted and is appropriate.

It works on the basis of ABC: **A**ntecedents, **B**ehaviour and **C**onsequences. Antecedents are things that happen beforehand whilst consequences, of course, are things that happen as a result. Take the example of a child who is taken through the check-out at the supermarket and who wants a packet of sweets. If the adult refuses the sweets some children will cry loud and long and the parent may give in and buy the sweets to save embarrassment. But what has happened from the point of view of operant conditioning theory? The child has displayed a behaviour (crying and shouting) and has then been given a packet of sweets. What effect do the sweets have? They act as a reward and reinforce the crying behaviour, making it more likely that the child will cry again in a similar situation.

In terms of ABC this is:

Antecedents: the sweets are encountered at the check-out

Behaviour: the child cries

Consequences: the child is given sweets and the crying is reinforced.

To change this behaviour a "two-pronged" attack is made: the unwanted behaviour has to be eliminated and the wanted behaviour has to be encouraged. To eliminate the unwanted behaviour, **extinction** can be used. The child's cries are simply ignored and if sweets are not given then eventually the behaviour will die out because it is not being reinforced. Of course, this is an easy thing to say but it is often difficult to ignore a crying child in a supermarket full of customers watching and tutting; in the long run, however, it will benefit both adult and child.

The second "prong" of this attack is to replace the crying with wanted behaviour. This requires a clear definition of what behaviour is wanted and a reward which is clearly given for that wanted behaviour, in order to reinforce it. It may be possible to define wanted behaviour in this situation as helping the adult to choose the goods and store them in the basket, and being quiet and calm in the supermarket. In this case, every few minutes in the supermarket the adult could give the child a reward, specifying what it is for (helping to put items in the basket quietly). The reward could be a positive comment like "You **are** being helpful and well behaved" or the adult may decide to give a sweet, or some other physical reward.

After a few visits to the supermarket when the desired behaviour has been adopted the adult should be able to reduce the level of reward and the child should get all the "normal" rewards which adults and other children get from being accepted by others and joining in with normal social interactions and conversations. Attention comes from positive behaviour here, not negative.

Health visitors often use a version of this to stop or reduce bed-wetting. A child is given a small poster of, perhaps, a farmyard scene and every time the bed is dry overnight the child is given a picture of a tractor or animal to stick on the poster. Some health visitors use gold stars to put on a chart and the child can be given a "real" reward like a toy or book or some other desirable item once ten starts have been collected. The star is truly a "token" because it can be exchanged for a "real" reward. Schools commonly use star, merit, house point, commendation or other systems and tokens to reward and reinforce desirable behaviour like punctuality and good work. In this case the token often leads to no more than another token (ten commendations in one term leads to a certificate of merit, for example), but some schools exchange the tokens for things like sweets or books.

**Token Economy**

Tokens are often used to modify the behaviour of patients in institutions like psychiatric hospitals or psychiatric wards of general hospitals; in this case they are often referred to as **"token economies"**. The tokens in this situation are often really plastic or metal tokens which can be exchanged at the end of the week for cigarettes, sweets, extra visits or other experiences like watching television which the patient interprets as a reward. Tokens are not always used; sometimes rewards are given directly and the patient is able to watch the TV for a period of time, at the moment the desired behaviour is displayed.

---

**Suggest a behaviour modification programme**

Imagine that you are managing a psychiatric ward and are asked to recommend a behaviour modification programme for Sally, a teenage girl suffering from anorexia (an eating disorder which leads people to eat so little that they will die if they do not increase their food intake). Sally has just arrived on the ward.

What is the undesirable behaviour?

What do you think may be reinforcing it?

What would you suggest is the desired behaviour?

What reward would you use to reinforce the desired behaviour?

How can behaviour shaping be employed in this situation?

There is a suggested answer in the Feedback section

---

## 3. Evaluation of Behaviour Changing Approaches

**Ethical considerations.** Ethics involves taking account of whether it is right to do the things we do.

- Can it be right to use techniques like making people sick or inflicting mild electric shocks on them? Should we be using flooding techniques (see lesson 13 on phobias) which involve confronting people with their worst fears? Do the ends (removing the phobia) justify the means (causing trauma and fear)?

- Who decides what behaviour is desirable and what is undesirable? Can we be sure that we do not just want to make people do what we want them to do? The techniques can be misused. For example, in the past, aversion therapy has been used to "treat" homosexual men by showing them pictures of naked men and administering electric shocks. Although it is unlikely that any psychologist would suggest this use today it does illustrate that the technique must be used carefully.

## Practical Considerations

- If aversion therapy works why are there any alcoholics? Behavioural therapies can be extremely powerful but many psychologists say that they will only work if the patient's thoughts are taken into account. This is known as **cognitive-behavioural therapy** and involves the patient being involved in their treatment and understanding what is happening.

- Are we treating the symptoms but not the causes? Some psychologists dismiss these types of treatment saying that even if we do manage to stop a child wetting the bed the child is only wetting it because of a psychological problem and if that problem is not identified and treated it will surface in another symptom like a phobia or difficult behaviours.

# 4. Programmed Learning

This involves taking knowledge to be learned, breaking it down into small parts or "frames" and presenting it to the learner in a predetermined sequence, usually on a computer. Additionally, the learner's understanding of each step is tested and if the learner gets the answer correct this acts as a reward; so the behaviour (giving the correct response to the stimulus) is reinforced and learning takes place. Reinforcement is also aided by praise from the programme, for example the phrase "Well done" may be shown when correct responses are given.

The learner's understanding is tested with a question and the learner usually chooses from a series of possible answers. Today's more sophisticated computers sometimes allow for learners to create their own answers and the programme searches the answer for key words and correct grammar, which it interprets as a correct answer.

If the learner gives the correct answer then the programme moves on to the next step but if the learner gets the answer wrong then the programme returns to an earlier frame and takes the learner through the sequence again. This type of programme is known as a **linear programme.**

Some programmes are more complex. If the learner chooses a wrong answer the programme goes to a series of frames which re-explain the material and re-test the learner. Each incorrect response suggests a different misunderstanding on the part of the learner so each one leads to a different sequence which is designed to cater for the different misunderstanding. This type of programme is known as a **branching programme.**

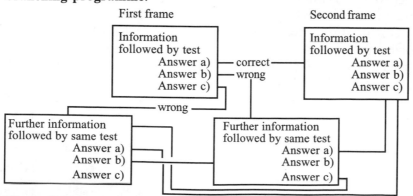

**Figure 1 The sequence of a branching programme**

Both types of programme work on the principle of rewarding correct responses and so reinforcing desired behaviour – correct responses.

**Evaluation of programmed learning**

> **Try these questions to prepare your own evaluation**
> 1. Do you think this type of learning is suitable for all subjects?
> 2. Do you think this type of learning is suitable for all learners?
> 3. Do you think this method requires much preparation on the part of the teachers?
> Some answers follow

1. It is suitable and appropriate for learning material which is factually based and which has right and wrong answers and can be broken down into small steps, e.g. knowing how to wire a plug or elementary algebra.

   It is not quite so suitable for subjects which have opinions, debates, or a wide range of answers in their material, e.g. philosophy, history.

2. Some learners may need the social interaction of the classroom and group to learn effectively. Programmed learning does not allow learners to ask their own questions and this can be important in helping people to understand a subject. Others may be happier with this more isolated learning experience.

3. This method requires a lot of painstaking preparation and piloting of the programme. All teaching requires good preparation, however.

Further points of evaluation are:

4. It allows learners to progress at their own pace instead of having to keep up with a group of other people or being kept back by the group.

5. Although early programmed learning used cumbersome machines or written texts, computers now offer very good facilities for delivering this type of learning.

## Feedback

### Suggest a behaviour modification programme

What is the undesirable behaviour? Avoiding eating

What do you think may be reinforcing it? Attention from others?

What would you suggest is the desired behaviour? Eating

What reward would you use to reinforce the desired behaviour? Perhaps television or visits from friends or family or books and magazines.

How can behaviour shaping be employed in this situation? Start with small and easily attainable behaviours like nibbling at food (even sniffing it may be worth trying in some situations) and reward that before moving on to taking mouthfuls and eventually eating whole dishes.

Explain the plan to the patient. Every time the patient takes a small amount of food (even a small bite of a biscuit will do) give the reward or a token. Continue, setting higher eating targets – perhaps setting a weight increase this time instead of specific mouthfuls – until we are rewarding normal eating behaviour.

# Lesson 15
# The Principles of Social Learning Theory

In this lesson the basic principles of Social Learning Theory are presented along with some of the evidence. This theory and further evidence also appear in a number of other lessons in the course, in particular in the lessons on Sex and Gender and in the lessons on Aggression.

Social Learning Theory starts with the idea that we tend to copy and imitate the behaviour of others ("models"), and then uses the principles of operant conditioning to explain how some behaviours become established through reinforcement.

## 1. Observation and Imitation

Youngsters in many species seem to observe and copy the behaviours of other members of the species. You may have seen ducklings following their parents in line. Human babies will observe and copy facial expressions when adults concentrate their attention on them and interact with smiles or tongue movements. Adults copy each other too. Fashions are example of copying behaviours, and the behaviours and language of actors, famous sports personalities and pop stars may be copied by their fans.

---

**Have you noticed copying behaviours?**
Reflect on these questions for a moment.
- Do you remember ever copying someone else's behaviour yourself?
- Do you remember someone else copying another person's behaviour, or perhaps your own behaviour?

---

Social Learning Theory suggests that as a natural process, young people in particular copy behaviours they observe in others. We seem to be pre-disposed to copy behaviours when we are young. People around us approve of some of the behaviours that we copy and they give us subtle rewards for producing these behaviours. According to the principle established by Thorndike, behaviours that are rewarded are more likely to be repeated so we tend to establish these rewarded behaviours.

**Bandura** reported a series of studies that have become well known in psychology. His studies were designed to investigate aggression (and so are also covered in the lesson on aggression). He used a bobo doll, which is an inflated, plastic doll about the same size as an average eight-year-old child. Its base is rounded and weighted so that if the doll is knocked over it rolls back up to a standing position.

In one of the studies Bandura caused a group of children to watch an actor performing aggressive acts towards the doll. Another group of children watched an actor with the same bobo doll but this time the actor did not act aggressively towards it. The first group, who watched the aggression, produced more aggressive acts towards the doll when they had the opportunity to play with it. This suggested that the idea that behaviour is copied is a valid one and seems to support the Social Learning Theory.

Bandura carried out more than this one, simple study and the findings are more complex and do not all support the theory in this straightforward way. For example, he compared a group of children who watched an actor performing aggressive acts and a group who watched a cartoon of the same behaviour. The group who watched the cartoon produced more aggressive acts than the group who watched the actor. We would, perhaps, expect the opposite to happen. As social learning theory is based on the idea that we have a natural inclination to copy other people, surely we would copy people rather than cartoons?

## 2. Vicarious Reinforcement

This refers to the idea that we do not necessarily need to be directly rewarded for a behaviour ourselves, for it to be reinforced. We may see other people rewarded for the behaviour and so the behaviour can be reinforced in ourselves. For example, we observe television characters achieving success by using violence. Their success is our reinforcement and so we imitate the behaviours.

Bandura's evidence did not support this notion, however. In the studies described above, he arranged for one group of children to observe the actor performing the aggressive acts with the bobo doll, as before, but another group observed the same thing followed by a researcher entering the room and rewarding the actor with praise and gifts.

> If the idea of Vicarious Reinforcement is correct, which group would we expect to show the most aggression – the one that saw the actor rewarded or the one that did not? The correct answer follows this box.

If the idea of Vicarious Reinforcement is correct, we should expect the children who observed the actor rewarded to show more aggression. Bandura did not find this to be the case, however. Both groups showed the same amount of aggression.

However, vicarious reinforcement does have some advantages as an idea. In the simple version of Social Learning Theory, a child observes and copies a behaviour and others give rewards for copying. For example, a child starts to walk and is immediately rewarded by parents and adults saying "Good girl". More subtle rewards are given when a child copies the helpful behaviour observed in last night's soap opera on television and is given respect for doing so by classmates.

Vicarious reinforcement, however, may explain some of the situations in which a person produces a behaviour that has not been directly rewarded. He or she has observed the model being rewarded but has not been directly rewarded him or her self.

> **Evaluation so far**
> Up to now, a number of advantages and disadvantages of Social Learning Theory and its concepts have been given. Can you spot some? Answers are in the Feedback section

## 3. Identification

Social Learning Theory acknowledges that our behaviour is more complex than a simple copying disposition. If we merely copied behaviours then there would be no variation and change in human behaviour. Also, like general conditioning theory, a simple approach like this would imply that we have no control over ourselves and that our thoughts, feelings, ambitions and motivations play no part in our behaviour – this seems unlikely.

One idea that takes some account of this is **identification**. In this idea we do not merely observe and copy a model's behaviour, **we put ourselves in the shoes of the model** and **act as though we were the model**.

For example, many of the role-playing games of children can be seen this way. Playing doctors and nurses, mummy and daddy, schools and so on, involves the child acting as though he or she were the model. The "teacher" child does not necessarily just produce the same words and behaviours that have been observed in the classroom, but instead produces the general behaviour of the teacher. When the "pupil" behaves in a certain way in the game so the child taking the role of the teacher acts as he or she thinks the teacher would act under those circumstances.

In this way the child **identifies** with the teacher and takes on the general behaviours of teachers. Vicarious reinforcement here may come from the power and esteem rewards that the child has observed the teacher enjoying. Not only does the child take on the behaviours of the model, he or she also takes on the attitudes, values and beliefs of the model.

## 4. Other features of Social Learning Theory

Bandura's studies also showed that certain characteristics seem to make imitation and identification more likely.

- **Appropriateness**: if the behaviour is seen as appropriate to the model and the situation then it is more likely to be imitated. For example, Bandura found that aggression is more likely to be imitated if it is observed in a male model rather than a female model. This is argued to be the result of society seeing aggression as more appropriate to male behaviour than to female behaviour.
- **Relevance and similarity**: if the behaviour is seen as relevant and the model seen as similar to the imitator, then it is more likely to be imitated. For example, Bandura found that boys were more likely to imitate aggression displayed by male models than were girls.

> **Further evaluation**
> Some further points can be made when evaluating Social Learning Theory:
> - The notion that our behaviour is the result of society rewarding us is still seen as suggesting that we are not in control of ourselves but subject to the manipulation of others.

> - Social Learning Theory does at least acknowledge some role for our motivation, personalities, attitudes and other internal processes when, for example, it acknowledges that we select some models and behaviours as more relevant or appropriate.

## Feedback

### Evaluation so far

**Advantage 1:** Bandura's study showed that children who had observed aggression in an actor produced more aggressive behaviours than children who had not observed the aggression.

**Advantage 2:** The idea of vicarious reinforcement would take account of the complexity of real behaviours and would explain why some behaviours are produced which have not been directly rewarded.

**Disadvantage 1:** Children who watched a cartoon of aggressive behaviours were more likely to produce aggressive behaviours than children who watched a real actor produce aggressive behaviours. We would expect the opposite.

**Disadvantage 2:** The idea of vicarious reinforcement was not supported by Bandura's evidence when children who had observed an actor being rewarded for aggression did not produce more aggression than children who had not observed this.

Social Learning Theory is also explained in the lesson on The Social Learning Theory Approach to Gender

# AQA Exam Style Questions: Learning

- **Answer all questions**
- **There is no time limit to this assignment**
- **When completed you may compare your answers with the example answers at the end of the book**
- **If you have tutorial support you should send a copy of your answers to your tutor to receive further feedback, comments and guidance**

1 Read the following letter and answer the questions that follow.

---

### Problem Page

Dear Masie,

   When I was two months pregnant with my first child I had some days when I felt I was going to be sick all day. My doctor told me that it was perfectly normal during early pregnancy. Usually, I didn't eat at all on those days because I was scared I would bring it all back up; I couldn't even cook because I felt sure I would be sick. On one of those days my mother in law came round and prepared a meal for my husband; it was smoked haddock. She asked me to try some and I didn't want to seem ungrateful so I tried to eat it. After the first taste of the stuff I vomited all over the place and caused an awful mess. I was so embarrassed.

   Now, two years later, I still cannot face smoked haddock. Every time I so much as see it I feel sick! The thought of it makes me sweat and the smell of it makes me retch. What is the matter with me and can I do anything about it?
Yours sincerely,
A fish lover.

---

(a) The following diagram can be used to explain how "A fish lover" was conditioned. **Fill in the empty spaces inside the square brackets** choosing from the terms in the box that follows.

|  | Pregnancy Sickness (UCS) | $\longrightarrow$ | Vomiting (UCR) |
|---|---|---|---|
| [    ] + (CS) | Pregnancy Sickness (UCS) | $\longrightarrow$ | Vomiting [    ] |
|  | Smoked Haddock [    ] | $\longrightarrow$ | Vomiting [    ] |

**Choose from these terms**
Smoked Haddock, Pregnancy Sickness, Vomiting
Unconditioned Stimulus (UCS), Conditioned Stimulus (CS),
Unconditioned Response (UCR), Conditioned Response (CR)
(4 marks)

(b) The writer does not feel sick when she has cod or tuna or other fish. Use your knowledge of classical conditioning to explain why this is. (3 marks)

(c) In her letter, "A fish lover" asks if there is anything she can do about her reaction to smoked haddock. Using your knowledge of conditioning, outline how a psychologist may remove her reaction. (2 marks)

(d) State **one** similarity between classical and operant conditioning (1 mark)

(e) State **one** difference between classical and operant conditioning (1 mark)

**2**   Choose **one** attempt to apply conditioning procedures to human behaviour.
(a) Name the procedure (1 mark)

(b) Describe the procedure. (5 marks)

(c) Evaluate the procedure (3 marks)

**Total possible marks = 20**

When completed you should compare your answers with the example answers at the end of the book. If you have tutorial support you should send a copy of your answers to the tutor for feedback, comments and further guidance.

# OCR Exam Style Questions: Phobias

- **Answer all questions**
- **There is no time limit to this assignment**
- **When completed you may compare your answers with the example answers at the end of the book**
- **If you have tutorial support you should send a copy of your answers to your tutor to receive further feedback, comments and guidance**

Source a Behaviour Psychology
Phobias

---

### Little Albert's Phobia

Two psychologists, Watson and Rayner, caused a small child, Albert, to be afraid of white, furry objects. They put a number of play objects in front of Albert. One of the objects was a white rat. Albert played happily with all the objects, including the rat. After some time Watson and Rayner banged a metal bar with a hammer every time he moved towards the rat and this caused Albert to cry in a fear response. They did this a number of times, waiting on each occasion until Albert started to play with the white rat before banging the metal bar.

After a number of trials, Albert was seen to cry when the rat was brought into his view, without the metal bar being banged. He had been given a fear of white rats. It was also noted that Albert would cry at the sight of other white, furry objects like cotton wool, a white rabbit and a white beard.

To rid Albert of the phobia, the experimenters let him see and then play with the rat many times without banging the metal bar. Albert lost his fear of other white, furry objects too.

---

1. Draw a line between the psychological term and the correct event or object

| Psychological Term | Event/Object |
|---|---|
| Unconditional Response | Banging the metal bar |
| Conditional Stimulus | Crying |
| Unconditional Stimulus | White rat |

(3 marks)

2. Little Albert developed a fear of white cotton wool. This is an example of which of the following? Put a tick in the correct box.

☐ Negative reinforcement

☐ Discrimination

☐ Extinction

☐ Generalisation

(1 mark)

3. (a) Give a definition of "phobia" (1 mark)

(b) Name and describe a common phobia.
Name (1 mark)
Description (2 marks)

4. In the past, some psychologists have argued that **all** human behaviour can be explained using conditioning theory. State **one** limitation to explaining human behaviour in terms of classical or operant conditioning. (1 mark)

5. Phobias can be explained in alternative ways to conditioning theory. Briefly describe **one** such alternative. (3 marks)

6. Social Learning Theory uses conditioning principles along with other concepts. Outline the basic principles of Social Learning Theory using evidence from psychological studies. (8 marks)

**Total possible marks = 20**

When completed you should compare your answers with the example answers at the end of the book. If you have tutorial support you should send a copy of your answers to the tutor for feedback, comments and further guidance.

# Lesson 16. Explanations of Aggression 1: Social Learning Theory and Psychodynamic Explanations

## What is Aggression?

*A Student's Dictionary of Psychology* defines aggression as "*a deliberate attempt to harm another being.*" (Stratton and Hayes, 1993).

However, the dictionary goes on to discuss the difficulties of defining the term; for example, is the act of defending oneself from attack aggression?

## 1. The Social Learning Theory Explanation of Aggression

The Social Learning Theory in general suggests that we observe other people as models and imitate their behaviour. If we see the model being rewarded for their behaviour then we are more likely to imitate it. Also, if we imitate some behaviour and then are rewarded for it, then we are more likely to repeat it.

Details of the social learning approach can be found in the lesson on "The Principles of Social Learning Theory". Also, this approach is used to explain

- gender behaviour – found in the lesson "The Social Learning Theory Approach to Gender" and
- moral development – found in the lesson "The Behaviourist and Social Learning Approaches to Moral Development"

---

**Review**
Take time now to read or review the lesson "The Principles of Social Learning Theory" in the section on Learning.

---

To proceed you should know the answers to these questions:

---

**Review Questions**
1. What is imitation?
2. What is identification?
3. What is a model?
4. What did Bandura find?
5. What is Vicarious Reinforcement?
Answers are in the feedback section at the end of the lesson.

---

Bandura's studies of Bobo dolls are the main evidence cited by psychologists to support the social learning theory of aggression. He carried out more than one study and they do not all support the idea in a straightforward way but they do form a sound body of evidence.

One of the criticisms cited by Brofenbrenner is the idea that the studies were not "real life". The children observed actors, not real people, and the actors and children did not interact – in real life children often interact with parents, peers, teachers and other models.

### Imitation in action

> Can you think of any models of aggression that children encounter? Suggestions follow the box.

- **Parents**: children may imitate aggression from parents, who may use aggression to discipline children, or as part of their ordinary behaviour. Parents may also reward children when they "stand up for themselves" and fight back, or even strike first in conflicts.
- **Peers**: friends and other children may act as aggressive models
- **Characters in the media**: even though they are fictional, children imitate characters in the media who act aggressively and appear to be rewarded for it. This includes a wide range, from Tom and Jerry cartoon characters to heroes of series who succeed by using aggression – Superman, Batman and so on and sporting heroes.

### Gender differences in levels of aggression

Researchers like Maccoby and Jacklin consistently report higher levels of aggression in males than in females. Social learning theory would predict that aggression would be imitated but why would boys imitate aggression more than girls would?

### Characteristics of models

Bandura's work shows that people are more likely to imitate the models in the above situation if the model's behaviour is:

- appropriate
- relevant
- performed by a model who is similar to the observer

This may account for the higher levels of aggression reported in boys. Boys see men as similar to them, society (and thus boys) see male aggression as appropriate (see the study by Rothart and Maccoby, below) and male behaviour is more relevant to the boy because of the similarity.

### Parent child-rearing practices

Rothart and Maccoby's studies showed that mothers accept aggression in boys much more than in girls. By studying the conversation between family members (a process known as discourse analysis), the researchers found that mothers accepted that their sons behaved aggressively but not their daughters. They were more likely to punish aggression in girls than in boys.

### Alternative explanations of gender differences

As mentioned in the **Biological Explanation** of aggression, the hormone **Testosterone** is associated with aggression and differences in the levels of this hormone in males and females may account for the gender differences in aggression.

**Cultural Differences in Levels of Aggression**

The Social Learning Theory may offer the best explanation of why some cultures seem to accept higher levels of aggression than others.

**(i) Social class cultural differences.** Newson and Newson studied a large group of children in Nottingham and found that working class parents were more likely than middle class parents to use physical punishment against their children (model of aggression) and were more likely to encourage their children to respond to aggression with aggression.

**(i) The studies of Margaret Mead** showed three tribes in the south pacific with markedly different levels of aggression in general – the Arapesh showed very low levels of aggression throughout the tribe, the Mundugamor showed very high levels of aggression throughout the tribe and the Tchambuli showed the opposite pattern to the western gender pattern – males were less aggressive than females.

These findings could all be accounted for by the idea that we learn aggression from those around us in one way or another.

**The Role of the Media in Aggression**

The social learning theory would at first sight support the notion that the media influences aggression.

**Evidence supporting the idea that the media causes aggression**

---

What piece of research supports the idea that aggression is copied from the media? The answer follows this box.

---

- Bandura's Bobo doll study showed directly how children would copy aggressive acts performed on the Bobo dolls. However, we have to remember Brofenbrenner's criticism that Bandura's study was not "real life".

Television and violent videos (or "video nasties") are probably the most studied media when it comes to aggression. However, just because we observe high levels of aggression in people who watch a lot of violence on the television, we cannot say that this proves that the television has caused the aggression: it could be that people who are naturally aggressive are attracted to a lot of violence on the television. It is difficult to separate cause and effect. Other methods of measuring the effects of the media have problems too. For example, see Parkes' study in the box below.

---

### Parkes' study of juvenile delinquents

In 1997 Parkes studied juvenile delinquent boys who were living in an institution divided into "cottages" – small groups living together with staff. He arranged for baseline levels of aggression to be measured in the boys, then showed violent films each evening for five evenings in one cottage but non-violent films in the other cottage. After a week the measures of aggression showed that the boys watching the violent films showed more aggression than the other boys.

---

At first sight this study seems convincing. It is naturalistic so we cannot say it is "unreal". However, we cannot rule out the idea that the boys may have been chosen for each cottage by the staff on the basis of how "difficult" their behaviour was. The idea that the more "excitable" boys should be put with staff who could handle that sort of behaviour may have been a policy of the institution. In this case it could be that Parkes accidentally chose the cottage with the more excitable boys and that the findings do not apply to "normal" boys or to girls at all, or to any children who are not delinquent and in a residential institution.

The Williams study in the next box is valuable evidence taken from a very unusual situation that provides further evidence on the effects of TV violence.

---

### The No-tel study

Williams observed children and rated their levels of aggression in a Canadian community in 1986, and also used ratings of aggression given by teachers and peers. Television had only just been introduced in the community and this group of children was compared to a group from a community in which there was only one television channel and another in which there were several.

Over a period of two years it was found that the levels of aggression in the "No-tel" community increased significantly but not in the other communities that already had extensive television access.

This suggests that the television caused the increase in aggression.

---

**Evaluation of the social learning theory explanation of aggression**
- Most of the evidence for this theory is based on artificial laboratory studies.
- The theory does not take account of biological evidence for aggression.
- More "real-life" (ecologically valid) studies of the effects of the media on aggression give good support to the theory and it does seem possible to reduce aggression levels by manipulating the media.

## 2. The psychodynamic explanation of aggression

Freud's work is described in two other sections of this course: "The Psychoanalytic Approach to Moral Behaviour" (p. 176) and "The Psychoanalytic Approach to Gender" (p. 286). If you have not already studied them then you may find it useful to read the sub-sections on the Id, the Ego and the Superego.

Freud said that the Libido is connected with the Id is an instinctive, unconscious, biological "energy" that drives us and is associated with sexual urges (it is in this sense that Freud can be seen as arguing that sex is behind everything). It takes the form of two opposing instincts: Eros, the life instinct and Thanatos, the death instinct. Aggression is associated with this death instinct or "death wish".

It seems self-evident that we have a life instinct, since so many people go to such extremes to ensure they survive and help others to survive. Eating, drinking, working – all of these seem to be natural and stem from an instinct to survive and prosper. However, an instinct to die? Could we really have such an instinct – and at the same time as the life instinct?

Freud pointed to the slaughter that takes place in mass wars – perhaps 30 million in the Second World War. He said that the willingness of soldiers to sign up – often voluntarily – and face the possibility or even the probability of death was evidence of this death instinct. The biggest single cause of death in young males in the United Kingdom is suicide at the moment. Freud would argue that this results from the victory of the death instinct over the life instinct.

Aggression, according to this theory, also results from the death instinct and is the individual's inclination to put him or herself into dangerous situations in which harm or even death may be a feature. Being aggressive towards others merely invites retaliation and the possibility that we may be injured.

Freud also suggested that aggression builds up like water behind a dam and needs to be released in a controlled way (like a dam) or it will spill over. If it is not released, it will cause psychological harm, like suicide.

This process of release is called **Catharsis** and can be achieved by, for example, taking part in sports.

### Evaluation of the psychodynamic explanation

- Freud's ideas are often criticised for lack of measurable (empirical) evidence. His ideas about aggression can be criticised in this way.
- Studies show that people are often **more** aggressive after playing sports rather than less aggressive – which would be predicted by the idea of catharsis.
- If aggression were instinctive, it would be difficult to explain cultural differences in levels of aggression since all cultures would have similar levels.

---

**Lesson Summary**
1. What do Bandura's studies tell us about aggression?
2. How can the concept of Identification explain aggression?
3. What do psychologists find is a common difference in behaviour between males and females, when it comes to aggression?
4. Give an example of a cultural difference in levels of aggressive behaviours.
5. State one possible explanation of these gender differences according to the Social Learning approach.
6. Name a researcher whose evidence seems to indicate that the media has a role in creating violence.
7. What, according to Freud, is Thanatos?
8. What evidence did Freud have for the existence of Thanatos?
9. Why does aggression result from Thanatos, according to Freud?
10. Give one criticism of Freud's ideas about aggression.

---

## Feedback

### Review Questions
1. Imitation is copying behaviours that are displayed by models.
2. Identification involves "putting oneself in the shoes" of the model and behaving as though one were that person
3. A model is a person who is imitated or with whom someone identifies.
4. Bandura's findings were complex but in general he found evidence that children will copy behaviour.
5. Vicarious reinforcement is the situation in which a person will copy a piece of behaviour that is seen to have been rewarded in the model.

**Lesson summary**

1.  That aggression results from imitating aggression in others.
2.  It would suggest that people take on the role of an aggressive person – they act "as though" they were an aggressive person and so display behaviour that would be expected of an aggressive person.
3.  In most studies, males usually display more aggression than females.
4.  Margaret Mead found that the Tchambuli tribe showed reverse gender patterns of aggression compared to the Western pattern of males being more aggressive.
5.  Child-rearing practices.
6.  Williams
7.  A death instinct.
8.  Suicide/people's willingness to go to war and face death.
9.  By being aggressive, we put ourselves in the position whereby we may be injured. We do this because we wish to die.
10. There is no empirical evidence.

# Lesson 17. Explanations of Aggression 2: Ethological and Biological Explanations

## 1. The Ethological Approach

Ethology is the study of animals in their natural habitat. The ethological approach to aggression is based on the idea that humans are animals and that aggression is natural in animals.

Ethologists, like Conrad Lorenz, suggest that animals' instincts to be aggressive have been selected by the process of evolution to give advantages to the species and allow it to "survive" in the sense of passing on its genes on to the next generation

What advantages to an animal could aggression have?

Using aggression an animal could:
- Fight off predators
- Kill prey to eat
- Keep other animals away from its territory so it can benefit from the food and shelter in it
- Dominate other members of the same sex to obtain the best partner of the opposite sex and so mate with it to produce the strongest offspring

You may be able to think of other reasons too.

### Evidence of instinctive aggression

Tinbergen studied the male stickleback and found that a specific pattern of behaviour is associated with aggression. He made a model of a stickleback and attached it to a rod, which allowed him to move the model around a fish tank. He put a real male stickleback in the fish tank then brought the model near it but found that the male did nothing. He noticed that in spring (when animals mate more often) the male's belly has a red mark on it so he painted a red mark on the model and brought it near the male. This time, the male stickleback attacked the model in a zig-zag pattern.

From this and other studies ethologists derived some principles:
- **Sign stimuli** – aggression is "triggered" in animals by some signal (the red spot on the male's belly in the case of the stickleback).
- **Fixed Action Patterns (FAP)** – the aggression is a specific series of behaviours repeated and rarely changed. For example, in a cat it includes an arched back, hissing, hair standing on end, crouching and so on.

Can you think of any disadvantages to animals of an instinct to be aggressive?

If an animal has an instinct to be aggressive every time it comes across a certain stimulus it may act aggressively towards another animal that it cannot beat in a fight. This would lead to animals becoming badly injured and dying – the opposite of what ethologists predict. So are ethologists wrong in thinking that aggression is an automatic, innate response?

Ethologists say that animals do work out when they are beaten by their opponent and have an innate mechanism for ensuring that they don't kill members of their own species. This is the "**appeasement ritual**". Dogs, for example, will roll on their backs and expose their jugular vein. The opponent could bite the vein and kill the dog but it does not. It simply "pretends" to bite the loser who gets up and walks off, leaving the winner to bark to announce that it has won. Ethologists say that the appeasement gesture acts as a sign stimulus to the winner to stop its aggressive behaviour.

Another way of avoiding the bad effects of aggression in animals is **Ritualised Behaviour**. This is the idea that a lot of aggressive behaviour is just "bravado" and does not really involve violence. For example, fighting cats will circle each other, hissing for quite some time and may never actually come to blows before one of them makes an appeasement gesture.

> Can you think of any parallels in human behaviour?

Studies of gang fights have found that a lot of what appears to be fighting is just threat. Even in knife fights, researchers (pretending to be gang members and carrying out participant observations) have found that opponents will circle each other a lot, saying things like "Come on then, let's see you try". These knife fights led, at worst, to the winner cutting the loser lightly and not stabbing him to death.

Another human parallel is the notion of "giving in". The loser may use these words or similar ones – particularly children when "play fighting".

## Evidence supporting the Ethological explanation in humans – Berkowitz's Study

Berkowitz, working with Le Page, suggested that we first feel angry but only show aggression if there is a "cue" in the environment to trigger it; this is the parallel to the sign stimulus for the human. This cue triggers the aggression just like the red spot triggers aggression in the stickleback.

Berkowitz created anger in three groups of participants by giving them mild electric shocks (to which they consented) after they solved a problem. The participants then had their turn to give shocks to a confederate but one group completed the procedure around a table with badminton rackets and shuttlecocks on it, a second completed the procedure around a table with a gun and a revolver on it and a third completed it around a table with nothing on it.

> Bearing in mind the idea of aggression being triggered by appropriate cues, can you predict which group gave the most shocks?

The group, which delivered the shocks around the table with the weapons on it, gave the most shocks. This is consistent with the idea that some form of "trigger" in the environment "encourages" aggression even if it is not the only cause.

**Criticisms of the Ethological Approach**

- Animals **do** kill members of their own species. Goodall observed two chimp colonies fighting with all males in one colony killed. Male lions commonly kill cubs and this occurs in other animals.

- Ritualised fixed action patterns of aggression in animals do exist but they are not always used.

- Human behaviour is moderated by other factors like conscious decisions not to fight or by taking account of the damage caused by aggression.

---

**Quick Quiz – Ethological Approach**

In the ethological approach to explaining aggression:
1. Name one thing that aggressive behaviour achieves for the animal?
2. What is a fixed action pattern (FAP)?
3. Give an example of an aggressive fixed action pattern for an animal.
4. Give an example of a sign stimulus for aggressive behaviour in an animal
5. Complete the sentence "Berkowitz showed that aggression can be triggered by . . . ."

Answers in the Feedback Section

---

## 2. The Biological Approach

This explanation is based on the idea that aggression is caused by hormone levels or brain structures, or a combination of the two.

**Evidence of the effects of hormones**

Many studies have found males more aggressive than females (e.g. Maccoby and Jacklin, 1974, found boys to be more aggressive physically and verbally). One possibility is that the difference comes from the higher levels of testosterone found in males. Further details of hormone differences can be found in the section on **Hormones** in the lesson "**Becoming Male or Female: the Influence of Biology**".

---

### Young's study of testosterone effects

Young injected testosterone into a pregnant female chimpanzee carrying a female foetus. The female behaved much more like a male when born, it fought with the other males and behaved in a more assertive manner than a normal female chimp.

---

### Adrenaline studies by Ax

Ax found that participants subjected to fear (created by wiring them up to machines that started to smoke!) produced increased adrenaline levels.

---

**Evidence of the effects of brain structures**

In the 1920's Hess stimulated the hypothalamus in cats' brains and found that they produced aggressive behaviour. Bard removed part of the cortex – the covering of the brain – and found a similar effect, suggesting that the cortex usually dampens down a "natural" inclination to be aggressive. Later investigations showed that the limbic system in the brain is involved in aggression.

**Temperature and aggression**

**Baron** found that riots tend to be correlated with air temperature. Riots occurred ~~most frequently at temperatures between 27° C and 29° C. He extended this~~ straightforward relationship to one in which "discomfort" is correlated with aggression. Discomfort can be a combination of temperature and negative emotion. His participants were given criticisms of a task they performed. They displayed most aggression when the criticisms coincided with slightly lower temperatures.

This suggests that biological factors alone are not enough to account for aggression; they must be combined with the right psychological state.

**Criticisms of the Biological Approach**
*   Just because aggression goes with high levels of hormones does not mean to say that the hormones have caused the aggression. It could be that the hormones are caused by the aggressive behaviour, not vice-versa. Males may be naturally more aggressive and produce high levels of testosterone as a result.
*   Studies on animals are not the same as studies on humans.
*   Some cultures are more aggressive than other ones. Biological explanations cannot account for this.

---

**Complete the sentence on Biological Explanations**
It may be that aggression results from biological factors like _____ levels or _____ structures. Evidence by Young from studies of _____ levels in chimpanzees shows that females with high levels of this hormone acted in a more _____ and _____ way. ____ was able to show that stimulating the hypothalamus of a cat produced aggressive behaviour and Bard showed that the _____ played a part too.

---

# Feedback

### Answers to Quick Quiz – Ethological Approach
1.  (Examples) Territory, a mate, food, the passing on of its genes.
2.  A sequence of fixed behaviours displayed by animals in response to a given situation.
3.  A cat will hiss, display its claws, arch its back and stand its hair on end when threatened or when attacking.
4.  The red spot on the belly of a stickleback.
5.  "Berkowitz showed that aggression could be triggered by *cues in the environment*"

### Complete the sentence on biological explanations – answers
It may be that aggression results from biological factors like *hormone* levels or *brain* structures. Evidence by Young from studies of *testosterone* levels in chimpanzees shows that females with high levels of this hormone acted in a more *assertive* and *aggressive* way. *Hess* was able to show that stimulating the hypothalamus of a cat produced aggressive behaviour and Bard showed that the *cortex* played a part too.

### Reference:
Stratton, P and Hayes, N (1993), *A Student's Dictionary of Psychology* (2nd ed) Edward Arnold.

# Lesson 18. Born to Be Wild
# – Or Trained That Way?
# Aggression and Child-Rearing Styles

This approach to explaining aggression is based on the idea that parents have a particular pattern of interacting with their children. It is this pattern that is responsible for aggression in the child.

## 1. The studies of Patterson et al

It is *probably* true to say that all families have arguments between members. *Probably* all parents shout at their children on some occasion. *Probably* all children are aggressive on some occasion. Patterson, however, found a distinct pattern of behaviours that some parents displayed consistently and saw how the children of these parents displayed far more aggression than other children.

---

### Patterson's study – do you know any parents like this?

Patterson observed the families of children who had been identified as overly aggressive. The observations were combined with interviews with the children, their peers, their parents and their teachers. These people also filled in questionnaires. The researchers collected the same data from children who were identified as not being aggressive but who had similar backgrounds – income, occupations, family size and so on.

Patterson found a distinct type of interaction that the parents used with their children and called it a **coercive home environment**. In this interaction, parents:

- controlled the child by punishing unwanted behaviour rather than rewarding good behaviour
- used physical punishment, aggression, shouting and teasing towards the child. Also,
- the family were constantly involved in conflicts amongst themselves and
- affection was not often shown towards the children.

---

**Evaluation**

This seems to be clear evidence that the way parents interact with their children can cause aggression. This does not mean that all aggression is caused by the way parents interact with their children. Also, we cannot be sure that once the children grow up or leave home their aggression continues.

## 2. The studies of Lewin, Lippitt and White

Lewin et al set out to create different styles of interaction between adults and children. They used an after-school model-making club for boys and asked the three "teachers" involved to adopt one of three styles as follows:

| The Three Styles Used by Adults in Lewin et al's Study | | |
|---|---|---|
| Democratic | Autocratic (Laissez-Faire) | Permissive |
| The boys were<br>• encouraged to make their own decisions<br>• allowed to choose their partners<br>**The adult**<br>• joined in with the group<br>• explained the reasons for his judgement of the work | The adult<br>• decided what would be made<br>• decided who would work with whom gave no explanations of why he thought the work was good or bad<br>• was "distant" and aloof | The adult<br>• Allowed the boys to do what they wanted<br>• Did not get involved unless the boys asked for help<br>• Made no comment on the work |

> **Can you predict the outcome**
> In which group would you predict that aggression would occur?

The outcome was as follows:

Compared to the autocratic group the boys in the **Democratic group**:
- got on better and were friendlier towards each other
- did slightly less work
- approached the adult for task-related matters
- showed more independence and cooperation
- carried on working when the adult left the room

In the **Autocratic group** the boys:
- were aggressive towards each other if work did not go well
- stopped work and were disruptive if the adult left the room
- did as much work as the democratic group

In the **Permissive group** the boys:
- were often aggressive towards each other but not as aggressive as the autocratic group
- did less work than the autocratic group
- were easily discouraged.

> Summarise here the adult behaviours that led to aggression according to the Lewin et al study. There is a suggestion in the Feedback section.

The Autocratic and Permissive groups showed the most aggression.

**Evaluation**

The sample was entirely boys. Although the boys showed aggression in the groups this does not mean that the aggression continued outside the class. The groups were very "unreal" situations and they only lasted for short periods; this is not "child-rearing" in the sense that parents may rear children on a long-term basis but it may be that parents tend to adopt these styles long-term.

## 3. Reducing aggression according to this explanation

> If aggression results from child-rearing practices, then we should be able to reduce aggression by teaching parents to alter the way they raise their children. This method is used successfully, often as part of a whole package of help for families in difficulty. Look back at Patterson's study and make a list of ways you think parents should raise children to avoid aggression in them. Then do the same for the Lewin et al study.

## Feedback

### Summary of adult behaviours leading to aggression

The autocratic group seemed to display the most aggression so the adult behaviours associated with this group are:

- **Controlling the child** – not allowing the child to make decisions
- **Instructing the child** – giving the child orders without consultation
- **Distancing the child** – keeping aloof and not being involved personally.

### Reducing Aggression

According to Patterson et al we should encourage parents to concentrate on rewarding good behaviour rather than punishing bad; do not use physical punishment, shout at or tease the child or be aggressive towards him or her; try not to argue amongst adults; show the child affection.

According to the Lewin et al study we should try to involve the child in decisions about his or her life, explain reasons for our decisions and form a close relationship with him or her.

# Lesson 19
# Ways of Reducing Aggression

**Recap**
Think back to the names of the different explanations of aggression you have read and make a note of them. Tick them off as you read through this lesson.

## 1. Social Learning Explanations
If aggression is learnt then we should be able to "unlearn" it by

1. Removing models of aggression and substituting models of non-aggressive learning.
- Parents can provide models of non-aggressive adult behaviour by altering their behaviour consciously to exclude aggression. Part of this would include not using aggression against their own children, of course.
- Access to violent television programmes can be restricted by parents monitoring closely the programmes that their children watch.
- The content of television programmes can be altered to reduce levels of violence, especially for children's programmes. For example, Forge and Phemister found that children who watched "Sesame Street" were more likely to take part in helping others.
2. Teaching non-aggression.
- Teachers can teach non-violence as a way of resolving conflicts and children are encouraged to report bullying. Bullies are also encouraged to examine their behaviour and find alternative ways of behaving.
- Prisons often offer aggression-control courses to encourage prisoners to alter their violent behaviour.

**Evaluation**
How likely to succeed are methods based on Social Learning Theory? Studies show how pro-social (the opposite of anti-social) television programmes have a positive effect on behaviour. Schools and prisons do run aggression-reduction courses. This suggests that altering models and teaching non-aggression are viable techniques for reducing behaviour.

## 2. The Psychodynamic Approach
According to this approach, aggression is natural and instinctive and "builds up" automatically, so the way to deal with it is to accept it and give it a channel for escape or dissipation. This technique is known as **Catharsis**.

To promote catharsis we could encourage people to take part in competitive sports – to "let off steam" as it is often known. Some people also argue that violent films and videos are cathartic because they allow someone to live through violent experiences without actually being involved in violence.

**Evaluation**

Evidence suggests that catharsis does not work. When levels of aggression have been measured before and after competitive games, it has been found that aggression has increased. Similarly, levels of aggression tend to increase after watching violent videos, not decrease.

## 3. The Ethological Approach

This approach gives two messages for the reduction of aggression. The first is that aggression is natural, instinctive and unavoidable on some situations. To reduce aggression we would have to reduce situations in which we compete for resources or mates.

The second message is that we should remove the "cues" to aggression, highlighted by Berkowitz – weapons, weapon-like toys, clothes that remind us of combat uniforms and so on.

**Evaluation**

It does seem feasible to remove weapons from everyday use – as happens in the UK – and public pressure can have effect on the availability of weapon-like toys. Attention to these aspects of everyday life could have an impact on aggression levels. Avoiding conflict situations could also be useful. For example, as part of the non-violence training undertaken by prisoners, particular pubs are often cited as a place where the prisoner has taken part in aggression. The pubs cited tend to have had a reputation for competitive aggression – as has the football match. For this person, therefore, avoiding these situations could have a reduction effect on their aggression.

## 4. The Biological Approach

If aggression results from brain structures or brain activity then we need to alter the structure or activity if we are to reduce aggression.

**Brain surgery (psychosurgery)**

This treatment grew out of experiments from the 1930s and became more common in the 1950s and 1960s. The Lobotomy involved severing the connections between the frontal lobes of the brain and the rest of it.

**Drugs**

Drugs like sedatives or major tranquillisers are administered to violent patients and some prisoners. They work by depressing the activity of the brain or some may depress activity in specific parts of the brain. They can only be prescribed by doctors and have side effects.

**Evaluation**

Brain surgery did often reduce aggression but it had severe side effects like personality changes (often causing people to become lethargic). Very rarely used nowadays, it is ethically difficult to justify unchangeable alterations to someone's brain.

Drugs are probably the commonest form of aggression control in mental health services and prisons. They are effective and relatively cheap though, again, ethical questions are raised – some people accuse prisons of using them as a "liquid cosh" to subdue prisoners.

Summarise the lesson by completing the table's empty cells. The answers are in the Feedback section

| Approach | Method of Aggression Reduction | Evaluation |
|---|---|---|
| Social learning | Manipulating models | Effective with media images |
| Psychodynamic | | |
| Ethological | | |
| Biological | | |

## Feedback

| Approach | Method of Aggression Reduction | Evaluation |
|---|---|---|
| Social learning | Manipulating models Teaching non-aggression | Effective with media images Effective with children and prisoners |
| Psychodynamic | Catharsis | Not shown to be affective |
| Ethological | Accept aggression or avoid cues like weapons | Can be used to an extent – e.g. avoiding cues |
| Biological | Brain surgery Drugs | Surgery ethically unsound Drugs effective but have side effects |

# Lesson 20
# What is Pro-Social Behaviour?

## 1. Definitions

**Pro-social behaviour** is behaviour that benefits others in some way. It is the opposite of anti-social behaviour. An example would be putting your litter in a bin.

**Altruism** is behaviour that benefits others without benefiting yourself, or even at a cost to you. For example, donating a kidney to a brother or sister would benefit your sibling but be a risk for you.

Some people argue that there is no such thing as altruism since even a kidney donor benefits from the self-esteem that comes from helping another. Some animal behaviours may at first sight be thought of as altruistic. For example, a rabbit thumps on the ground when it sees a fox and this acts as a signal to other rabbits who disappear down their burrows – but the rabbit that thumped has drawn the fox's attention and may become its next meal as a result. Ethologists argue that this rabbit is benefiting because it is helping to preserve its own genes by saving the lives of its relatives, who share some of its genes.

**Empathy** involves understanding the feelings of another person and identifying with the person and the feelings. An example would be understanding that a friend is disappointed at not getting a job. To empathise is to feel empathy for someone.

> **What is being described here** – Pro-social behaviour, Altruism or Empathy?
> 1. The parable of the thirsty soldier who gave his last drink of water to an injured colleague because "Your need is greater than mine"
> 2. Helping an elderly person as you cross the street
> 3. Feeling sad because your friend has split up with a partner
> Answers are in the Feedback section

## 2. The Development of Empathy

### Hoffman's Stages of Development of Empathy

Hoffman observed behaviour that would indicate empathy and suggested the following stages with age guidelines that vary from person to person:

- **Global Empathy** (Under 1 year old). Have you ever observed a child cry because another child has done so? At this stage, children's experiences are still unsophisticated ones like general happiness or sadness. A child will cry if in the company of other crying children so this suggests that it experiences empathy. Children this young will probably not pick up subtle feelings like guilt so cannot empathise with them.
- **Egocentric Empathy** (1 to 2 years old). In this stage, empathy is combined with a baby's view that the world revolves around it (a somewhat crude

definition of "egocentric"). The child will assume that others should feel the same as it does itself and will behave in such a way as to make people feel the same; for example, Hoffman describes a child offering its own doll to an adult who is unhappy.

- **Empathy For Another** (3 to 6 years). As the child experiences a wider range of emotions he or she can empathise with a wider range too. Also at this age language is becoming sophisticated enough to understand and communicate ideas like guilt, and this adds to the child's ability to empathise. The child is maturing towards adult levels of empathy.
- **Empathy For Another's Life Condition** (from 7 years). Children begin to understand concepts like "the poor" or "the unemployed" as groups of people who exist but cannot be readily seen as an identifiable group, like the people who live in the next street. At this stage children may start to get involved in charity activities; the success of television's Blue Peter charity appeals demonstrates this stage.

---

**Progress test**

Which of Hoffman's four stages is being described in each of the following?

1. Rehana watches a soap opera and turns to her mother saying, "Jolene must be very jealous of Ronette – first she stole her boyfriend and now she's won the Student of the Year award".
2. Alan cries at the sight of a huge dog running into the room; Joey starts to cry too.
3. Alan cries at the sight of a huge dog running into the room; Joey tries to put a biscuit into Alan's mouth as he cries.
4. Sarah turns to her teacher and asks "Miss, if we bought more African food at Sainsbury's, it would help the poor families in African countries wouldn't it?

---

## 3. Factors Affecting Pro-Social Behaviour

A two year-old dropping a sweet wrapper perhaps cannot be expected to know that it is acting anti-socially but a ten-year old can. Clearly, then, age, level of maturity and cognitive ability (thinking ability) affect pro-social behaviour. The other factor that affects this behaviour is whether or not the child has been taught to put sweet wrappers in a bin – so socialisation plays a part too.

### Socialisation

Children learn pro-social behaviour – some more than others. They may do this through a combination of social learning in which they imitate others or through having behaviour directly reinforced – say by their parents or teachers. The study in the box below demonstrates this.

---

## Socialisation Affects Pro-Social Behaviour

**Rosenhan** studied American civil rights workers who were active during the 1960s civil rights for Blacks movements. One group was classified as "fully committed" – they gave up jobs and normal life/career patterns to devote their time to the movement. The other group were classified as partially committed – they spent a significant amount of time working for civil rights but did not give up their careers or normal life patterns.

He found that there were distinct differences between the socialisation patterns of the partially and fully committed groups. For example the fully committed group had:

- Closer relations with their parents
- Parents who were more likely to voice opinions against injustice in civil rights
- Parents who were more likely to put their beliefs into practice. This suggests that parents' socialisation of their children made a difference to the degree of commitment to civil rights (pro-social behaviour).

Parents acted as both models and instruments of reward and reinforcement.

**Critical analysis**: Have the parents caused the children to be more pro-social or have the children caused the parents to show the characteristics they display? For example, have young people with a tendency to display pro-social behaviour also stimulated a closer relationship with their parents? Cause and effect may be the reverse of what they appear.

### Social Norms

Social norms are accepted ways of behaving in given situations. In the context of pro-social behaviour, the important factor is what level of pro-social behaviour is the norm?

- In some communities, isolation may go hand in hand with a lack of commitment to pro-social behaviour. If it is normal for people to "keep themselves to themselves" then pro-social behaviour will be less.
- Justice may also play a part. If a community has a strong sense of justice then people who grow up in it are likely to display more pro-social behaviour to ensure that everyone experiences justice in their lives laws may set the norm. For example, if a community believes in equal opportunities then support organisations like the Equal Opportunities Commission are likely to help minority groups.

**Critical analysis**: innate or learned personality differences may have an effect on individuals' levels of pro-social behaviour and may override the norms; but if societies differ in their levels of pro-social behaviour then this could be because social norms override other factors.

## Feedback

**What is being described here?**

1. Altruism
2. Pro-Social behaviour
3. Empathy

**Progress test**

1. Empathy for another
2. Global Empathy
3. Egocentric Empathy
4. Empathy for another's life condition

# Lesson 21
# Pro-Social Behaviour
# and Bystander Intervention

## 1. Recap
Bystander behaviour has been discussed before in the lesson "Why Bystanders Don't Help". You should make sure you are familiar with the sort of incident that concerns bystander behaviour.

Look back over the lesson (or cover it before continuing, if you have not already done so) and recall:
- the "smoke studies" that indicated how people have to define a situation as an emergency before they will help a victim
- the "falling" studies that indicated how we take our cues from others and don't react if others don't
- the "intercom" studies that showed how the more bystanders, the less likely someone is to help a victim.

Now read on.

## 2. Factors that affect bystander intervention: Preview
In the rest of this lesson you will read of studies that show the sorts of factors that can make a difference to whether or not someone intervenes. The factors are:
1. Whether or not the bystander defines the situation as an emergency, influenced by the behaviour of other people.
2. The number of other bystanders
3. How competent the bystander feels to deal with the situation
4. Characteristics of the victim
5. Characteristics of the bystander
6. The costs and rewards of intervening

## 3. Factors that affect bystander intervention
**1. Latané and Darley's "smoke" studies and falling studies** support the notion that we need to define the situation as an emergency.

**2. Latané and Darley's "intercom" studies** support the notion that the number of other bystanders affects whether or not we intervene.

### 3. How competent the bystander feels to deal with the situation
Related to this idea is the suggestion of competence; we are less likely to take responsibility if we do not feel competent to intervene. If we have some first aid training and know how to deal with someone undergoing an epileptic fit then we are more likely to go to his or her aid.

#### 4. Characteristics of the "victim".

The victim in the situation may be one of the variables that affect the likelihood of intervention. Studies by Piliavin on the New York subway have shown that people are far less likely to help a victim acting drunk than one acting sober. Researchers went onto the subway dressed as one of two characters: a drunk who smelled of alcohol and carried a bottle in a brown paper bag, or a person carrying a cane and not smelling of alcohol. As the train pulled out of the station the researcher pretended to stumble to the floor. Intervention was as follows:

- The researcher with the cane was helped immediately on 62 occasions out of 65 (95%)
- The researcher with the alcohol was helped on 19 occasions out of 38 (50%)

#### 5. Characteristics of the bystander

Other studies by Piliavin have found that men are more likely to intervene than are women and that bystanders tend to help victims of the same ethnic group.

#### 6. The costs and rewards of intervening

Piliavin has suggested that whilst the situation of a victim is likely to **arouse** us to intervene, we also take into account the balance of **costs and rewards** of helping.

---

> Can you think of one cost and one reward of intervening for the bystander?

---

Examples of costs might include:

- The time spent in helping the victim (more important if you are in a hurry – on your way to work perhaps)
- The embarrassment of "making a spectacle of yourself" by drawing other people's attention to yourself

Examples of rewards might include:

- An increase in self esteem from knowing that of all the bystanders, you were the one who helped
- Thanks from the victim

If the **balance of costs and rewards** is in favour of costs, then the likelihood of us intervening is decreased. If the balance is in favour of rewards, then the likelihood is increased. However, this balance must itself be weighed against the level of **arousal**. Victims who are suffering visibly will increase our arousal to help them, so this may outweigh any cost balance and cause us to intervene.

**Evaluation of the theory**: whilst the theory does seem sensible it may be difficult to accept that people are as "calculating" as the theory implies. Also, people tend to react quickly in intervention situations and we would have to question whether they have the time to take all these factors into account and make a calculation in this way.

**Evaluation of the studies of bystander intervention**: the "smoke studies" and "subway studies" were observations with some degree of **ecological validity** (true to life) and a manipulated situation. Like other observations they suffer from observer bias but using inter-observer reliability offset this. The "Intercom Studies" were correlations but unusually, the cause-effect direction is unambiguous (the perceived number of participants caused the speed of reaction as the reverse could not be the case) so the studies have some level of credibility.

> **Complete the following paragraph:**
> Psychologists see bystander behaviour as an example of _____
> _____ because it represents a situation in which people can make
> a contribution to society. Many of us have faced situations in which we
> have to choose whether or not to help a stranger in public. Psychologists
> have shown that the decision to intervene can be influenced by factors
> such as the characteristics of the victim and the characteristics of the
> _____. Apart from other factors, Piliavin suggested we also
> take into account the balance of the _____ and the _____ of
> helping a victim.

## Feedback

**Complete the paragraph:**

Psychologists see bystander behaviour as an example of pro-social behaviour because it represents a situation in which people can make a contribution to society. Many of us have faced situations in which we have to choose whether or not to help a stranger in public. Psychologists have shown that the decision to intervene can be influenced by factors such as the characteristics of the victim and the characteristics of the bystander. Apart from other factors, Piliavin suggested we also take into account the balance of the costs and the rewards of helping a victim.

# AQA Exam Style Questions:
# Anti-Social Behaviour

- **Answer all questions**
- **There is no time limit to this assignment**
- **When completed you may compare your answers with the example answers at the end of the book**
- **If you have tutorial support you should send a copy of your answers to your tutor to receive further feedback, comments and guidance**

---

## Aggression Spills Over at World Cup

City shoppers took to their heels yesterday when fans attacked each other at the world cup final. Shop windows and street furniture were badly damaged in the City's main shopping district when rival fans left the bars in which they had been drinking all day and confronted each other, responding to taunts from the opposite side by throwing bricks from a city centre construction site. A total of about eighty men were arrested as police in riot gear fought the fans for two hours.

---

(a) What is "aggression"? (1 mark)

(b) The ethological approach is based on the idea that aggression is instinctive. Objects or events called "sign stimuli" trigger fixed action patterns. Give an example of an aggressive fixed action pattern with which you are familiar. (2 marks)

(c) Appeasement gestures may be used to terminate aggression. Give an example of an appeasement gesture in human behaviour. (2 marks)

(d) Give one criticism of the ethological approach to explaining human aggression. (1 mark)

(e) Aggression may be the result of biological factors in a person. Name **one** brain structure that has been implicated as a cause of aggression (1 mark)

(f) Some psychologists have found that hormones may affect levels of aggression. Name **one** hormone that has been implicated as a cause of aggression. (1 mark)

(g) Give **one** criticism of the biological explanation of aggression (2 marks)

(h) Using the idea of the life instinct and the death instinct, explain why we show aggressive behaviour according to Freud. (3 marks)

(i)  Using your knowledge of psychology, outline the social learning theory of aggression (5 marks)

(j)  Outline **one** method of reducing aggression according to the social learning theory approach. (2 marks)

**Total possible marks = 20**

When completed you should compare your answers with the example answers at the end of the book. If you have tutorial support you should send a copy of your answers to the tutor for feedback, comments and further guidance.

# AQA Exam Style Questions:
# Pro-Social Behaviour

- **Answer all questions**
- **There is no time limit to this assignment**
- **When completed you may compare your answers with the example answers at the end of the book**
- **If you have tutorial support you should send a copy of your answers to your tutor to receive further feedback, comments and guidance**

Read the following transcript of a conversation between a new arrival in the town and a long established resident:

**Resident:** "What do you think of the town then?"
**New arrival**: "Well the shopping centre is just like the one I left but the bus service is good round here and I like the market. I haven't seen much of the social life yet though so I don't know about that".
**Resident**: "And what about the people?"
**New arrival**: "I've only met a couple of people including you but I can tell that people are really helpful".
**Resident**: "How do you reckon that?"
**New arrival**: "You can tell by the way that people do things like look round to see if there's anyone behind them then hold the door open when you're going into a shop, for example".

(a) What is "Pro-social behaviour"? (1 mark)

(b) Give an example of "Empathy" (2 marks)

(c) Outline Hoffman's four stages of Empathy (6 marks)

(d) Pro-social behaviour can be affected by a variety of factors including socialisation and social norms. Take **one** of these factors and describe how it can affect pro-social behaviour. (4 marks)

(e) Give a critical analysis of the factor you have described in question (d). (2 marks)

(f) Outline and evaluate **one** study of bystander behaviour. (5 marks)

**Total possible marks = 20**
When completed you should compare your answers with the example answers at the end of the book. If you have tutorial support you should send a copy of your answers to the tutor for feedback, comments and further guidance.

# OCR Exam Style Questions:
# Aggression

- Answer all questions
- There is no time limit to this assignment
- When completed you may compare your answers with the example answers at the end of the book
- If you have tutorial support you should send a copy of your answers to your tutor to receive further feedback, comments and guidance

**Source a Behaviour Psychology**
**Aggression**
Researchers asked parents to list all the programmes a child watched in a week then, using this information, they added up all the hours the child spent watching programmes considered to be aggressive. The researchers also asked the child's peers to rate how aggressive they thought the child was on a scale from 1 to 10, where 1 is "not aggressive" and 10 is "very aggressive". The results are displayed in the following scattergram.

Hours per week watching aggressive TV programmes

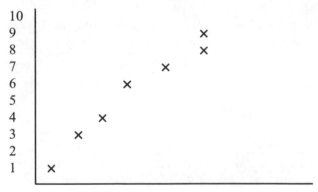

**Scattergram showing the relationship between the time a child spends watching aggressive programmes on the television and a rating of aggressiveness in the child, supplied by the child's peers.**

(a) What is the peer rating of aggressiveness for a child who watches 1 hour of aggressive television programmes per week? (1 mark)

(b) What do the results show is the relationship between television watching and aggression in the children? (2 marks)

(c) Why can we **not** say from the above results that watching aggressive television programmes causes children to be aggressive? (1 mark)

(d) What is meant by "cultural differences in the levels of aggression"? (2 marks)

(e) Outline the findings of a study of cultural differences in levels of aggression (3 marks)

(f) Most studies investigating gender differences in aggression find that males show more aggressive behaviours than females. How would the social learning theory explain this? (3 marks)

(g) Give **one** criticism of the social learning theory explanation of aggression (2 marks)

(h) Outline and evaluate the psychoanalytical approach to aggression (6 marks)

**Total possible marks = 20**

When completed you should compare your answers with the example answers at the end of the book. If you have tutorial support you should send a copy of your answers to the tutor for feedback, comments and further guidance.

# Lesson 22. Is Your Mother Really Necessary? The Development of Attachment

## 1. Do babies need mothers to look after them?

You may already have an opinion about this question. If you have, make a note of it.

Of course, babies need *someone* to look after them, as they are completely dependent on others to feed them and look after their medical needs. But does it have to be the baby's mother who does this job? Is there a link created by nature between mother and child? This question can stir up a real hornet's nest of disputes because all sorts of interests are at stake. If babies need mothers then what does that say about mothers who leave their babies when they go out to work? Where does it leave the father and his role? What about women who don't get on with their babies – are they failures?

## 2. What is Attachment?

The word refers to a close emotional relationship between two people, but most psychologists use it to refer specifically to a close emotional relationship between mother and baby. The word "bond" may sometimes be used interchangeably with the word "attachment", though "bond" or "bonding" tends more often to refer to the *process* in which an attachment is formed. A mother and baby who have bonded well will have a strong attachment. This does not mean to say that fathers do not have attachments with babies.

## 3. Studies of Attachment: Mary Ainsworth's work

Ainsworth invented **The "Strange Situation"** in which children's reactions to certain standardised situations are observed and recorded either through a two-way mirror or a camera. The situations involve the baby with its carer (mother, father or other person) who is asked to allow the baby to move around freely. A fixed pattern of events is carried out – the sequence is always the same.

A stranger enters the room and remains silent at first, then talks to the carer, then approaches the baby. The carer leaves the room so the baby and stranger are alone together. Various other combinations of events take place. For example, the baby is left alone for a period or the carer returns and is left with the baby. The procedure takes about half an hour and trained observers record the baby's behaviour at each stage.

Babies have various reactions to these situations; they may cry, play, act indifferent towards the stranger or allow themselves to be comforted by her. Ainsworth classified the relationship between mother and child according to the baby's reactions, and classified the mother according to the reactions also. Three types of reaction were noted:

- **Securely Attached:** Baby plays happily when carer is present. Distressed by carer's absence and can only be comforted to a small extent by the stranger. Goes to carer upon her return and is quickly comforted by her. Interacts with stranger in presence of carer.
- **Insecurely Attached:** Child tends to cling to carer and is not content to explore the room and toys. Distressed by absence of carer. Takes some time to be comforted upon carer's return. Reluctant to interact with stranger.
- **Anxious-Avoidant:** The child does not really differentiate between the carer and the stranger and can be comforted equally by either; child is not distressed by absence of carer but by being left alone.

Ainsworth's observations suggested two classifications of mother: **sensitive** and **insensitive**.

- The **sensitive** mother, according to Ainsworth, can see things from the baby's point of view and is sensitive to its needs, understanding the baby's messages, accepting the baby and paying attention to it. A separate study by Bell and Ainsworth observed how quickly mothers responded to the crying of babies during the first year. The most important factor in reducing crying was the promptness with which the mother picked up the baby. Sensitive mothers picked up the baby earlier and Bell and Ainsworth felt that later emotional and social development was affected by this – sensitive mothers having children with more emotional stability and better social skills.
- The **insensitive** mother, on the other hand, organises her interactions with the child to suit herself rather than the baby. She allows her moods to affect her relationship and can interpret the baby's communications as personal attacks or negative comments on herself. In the Bell and Ainsworth study of crying, insensitive mothers took longer to respond and had children who were not as emotionally stable as those of sensitive mothers nor as capable socially.

It is likely that most mothers show some behaviour from both types above. Even the most sensitive mother probably feels the need to ignore her child on some occasions.

## 4. Early fearful reactions to strangers

Other psychologists have suggested a general pattern of reactions to strangers in the early months, for all children.

**0 to 3 months** – the child will treat strangers the same as it treats its carers or anyone else.

**4 to 5 months** – the child tends to stare at strangers, suggesting it has recognised them as people who it does not normally see.

**6 months** – the child will "freeze" if a stranger approaches it. This reaction will die out as the child develops.

This pattern of reactions serves as evidence of the idea of attachment too. If the baby reacts to strangers in a way that is different from the way it reacts to its caregiver, then this suggests that a special relationship has formed with the caregiver – attachment.

As can be seen from the Ainsworth studies these reactions also depend on how securely the child is attached to its caregiver. A securely attached infant is likely to react to an approach by a stranger in the way shown above, whilst an anxious-avoidant child will probably not react differently to a stranger at six months.

The behaviour of the stranger will also make a difference to the child's reaction and so will the location of the interaction – the baby is less likely to react negatively if it is in familiar surroundings.

---

**Quick Quiz**

See if you can answer these questions without looking back at the materials.
1. What is "attachment":
2. What is "bonding"?
3. Who investigated the Strange Situation?
4. Name the three types of reaction to the strange situation
5. At what age do securely attached infants "freeze" at the approach of a stranger?

Answers are in the Feedback section.

---

## 5. The pattern of development of attachments
### Birth
There is some evidence that suggests attachments start from the moment of birth. Klaus and Kennel carried out a study in the mid 1970s that started changes in the way many maternity hospitals dealt with the birth of children.

At the time, the normal practice in hospitals was for the baby to be taken away from the mother a few minutes after birth. While the baby was checked, cleaned, wrapped and looked after by staff, the mother would also be checked and encouraged to rest. The baby was normally brought back to the mother some hours later. In Klaus and Kennel's study the baby was not taken away from one group of women and the women were encouraged to hold the baby from the moment of birth. This group was compared with another group who were treated in the normal hospital routine.

The women who were kept with their babies throughout, were found to have a different quality of relationship with the baby. One month later, the researchers found that the mothers held the babies closer when they fed them than did the group who were treated in the normal way, and were emotionally closer to them. This difference held almost a year later when the researchers found that these mothers cuddled and their babies more and that the babies were more mature and sociable.

### The early months
Despite the work of Klaus and Kennel, it appears that babies do not mind who looks after them for the first few months. Look back at the child's reaction to strangers in the section above and it can be seen that in the first three months babies treat strangers like others, so the baby does not appear to display any special attachment behaviour.

By five months, however, babies react differently to strangers and by six months they will choose the attachment figure in preference to others and will actively seek to be close to that person.

**Later**

By eighteen months children will form closer relationships with people who enjoy their company. Playing with, talking with and being happy with the child at this stage will help to form the secure attachment described by Ainsworth.

## 6. Practical applications of these findings

The lesson parents can learn from these studies, is that being sensitive to children and responding to them as soon as possible is beneficial in the long term.

- Many parents want to know whether it is best to ignore a crying infant in case picking it up "spoils" it. In general these studies tell us that it is better to pick the child up straight away, though there may be times when parents find this difficult.
- Being sensitive to the child's needs, taking its concerns seriously and responding to its cries for help throughout childhood are important aspects of parenting skills that follow from these studies.
- Attachment is important for young children and parents should pay as much attention to encouraging the attachment as possible. If parents are unable to devote the time to their child that they would like, then finding a substitute is the best thing for the child. Grandparents and other willing relatives can also form attachments with children and the quality of the child's relationship with the parents will be enhanced, not spoiled, if the substitute is used.
- Psychologists and others can train parents in these skills. Insensitive parents can be trained to put the baby's needs before their own, relate to a baby in a consistent way no matter how they (the parents) feel at the moment, and re-interpret the baby's actions as expressions of its needs rather than comments on the parents.

## Feedback

### Quick Quiz

1. A close emotional relationship between mother and baby
2. The process of forming an attachment
3. Mary Ainsworth
4. Secure, insecure and anxious-avoidant
5. 6 months.

# Lesson 23. Bowlby's Work on Attachment

## 1. The background to Bowlby's work

Bowlby's work on attachment concerned investigating what happened to children when the attachment process was prevented from happening properly. It was, therefore, involved with separation of mother and baby. Other psychologists investigated what happened when mother and baby experienced separation and we shall start this lesson with a look at this other work.

## 2. Comparisons with animals

Studies of animals in their natural surroundings are known as **ethological** studies. **Ethology** is the study of animals in their natural settings. What constitutes a "natural" setting is debatable, however and sometimes these studies are closer to laboratory studies; for example, is a stickleback in a well-stocked fish tank in a "natural setting"?

Even so, many psychologists argue that we can learn a lot about human behaviour by studying animal behaviour, and there may be times when we can study events in animal life which we could not manipulate in humans. What happens when an animal is separated from and brought up without its mother, for example? This is something we could do with a kitten but not with a child.

### Lorenz's studies of Imprinting

In the 1930s Konrad Lorenz studied the way in which goslings followed their mothers around so faithfully. He wondered whether it was an effect produced only by mother geese or whether goslings would do this with other animals.

Eventually, he took a clutch of goose eggs on the point of hatching and kept half with the mother goose and the other half with himself. After hatching, the goslings that were kept with the goose followed her and the half that were kept with Lorenz followed him. He mixed them together in an upturned box then released them. He found that "his" half continued to follow him and the "mother's" half followed her again. He concluded that the geese would follow the first moving object they saw when they hatched.

He called this process of following the first moving object **imprinting** and later studies showed that the geese would follow other objects, from Wellington boots to models of animals. Most animals that moved about soon after birth or hatching are shown to exhibit imprinting.

He also found that there was a **critical period** after hatching during which the animal would imprint; this lasted for some hours and if no moving object was presented to the gosling during this period it would not imprint. Attempts to allow the gosling to imprint after this period would fail. Later studies by Sluckin suggested that this critical period could be varied and so it became referred to as a **sensitive period** instead of a critical one.

Lorenz considered that the imprinting process produced a special bond between the mother goose and the gosling; this bond is referred to as an **attachment**. The implication of these studies is that a similar bond may develop between human mothers and their babies even though babies obviously cannot move around soon after birth.

> Can we compare babies to other animals? Is the evidence from studying goslings useful in coming to conclusions about human babies? Try to think of two ways in which human babies and children are the same as other animal young and two ways in which they are different.

You may have chosen to point to similarities like the way in which babies and goslings both need to be looked after when born, and the way in which they both need to learn about the world around them (goslings need to run from foxes for example, babies need to suck in the right place to find milk).

Your differences may include ideas like goslings can do some things for themselves straight away (like walk), whilst babies cannot, and that goslings will never grow into the level of sophisticated being that babies will grow into.

If we **are** willing to accept that there are at least parallels between goslings and humans then we have some evidence to suggest that babies are born with a capacity and a need to form some sort of attachment with another being: Lorenz's studies would seem to indicate that it does not have to be a specific mother, however.

## 3. Comparisons closer to humans

Harlow studied the effects of separating rhesus monkeys from their mothers soon after birth. These studies are closer to the situation we are trying to investigate, because monkeys are closer to humans than are goslings. Their brains are closer to human brains, their ability to learn is closer to a human's, their ability to manipulate things around them is closer to a human's ability and their social groupings are closer to the varieties we might find with humans.

These studies have now become famous in psychology and other fields. Harlow reared monkeys with two "surrogate mothers" instead of their real ones. The surrogates were actually two wire models; one was covered in cloth and had no milk supply, the other was just bare wire but had a supply of milk in a bottle which the monkey could obtain when it wanted. Young monkeys usually cling to their mothers for long periods of time.

> Which model would you predict the monkeys would spend most time clinging to?

You may have thought the monkey would cling to the wire model because it was the one that supplied the milk or you may have thought the monkey would cling to the cloth one because it felt more like the "real" mother would feel. The monkeys actually did cling to the cloth model for most of the time and went over to the wire monkey only to feed on the milk.

When the monkeys were off the model exploring, the cage a mechanical toy was placed in the cage by the researchers. The monkey became frightened and ran back to the cloth model for safety, not the wire model.

Harlow's studies suggest, then, that the monkeys needed to attach to an object that supplied some sort of warmth and comfort. Neither of the models moved, as in Lorenz's studies of goslings, but Harlow's studies show both the need for attachment and the type of model preferred for attachment.

---

**Review**

Complete these sentences to summarise the major findings so far:

1. Lorenz found that goslings would _____

_____ .

2. Harlow found that rhesus monkeys would _____

_____ .

(Suggested answers can be found in the feedback section at the end of the lesson)

---

## 4. The work of John Bowlby: Studies of human babies and mothers

If the work of Lorenz and Harlow points to the idea that, yes, babies do need mothers, what are the results from studies of babies and their mothers?

**Bowlby's Theories**

The theories and studies published by John Bowlby are probably the most fiercely debated area of this topic of attachment. Bowlby argued that:

**Theory of Attachment**

- Children need to form attachments as much as they need food
- Attachments result from instincts in both the mother and the baby
- As children develop they increasingly focus their attachment on one person – usually, though not necessarily, the mother (this is known as monotropy)
- A critical period exists: attachment has to happen within the first 1 to 3 years of the baby's life

**Theory of Maternal Deprivation**

- Maternal Deprivation will occur if the attachment to the mother is interfered with during this period
- Maternal Deprivation leads to damage to the child's social, emotional and intellectual development

Bowlby was clearly influenced by the work of people like Lorenz and Harlow and their conclusions that animals need to attach, but he was also trained in the theories of Sigmund Freud. Freud's theory of human behaviour and experience is known as the **psychoanalytical** approach. For the moment it is worth knowing that Freud considered the following ideas about early childhood to be important:

- We are "driven" by our desire to satisfy our biological needs
- Babies can satisfy these needs best by using their mothers to supply them with nourishment

Putting both of these influences together, **ethological studies** and **psychoanalytical theories,** it is easy to see how Bowlby came to the conclusion he reached.

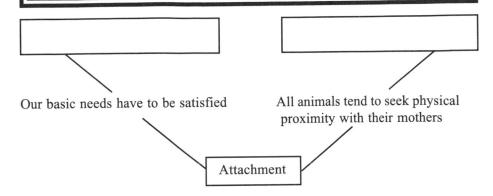

Write these two phrases (ethological studies and psychoanalytical theories) in the appropriate box to complete the flow-chart below. The correct solution is in the feedback section.

## Bowlby's Studies
## Affectionless Psychopathy

In the mid 1940s Bowlby published a study of 44 juvenile thieves which formed the basis of some of his ideas. 14 of the juveniles displayed a type of characteristic that Bowlby referred to this as **"affectionless psychopathy"**. We could translate the word "psycho" as "self", and the rest of the word ". . .pathy", comes from "pathological" meaning "ill". Hence the phrase "affectionless psychopathy" can be seen as meaning somebody with an illness of the self which lead them to lack affection. Bowlby went further than this, suggesting that this group of juveniles lacked any feeling for others and so were not able to form relationship with others. This condition also included an inability to feel guilt at doing something wrong.

Harlow found that the monkeys raised on wire and cloth models were unable to form attachments with other monkeys later in life and Bowlby found that these juvenile delinquents had also experienced separation from their mothers when young. Of these 14 juveniles, 9 had experienced prolonged separation from their mother during the first five years of their life. Bowlby therefore concluded that separation in early childhood led to affectionless psychopathy later in life.

The study as described so far contains elements that lead us to question the conclusions that Bowlby arrived at. Can you suggest two points that do this? Answers follow.

- Firstly, how would Bowlby explain the fact that only 9 of the 14 had been separated from their mothers; how would he explain the affectionless psychopathy of the other 5?
- Secondly, we have to ask why the children were separated:

If this was because their families had not been able to afford to look after them and they had been taken into care, could it be poverty that is linked to this condition of affectionless psychopathy rather than separation?

Had the children been separated from their mothers because of family conflict and, if so, could it be the family conflict that led to the condition?

### Developmental Retardation

Bowlby suggested, as did some other writers such as Spitz and Goldfarb, that maternal deprivation also led to a lack of intellectual development. That is to say that a child's ability to think, talk and act intelligently would be affected by maternal deprivation. We would not expect the child to perform as well at school, nor would we expect good problem-solving skills or communication ability.

---

**Quick Quiz on Bowlby's Theories and Studies**
Try this quick quiz to summarise the work of Bowlby
**Bowlby's Theories**
1. Lorenz used the phrase "imprinting" to refer to the process involving goslings following their mothers. What term is used to refer to a similar process emphasised by Bowlby, involving mothers and children? (1 mark).
2. Bowlby referred to any significant interference with this process as _ _. (1 mark)
3. What is a critical period? (2 marks)
4. Name two results for the child of the failure in the process (2 marks)
5. On which study did Bowlby base his ideas about the effects of separation from the mother? (1 mark)
6. Give one objection to the way in which Bowlby came to his conclusion from this study. (2 marks)
7. Another of the effects of separation which Bowlby referred to was "intellectual retardation". What did he mean by this? (1 mark)
**Total marks = 10**

---

## Feedback on Attachment and Separation

### Suggested answers to the review

1. Lorenz found that goslings would follow the first moving object they encountered within a particular time span after hatching.
2. Harlow found that rhesus monkeys separated from their mothers would cling to a fur-covered model rather than to a wire one supplying milk.

**The correct solution to the flowchart in the section "The work of John Bowlby"**

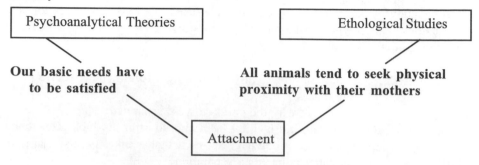

**Answers to the Quick Quiz on Bowlby's Theories and Studies**

1. Attachment (some writers use "bonding") (1 mark)

2. Maternal Deprivation (1 mark)

3. A period of time during which attachment can take place. (2 marks)

4. Affectionless Psychopathy and Intellectual Retardation ( 2 marks – one mark for each one correct).

5. His study of 44 juvenile delinquents (1 mark)

6. Any choice from:

(i)     He failed to explain why the remaining 30 delinquents, who had been separated, did not show affectionless psychopathy

(ii)     The separation may have occurred because of a third factor like poverty or family conflict which could also have been the cause of the affectionless psychopathy

(iii)     He failed to explain the affectionless psychopathy of the 5 juveniles who had not been separated.

     (2 marks)

7. The ability to talk, think and act intelligently is affected. (1 mark)

**Total marks = 10**

# Lesson 24
# An Evaluation of Bowlby's
# Evidence and Theory

## 1. Evaluating Bowlby's theory of attachment
### Multiple attachments: Schaffer and Emerson

Babies often form attachments with more than one person. Schaffer and Emerson studied 60 babies in Glasgow. They visited the family home every four weeks and asked the adults questions about whether the baby cried when left alone in a room or outside a shop etc.

As the babies got older the number of attachments they had formed **increased**. By the age of 18 months only 1 child in 8 had only one attachment; the remaining children had all formed more than one attachment. The majority of children formed solid attachments with brothers, sisters, grandparents and others. It seems that several people can share "mothering" without any loss in the quality of the care or relationships.

This evidence does not support Bowlby's idea of **monotropy** in which the baby will only form an attachment with one person. Nor does it support the idea that bonding with the mother is instinctive; we can see that babies will bond with people other than the mother.

**Contradiction 1:** Schaffer and Emerson showed that children can develop attachments with other adults and children, not just the mother. The other attachments will affect the child's reaction to separation and this also undermines Bowlby's predictions about the effects of maternal deprivation.

**Rutter** pointed out that other observations support Schaffer and Emerson's findings. Children will show the same reactions to a variety of people leaving the room, not only the mother. These indicators of attachment (crying, searching behaviour etc.) can be displayed after the departure of fathers, siblings, other relatives and family friends who have become familiar to the infant.

**Parke** pointed out that we have no real reason to believe that only the mother can supply the support that a baby needs.

There are **alternatives to Bowlby's psychoanalytical approach to attachment.** These include:

- Learning theories. The bond is formed between the infant and caregiver because the infant is rewarded for intimate emotional and physical contact. When a baby is fed, for example, either by bottle or by breastfeeding, the process involves warm, intimate contact and the food acts as a reward. Rewarded behaviour tends to be repeated according to learning theorists.
- Ethological Theories. These theories argue that forming an attachment is an

instinctive behaviour for both mother and baby. Bowlby's theory can also be seen as an ethological one. Lorenz's gosling study shows how some other animals do seem to be pre-programmed with this behaviour. It fits the notion that behaviour which leads to survival for the animal (or the animal's genes) is inherited. Babies who form a close bond with the mother are more likely to survive.

## 2. Evaluating Bowlby's theory of Maternal Deprivation

### Privation and *De*privation: Michael Rutter

Rutter pointed out that the children studied by Bowlby differed from the monkeys studied by Harlow in a crucial way. Harlow's monkeys had not had the opportunity to form bonds with their mothers but Bowlby's juveniles **had** formed bonds with their mothers and those bonds had later been broken by separation. These are two different situations and are now referred to with two different labels. The situation in which children form no bonds (which has been known to happen when children are brought up in institutions, for example) is known as **privation**. The other situation, when children are separated from their mothers after forming an attachment, is known as **deprivation**.

**Contradiction 2:** Rutter suggested that Bowlby had failed to differentiate between privation and deprivation and so failed to find a human equivalent of the animal studies he identified as important.

### Confusing the Cause and the Effect: Michael Rutter

Rutter studied a group of boys on the Isle of Wight and in London. All the boys had been separated from their mothers for a significant period of time at a similar age. They fell into two groups: one group were reported to be maladjusted whilst the others were reported to be well adjusted. The maladjusted group had been separated because of family conflict or psychiatric disorders of the parents, whilst the well-adjusted group had been separated because of physical illness of the mother or housing difficulties or other difficulties, all of which had been resolved later on.

The key difference here seems to have been that stress and discord in the family led to the maladjusted behaviour, not separation from the mother: separation was the effect of the problem, not the cause. If the family could overcome the problem that had led to the separation, then the separation had no lasting effect.

**Contradiction 3:** Rutter also suggested that Bowlby had failed to differentiate between cause and effect; stress on the family was the cause of both the separation and the maladjusted behaviour. The separation was not the cause of the maladjusted behaviour.

### The causes of intellectual retardation: Goldfarb

Bowlby's research pointed to the way in which the maternal deprivation led to intellectual retardation – a deterioration in mental ability compared to how we might expect the child to perform. Goldfarb compared two groups of children from the age of six-months, who had to be raised away from their parental homes. One group was fostered straight away whilst the other group spent three years in institutions before being fostered.

The group who were placed in an institution before fostering were shown to be performing at a lower intellectual level than the group who were fostered straight away. For example, the language abilities of the fostered group were better than the language of the other group. When Goldfarb investigated the circumstances of the institution he found that children lived in an unstimulating environment with little attention from adults and few games, books or other intellectual pursuits. Their physical care was well catered for but staff were not trained to look after the emotional and intellectual needs of the children. They were not given as much opportunity to talk to adults and older children so weren't able to practise their language skills, for example.

Bowlby's juveniles had been raised in institutions during the separation from their mothers and it would seem from Goldfarb's study and many like it that their intellectual retardation could easily be accounted for by their institutional environment rather than the maternal deprivation.

**Contradiction 4:** Goldfarb's studies show that intellectual retardation is more likely to be the result of institutional care than the maternal deprivation which Bowlby blamed.

### Further criticism of the Maternal Deprivation theory

Bowlby's theory of Maternal Deprivation has also been criticised on the basis that it was merely an idea designed to encourage women to leave their jobs so that men returning from war could take up their jobs again. As the World Health Organisation published the theory after the Second World War, it did seem to fit this accusation.

If this makes it sound as though we are accusing Bowlby of conspiring with governments against women then it could at least be said that the theory does seem to be unduly influenced by the cultural setting of the time. Even today, many theorists dismiss Bowlby's theory of attachment and maternal deprivation on the grounds that it simply makes mothers feel guilty about wanting to have their own achievements.

---

**Summarising the debate on Bowlby's Evidence**
Below is a list of topics concerned with the work of John Bowlby or writers who have debated his ideas. The list is in alphabetical order. Take a piece of paper and put two headings: *"Supports Bowlby's Ideas"* and *"Contradicts Bowlby's Ideas"*. Place each of the topics under one of the headings. A correct list appears in the Feedback section.

Affectionless psychopathy
Ainsworth's Studies of the
   "Strange Situation"
Attachment
Critical period
Developmental retardation
Ethological studies
Goldfarb's studies of institutions
Harlow's studies of monkeys
Imprinting
   There are alternative theories

Just encourages women to stay
   at home
Lorenz
Privation v deprivation debate
Psychoanalytical approach
Rutter's Isle of Wight study
Schaffer and Emerson's multiple
   attachments study
Senstitive period
Study of 44 juveniles

## Feedback

**Summarising the debate on Bowlby's Maternal Deprivation. Correct answers:**

| Supports Bowlby's ideas on | Contradicts Bowlby's ideas on |
|---|---|
| **Maternal Deprivation** | **Maternal Deprivation** |
| Affectionless psychopathy | Ainsworth's studies of the "Strange Situation" |
| Attachment | |
| Critical period | Goldfarb's studies of institutions |
| Developmental retardation | Privation v deprivation |
| Ethological studies | Rutter's Isle of Wight study |
| Harlow's studies of monkeys | Schaffer and Emerson's multiple attachments study |
| Imprinting | |
| Lorenz | Just encourages women to stay at home |
| Psychoanalytical approach | |
| Sensitive period | |
| There are alternative theories | |
| Study of 44 juveniles | |

# Lesson 25. Breaking Attachment Bonds – The Effects of Deprivation and Privation

Sometimes it is impossible to avoid separating a child from its mother or caregiver. Day care, hospitalisation of the child or the parent, imprisonment, parental separation or divorce and death are the commonest causes of long – term separation. What has psychology learned about the effects of these situations?

> Do you have a memory of being separated from your parent or other caregiver? Do you remember your feelings during and after the separation? Make a note of the main memories if you can.

**Reminder**
- **Deprivation** involves separating child and caregiver **after** attachments have formed
- **Privation** involves separating child and caregiver **before** attachments have formed

## 1. Short term effects of deprivation

One of the best known studies of children separated from their parents for a short time is that of Robertson and Robertson's "Young Children in Brief Separation". This was a filmed study of children up to two years old in different circumstances. It included children being brought into a residential nursery, admitted to hospital or looked after by the Robertsons themselves in their own home.

The researchers noted the same syndrome of reaction, known as **separation anxiety** or **syndrome of distress**, in many cases. This syndrome consisted of:

1. **Protest** The child reacts to the situation of being left – e.g. as the parent departs – with crying, screaming, kicking, struggling to escape etc.
2. **Despair** The child eventually calms down and appears to be apathetic and sad. It rejects attempts to console it and prefers to be alone, often rocking or thumb sucking.
3. **Detachment** The child seems distant from others though he or she may interact on a superficial level. If the mother returns when the child is in this stage he may ignore her. It seems as though he has to re-learn his relationship with her.

Children vary in the extent to which they show this syndrome. This variation can be affected by:

- **Age of the child** The biggest reactions are found in children aged 7 or 8 months to 3 years old. Attachments have formed by the 7-8 month stage, so separation will have an effect but the child in this age range does not have the language to understand ideas like "only for a few days".

- **Sex** The Robertsons reported that boys are more distressed by separation than girls.
- **Relationship with mother** Children who have a good relationship with the mother before the brief separation are more likely to cope. This reflects Ainsworth's study of securely and insecurely attached children.
- **Experience of previous separations** Children who have experienced "successful" separations previously are more able to cope with new ones.
- **Multiple attachments** Children who have formed multiple attachments will find it easier to be separated from one person.
- **The quality of childcare** Some childcare arrangements during separation offer the child better support. These include the substitute caregivers being able to offer affection and attention.

**The effects of day care**

When both parents work, the child can experience a combination of short-term and long-term separations since the child is not with its attachment figures for up to eight hours (the short-term element), but this can go on for the whole of the child's infancy (the long-term element).

One large-scale study by Kagan and others followed children in day care over a period of five years. They were compared to children who were brought up at home. Kagan found no significant differences between the two groups when good quality day care provision was used. However, poor day care facilities showed up in poorer language and social development.

In itself, then, this form of separation is does not lead to a detrimental effect on the child.

---

**Short Term Effects of Deprivation – Exercise**

1. What was the name of the researchers quoted in the lesson as studying children in brief separation?
2. Name all three stages of separation anxiety.
3. Name two factors that may affect a child's reaction to separation.
4. Did Kagan find that children in good quality day care were behind in language skills compared to children brought up at home?

Answers in the Feedback section

---

## 2. Long term effects of deprivation

Probably the commonest form of deprivation for children is the loss of the father because of divorce. It has been estimated that 20% of children experience divorce and only one divorced father in three maintains contact with his children.

**General possible outcomes**

*Bowlby's suggestions:* the anxiety created by the fear that separation will happen again may result in a variety of effects including:

- **Detachment** – the child becomes self-contained so that it does not have to suffer if separation occurs again.
- **Clinging** – in contrast to detachment, the child may find it difficult to be without the remaining parent and may cling obsessively. Children may even

veer between the extremes of detachment and clinging.
- **Psychosomatic disorders** – again, this is a very psychoanalytical idea that reflects the general approach of Bowlby. In this case, children develop symptoms of illnesses as a result of the separation.
- **Aggression** – some children may develop aggressive behaviour.

*Rutter's contribution.* In his study of boys in residential care on the Isle of Wight, Rutter found that deprivation itself does not lead to maladjusted behaviour. His group of boys included some whose separation from their mother was caused by family discord and conflict – they were shown to be maladjusted. The other boys were separated because their mothers had been taken into hospital or because they had housing problems – they were not maladjusted. Being separated did not, itself, cause behaviour problems then, only the conflict in the family was linked to it.

## Divorce studies

The effects of divorce depend on many factors apart from the divorce itself.

---

**Can you anticipate the factors?**

What factors do you think might make a difference to the effects of divorce on the child? If you can think of any, make a note of them.

---

You may have included in your list the idea that children may actually **improve** their general well-being if the parents had argued a lot and created an unhappy atmosphere before the divorce. Rutter found that disturbed behaviour in children is linked with unhappy parents living together.

Other factors found to have an effect include:
- The age of the child – the older the child, the less the effect in general
- The relationship between the child and each parent – perhaps the best situation is the one in which the child is well adjusted to both parents
- The relationship between the parents after the divorce. A reasonable level of harmony between the parents seems to be the least disruptive situation for the child.

You may also have included factors like
- the support offered by other members of the family – including siblings – and the school and
- the emotional temperament of the child
- the sex of the child – perhaps girls cope better than boys?

**Heatherington** identified two phases of the reaction after divorce in children who were four years old when the divorce occurred:
1. **The Crisis Phase**. In this period, the child became more aggressive and inflexible, possibly depressed and disobedient.
2. **The Adjustment Phase**. The child's behaviour became similar to the way it had been before the divorce. Aggression reduced.

Heatherington also found sex differences. Children usually stay with the mother after divorce and this may lead to girls experiencing less disruption if they identified with the mother. Boys, on the other hand, will experience more loss if they identify with the father. The study found that girls had recovered from the divorce after two years in general but boys were still affected by it at this time. Other studies have found this not to be the case and it seems that a critical factor in this is whether the boy really does have a closer relationship with the father.

Heatherington's study also confirmed that children with parents who were unhappy before the divorce were generally happier a year after the divorce than they were before the divorce.

---

Long term Effects of Deprivation – Exercise
1. List three general possible effects of long-term deprivation
2. What two phases of reaction to deprivation did Heatherington identify?
3. Are there sex differences in children's reactions to divorce?
Answers in the Feedback section

---

## 3. Long term effects of privation

### Intellectual performance

The work of Goldfarb was outlined in the previous lesson. From this we can see that children raised from the age of six months with foster parents (and so allowed to develop attachments with them) had better intellectual skills than those raised in an institution from six months to three years (making it difficult to form attachments) and then placed in foster homes.

### Emotional and social skills

Harlow's studies of monkeys have also been outlined in the previous lesson. They showed that monkeys raised without a mother were unable to form relationships with other monkeys and failed to rear their own young normally. But monkeys are not humans. What happens if human children are brought up without the mother or mother figure?

Of course, we cannot take babies from their mothers just to see what the effect will be but there are cases of children apparently growing up without adult humans. These children are reported from time to time. An example is the "Wild Child of Aveyron" from France. Found in the nineteenth century running on all fours naked in the forest aged about ten years, it was suggested that this boy had been abandoned by his parents at birth but had been suckled and reared by wolves. He ran with a pack of wolves when found. He was captured and brought back to civilisation but never learned to speak, hold cutlery, or use a toilet. From the psychologist's point of view he was intellectually socially and emotionally retarded.

However, the Wild Child may have been abandoned in the first place as a much older child than new born. It may be that his parents recognised that the boy was not going to grow normally and so abandoned him at a much later age. His behaviour may have turned out like this anyway.

Other similar cases have been reported in which the children do make up for earlier privation. The Koluchova twins, for example, were found at about age eight locked by their parents in a cupboard, which had been their home all their lives. They showed intellectual, emotional and social retardation but later, with the help of remedial programmes and support from adults, they recovered to a more or less normal level. Other well documented case studies like these have been reported, though not all have recovered to the same extent.

These are good examples of the case-study method, and as such they suffer from the problems of this method. For example,

- each case may not apply to other people
- the form of isolation experienced by the subjects of the studies are not necessarily comparable with children who are deprived of attachments "normally"
- we have no authentic details of the people before they were found
- there are no controls to compare the person with.

However, some generalisations can be made. All these children demonstrated some degree of intellectual, social and emotional inadequacy and some of them were able to recover from it with structured help.

---

**Long-Term Effects of Privation**
1. What did the work of Goldfarb show?
2. Do "abandoned children" regain their intellectual and social skills?
3. Give one problem with the studies of abandoned children as evidence for privation
Answers in the Feedback section

---

## Feedback
### Short Term Effects of Separation Exercise
1. The Robertsons
2. Protest, despair and detachment
3. (e.g.) Age of child and sex.
4. No
### Long Term Effects of Deprivation – Exercise
1. (e.g.) Detachment, clinging, aggression.
2. Crisis and Adjustment
3. Yes, though other factors can affect this.
### Long-Term Effects of Privation
1. That children in privation had less intellectual ability than attached children.
2. Sometimes, but not always.
3. (e.g.) We are not always sure that they were of normal capacity in the first place.

# Lesson 26
# Cultural Variations in Childcare Practices

## 1. The right way to bring up children

There is no single right way to bring up children. Societies are different and the way they care for children is different. Cultures are collections of attitudes, values, beliefs and language shared by a group of people. Virtually any group has its own culture – from Hell's Angels to Boy Scouts – but we shall be looking at the cultures of large groups of people like societies.

> Perhaps there are certain principles that you think are important in bringing up children. Would you be able to list two or three important principles in the way you think that children should be cared for? If so, make a note of them.

You may have put things like:
- To be honest
- To be friendly
- To stick up for themselves
- To try their hardest

and so on. If you ask a couple of friends what they would put, without discussing it with them first, it is likely that you will get two different lists.

Whilst individual people will have different ideas, it is still possible to find general patterns of bringing up children that are common to most people in a culture. Also, studies have shown how cultures vary in the way they care for children – even though people may never have discussed how to bring up children, they still tend to do it in the same way as other members of their culture. Here we shall look at some of those variations in childcare that exist between cultures.

## 2. Examples of cultures where separation is normal

In the previous lessons we examined the debate about what happens when children are separated from their carers – often from their mother. To an extent this debate starts from the idea that it is natural and desirable for children to be cared for by their mothers. But in some cultures an element of separation between mother and child is quite the normal way to bring up children.

**i) Kibbutzim in Israel.** a communal way of living has been practised by some groups for many years. It does not seem as popular as it once was but there are still many of these communities. The members share goods produced by the kibbutz so everybody has the same standard of living. Other practices include all members eating together and leadership roles being elected – so the members will elect the manager of the farm. All members own the machinery and tools. On some Israeli kibbutzim, children are cared for in a house dedicated to looking after children. So the children grow up together with adults who specialise in caring for the community's children, and both parents go out to work during the day.

This does not mean that parents and children do not meet. There are many different arrangements on kibbutzim. Sometimes the children go back with their parents in the evening to sleep in their accommodation. Or the arrangement may be that parents visit the children in the evening. There are other arrangements too.

---

What would you see as the advantages and disadvantages of these ways of caring for children?
Try to note two advantages and two disadvantages

---

For advantages you might have noted things like:
- Parents will not be harassed when they are with their children – when they do see the children they can them their full attention.
- Children can receive specialised care focused on their needs with adults who have learned about caring for children.

For disadvantages you may have noted things like:
- The children may grow up closer to their carers (known as metapelets) then their parents.
- Parents may not be able to observe all the changes in their children that they would see if the family lived together.

One of the most famous writers on Israeli children, Bruno Bettelheim, found that children in kibbutz did not suffer the sorts of problems that Bowlby would predict; although a study by Sidell showed that the kibbutz children tended to be more aggressive than other children.

ii) **The Shona of Zimbabwe.** Gelfand found that the Shona also have a pattern of childcare which involves separation of parents and children. When the child reaches about eighteen months to two years, it is normal for it to go to live with its grandparents who will care for it and raise it. Although the child may see its mother it does not live with her but in the home if the grandparents. The grandfather takes responsibility for a boy and the grandmother looks after a girl. Later on, when the child reaches perhaps seven or eight, it will return to the mother's house to be raised to adulthood by her.

## 3. Cooperation vs. Competition

One aspect of cultural variation in childcare that has been well researched is the idea that some societies encourage their children to cooperate whilst others encourage them to compete. As you may imagine, the children of the kibbutz mentioned above are very much encouraged to cooperate, but this value is common in other societies like China too.

---

Think for a moment about your own childhood experiences at school. Can you point to one example of being encouraged to cooperate and one example of being encouraged to compete?

---

The sort of example you may have cited for competition is sports activities where you were competing for the best result in, say the 100 metres race, or you may have attended a school where you knew who was "top of the class".

The sports field may have figured in your example of cooperation too. For example, you may have been encouraged to forgo individual "glory" so that you could be a good member of a team and promote the team's success, rather than your personal success.

Did you find it more difficult to think of an example of cooperation? British society tends to follow the pattern of most western societies and promote competition as a cultural value, so that would suggest that competition would be a more common aspect of school life.

**Bronfenbrenner** compared the childcare styles of America with those of the USSR (the former alliance of eastern countries dominated by Russia). He found the USSR encouraged a set of cooperative values in children. For example, children were taught to do their best not so that they could benefit personally but so that the whole class, team, school or society could benefit. Examples of good behaviour held up to children, tended to be those who had benefited the whole group. It was common for teenagers to join youth groups which reflected society's aims – they would work together on community projects for example.

By contrast, the emphasis in American culture tended to be on individual success and on "standing out from the crowd". Children who beat others in school grades were held up as good examples. Violence was found to be more prevalent in children's experiences (entertainment for example) and success through violence featured in the media often (police officers winning by countering violence with "better" violence, for example). Bronfenbrenner found it was common for teenagers to join groups of other teenagers who were antagonistic towards society's values.

---

**Quick Quiz**
1. What is meant by "culture"?
2. What is the name of communities in Israel where people own the machinery, land, buildings and tools communally?
3. Describe an example of a common approach to childcare in these Israeli communities.
4. What do these communities and the Shona people of Zimbabwe have in common in terms of childcare?
5. What dimension of childcare did Bronfenbrenner investigate in the USSR and America?

---

# Feedback
## Quick Quiz
1. Attitudes, values, beliefs and language shared by a group
2. Kibbutzim
3. Children are cared for by Metapelets in houses devoted to childcare instead of by their parents
4. Children are normally brought up separately from their mothers/parents
5. Competition and Cooperation.

# AQA Exam Style Questions: Attachment and Separation

- **Answer all questions**
- **There is no time limit to this assignment**
- **When completed you may compare your answers with the example answers at the end of the book**
- **If you have tutorial support you should send a copy of your answers to your tutor to receive further feedback, comments and guidance**

Read the description of a child's behaviour, below, and then answer the questions that follow.

---

## Hospital Visit

Baby X was brought into the hospital waiting room by her mother who pointed out the toys to the child. The mother attempted to encourage the child to look at and play with the toys but the child was clinging to the mother and would not allow himself to be put down. The assistant entered the room and the child ignored her. The mother put the child on the floor and the child cried bitterly. The mother left the room to go for her x-ray and the child continued to cry. The assistant tried to comfort the child but the child ignored the assistant and continued to cry. The mother returned from her x-ray and picked up the child who continued to cry. The child would not stop crying for quite some time despite the mother's attempts to comfort him.

---

(a) How did the baby behave when the mother showed him the toys? (1 mark)

(b) What type of attachment does the child's behaviour reflect? Tick the correct box.

☐ Securely attached

☐ Insecurely attached

☐ Anxious avoidant

(1 mark)

(c) Using your knowledge of psychology, give **one** practical application of the study of attachment. (2 marks)

(d) Describe Bowlby's work relating to Maternal Deprivation (6 marks)

(e) Give **two** criticisms of Bowlby's work on Maternal Deprivation (4 marks)

(f) Using your knowledge of psychology, outline the reaction we might expect from a young child if it has to be taken into hospital for a period of three weeks. (3 marks)

(g) Describe what Rutter found about the long-term effects of breaking attachment bonds. (3 marks)

**Total possible marks = 20**

When completed you should compare your answers with the example answers at the end of the book. If you have tutorial support you should send a copy of your answers to the tutor for feedback, comments and further guidance.

# OCR Exam Style Questions: Attachment

- **Answer all questions**
- **There is no time limit to this assignment**
- **When completed you may compare your answers with the example answers at the end of the book**
- **If you have tutorial support you should send a copy of your answers to your tutor to receive further feedback, comments and guidance**

Source a Developmental Psychology
attachment

---

## Hospital Visit

Baby X was brought into the hospital waiting room by her mother who pointed out the toys to the child. The mother attempted to encourage the child to look at and play with the toys but the child was clinging to the mother and would not allow himself to be put down. The assistant entered the room and the child ignored her. The mother put the child on the floor and the child cried bitterly. The mother left the room to go for her x-ray and the child continued to cry. The assistant tried to comfort the child but the child ignored the assistant and continued to cry. The mother returned from her x-ray and picked up the child who continued to cry. The child would not stop crying for quite some time despite the mother's attempts to comfort him.

---

(a) How did the baby behave when the mother showed him the toys? (1 mark)

(b) What type of attachment does the child's behaviour reflect? Tick the correct box.

☐ Securely attached ☐ Insecurely attached ☐ Anxious avoidant (1 mark)

(c) Describe Bowlby's work relating to Maternal Deprivation (6 marks)

(d) Give **two** criticisms of Bowlby's work on Maternal Deprivation (4 marks)

(e) Describe **one** study of the long-term effects of breaking attachment bonds (3 marks)

(f) State the difference between deprivation and privation (2 marks)

(g) Using your knowledge of psychology, outline an example of a cultural variation in childcare practices (3 marks)

**Total possible marks = 20**

When completed you should compare your answers with the example answers at the end of the book. If you have tutorial support you should send a copy of your answers to the tutor for feedback, comments and further guidance.

# Lesson 27
# Piaget's Theory of Cognitive Development

## 1. Piaget's Theory of Cognitive or Intellectual Development

At first sight the word "cognitive" seems unusual and is certainly not a word commonly used in everyday language. It is very similar to the word "recognise", however, which **is** used in everyday language. To recognise is to re-cognise or to "cognise" again. When you recognise someone in the street you "know them again".

**Cognitive development** refers to the way in which our ability to know about the world develops from birth.

The word **intellect** tends to be used when we are referring to thinking or reasoning. Some writers refer to **cognitive development** whilst others refer to **intellectual development** but both are talking about the same processes.

In this lesson, Piaget's theory of cognitive or intellectual development is examined and it makes the assumption that we all pass through certain **stages** of development.

## 2. Piaget's Studies of Children's Thinking

It is sometimes difficult to realise that the way children think can be very different from the way that adults think. Piaget was the first psychologist to show this difference systematically.

**Differences between adult and child reasoning**
You may be able to illustrate this difference yourself if you are able to spend a little time with a child of about 4 to 5 years old. If the child is not your own you must be sure to obtain the permission of the parent or guardian before you do this and to explain what you will be doing with the child.
1. Allow the child to watch as you fill two milk bottles with water
2. Ask the child if the bottles contain the same amount of water. The child will say "yes" or you may have to put more in one bottle before he or she will say "yes".
3. Again, allow the child to watch as you pour the water from one bottle into a wide, shallow container – like a salad bowl or baking tray
4. Ask the child which container has the most water in it: the milk bottle or the salad bowl/baking tray

Many (most) 4 or 5 year olds will say that the milk bottle holds the most water. You should not try to contradict the child or imply that he or she has made a mistake or is somehow inadequate for giving that answer. Just say thank you and carry on with something else.

Most adults will be surprised that children will make the mistake outlined in the box above.

- Even though the child saw you filling the bottle then pouring from the bottle to the bowl he or she will not assume that the amount of water has remained constant. You, however, know that it cannot change.
- The child will consistently choose whichever container is the tallest as the one holding the most liquid.

This little investigation was one of the pieces of research carried out by Piaget demonstrating that children do not just think "less" than adults but that there is a difference in the **quality and type** of their thinking. He studied children's thinking by setting them tasks and asking them questions that revealed their thinking; this method of gathering information from the children is sometimes known as the **clinical interview**.

In particular three aspects of intellectual activity that Piaget showed were different in children and adults can be seen below.

**Three important aspects of cognition**

(1) **Conservation** Adults know that although the *appearance* of a substance may change, this does not necessarily mean that the *amount* changes. The illustration of the water changing from a milk bottle to a salad bowl is an example of this – the shape of the water has changed but the amount stays the same.

Similarly, Piaget showed how we can roll out a sausage of plasticine and then alter its shape into a longer, thinner one: the child will say the longer, thinner one has more plasticine in it.

Also, he arranged five counters in a row and then put down an identical row of five more beneath them: when the second row was re-arranged to make it more spread out, children would say it contained more counters.

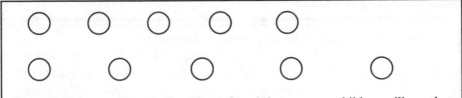

**Piaget's Conservation Studies** Piaget found that younger children will say that the bottom row has more counters than the top row – simply because it is longer.

Young children, then, fail to **conserve**. This applies to liquids, solids, number, length, weight, area and volume.

(2) **Egocentrism** To be egocentric means to see things only from your own point of view and Piaget showed how young children were egocentric in a very real way.

Adults have the ability to imagine that they are sitting in another part of the room and to imagine what the room looks like from that point of view. Some objects can interfere with the line of sight of a person in the "other" position, so some of the things you can see now may not be visible from the imagined point of view and vice versa. Young children do not have this ability.

Piaget constructed a model of some mountains (he did live in Switzerland so mountains are a natural part of the landscape which children may encounter daily in their lives). He placed various objects on the "mountains" and asked the child which of them he or she could see from where he or she sat. Then he placed a doll at one point in the scene and asked the child to consider what the doll could see. Could it see the church from where it stood? In general, young children could not carry out this task successfully. Also, they could not look at photographs of the scene taken from different points of view and identify which ones were taken from which viewpoints.

In this way, Piaget illustrated how children are **egocentric**.

**(3) Inferential Reasoning** The ability to abstract from the real, concrete world and manipulate those abstract ideas, eventually inferring a conclusion, is a powerful and complex ability. For example, if n plus 2 equals five, then we infer that n must be 3 because we have to add 3 to 2 to make 5. We do not have to specify 2 "what", we can appreciate 2 as an abstract symbol that could stand for 2 anything. This ability is behind much of a human's reasoning ability. We can discuss imaginary events and objects (e.g. tomorrow) and predict what will happen under certain circumstances (e.g. if I put that apple on that sloping table it will roll off).

Some elements of **inferential reasoning** are present in children but the full ability only develops with age, as shown by some more of Piaget's studies discussed below.

---

**Check your understanding – Aspects of Cognition**
(Answers in the Feedback section)
Match the following three terms to the types of cognitive abilities given below
1. Conservation, 2. Egocentrism, 3. Abstract Reasoning
A. Ben is unable to select the correct picture showing what a room looks like from the window
B. Shagufta is able to understand that it **is** possible to subtract 4 from 3 and have an answer of -1
C. When asked how long her tape measure is if it is rolled up, Tracy says it is still one metre, just like it was before it was rolled up

---

# 3. Piaget's Theory of Intellectual or Cognitive Development

Through studies like those described above, Piaget suggested that we all go through four major steps in the development of our thinking ability. These form a distinctive pattern of stages through which we all pass; you cannot alter the sequence – everyone goes through it in the same order and at roughly the same age. You cannot "speed up" your passage through these stages but will pass from one to the next when you are ready to do so – as you mature. Later he suggested that the age may differ from person to person and that not everyone reaches the final stages.

**Stage 1 The Sensory-Motor Stage** (0 to 2 years)

In this stage the baby comes to know and understand the world by its senses and by motor activity (movement). The baby learns to follow moving objects with its eyes, grasps objects in its view, later bangs them, testing the feel and noise of the object. It puts objects in its mouth to explore the taste.

There is a big difference between a new-born baby and a 2 year old so this stage, like all others, does allow for change through development. What the new-born and the 2 year old do have in common is their attempts to understand the world by direct experiences with their senses.

An interesting feature of this stage is **object permanence**. If you are looking out of the window and someone draws the blind you do not assume that the window and scene outside have disappeared – yet this is precisely what babies seem to do at the beginning of this stage. A baby in the first part of this stage will reach out for a toy and immediately stop if the toy is covered with something. Yet by the later part of this stage the baby will continue to reach for it and make sounds to communicate its continuing interest – all evidence that it has begun to understand that objects have a permanence – they still exist even when the baby cannot see them.

**Stage 2 The Pre-Operational Stage** (2 years to 7 years)

Again, there is a lot of difference between the ability of a seven year old and that of a 2 year old but, again, there are things they have in common. For example, both are **egocentric** and both are **unable to conserve** (see above).

**Symbolic thinking** is the ability to let something "stand for" something else. This can provide a range of possibilities. For example, a stick may stand in for a gun, a doll may stand in for a baby, another doll may symbolise mummy and so on. Two jumpers may symbolise a pair of goal posts and a cardboard box can symbolise a car.

This is a powerful development because language (in its spoken and written form) is also symbolic. The symbol "100" means "one hundred" the squiggle "a" means the word "a". Language, art, maths – all these are symbols but they are powerful in the sense that they allow the child to abstract from the "real" world and consider or discuss it. The child at this stage can discuss with an adult the cycle of the four seasons. Compare this with the way in which the child could only understand the world by sucking it in the previous stage!

This stage is an important one in preparation for abstract thinking. It is during this period that the most development in language takes place.

Another interesting feature of this stage is the child's inability to **classify** objects in the same way that an adult can. Given a box of wooden shapes and asked to put them into groups, an adult may, for example, put all the squares together, all the circles together, all the triangles together and so on. Further, an adult could work with two criteria and put all the red squares into one pile and all the green squares into another and so on. If asked, the adult could also ignore the shapes and put all the red objects together, all the green together and so on. This ability of **classification** is eventually achieved in the Formal Operational Stage later on.

Children at the Pre-Operational stage cannot do these tasks. If asked to classify by shape, they may start by correctly putting a red triangle with a blue triangle but then put a blue square in the pile (because the previous object was blue – even though it is the wrong shape) and then perhaps a red square (because the previous object was a square) and so on.

**Stage 3 The Concrete Operational Stage** (7 years to 11 years)

At this stage, children become **able to conserve.** They also develop the ability to **decentre** (to see things from other people's viewpoint – both physically and psychologically too). The word **"concrete"** in the name of this stage tells us about one of its features. Whilst the child can carry out "operations" about the world ("think" about the world) he or she still needs concrete examples of what is being manipulated in order to understand. For example, the child attains the concept of **reversibility** at this stage – this means that the child understands that logical sequences can be reversed. For example, if you add two to three you will get five; similarly, if you take away two from five you will get three. Although the child comes to understand this idea, he or she will still benefit from actually seeing five counters on the desk from which two can be removed. Concrete examples will also allow a child to solve the following problem:

*Anne is bigger than Stacey; Stacey is bigger than Lee. Is Anne bigger than Lee?*

If the child has three differently sized dolls and allows each to "stand" in for the children in the puzzle, then the correct answer ("Yes") can usually be achieved. Being able to work through this type of puzzle without needing concrete examples is known as **Transitive Inference**.

**Stage 4 The Formal Operational Stage** (11 years and older)

In this stage abstract thinking is possible, this is the ability to abstract from the real, concrete world and manipulate those abstract ideas, eventually reaching a conclusion. Algebra is only possible only if this stage has been reached, since it involves using abstract symbols (letters – sometimes Greek ones) to symbolise numbers and mathematical processes. Transitive inference is achieved without concrete symbols. Classification can also be achieved.

Scientific advances can only be made using this type of thought – abstract ideas like the composition of the air around us, the use of music as a form of therapy or the way in which one artistic school precedes another can only be made if we are able to abstract from our concrete experiences and consider what may be. Adults vary in the degree to which they reach this stage and how far into it they progress.

**Complete the following table: the first row has been completed for you**

| STAGE | AGE | CHARACTERISTICS |
|---|---|---|
| Sensory-motor | 0 to 2 years | Motor activity<br>Physical manipulation of objects<br>Objects put in mouth<br>Object permanence develops |
| | | |
| | | |
| | | |

# Feedback

**Table of Piaget's Theory**

| STAGE | AGE | CHARACTERISTICS |
|---|---|---|
| Sensory-motor | 0 to 2 years | Motor activity<br>Physical manipulation of objects<br>Objects put in mouth<br>Object permanence develops |
| PRE-OPERATIONAL STAGE | 2 years to 7 years | Egocentric<br>Unable to Conserve<br>Symbolic Thinking |
| CONCRETE OPERATIONAL STAGE | 7 years to 11 years | Able to conserve<br>Able to decentre<br>Reversibility<br>Seriation<br>Concrete examples needed |
| FORMAL OPERATIONAL STAGE | 11 years and older | Abstract Thinking<br>Classification<br>Transitive Inference |

# Lesson 28
# The Processes of Cognitive Development

## 1. The Processes Involved in Development

Development from one stage to the next is a natural process of maturation, according to Piaget. He made suggestions about the way in which the development occurred as follows:

**Schema** (plural "schemata") Piaget suggested that we have a store of information about things and about how to do things. This store is a schema. The store acts as a basis upon which we decide how to act towards things. For example,

- a baby would build a schema of grasping, which it would use as a strategy for dealing with objects;
- an adult may have a more complex schema for riding a bicycle.

**Assimilation** New information is "fitted into" a schema so that it can be understood. For example,

- the baby's grasping reflex may have been developed from experience with a round object but it will cope with the first cube it comes across by using the same schema.

**Accommodation** Sometimes a schema has to change to handle new information: it has to accommodate itself to new experiences. The baby's grasp may have to be two-handed to cope with a large object:

**Adaptation** When the child has assimilated new a new object into its current schema and accommodated the schema to cope with new objects that are too different for its current ones then it will **adapt** its behaviour appropriately, rattling a new rattle like the old one (assimilation), or banging its first rubber hammer correctly to achieve the right sound from it (accommodation). These changes in behaviours are known as **adaptation**.

**The individual experiences equilibration** When a schema fails to cope with a new situation, a sense of discomfort or "disequilibrium" is felt. Assimilation and accommodation take place to alter the schema and this brings the person back to the feeling of equilibrium experienced previously. This process of bringing a person back to a sense of balance is equilibration.

The Development of Schema By this process of assimilation, accommodation and equilibration, schema are constantly developed and changed. The process must be intensive early on in life, since babies have so much to develop. Some psychologists would argue that babies and children sleep so much more than adults because their minds are tired from this work. Although many schemas are developed and established by adulthood, some of the examples given in this lesson illustrate the idea that the development process continues into adulthood.

**Progress Check: Schema, Accommodation, and Assimilation**

Louise starts college and joins the Learning Centre where she hopes to word process her assignments. However, the software package on the Learning Centre's computer is different from the one she learned at school. She enrols in the IT workshop to learn the new word processing software but discovers that it is very similar to the one she used at school. The principles are exactly the same, only the layout of the screen is slightly different.

In the accounts lesson, however, Louise has to learn to use a spreadsheet software package. She has never used spreadsheets before but sees that it has familiar aspects – for example, it can be run on the same computer as the word processor and has a Help facility, just like the word processor.

In your opinion, what aspects of the above account of Louise's experience represent:
1. Schemata?
2. Assimilation?
3. Accommodation?
4. Adaptation

Suggested answers can be found in the Feedback section

## 2. Evaluation of Piaget's Theory of Intellectual Development

**Positive points**

- **Reveals children's thinking.** There is no doubt that Piaget's studies showed us just how differently children think when compared to adults. His work shows a systematic pattern of thinking markedly different from adults' patterns.
- **Applications to education.** Piaget's ideas had an impact on education, ranging from pre-school to secondary. The implications for the classroom of what he found are discussed later in this lesson; they are major implications and still affect the way that children are taught in schools.
- **Stimulated further research.** The work of Piaget has stimulated debate and further investigations along similar lines.
- **Children as scientists.** Piaget gave us a new way of looking at children as people striving to understand the world in which they were developing.

**Criticisms**

- **Contrary Findings.** Some researchers have found that, given the right circumstances, children **are** able to employ thinking which is supposed to be displayed only by older children and adults. For example:
  - **McGarrigle and Donaldson** carried out the conservation task with two rows of counters, as described earlier. In their study, however, they used a soft toy, which they called "Naughty Teddy" and acted out a little scene in which Naughty Teddy came along and messed up the second row of counters. When the children were asked whether the two rows still held the same number of counters, on this occasion, they were much more likely to say "yes", revealing that they understood conservation and contradicting Piaget's findings.

- **Hughes** carried out a parallel study to the mountains one, in which children had to see this scene from a different viewpoint. Although Piaget found that 3 to 5 year olds could not do this, Hughes found that, given the right circumstances, they could do this. He constructed equipment in which a model boy could be placed behind intersecting walls to "hide" from model police officers. Children of this age **could** place the boy doll in such a position that the police officer dolls would not be able to see it. This contradicted Piaget's findings.

Both the Naughty Teddy study and the Police/Boy study illustrate the way in which the **social context** of the tasks affects the child's answers. In the case of Naught Teddy, the play nature of the task seems to have allowed the child's "true" thinking to be revealed. Hughes argued that the use of mountains by Piaget was not part of children's ordinary thinking (even though they **did** live in Switzerland!), so putting the task in a more realistic setting also seems to have revealed the "true" thinking of the child.

- **Ages for stages.** There does seem to be a wide variation amongst children in the age at which Piaget's stages may be attained. Piaget did concede that the ages were only guidelines and that variation did occur. Also, people may be at different stages of development for different aspects of their thinking.
- **Method.** The clinical interview can be intimidating for children. It may have inhibited both their thinking and their responses to questions. When Piaget asked, "Are you sure?" in response to a child's answer, for example, children may think to themselves that this must mean they are wrong and they may change their answer as a result.

## 3. Applications of Cognitive Development Theories to Education

Piaget's findings in particular have been taken into account by teachers, and his ideas and their implications form an important part of most teacher training courses.

- **Readiness.** The idea that it is no good trying to teach children ideas beyond their stage of cognitive development is accepted by many teachers (But see "Accommodation and Assimilation", below). Using ideas and materials that are appropriate to their stage of development is practised in the classroom. If children cannot think symbolically then it is no good trying to teach them algebra which depends upon symbolism (where letters stand for numbers) and it is common to find algebra being taught at an appropriate age (about 11 years upwards).
- **For younger children.** In the concrete operational stage it is helpful for them to have concrete objects to manipulate in number work, e.g. using cubes to stand for units and rectangular bars ten times longer to stand for tens in number work. Playgroup practices incorporate these principles – the equipment they use like sand and water encourages "discovery learning" and focuses on sensory-motor activity, as do the toys available for under twos, which encourage the children to make noises by rattling them or to push them along to see them go.
- **Assimilation and Accommodation.** Despite the principle of waiting for children to be ready before expecting them to work at a higher level of cognitive

function, teachers also present children with challenging experiences and problems which allow them to accommodate, and so develop, their schemata. Ideally, the children also need the opportunity to push forward the boundaries of their functioning and assimilate new experiences into their current schemata too.

- **Early experiences.** In the early years of formal education materials like sand, water, clay, paper, paints, building blocks and other equipment play an important part in allowing children to learn through sensory motor experiences. As mentioned earlier, the need for concrete experiences also guides teachers in later years even in maths or languages lessons.

- **Discovery learning.** If Piaget is correct and children are scientists struggling to understand their world, then a major theme in education should be the provision of materials and experiences which support children in finding things out for themselves, rather than simply being told.

- **Multi-sensory learning.** Children with learning differences, in particular, benefit from the experience of learning a point through all senses simultaneously. The research shows that we learn through a range of experiences: sensory-motor (enactive), iconic, concrete, symbolic/formal and other modes of representing the world and thinking. A point that is learnt through many different senses simultaneously should be learnt more thoroughly and more easily, especially if the child has difficulties learning normally.

## Feedback

### Progress Check: Schema, Accommodation, and Assimilation

1. The skills that Louise uses to operate the computer and software – e.g. typing, using delete keys, taking breaks to prevent her eyes becoming strained.
2. Probably the use of the new software for word processing can be seen as assimilation since Louise only has to alter slightly what she already practices in her word processing skills to fit the new software into her existing schema for word processing
3. Probably the new skills required for the new spreadsheet software can be seen as accommodation because Louise is not just fitting new experiences into existing schemata for word processing but she is making significant changes to her schemata for using computers by accommodating them to new ones for using spreadsheets.
4. Louise's correct use of the new word processing and spreadsheet software.

# AQA Exam Style Questions: Cognitive Development

- **Answer all questions**
- **There is no time limit to this assignment**
- **When completed you may compare your answers with the example answers at the end of the book**
- **If you have tutorial support you should send a copy of your answers to your tutor to receive further feedback, comments and guidance**

Read the description of the study below.

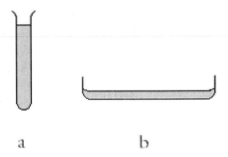

a                    b

A student was describing the work that she did in her chemistry class at school to her four year old sister. She had some equipment from a chemistry set and she demonstrated a test tube (a in the diagram) and a wide, shallow glass dish (b in the diagram). She put some water in the test tube to show her sister how they used them at school then poured it into the wide glass dish. During their conversation the older sister asked the younger one if the two containers had the same amount of water in. Even though the younger one had seen the older sister pour the same water from a to b, she still said she thought there was more water in the test tube than in the dish. The older sister was surprised.

(a) In Piaget's theory of intellectual development, what did he mean by a schema? (1 mark)

(b) In the table below, match the definitions to the terms by drawing a line between the boxes. One of them has been done for you.

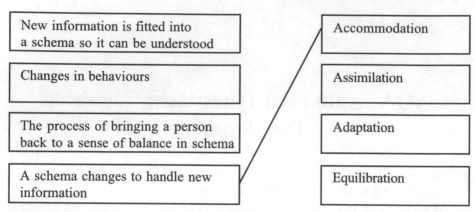

(3 marks)

(c)  Piaget suggested that the concept of object permanence did not exist at the sensory-motor stage. Outline what Piaget meant by "object permanence". (3 marks)

(d)  Outline the **Concrete Operational stage** of Piaget's four stages of development. (5 marks)

(e)  Outline **one** piece of evidence that suggests Piaget's theory may be inadequate to explain all aspects of cognitive development. (4 marks)

(f)  Piaget's work has been applied to various aspects of working with children. Describe one such application. (4 marks)

**Total possible marks = 20**

When completed you should compare your answers with the example answers at the end of the book. If you have tutorial support you should send a copy of your answers to the tutor for feedback, comments and further guidance.

# OCR Exam Style Questions: Cognitive Development

- Answer all questions
- There is no time limit to this assignment
- When completed you may compare your answers with the example answers at the end of the book
- If you have tutorial support you should send a copy of your answers to your tutor to receive further feedback, comments and guidance

**Source a Development Psychology**
**Cognitive Development**

> Egocentrism is the tendency to see the world only from our own point of view. Piaget's theory of how our thinking develops as we get older suggests that up to the age of about 7 years, children can only see the world from their own point of view. He discovered this by making a model of mountains and placing various objects on the model to represent buildings for example. He asked children to look at the model from one point of view and choose a photograph that corresponded to how the scene would look from a different point of view. In general, children up to age 7 could not do this and tended to choose the picture of the scene as they saw it themselves at that moment. After the age of about 7, however, children could perform this task successfully.

(a) According to the source, what does egocentrism mean? (1 mark)

(b) In Piaget's test what would a child of 12 years usually do if asked to pick correctly a photograph showing the scene from a different point of view? (1 mark)

(c) What is the name of the stage at which children become able to decentre? (1 mark)

(d) Describe **one** other feature of this stage of cognitive development. (2 marks)

(e) Piaget also carried out studies that led him to propose the idea of **conservation**. Describe **one** such study. (3 marks)

(f) Outline **one** criticism of the study you described in (e) above. (2 marks)

(g) Piaget suggested that cognitive development occurs through the processes of **assimilation** and **accommodation**. State what each of these concepts means.

**Assimilation** (2 marks)
**Accommodation** (2 marks)

(h) Outline **one** study that produced findings that question Piaget's theory. (4 marks)

(i) Give **one** criticism of Piaget's theory other than the existence of contrary findings from other studies. (2 marks)

**Total possible marks = 20**

When completed you should compare your answers with the example answers at the end of the book. If you have tutorial support you should send a copy of your answers to the tutor for feedback, comments and further guidance.

# Lesson 29 Behaviourist and Social Learning Approaches to Moral Behaviour

## 1. Do the right thing – what is moral behaviour?

> **What would you do if. . . ?**
> What is the right thing? Do you always do it? Consider the situations below and make a note of your response.
> 1. Have you ever been given too much change in a shop and noticed it? What did you do? Did you keep the extra or give it back? Why?
> 2. What would you do if you were getting money out of a cash machine and it gave you £50 too much but only recorded the amount you asked for? Would you keep it? What is the right thing to do? Why?

Now look at the factors you took into account when you made your decision.
- In the shop change question, did you consider the size or locality of the shop? Would you have kept the change if it had been a national chain and returned it if it were a small, local shop?
- Would you keep the money from the bank because banks can afford to lose £50, or return it because keeping it would be stealing and/ or you would feel guilty or suspect that they could trace it to you?

Adults often do take account of subtle ideas like this when they are making these decisions about what is right and wrong and this can be quite different from the way children think.

When we study morals we study the way people decide what is right and what is wrong. We do not set out to establish what **is** right and wrong, just how people decide for themselves.

**Definition: Moral behaviour is behaviour that is considered right and good.**
Of course, people often have different ideas about whether a particular piece of behaviour is moral or not.

## 2. The Behaviourist approach to moral development

The Behaviourist approach is based on the idea of **reinforcement**: rewarding good behaviour. Most parents will set out to "teach the difference between right and wrong" to their children, so we already seem to accept that learning plays a part.

This approach assumes that all behaviour can be explained in terms of learning and moral behaviour is no exception. The lessons in the section on Learning explain the principles and the ideas of **classical** and **operant** conditioning and reinforcement. In short, conditioning suggests that behaviour that is associated with a pleasant experience will tend to be repeated; behaviour that is associated with an unpleasant experience tends not to be repeated. Parents and other adults confer rewards and punishments on children for morally good or bad behaviour

> Aronfreed punished one group of boys by telling them off **before** they touched some toys and he punished another group by telling them off **after** they had touched them. The boys who had been punished before were found to be less likely to touch the toys later when given the opportunity. The act of reaching out to touch the toys had been associated with a negative experience.

- Children who are told "good girl" or "good boy" when they produce behaviour seen as morally correct by others, will tend to repeat that behaviour. Some writers suggest that children say "good boy" or "good girl" to themselves and so continue to practise the behaviour even when the parents are not present.
- Eysenck argued that we feel guilty when we contemplate or carry out "bad" behaviour because we have been punished in the past for bad behaviour and so associate punishment with the bad behaviour. The feeling of guilt is the conditioned response of anxiety, which has a biological basis.

## 3. The Social Learning approach to moral development

Social learning theory involves **observation** and **imitation**. Children
- observe other people being rewarded or punished for behaviour and so develop the idea of what is right and wrong from others' experiences an
- imitate the observed behaviour when they are in a similar position.

> In a study by Bryan and Test, motorists were found to be more likely to stop and offer to help a woman whose car tyre was flat if she was already receiving help from another passing motorist. The first helper acted as a model for other motorists to imitate. Note here that adults are responding, not children.

Were you ever asked to "set a good example" to younger brothers or sisters, or to younger children at school? Again, this idea of modelling and imitation seems to be accepted by many parents and teachers in bringing up children.

Many children's heroes and heroines play a role in setting examples of good behaviour for children to follow – often saving somebody from a terrible fate then acting modestly when offered praise.

> **Relive your childhood!**
> Cast your mind back over your early childhood and make a note of:
> - An example of a time when you were taught the difference between right and wrong. Did you receive a reward for being good (helping somebody or doing something morally good (not just completing your homework) or a punishment for being bad?
> - Somebody who was presented to you as a "good example". What was it the other person did to be good?

## 4. Evaluation of these approaches

**Praise**

- There is a considerable body of evidence to support the principles of the learning approach and the social learning approach in general. It would seem logical to apply these principles to moral behaviour.

- Teaching children the difference between right and wrong seems to be a feature of most societies so it appears that one line of support for the theory is the fact that it can be applied to real life.

**Criticism**

- As can be seen from the lesson on cognitive approaches to moral development, children seem to pass through universal stages of development in their moral reasoning and there would be no reason for this if moral development were simply a question of learning, since there would be no reason why we would all learn in the same pattern or sequence of stages.

---

**Complete the following sentences**

Moral behaviour is behaviour that is considered _____ or _____.
Reinforcement is part of the _____ approach to explaining moral development. A study by _____ showed how moral behaviour is affected by conditioning. Many parents practise the behavioural approach without realising it by saying phrases like "_____ _____" when their child does something seen as being in line with their moral code. When children watch "good" behaviour on television then go out and copy it, they are _____ according to the social learning theory. A study by _____ and _____ showed how even adults are influenced by processes of modelling when they stopped to imitate the model of a helpful motorist.

---

## Feedback

**Answers to "Complete the following sentences"**

| | | |
|---|---|---|
| Right or Good. | Behaviourist Aronfreed | Good boy/girl |
| Imitating | Bryan and Test | |

# Lesson 30
# The Cognitive Approach to Moral Behaviour

## 1. How do you play marbles? Piaget's Stage Theory of Moral Development

To children, the idea of what is right and what is wrong often seems to be decided by other people. Piaget investigated the way that children saw the rules about right and wrong by asking them about the rules of marbles. He asked the children

- what the rules were,
- where the rules came from,
- whether or not they could be changed,
- whether or not they ever broke them
  – and other questions.

> Jot down your answers to these questions so you can compare them to Piaget's findings

From children's answers to these questions, Piaget felt he could paint a clear picture of how moral development occurred in children.

Your answers to two of the above questions would probably be that other children made the rules of marbles and that they could be changed as long as all the players agreed. Piaget found a pattern in children's reasoning, they thought of the rules as follows:

- **under fives** did not follow rules but just pushed the marbles as they pleased or aimed them randomly for pleasure
- **5 to 8 year olds** (approximately) knew the rules and thought they came from God or older children or some other authority. They were seen as unchangeable.
- **9 year olds or older** (approximately) knew that although other children had started the rules of marbles it was possible to change them if all the players agreed.

Piaget also investigated children's thinking of what they see as right and wrong, like the box on the previous page. He presented children with moral dilemmas – stories like the one below – and analysed the children's answers.

## Who is Naughtiest?

Piaget asked children to say which of the characters in the following two stories had acted in the naughtiest way

**Story 1** A child called John was called to tea by his mother. He went into the dining room but as he pushed open the door it knocked over a tray that was behind it and all fifteen of the cups on the tray fell to the floor and broke. John did not know that the tray was there.

**Story 2** A child called Henry waited till his mother was out and then climbed onto a chair to reach a cupboard so he could get out a jar of jam that was there. He could not reach the jam but as he stretched up he knocked over a cup and it fell to the floor and broke.

> What would you say? Was John or Henry the naughtiest?

- Some adults would say that neither child was naughty because neither intended to break the cup or cups.
- Some adults would say that Henry was the naughtiest because his intention was to take jam that he should not have been taking.

Both of these answers take into account the **intention** of the child when deciding on guilt. Piaget found that children up to about eight years ignored the intention of John and Henry when deciding on guilt but instead they took into account **only the consequences** – John was the naughtiest because he broke fifteen cups and that is the most damage so he is the most naughty!

Piaget referred to the type of reasoning that the younger children employed and that took only consequences into account as **moral realism**. He said children use this type of reasoning at the **heteronomous** stage. Heteronomous means that others are in charge. The other type of reasoning, which took into account intention was called **moral relativism**. He called this stage the **autonomous** stage. Autonomous means we set our own rules.

---

**Try it out**

If you are able to obtain the permission of parents you may like to tell the above stories to children of different ages and see what response you get. Do not give any of the children the impression they have done anything wrong if they give the moral realism type of answer.

---

His theory is a **stage** theory; this means:
- children pass through stages in their reasoning about what is right and what is wrong,
- the stages are **universal** – they apply to everyone,
- the stages are **invariable** – everyone goes through them in the same sequence.

Putting all Piaget's work together, we can construct a table that describes his findings. Try to complete the table below from the explanation you have read so far. The completed version is in the Feedback section at the end of the lesson.

| Stage of Moral Development | Heteronomous | Autonomous |
|---|---|---|
| Approximate Age | | |
| Type of moral reasoning employed | | |
| Child's Ideas About Rules | | |
| Guilt Takes Into Account: | | |

**Criticisms** Piaget used interviews with children about the rules of marbles and about moral dilemmas, as the evidence for his model.

- The children were an opportunity sample (a convenient group of people who just happened to be accessible) and included his own children. They were not particularly representative of all children and Piaget's relationship with some of them could have been a source of bias in their responses and in his account of their responses.
- Marbles are a very limited aspect of life. Studies of marbles or similar games may not be all that useful when applied to other aspects of life. Marbles tends to be played by boys and this shows a gender bias in Piaget's methodology.
- Are **two** stages of moral development enough to account for the differences between the moral decisions of all adults and all children? Are teenagers likely to make the same moral decisions as middle-aged people or the elderly? It seems unlikely that two stages differentiate between different ages sufficiently.

**Praise**

Piaget's theory fitted well with the evidence he collected and with his theory of cognitive development.

## 3. Kohlberg's Model of Moral Development

A more complex model was suggested by Kohlberg. He also used moral dilemmas to ascertain how people would behave under certain circumstances. Each dilemma involved having to choose between two principles. The one below asks us to choose between upholding the law and saving someone's life.

---

**What should Heinz do?**

**One of Kohlberg's dilemmas**

Heinz's wife was dying from a special form of cancer but there was one drug that could save her. The drug was made by a local chemist; it was expensive to produce but the chemist was charging ten times what it cost him to make. The chemist wanted $2000 for a small dose but Heinz could only get together about $1000 – even though he had borrowed as much as he could from his friends.

    Heinz told the chemist that his wife was dying and asked him to let him have the drug for $1000 or to let him pay the remainder later. The chemist refused, saying that he had invented the drug and had a right to make a profit from it. Heinz became desperate and broke into the chemist's to steal the drug.

Should Heinz have done this?

Is the chemist right to charge what he likes?

Should Heinz have done the same thing for a stranger?

---

On the basis of people's answers to these sorts of dilemmas, Kohlberg constructed a more complex model than Piaget's. He suggested that people made decisions about what is right and wrong on the basis of certain principles as shown in the following table:

| Level | Stage | Guiding Principle |
|---|---|---|
| Level 1 Pre-conventional | Stage 1 (Punishment/ obedience) | The right thing to do is whatever gains a reward; the wrong thing to do is whatever is punished. |
| | Stage 2 (Instrumental) | The right thing to do is whatever is in your own best interests. |
| Level 2 Conventional | Stage 3 (Interpersonal Concordance) | Gaining approval of others. The right thing involves doing whatever makes people think you are "good". |
| | Stage 4 (Law and Order) | Maintaining law and order. The right thing is whatever is good for society. |
| Level 3 Post-conventional | Stage 5 (Social Contract) | Although laws should be obeyed, there are times when they are overridden by the rights individuals |
| | Stage 6 (Universal-ethical) | What is right and wrong is decided by our own ethical principles which we arrive at by reason and thought. |

Note how the Pre-conventional stage seems to be concerned with individuals gaining benefits for themselves; the second is concerned with individuals fitting in with others; the third is concerned with justice and individual rights.

> Using the table, say what answer would be given to Heinz's dilemma by someone at each stage in Kohlberg's model. Put your answers in the table below. The answers are given after the table.

| Stage of moral reasoning | Guiding Principle | Should Heinz steal the drug? |
|---|---|---|
| Stage 1 (Punishment/ obedience) | The right thing to do is whatever gains a reward; the wrong thing to do is whatever is punished. | |
| Stage 2 (Instrumental) | The right thing to do is whatever is in your own best interests. | |
| Stage 3 (Interpersonal Concordance) | Gaining approval of others. The right thing involves doing whatever makes people think you are "good". | |

| Stage 4 (Law and Order) | Maintaining law and order. The right thing is whatever is good for society. | |
| Stage 5 (Social Contract) | Although laws should be obeyed, there are times when they are overridden by the rights of individuals. | |
| Stage 6 (Universal-ethical) | What is right and wrong is decided by our own ethical principles which we arrive at by reason and thought. | |

We can see how Heinz's dilemma would be seen differently by people at different stages of moral development in this model. Kohlberg found that younger children tended to say that Heinz should not steal the drug. This would correspond to Level 1 and Level 2 thinking; the law should not be broken – breaking it brings punishment, it is not in your interests to break the law, you do not gain the approval of others by breaking it and it is not in the interests of society to break laws. The answers for stages1 to 4, therefore, are "No".

By the time the interviewee is reaching Level 3, however, the decision is different. Kohlberg found that older teenagers and adults tended to say that Heinz should steal the drug. Again, this corresponds to his model. The laws against theft can be broken under certain circumstances and the principle of life is more important than that of a small amount of personal property. The answers for stages5 and 6, therefore, are "Yes".

**Evaluation** Kohlberg's model has some **advantages** over Piaget's:

- its more sophisticated levels account for the subtle differences that do seem to exist between different age groups; for example, differences can be seen between adolescents' reasoning and that of middle-aged people – both groups may have developed different ethical principles in stage 6; adolescents may value liberty highly whilst the middle-aged may place more importance on stability.
- these principles seem more appropriate to real life, taking into account ideas like maintaining law and order and balancing them with occasions when they can be overridden.

**Criticisms** Kohlberg's model is often criticised for its dependence on Western values. The "peak" of moral reasoning is very much biased towards the individual: the height of morality occurs when individuals decide what their own ethical principles will be. In other cultures the individual is never seen as superior to the group; the family or community or kinship is seen as always overriding the needs of the individual and stage 6 would be seen as inferior to stage 4.

## Feedback
**Summary Table of Piaget's Moral Development Model**

| Stage of moral development | Heteronomous | Autonomous |
|---|---|---|
| **Approximate age** | Up to eight years approx | Over eight years approx |
| **Type of moral reasoning employed** | Moral Realism | Moral Relativism |
| **Child's ideas about rules** | • Made by authority figure<br>• Unchangeable | • Made by other children<br>• Can be changed to suit situation |
| **Guilt takes into account:** | Consequences | Intentions |

# Lesson 31
# The Psychoanalytic Approach
# to Moral Behaviour

## 1. Freud's Psychoanalytic approach to moral development

The picture of moral development portrayed by Freud's **Psychoanalytic** theory is centred on his idea of the **Superego**. Freud's psychoanalytic theory informs many topics in psychology and you may like to read about his approach in Sex and Gender, but the relevant parts as far as moral development goes can be summarised as follows:

**The unconscious mind:** Most of out thinking is "under the surface" of conscious thought. We are not aware of our unconscious thoughts but they play the most important part in out thinking and we can get access to these thoughts via dreams, hypnosis, free association and other routes.

**The Id:** We are born as a collection of biological needs: the need for food, drink, warmth, sexual gratification, physical contact, urination, defecation and possibly some others. These needs are driven by the force of the Id, which expects immediate gratification.

**The Ego:** As babies we can obtain gratification for these needs immediately. If we are hungry we can cry and expect to be fed. We can urinate and defecate at will. However, as we grow older we are expected to wait until an appropriate time to be fed and to use a potty rather than nappies. Our Ego develops as a part of our mind that organises our thoughts and behaviours in such a way as to satisfy the desires of the Id but in a socially acceptable way. It is the part of us that makes us wait until we can buy some food rather than just take that of the person sitting next to us on a train.

**The Superego:** Further development brings with it the development of the Superego. This is the part of the mind that causes us to ask ourselves whether what we are doing is morally the right thing to do. It contains the **conscience** which administers **guilt** when we do something it disapproves of and boosts our **pride** and **self-esteem** when we do something it approves of.

**The Phallic Stage of Psychosexual Development** is the third of five stages of development through which all people pass. It occurs at about the age of five years and is the point at which we have to resolve the **Oedipus Complex**. This complex results from the child falling in love with its opposite sex parent; "falling in love" includes the real desire to have a sexual relationship with the opposite sex parent. Boys, therefore, realise that they are rivals with their fathers for their mother's love. Girls realise that they are rivals with their mothers for their father's love.

Boys and girls resolve this complex by becoming more like their same sex parent. Boys become like their fathers so that they can win their mother's love and at the same time put their fathers off the scent; if the father feels flattered by the fact that the boy is becoming more like him, he is less likely to see him as a rival for the mother's affections. Freud said that the boy is motivated to do this by the fear that the father will castrate him if he realises that he (the boy) is in love with the mother. This is a powerful motivating factor, so the boy will put a lot of energy into becoming like the father.

This process of becoming like the father is **internalisation**. The boy internalises the whole parent and this includes the parent's moral code. Hence, moral development occurs at this stage in children and consists of taking on (or internalising) the father's moral code.

Girls do not have as much to lose. They believe they have already been castrated and so do not fear castration. Instead, Freud suggested that they fear losing their mother's love if the mother finds out that the daughter is in love with the father and desires him sexually. Girls do present the same process (Freud referred to the process as the Oedipus Complex in both boys and girls though later writers used the term Electra Complex for girls). Freud reasoned that because they do not fear castration they are not as strongly motivated to internalise the mother as is the boy motivated to internalise the father. One result is that girls do not have morals as strongly ingrained as do boys.

For both boys and girls, the conscience is the internalised parent and this is the source of moral decisions. It takes the place of parents in punishing and rewarding behaviours.

**Evaluation** Some of the points which can be made about Freud's ideas include:
- It does not seem to fit with everyday experience that children do not have a conscience until about the age of 5 years and that it suddenly appears as a finished product. Rather, it seems to be something that develops and changes over time well into adulthood.
- Children are exposed to many other sources of influence about what is right and wrong apart from parents. The media, "soap operas", school and a host of other agencies probably play a part in this development.
- It is difficult to establish that unconscious thoughts exist, let alone a separate part of our self devoted to moral behaviour – the conscience.
- There is no evidence that girls are less moral than boys.

---

**Insert the missing words in the following paragraph to help establish and check your understanding of Freud's idea.** The correct answers are in the Feedback section at the end of the lesson.

"Freud's model of moral development is based on one of three structures in the _____ mind – the Superego. This part of the mind develops with the function of checking whether the behaviour and thoughts of a person are morally_____. If the person does something immoral the _____ will punish the person with feelings of _____. If the person does the right thing it will reward the person with feelings of pride or self-esteem.

> The Superego develops during the _____ stage of psychosexual development when the _____ Complex needs to be resolved. During this stage the child internalises the same-sex parent and so also internalises the _____ _____ of the parent. This allows the Superego to be seen as the _____ Parent.

## Feedback

"Freud's model of moral development is based on one of three structures in the **unconscious** mind – the Superego. This part of the mind develops with the function of checking whether the behaviour and thoughts of a person are morally **good** or **right**. If the person does something immoral, the Superego will punish the person with feelings of **guilt**. If the person does the right thing it will reward the person with feelings of pride or self-esteem.

The Superego develops during the **phallic** stage of psychosexual development, when the **Oedipus** Complex needs to be resolved. During this stage the child internalises the same-sex parent and so also internalises the **moral code** of the parent. This allows the Superego to be seen as the **internalised** parent.

# Lesson 32
# Evaluation of Studies of Moral Development

## 1. Recap of criticisms up to now

Each description of an approach to explaining the development of moral behaviour given in previous lessons has included an evaluation of the approach and its methodology. For example,

- the description of Piaget's approach included criticism of the methods he used. He used interviews with children, which can be flawed – children may be more likely to give an answer they think the researcher wants to hear. Also, Piaget used his own children at times and they are even more likely to be biased towards giving a "desirable" answer.
- Similarly, Kohlberg interviewed participants when they were children (as well as when they grew to adulthood) but also he set them dilemmas and asked what they would do in these situations. The children and adults may say they will do one thing but if they were faced with the dilemma in real life they may actually do something entirely different.

Some investigators have used different methods. For example, the Social Learning approach is supported by the Bryan and Test study of motorists stopping to help a driver whose car had apparently broken down. A number of studies have observed children who believe they are alone to see if they succumb to temptation and break a rule they are asked to observe (e.g. not eating a sweet from a bowlful). These studies have given good evidence for their corresponding theories.

Two further writers will be considered in this lesson to evaluate theories of moral development in general. They are Carol Gilligan and Nancy Eisenberg.

## 2. Gilligan's contribution – gender makes a difference

- Freud's suggestion that women's morals are not as strong as men's morals has been a source of controversy for some time. Its implication that women are naturally inferior to men in this way has annoyed many writers.
- Carol Gilligan noted that not only did Freud's ideas give women a lower moral strength than men but also, Kohlberg's studies put most women at level 3 of his stages – which is lower than most men reached and a long way off the maximum level of 6, but perhaps more importantly if focused on the idea of people and personal relationships.

She therefore set out to obtain the views of men and women on a number of different moral issues and concluded that **there is a difference in the way that men and women think about morals** but not in the way that Freud's work suggests.

Gilligan found that men tend to make moral decisions around the notion of justice. For men, the right thing to do is what is "just" and **fair**. Women tend to be more concerned with the **care** of others. What is the right thing to women is what involves caring for people and moral decisions are those that take into account the best interests of the people involved, even if that means that the decision is not necessarily fair.

Gilligan's idea that men and women are different in morals but not inferior or superior also draws attention to Kohlberg's bias towards males. His sample was largely male and the central characters of his dilemmas were mostly males. Things look different when moral development is considered from a female point of view.

### 3. Eisenberg's contribution – the dilemma makes a difference

Eisenberg pointed out the dilemmas used by Piaget and Kohlberg always involved consideration of some form of rule or law.

- Piaget wanted to know who had been the naughtiest or what the rules of marbles were
- Kohlberg wanted to know whether it was right to break some rules sometimes.

Eisenberg pointed out that most real moral dilemmas did not concern breaking rules. Instead they concerned balancing our own needs with the needs of other people. For example:

- Should I eat the last biscuit in the tin or leave it for George, who's had none?
- Should I spend time helping this elderly person carry luggage up the steps when I may miss the train?
- Should I offer to pay my friend for the lift home?

She followed the tradition of other investigators and gave them little stories that were dilemmas like the ones above, asking them what they think the characters should do. From her investigations she also constructed a theory based on a series of stages. Her stages are shown in the following table.

| Stage 1: Hedonistic | Hedonistic means something that is concerned with satisfying our own needs. At this stage, people solve dilemmas by referring to what is best for the person who has to make the decision (Yes, I should eat the last biscuit because I like them) |
|---|---|
| Stage 2: Needs of Others | A swing from stage 1 to the opposite extreme. The needs of others are put first. (I should offer the last biscuit to George because he's had none) |
| Stage 3: Approval | Based on stereotypes of moral behaviour – the sort of thing a comic book hero would do. (I should give my brother the last biscuit because it's the sort of  thing Superman would do) |
| Stage 4a: Empathic | Empathy involves feeling the same thing as someone else is feeling. Based on an element of sympathy for the other person. (I should give my visitor the last biscuit because I know how pleased she will be and I will only feel guilty if I don't). |
| Stage 4b: Transitional | Based on a generalised but slightly vague idea that this is the right thing to do. (The older sister should look after the younger brother – it's only right to give him the biscuit). |
| Stage 5: Strongly Internalised | A much stronger and clearer idea of what is right and an obligation to oneself to maintain standards of morals. (I shall offer my mother the last biscuit as elderly people deserve to be looked after and it is my responsibility to do so). |

Eisenberg studied a group of people over a period of time and found that, although it was not a perfect fit, their behaviour did tend to match the pattern of the above table which was based on their responses to moral dilemma questions.

## 4. Eurocentrism

Writers have pointed out other criticisms of these models

- **Eurocentric** Kohlberg suggested that his model was universal; that is to say that everybody from every culture in the world passed through the same stages. Critics of this view argue that it assumes that European and Western forms of democracy and thought are superior to other cultures' forms since those forms are typical of the "top" stages of the moral development rather than, say, "Following God's word", which may be considered the highest moral principle in a different culture.

---

**Summary Exercise on Evaluation**

1. Give two criticisms of using children in investigations of moral development. (2 marks)
2. Gilligan made criticisms of Freud's ideas and Kohlberg's ideas from the point of view of what they said about women. What were the two criticisms? (2 marks)
3. What did Gilligan find was the centre of women's reasoning when it came to morals and what did she think was the centre of men's reasoning? (2 marks)
4. What did Eisenberg suggest was the basis of most moral dilemmas faced by real people in real life? (2 marks)
5. Name the first and last stages of Eisenberg's model of moral development. (2 marks)

---

## Feedback

### Answers to summary exercise

1. Children may give the answer they think the adult wants. Children may not have the necessary language skills they need to express their reasoning.
2. Freud suggested that women had weaker morals than men. Kohlberg's view always left women at a lower stage than men's when their morals were "measured".
3. Women centred on caring for others. Men centred on "justice"
4. Balancing our own needs and the needs of others.
5. First = Hedonistic. Last = Strongly Internalised.

# AQA Exam Style Questions: The Development of Moral Behaviour

- **Answer all questions**
- **There is no time limit to this assignment**
- **When completed you may compare your answers with the example answers at the end of the book**
- **If you have tutorial support you should send a copy of your answers to your tutor to receive further feedback, comments and guidance**

*The Unlikely Daily News*

---

### Cabinet Minister in lie shock!

A cabinet minister's career lay in ruins today as his daughter revealed that he had lied to her as a child. Minister X's daughter, Little Miss X said to a packed press conference:

"My father told me that my Christmas presents were delivered by a man in a red suit with white fur round it and black boots. In fact, I now know that he and mother bought the presents and placed them at the foot of the bed themselves!"

---

Is it right to lie to children under some circumstances? We often face problems in deciding whether our behaviour is **Moral** or not.

1. Give a definition of **Moral behaviour** (1 mark)

2. The **Cognitive** approach to explaining moral development involves stages. Piaget's theory suggested that we pass from a **Heteronomous** stage to an **Autonomous** stage.

(a) At approximately what age do we pass from the heteronomous stage to the autonomous? (1 mark)

(b) Give a definition of each term heteronomous and autonomous
**Heteronomous** (1 mark)
**Autonomous** (1 mark)

(c) Briefly describe a study that illustrates Piaget's cognitive theory of moral development. (3 marks)

(d) Give **two** criticisms of the Piaget's cognitive approach to explaining moral development. (4 marks)

3. Describe **one** other theory of moral development. (6 marks)

4. Describe **Gilligan's** contribution to the evaluation of theories of moral development. (3 marks)

**Total possible marks = 20**

When completed you should compare your answers with the example answers at the end of the book. If you have tutorial support you should send a copy of your answers to the tutor for feedback, comments and further guidance.

# OCR Exam Style Questions:
# Aspects of Morality

- Answer all questions
- There is no time limit to this assignment
- When completed you may compare your answers with the example answers at the end of the book
- If you have tutorial support you should send a copy of your answers to your tutor to receive further feedback, comments and guidance

Source an Individual Differentiation
Aspects of Morality

---

## Androcles and the Lion

*In this famous fable, a slave, Androcles, helps a lion and is rewarded.*

Androcles was fleeing from the Romans when he hid in cave. As he went further into the cave he saw a lion and was overcome with fear as the lion suddenly let out a tremendous roar. Androcles thought the lion would kill him but he noticed that it was holding its paw strangely so instead of escaping he looked carefully and saw a thorn in the paw. He removed the splinter and the lion's roaring stopped. Androcles then ran from the cave but fell straight into the arms of the Romans.

About a year later the Romans took Androcles to fight as a gladiator in the great Coliseum. He was full of fear as he was pushed into the arena and the gates locked behind him. In front of him a huge lion paced around the arena then ran towards him roaring for blood. But the lion suddenly stopped. It was the same lion that Androcles had helped in the cave. The lion licked and caressed Androcles instead of eating him. The crowd was so amazed at the lion's behaviour that they thought Androcles must posses some special qualities and the Emperor released him.

---

1. What did Androcles do to help the lion? (1 mark)

2. What reward did Androcles receive for helping the lion? (1 mark)

3. An important principle in the Social Learning theory of moral development is "imitation". How might this principle play a part in children's moral development if they are told the story of Androcles? (2 marks)

4. From your knowledge of psychology, give an example of a study that supports the principle that people imitate morally good behaviour. (4 marks)

**5.** Piaget considered that moral development occurred through fixed stages. In the table below, enter the information about his theory in the blank spaces. One space has already been completed.

| Stage of Moral Development Approximate Age | | Autonomous |
| --- | --- | --- |
| | | |

(3 marks)

**6.** Give **one advantage** and **one disadvantage** of Piaget's theory
**Advantage** (2 marks)
**Disadvantage** (2 marks)

**7.** Outline possible methodological and gender biases in research into moral development. (5 marks)

**Total possible marks = 20**

When completed you should compare your answers with the example answers at the end of the book. If you have tutorial support you should send a copy of your answers to the tutor for feedback, comments and further guidance.

# Lesson 33
# Prejudice Definitions

## 1. Definitions

**Prejudice**

Prejudice refers to **pre-judgement**: to judge something before we know very much about it. In psychology it means a little more than this, however.

- Firstly, it usually refers to a **pre-judgement of a person or a group.**
- Secondly, it is a judgement that may **contradict the facts** about the person or group.
- Thirdly, a person may **continue to hold the prejudice** even though contradictory facts are shown to be true.

Prejudices may be **positive** or **negative** but psychologists tend to deal more often with negative ones

A **definition** of prejudice would be: "A negative pre-judgement of a person or group which may contradict the facts about them and continue to be held even though the holder is aware of the contradictory facts."

Prejudice is an attitude towards the person or group and as such contains three components:

i. a belief about the person (psychologists call this the **cognitive component**)
ii. a feeling about the person (psychologists call this the **affective component**)
iii. a way of behaving towards the person (psychologists call this the **behavioural component**)

In the 1930s La Piere showed that the three components of prejudiced attitudes do not always coincide. At the time, it was common in some parts of the USA to hold prejudices against people of an oriental ethnic origin. La Piere travelled 10, 000 miles around America with an Oriental couple and stayed in a large number of hotels. Six months later he wrote to the hotels asking if they would accept Orientals as clients. Over 90 percent said "No".

> In this example, what is the cognitive component, and what is the behavioural component? Answers in the Feedback section at the end of the lesson.

**Stereotypes**

Stereotypes are simplistic (too simple) beliefs about what a particular group of people is like. For example, Irish people are stupid, English people are cold, Scottish people are mean, women are scatterbrained, men are unemotional, black people are naturally musical, Asian men all want to be doctors, Jews will trick you out of money etc.

We tend to think that any one individual from the group carries the characteristic of the group – so the woman driving the car in front is probably a bad driver because she is a member of the category "woman".

Prejudices are often based on stereotypes: they are pre-judgements, they contradict the facts and they are still held besides contradictory evidence (e.g. insurance companies think so highly of women's driving that they often offer them lower premiums).

## Ethnocentrism

This refers to the practice of seeing the world entirely from the point of view of one's own ethnic group or culture. Seeing it "centred" around a particular culture. An example of ethnocentrism would be:

- today's popular Australian soap operas give the impression that Australia is composed almost entirely of white people who use English as their first language. In fact non-white, ethnic minorities who use English as a second language make up a significant proportion of the Australian population and the soap opera view of the country is centred round a European culture's view.

## Discrimination

Discrimination involves the behavioural component of prejudice. It refers to "a set of behaviours toward members of a . . . group which are unfair in comparison to members of other groups" (Cardwell, 1996)

Making a negative pre-judgement of a person or group is likely to cause us to behave negatively towards them if we are in a position to do so.

Discrimination leads to a group being treated unfairly compared to another group. It can occur in the provision of public services such as housing or health or it can occur in areas of life such as employment or legal services. Apart from the injustice of one group failing to obtain their rightful share, the experience of being discriminated against leads to frustration anger and other negative feelings in the victims and leads to a loss to society of the skills and talents of the group who suffer in this way.

### i. Racial discrimination (Racism)

Researchers have often used a standard way of measuring and uncovering discrimination in employment. It consists of submitting two or more applications for an advertised job. The applications are identical except for the applicant's name; on one form a white name is used and on the other an ethnic minority name is used. Discrimination occurs when the employer gives a positive response to the white name (e.g. an invitation to an interview) whilst giving a negative response to the ethnic minority name (e.g. not inviting the applicant to an interview or telling the applicant that the post has been filled).

As recently as June, 1997 the Commission for Racial Equality published the outcome of a large-scale investigation of a similar nature, showing that employers were still practising this form of discrimination, inviting "white" applicants for interview and telling others that the post was filled.

### ii. Gender Discrimination (Sexism)

Most research shows gender discrimination against women but it also occurs against men. Employment is, again, a common area for discrimination and has been shown at top and bottom levels of organisations.

At management level, research has shown women to be under-represented;

the proportion of women at this level is very low. The term "glass ceiling" has been used to describe the experience of women who find that there seems to be a limit to the level to which they gain promotion. Although firms have no written policy there seems to be an unwritten agreement amongst higher managers that women will not be promoted above a certain level. The ceiling to promotion seems to be there, but like glass, it is not visible.

At lower levels in organisations women at interview may still be asked about their home responsibilities for children whilst men are not, and even today women are still having to ask courts to award them the same wages as men for the same work. As recently as June, 1997 a local authority had to be ordered by a court to pay the same rate for female care-workers in homes for the elderly, as it paid males.

In the case of discrimination against men, some jobs are still seen as the reserve of women and employers are reluctant to appoint men to jobs when they believe that a man could upset the female workgroup or that customers may be disturbed by males in certain posts or hold the prejudice that men are simply not as good at a job as women are.

### iii. Sexual Orientation Discrimination (Homophobia)

Research has shown that children raised by lesbian couples are not more likely than children of heterosexual couples to be homosexual when they mature. Newspaper articles sometimes present lesbians who seek sperm donors to father children as unworthy of motherhood on the grounds that their sexual orientation will be an unsuitable environment for the child who is more likely to grow up homosexual.

Gay men in long-term, stable relationships find it difficult if not impossible to foster and adopt children. It is often assumed that their relationship is an unhealthy environment for raising children or that they may sexually abuse them.

Lesbians and Gay men find prejudice leading to discrimination in other walks of life too; the law does not acknowledge a partner's right to property upon the death of one of the couple, nor does it confer a legal status to vows and agreements that parallel marriage. Gay men were, until recently, assumed by the law to be incapable of consenting to sex until they were 18 years old whilst heterosexual men were assumed to be capable of deciding at 16 years old. The laws governing sex also place different conditions on who may not have homosexual experiences (members of the military forces) and where they may have them ("in private"). The word "phobia" refers to a fear and the assumption behind the word "homophobia" is that people are prejudiced against homosexuals because they are afraid of homosexuality.

### iv. Age Discrimination (Ageism)

One fear sometimes held by people over the age of 50 is that they will be made redundant. This fear is a result of reports that many employers will not appoint people to new jobs after the age of 50 because they think of them as "over the hill". Hospitals have to ration treatment and facilities and one of the things they take into account is age. A person over the age of 70, for example, is less likely to be treated for some illnesses in hospital because staff believe that it is better to give the rationed treatment to younger people who will be able to benefit from it for longer.

| From the following list, put the correct terms in the blank boxes: Stereotypes, Ethnocentrism, Racism, Sexism, Homophobia, and Ageism. Some boxes could have more than one term. Answers are in the Feedback section below. | |
|---|---|
| Why do women have small feet? So they can get closer to the kitchen sink! | |
| Aren't scientists such dull people? | |
| Nurse, make sure you put "high risk of AIDS" on that patient's notes – he's gay. | |
| Just a minute son, I want to serve the woman behind you in the queue. | |
| "Vacancies – no blacks or Irish" | |
| We should all be singing from the same hymn sheet | |

## Feedback

### La Piere study of prejudice against Orientals

There are a number of possible interpretations here. The behavioural component is the acceptance of the couple at the hotels. The cognitive component is the belief, expressed by hotel managers, that they would not accept the Oriental couple.

| Why do women have small feet? So they can get closer to the kitchen sink! | Sexism (also, stereotypes) |
|---|---|
| Aren't scientists such dull people? | Stereotypes |
| Nurse, make sure you put "high risk of AIDS" on that patient's notes – he's gay. | Homophobia |
| Just a minute son, I want to serve the woman behind you in the queue. | Ageism (also stereotypes? Perhaps the woman's shopping is seen as more "valid" than the boy's?) |
| "Vacancies – no blacks or Irish" | Racism |
| We should all be singing from the same hymn sheet | Ethnocentrism |

## References

Cardwell, M (1996) *The Complete A-Z Psychology Handbook* Hodder and Stoughton.

# Lesson 34
# The Causes of Prejudice

This lesson describes a range of theories that attempt to explain why prejudice occurs. The theories do not necessarily "compete" in the sense that only one is "true"; rather, one theory may be more appropriate to explain one incidence of prejudice and another theory to explain another incidence.

## 1. The Authoritarian Personality – Individual Explanation

American investigators Adorno and his colleagues suggested that we can examine individual personality characteristics to explain prejudice. The prejudice lies within the person in this theory. It is the result of a collection of characteristics which he referred to collectively as the authoritarian personality.

This work was published just after the Second World War and it was directed towards investigating the anti-Semitism (anti-Jewish) and fascism which were key aspects of the conflict with Germany. The work looked for a relationship between personality types and prejudice. Adorno developed ways of measuring certain features of personality. This involved asking subjects to rate how much they agreed with statements that were designed to reflect those features of personality. Here are some examples of the statements: the corresponding features of personality are in brackets.

- I can hardly imagine myself marrying a Jew. (Anti-Semitism)
- America may not be perfect but the American Way has brought us about as close as human beings can get to a perfect society. (Ethnocentrism)
- A child should learn early in life the value of a dollar and the importance of ambition, efficiency and determination. (Conservatism)
- Obedience and respect for authority are the most important virtues children should learn. (Fascism)

The work found that people who scored very highly on the Anti-Semitism scale also scored high on the Ethnocentrism scale so it would be possible to predict within limits that anyone who was very ethnocentric would also be anti-Semitic. Similarly, a high score on Ethnocentrism also predicted a high score on Fascism.

Adorno and his colleagues came to the conclusion that there was indeed an authoritarian personality type and that this person was far more likely to be prejudiced against other races or ethnic groups. Characteristics of this personality included conservatism (disliking change or difference), anti-Semitism (disliking Jews), ethnocentrism (seeing everything from your own culture's point of view) and Fascism (extreme right-wing political beliefs).

Further work lead Adorno to conclude that the reason that a person developed an authoritarian personality was a strict and highly disciplined upbringing as a child.

**An evaluation of the theory of the Authoritarian Personality**

It is possible for whole societies to be more prejudiced or less prejudiced. It does not seem possible that whole societies can have the same personality so there must be a factor which overrides individual personality in this case. Examples of whole societies being prejudiced include the attempted genocide (extermination of a whole group) of Jews in Nazi Germany with the likely collusion of most of the non-Jewish population and a study by Pettigrew, mentioned later, showing that prejudice against blacks in the north of the USA was less than prejudice in the southern states.

There are also criticisms of the way that the statements the subjects had to express agreement or disagreement with were easier to agree with and so were not a true measure of people's characteristics.

---

**To help you understand and recall**
- Make a list of three people that you know quite well.
- Ask yourself to what extent you feel that each of the three fits the following outline:
    - i.   acts in a hostile way towards people of a lower status
    - ii.  acts in a servile way towards people of a higher status
    - iii. dislikes people who are seen as "weak"
    - iv.  is rigid and inflexible
    - v.   likes things to be "clear cut", not ambiguous
    - vi.  does not like to talk about feelings
    - vii. likes to uphold conventions and normal ways of life.
- The person who best fits this outline is the most authoritarian according to Adorno's ideas. Is the person you have identified also prejudiced as far as you know? Adorno's theory would predict that the person who fits this list would also be prejudiced. Perhaps you were not able to spot any of these characteristics in the people you listed. You may like to consider the extent to which you fit the characteristics yourself.

---

## 2. Conformity – Interpersonal Explanation

This explanation of conformity suggests that prejudice and discrimination result from people merely behaving like the rest of the group. If someone is brought up surrounded by a family and wider community that expresses prejudice against a particular group as a normal part of life then it is likely that the individual concerned will adopt those attitudes of prejudice. When Adorno was publishing his work it was still normal practice in some of the Southern states of America for restaurants, schools and businesses to admit whites only and to display notices to that effect. Black people were expected to stand for whites if seats were taken on buses. This was legal in the USA at that time. In the United Kingdom it was also perfectly legal to display notices offering rooms to rent but "No Irish or Coloureds". In surroundings like this it is argued that prejudice is simply the norm (an accepted way of behaving) to which people will conform.

In a study of attitudes towards different ethnic minorities, Pettigrew found that people in the northern states of the USA were less prejudiced against blacks than people in the southern states. He also found, however, that attitudes towards other minorities did not differ; there was no more anti-Semitism in the north or south for example. This finding contradicts the idea that prejudice results from personality and gives some support to the idea that people are merely conforming to social norms when they express prejudice – especially when the general behaviours like segregated restaurants and schools mentioned above are taken into account.

---

**Question**

Why does Pettigrew's study of prejudice in the USA contradict the idea that prejudice results from a type of personality?

A suggested answer appears in the Feedback section at the end of the lesson

---

## 3. The Group – Intergroup Explanation

### (i) Minimal Groups

Some research has shown that the simple fact that we think of ourselves as a member of one group (the "in-group") can cause us to be prejudiced against another group (the "out-group") – even if the groups don't really exist!

For example, Tajfel asked boys to estimate the number of dots on a screen and then told each one (without any real basis) that they were either "over-estimators" or "under-estimators". In reality the classification into "over-estimators" or "under-estimators" was completely random but each boy perceived the group he was in as the "in group" and the other as the "out group". Each boy then played a game in isolation in which he had to award "points" to other boys.. They consistently awarded more points to boys who had been classified into the same group as themselves – the "in group" and they awarded fewer points to those in the other group.

### (ii) Social Identity Theory

Tajfel suggested reasons why the minimal groups effect occurred, based on his Social Identity Theory. A starting point of this theory is the idea that

- we try to achieve and keep a positive self-image. A positive self-image is the thought and feeling that I am a "good", "useful", "attractive" person (and lots of other positive characteristics).

The self-image has two parts:

- a personal identity (which comes from our personality, our relationships with other people etc. – e.g. I am an intelligent, warm person, well-liked by others)
- a social identity (which comes from the groups to which we feel we belong – e.g. I am a school prefect, a member of the hockey team and hang around with some of the "in crowd")

If we want to have a good self-image it is in our interests to see ourselves as belonging to high status groups with lots of good characteristics. One way to keep this belief is to believe that other groups are **low** status and have **bad** characteristics (e.g. "the group that hangs around with Naseem is trash" or "those school prefects are sad"). Tajfel argued that it is, therefore, natural for us to be prejudiced against many other groups because it maintains our own positive self-image.

(iii) **Intergroup Conflict**

Sherif studied two groups of boys at a summer camp and showed how they acted in a prejudiced way when conflict between the two groups was set up. Details of the study are given in the next lesson but for now we can simply draw on the conclusion that when the goal of two groups is the same and only one can achieve the goal, then hostility arises between the groups and the members become prejudiced against each other – in other words, Leeds United fans will never welcome Arsenal fans!

## 6. Prejudice and Discrimination in everyday situations

At the beginning of the lesson the point was made that the theories about the causes of prejudice are not necessarily in competition; it is likely that each explanation of prejudice can be important in different settings.

There is no doubt that prejudice and discrimination against Jews was widespread in Germany in the years leading up to the Second World War. Businesses were boycotted, then taken over or destroyed, their property was stolen, an attempt was made to exterminate the whole of the Jewish population and it was perfectly acceptable to denigrate Jews in public. Clearly, this was not the result of authoritarian personalities as it is unlikely that the majority of the German population suddenly became authoritarian, and there is plenty of evidence to support the idea that anti-Semitism was common in other parts of Europe.

An event like the anti-Semitism of the 1930s and 1940s in Germany then is probably more realistically explained by referring to conformity. Pressure was put on the German population to adopt these prejudiced attitudes, as the film and newspaper propaganda from the period shows. Interestingly, however, not everybody did adopt these attitudes so this must also be explained. Holland was occupied by German forces for a period and an order was issued for all Jews to wear a large star of David on their coats to identify them in the streets. The non-Jewish population also started to wear the star in the streets in sympathy with the Jews and to defeat the objective of identifying them (the order did not say that non-Jews could **not** wear the star). There are also many case-studies of individual non-Jews who risked their lives to save Jews in Germany. These ideas put a limit on conformity as an explanation too.

Social Identity Theory has support from laboratory studies. It is also capable of explaining a wide range of prejudices that do not seem to have any other explanation (e.g. why the fans of one band dislike the fans of another band). It may be that some people are more likely to use this as a strategy. For example, people who feel less adequate than others or who experience feelings of inferiority.

Finally, whilst rivalry and competition between groups may explain some prejudice, there are examples of studies which show members of rival groups who do not hold prejudiced attitudes towards each other and who remain friends despite their groups' rivalry.

**Review: Causes of Prejudice**
(Suggested answers in the Feedback section)

---

i.   What did Adorno suggest was the cause of prejudice (1 mark)

ii.  Name two of the features of an authoritarian personality according to Adorno (2 marks)

iii. Why is the Authoritarian Personality a poor explanation for prejudice in some cases? (2 marks)

iv.  Identify a study which supports conformity as an explanation of prejudice (1 mark)

v.   What are the two components of a positive self-image according to Tajfel? (2 marks)

vi. According to Social Identity Theory, what eventual function does prejudice serve? (1 mark)

vii. Tajfel suggests that merely belonging to one group will cause us to be prejudiced against another. What is another cause of prejudice that is suggested on the basis of groups? (1 mark)

**Total Possible Marks = 10**

---

# Feedback

**Practice Question:** suggested answer

Pettigrew found a higher level of prejudice against blacks in the south of the USA than in the north. Also, he found the same level of prejudice against Jews in both the north and the south. If prejudice results from personality, the people with a high level of prejudice against blacks should also have high levels of prejudice against Jews.

**Suggest a study**

One idea would be to measure the level of prejudice in a group of parents and in their offspring (perhaps adult rather than children). If people learn prejudice then parents with high levels are likely to have offspring with high levels and vice-versa.

**Review: Causes of Prejudice**

i.   An authoritarian Personality (1 mark)

ii.  Any two of: Anti-Semitism, Ethnocentrism, Conservatism and Fascism (1 for each of two correct)

iii. It fails to explain why whole societies can display prejudice (2 marks)

iv.  Pettigrew's study of prejudice in the north and south of the USA (1 mark)

v.   Personal Identity and Social identity (1 mark for each)

vi.  It promotes a positive self-image (1 mark)

vii. Inter-group conflict (1 mark)

**Total Possible Marks = 10**

# Lesson 35
# Reducing Prejudice

**Sherif's Study "The Robbers' Cave"**

A well-known study carried out by Sherif in 1961 provides some interesting evidence about the way that prejudice arises and the way in which it can be modified. Sherif and his colleagues organised a summer camp along the lines of a typical American summer camp, for twenty-two boys. The boys were randomly assigned to two groups but neither group was aware of the other's existence for the first few days and the cabins they occupied were in separate areas. This allowed each group to develop its own identity and norms; one group chose the name "The Rattlers" for itself and the other decided on "The Eagles".

Eventually the groups discovered each other and the staff/investigators announced a competition between the two with prizes for the best kept camp, sports events and so on. Sherif noted antagonistic behaviours and language used by the groups towards the outgroup. He noted their views on the outgroup and found name-calling and negative stereotypes held by the boys, about the other group. Boys who had known each other before the camp cut their friendships in favour of allegiance to the group. Sherif accounted for this prejudice with the idea that the two groups were in competition for the same prizes and concluded that competition was a source of prejudice. The behaviours became extreme at some points and staff had to break up potential fights.

## Reducing Prejudice
## 1. Working towards Common Goals

Sherif and his colleagues manufactured situations in an attempt to reduce prejudice and reported success in their attempts. In one situation, Sherif fixed the camp bus to appear as though it had stuck in some mud and the boys had to co-operate to pull it out. In another, he caused the water supply to the camp to break down and the boys had to co-operate to locate the fault and repair it. Both groups offered to share the cost of an end-of-camp treat – hiring a film, which was the only way that it could have been afforded. Sherif reported a different set of attitudes held by the boys by the time the co-operative activities were finished. Sherif concluded that co-operation between two or more groups towards one "**superordinate**" goal is one means of reducing prejudice.

> Can you think of an objection to concluding from Sherif's study that prejudice can be reduced in society by working towards a common goal?

Twenty-two American boys do not really represent a good cross-section of society

so it is difficult to accept that Sherif's study is one on which we can base many conclusions. Also, the boys in the study were
- all of a similar age,
- all middle-class,
- all Protestant and
- many knew each other before the study.

## 2. Equal Status Contact

If two groups of people have little or no contact with each other then they do not have the opportunity to see what the other group is really like. They do not have the opportunity for their stereotypes of each other to be tested. Nor do they have the opportunity to see how the other group experiences something: they cannot see it from the other's point of view. Under these circumstances prejudice is likely to continue unchecked. If the two groups are brought into contact then these aspects are likely to change and prejudice may reduce.

However, contact alone may not be enough. Aronson pointed out that in the USA for example, blacks and whites do come into contact frequently but usually when the black person is in an inferior role such as a cleaner. In South Africa until recently black people would only ever have come into contact with whites in superior roles – employer, police officer, state official, supervisor etc. In this case it is likely that the "contact" is superficial and that the prejudices are confirmed rather than dispelled. If contact is to be any use in reducing prejudice, therefore, it has to be contact at a level of equal status.

A famous study by Deutsch and Collins in 1951 examined two American housing estates. In one estate the tenants were placed in accommodation randomly on the basis of the next available property. In the second estate the accommodation was segregated so black people were given property in one area and whites were given property in another. The views of each group were obtained by interview and as may be predicted the integrated estate reported much more casual contact between the groups and much less prejudice. Psychologists have also found that individuals tend to be attracted to other individuals who they come into contact with most frequently, so these findings are consistent. In this case, was there contact on the basis of equal status? Everyone in the integrated estate was in accommodation of equal status though it is likely that other status differences did exist between the black residents and the whites.

Minard studied a group of miners in West Virginia, America, in 1952 and found that attitudes and behaviours were much less prejudiced below ground than above ground. It was concluded that when they were below ground the miners were of equal status and it can also be said that they pursued the common goal of safety – each miner's life depends on the actions of the others.

If equal status contact is a good way of reducing prejudice, then the desegregation of American schools in the 1960s should have led to a fall in prejudiced attitudes of black and white people towards each other, but a review of a number of studies by Stephan in 1978 concluded that this had not happened, so prejudice is not so easily controlled.

## 3. Changing the Authoritarian Personality

If prejudice results from an authoritarian personality, as Adorno's research concluded, then it may be possible to change someone's personality so that the prejudice is removed.

In theory it should be possible to use psychoanalysis to change the personality and help to remove the source of the prejudice but in real life psychoanalysis is not as predictable or certain as this. Also, it would be very difficult to organise the psychoanalysis of a large group of people over a very long period time; many would not agree to undergo it. Alternatively, it may be possible to reduce prejudice in the next generation by discouraging the strict upbringing which is associated with this personality but in reality it would be a difficult thing to identify and alter people's child-rearing habits.

## 4. Manipulating Stereotypes – Providing positive images

Prejudice and stereotypes go together. The pre-judgement of a person (prejudice) can be based on a stereotype – the belief that the person holds all the perceived characteristics of a group – usually negative characteristics. If the belief about the characteristics can be changed then the prejudice may be reduced.

We often come into "contact" with a group through the media – in fact it may be the only source of information about many groups for us. Ensuring that images of groups in the media give a fair representation of the group can be one way of reducing prejudice. For example, images of black people in the cinema were at one time mainly of "simple" poor, unintelligent almost child-like people whose only saving virtue was musical ability. At the time (the 1930s, 1940s and 1950s) the cinema was probably the most influential medium – more people visited it than watched television or listened to the radio – but black people only played secondary roles such as servants, musicians, waiters or cleaners.

Today, black people play lead characters and are stars in their own right. Some American and British situation comedies are all black. Dramas have black heroes as well as villains. It is believed that this portrayal of **positive** images and stereotypes can play a part in reducing prejudice, though they can sometimes be accused of being "politically correct" and may create an element of resentment in other groups which may have an unwanted, negative effect of reinforcing prejudice. The introduction of the first two gay characters into the television soap "Eastenders", for example, resulted in many negative comments in the press and it may be no coincidence that the two characters did not last long in the series. Gay pressure groups may still argue that this experience is better than no gay characters or stereotyped, "limp-wristed" ones. Research into this area of the effect of media manipulation is still uncommon.

## 5. Positive Discrimination

Institutions, government organisations and companies sometimes adopt policies to reduce prejudice within the organisation. In some cases this may be no more than asking all committees to ensure that an item like "Equal Opportunities" appears on all committee meeting agendas. In other cases, an organisation may adopt a policy of actively appointing and promoting a particular minority. It is common for women to be under represented on the board of a company and in the higher tiers of management for example, and a company may make a decision to appoint only a woman to the next available post.

There may be a quota established to ensure that a minority is represented in a police force, for example, so that a specific number of, say, Hispanic applicants is accepted into the Los Angeles police. This may cause resentment in majority groups. For example, the entry requirements for Hispanics is lower than for white applicants to ensure that the quota is met, so Hispanic police officers may be resented and thought of as of poorer ability than white officers. This "backlash" may have the opposite effect and prejudice may actually be increased by such a policy instead of being reduced. In California the backlash has led to a law that forbids such positive discrimination in government organisations.

---

**Short Exercise**
**Try this exercise to improve your understanding and memory for this section. Check it against the example answer in the Feedback section below.**
Write a list of each suggested method of reducing prejudice. Under each item in the list write a short account of why the method may **not** be regarded as realistic in a real-life situation.

---

## Feedback
### Short Exercise: example answer
i.   Working towards common (superordinate) goals
     The evidence for this method is based on a sample which is not really representative of the population as a whole
ii.  Equal status contact
     Ensuring equal status is not easy. Other factors which are not controlled by the experimenter may override the attempt to establish equal status. Also, the desegregation of American schools should be an example of equal status contact but it does not seem to have led to a reduction in prejudice.
iii. Changing the authoritarian personality
     Psychoanalysis of large numbers of people who may not agree in the first place is unrealistic. Changing the child-rearing styles of large groups of parents is also very difficult.
iv.  Manipulating stereotypes
     This may be seen as an obvious technique by the majority group and "politically correct" (implying that the presented stereotype is not valid). It may reinforce the original negative stereotype as people may believe it must be true if those in authority are trying to manipulate it.
v.   Positive discrimination
     The majority population may resent what they perceive as the relative ease with which the minority group has attained its position and this may lead to a backlash resulting in a reinforcement of the original stereotype and prejudice.
**Marks**: try to judge the extent to which you have answered the question as fully as the above. Allow two points for each of the above answers: if you have made less than five points then you cannot attain full marks. For each answer, award two marks if it contains as much information as above, one mark if it does not contain as much. The maximum possible score is, therefore, ten.

# AQA Exam Style Questions: Prejudice and Discrimination

- **Answer all questions**
- **There is no time limit to this assignment**
- **When completed you may compare your answers with the example answers at the end of the book**
- **If you have tutorial support you should send a copy of your answers to your tutor to receive further feedback, comments and guidance**

Read the following conversation

---

### Welcome to the club!

"Hi Asif, welcome to the club"

"Huh; hi"

"You look down Asif, what's the matter?"

"Its nothing, just the bus journey over here"

"What about it?"

"Well, I travelled all the way from town and the bus filled up and I was the only non-white on it."

"So what?"

"So there was one empty seat and it was next to me but nobody took it, that's what. Two elderly people even stood at the front rather than sit next to me. I felt like rubbish"

"What, no-one at all sat on it?"

"Well there was a bloke who sat on it just before I got off – but he looked gay!"

---

(a) What do psychologists mean by the term *prejudice*? (2 marks)

(b) What do psychologists mean by the term *discrimination*? (2 marks)

(c) Adorno explained prejudice in terms of the Authoritarian Personality. Describe one characteristic of the Authoritarian Personality according to Adorno (2 marks)

(d) Outline **one** criticism of Adorno's explanation of prejudice. (2 marks)

(e) Outline **one** other psychological explanation of prejudice. (3 marks)

(f) Give **one** criticism of the explanation you have outlined in (e) above. (2 marks)

(g) Describe **one** psychological study in which the reduction of discrimination was investigated. Indicate in your answer the method used, the results obtained and the conclusions drawn (4 marks)

(h)  Assess the likely success of the technique of prejudice reduction which follows from the study you outlined in (g) (3 marks)

**Total possible marks = 20**

When completed you should compare your answers with the example answers at the end of the book. If you have tutorial support you should send a copy of your answers to the tutor for feedback, comments and further guidance.

# OCR Exam Style Questions: Attitudes of Prejudice

- **Answer all questions**
- **There is no time limit to this assignment**
- **When completed you may compare your answers with the example answers at the end of the book**
- **If you have tutorial support you should send a copy of your answers to your tutor to receive further feedback, comments and guidance**

**Source A Individual Differentiation**
**Attitudes of Prejudice**

---

### Welcome to the club!

"Hi Asif, welcome to the club"

"Huh; hi"

"You look down Asif, what's the matter?"

"Its nothing, just the bus journey over here"

"What about it?"

"Well, I travelled all the way from town and the bus filled up and I was the only non-white on it."

"So what?"

"So there was one empty seat and it was next to me but nobody took it, that's what. Two elderly people even stood at the front rather than sit next to me. I felt like rubbish"

"What, no-one at all sat on it?"

"Well there was a bloke who sat on it just before I got off – but he looked gay!"

---

(a) Why did Asif feel that other passengers were prejudiced against him? (1 mark)

(b) What do psychologists mean by the term *prejudice*? (2 marks)

(c) Each of the terms in the following list corresponds to one of the words in the left hand box below describing the components of prejudice. Put the correct term from the list in the right hand box.

**List**: discrimination, stereotyping, dislike.

| Affective component | |
|---|---|
| Behavioural component | |
| Cognitive component | |

(3 marks)

(d) Ethnocentrism involves seeing the world only from your own cultural point of view. Give an example of ethnocentrism that you have studied. (2 marks)

(e) What do psychologists mean by *stereotyping*? (2 marks)

(f) Describe and evaluate **one** psychological theory of prejudice with which you are familiar. (7 marks)

(g) Describe **one** means of reducing prejudice according to psychologists. (3 marks)

**Total possible marks = 20**

When completed you should compare your answers with the example answers at the end of the book. If you have tutorial support you should send a copy of your answers to the tutor for feedback, comments and further guidance.

# Lesson 36
# What is Memory?

## 1. Astounding Feats of Memory

There is no doubt that some people can perform outstanding feats of remembering. They remember information like the winners of virtually every important horse race in the last fifty years.

A Russian psychologist, Luria, documented the case study of such a "mnemonist" as these people are called (the first "m" is not pronounced). He would read out a list of numbers or letters which would be fifty, seventy, one hundred or two hundred items long; the mnemonist, referred to only as S, would concentrate for a moment as though "collecting" his thoughts and then recall every number correctly, in one case, even after eleven years.

"Photographic" memories have also been documented. In this case, people can open a textbook at the beginning, turn the pages at the rate of about one per second, scanning the contents, then, when finished, "project" the pages onto a blank sheet or wall in their mind and "see" the page, telling an enquirer the tenth word on the seventh line of page 49 and so on.

---

Consider your own memory for a moment. How good do you feel it is?

---

You may have thought your memory is poor or good but look at the sort of things you remember:

- Language: how many tens of thousands of words are there in your vocabulary?
- The people you know. Thirty or more pupils in a school class; dozens of people at work; friends; acquaintances; characters in television programmes; musicians;
- Films and books you have seen and read. Songs and their words;
- Places you have been; things you have seen – the Eiffel Tower, Blackpool Tower;
- The things that have happened to you. Last Christmas, your last birthday;

The list of things you remember would be impossible to write down. Whatever you think of your memory the evidence is that, given patient training, everyone's memory can perform feats that would surprise and impress you.

Memory is not only this conscious effort to memorise and recall numbers from a telephone directory or sequences of cards, however. It is a mechanism that we use virtually all the time, usually without noticing. As you read this you are using your memory of what all these marks on the page mean, what a "page" is, why you are reading, what that ringing sound means when you are interrupted by a phone call, where this lesson fits into your other plans for the day and so on.

Even people who "lose" their memory in fact remember a tremendous amount including their language, the "rules" of how to live (how to address people, how to hold a knife and fork, how to turn on the television, write and so on).

**Encoding, Storage and Retrieval**

The first element of memory, encoding, is not one that is often considered by the layperson but to the psychologist it is an important one. Memory involves all three of these elements; we encode information, store it then retrieve it when it is needed.

---

**Definition of memory**

For the purposes of this section, the following definition will be useful: "The term given to the encoding, storage and subsequent retrieval of information".

---

## 2. Encoding

If you are asked to store information – say something simple like a recipe for a chocolate pudding, then you will have to use some medium in which to store the recipe. For most people, it will be written in ink on a piece of paper but a school teacher may write it in chalk on a chalk board whilst others may store it by speaking it into a tape recorder so it is a magnetic impulse on a cassette tape, in Braille, which is a pattern of tiny "bumps" on a piece of thick paper, as magnetic impulses on a computer disk. The recipe is stored in some form, some code.

Similarly, memories need to be stored in some form; they need to be encoded. Encoding is the process of representing an item in some form in the memory; it may be in the form of a "sound" heard in the mind, a "picture" seen in the mind or a "meaning" held in the mind.

---

Imagine for a moment that you have called directory enquiries for a telephone number. As the recorded voice tells you the number ("The number you require is....") can you think how you keep it in your memory whilst writing it down?

---

Most people say it over to themselves a couple of times until they have written it down. This is an example of encoding the information. In this case, it is encoded in the form of a sound. You "hear" your voice in your head whilst you repeat it. Psychologists often refer to this as **acoustic coding**.

---

What word comes before the line "Send her victorious...." in the song "God Save the Queen"?

---

It is most likely that you answered that question by singing the first few lines to yourself, probably without making any real sound. In this example, you have encoded the information acoustically and you used this mode to recall it. Other memories may be encoded in different modes. Try answering the questions in the following box as quickly as possible.

---

1.  What colours are used in the Union Jack flag?
2.  Where on the page was the question box on page 1 of this lesson (no peeking)
3.  What is the name of the monarch's sister?
4.  What was the name of your favourite book as a child?

The answers to these questions are not as important as the way in which you came to the answers.

- For question 1), did you imagine the flag and "look" at the colours? Many people would.
- For question 2), did you try to imagine the first page and "look" at where the box was on the page but in your mind? Again, most people would.

Psychologists argue that this information tends to be encoded in a **visual** mode and that is the mode you use to look it up again. This is an example of **visual coding**.

Questions 3) and 4) are not quite so clear-cut or easy to demonstrate as 1) and 2) but it is likely that you had to "think them through": who is the monarch?

- What is the sister's name?
- What book stands out in my mind?
- Was there a better one? and so on.

This is also complicated by the idea that you may have used visual cues too. Perhaps you "saw" a picture of the monarch and her sister or the cover of your favourite book. Putting aside the pictures for a moment, this last form of encoding is called **semantic coding**; the word "semantic" refers to the idea of the meaning of something and psychologists suggest that some information is encoded as a meaning rather than a sound or a picture (acoustic or visual). Semantic coding is much more of an abstract idea than acoustic or visual of course but further ideas about it will be put forward later in the lesson.

It is possible that other forms of coding are used (smell, perhaps or taste) but these three forms have been studied by psychologists quite extensively.

---

**Quick Quiz 1**
What three forms of encoding take place in the human memory? (3 marks)

---

answer = Acoustic, visual, semantic.

In subsequent lessons you will see that important aspects of encoding include its **organisation** (which is often in categories or hierarchies), the **elaboration** of the item to be encoded (the more it is elaborated on, the better it is encoded) and the **context** in which the item is encoded (we don't just encode the item, we encode the context too).

## 3. Storage

There is quite a lot to consider about the storage of information: the amount stored, the length of time it is stored, the way it is organised when it is stored. These aspects differ from one part of memory to another and it is easier to explain and understand them at the same time as considering the models of memory, which are explained in the sections below, so we shall return to these aspects of storage under the heading "Models of Memory" later.

## 4. Retrieval

Having encoded information and stored it we need to be able to get it out again – to retrieve it. This can be done in a number of ways:

- **Recall:** This is the form of retrieval most often associated with remembering.

In this form we search our memories for an item. What is the capital of Peru? We think and ponder and come up with the answer from "somewhere in our memory" – Lima. In the psychology laboratory this method is often used. "Please try to recall as many of the words in the list as possible."

- **Recognition:** In this method we are presented with items and asked if we remember them. "Was this the dress you brought in for cleaning last week?" Have I seen this episode before?" This method can be used in the psychology laboratory too: "Tick the words in the following list which were also in the list you were asked to remember"

- **Re-learning:** This is an interesting example of retrieval because it demonstrates that we are not always conscious of what we have remembered. If we learn a piece of music as a child, for example, then come across it again as an adult we may have to re-learn it but it will not take as long to do so as it normally would to learn a comparable piece.

> Which of the above three methods of measuring retrieval would you consider to be the best one to use in the laboratory and why? Which one would you think is the least easy to measure and why?

### Research Data

To illustrate some ideas about memory later, it would be useful to have some research data to examine. To create the data you could either complete the task in the box below yourself or ask someone else to act as a participant, remembering to inform the other person of the purpose of the task, obtain their complete consent to the task, offer them the opportunity to withdraw at any point or to withdraw their data if they want to and to tell them what the outcome is if they want to know! (See the lesson on ethics in the Methods section of the materials)

> **Memory Task**
> **Apparatus Required**
> - A clock, watch or stopwatch to time a three minute period
> - A piece of blank paper and a pen
> - The list of words below
>
> **Instructions**
> Allowing three minutes, look at the list of words below and attempt to memorise them. When the three minutes are up, cover the list and write down as many of the words as you can remember on the blank sheet of paper. Allow 3 to five minutes to recall the words or until you are not going to recall any more. The order in which you recall the words is not important.
> **Start when you are ready; then go on to the next lesson**
>
> | carpet    | garden   | seaside | poker   |
> |-----------|----------|---------|---------|
> | jacket    | London   | chicken | country |
> | sparrow   | tarmac   | tennis  | alcohol |
> | hairnet   | computer | mother  | kettle  |
> | waist     | picture  | bottle  | shoes   |
> | coastline | tower    | clouds  | hotel   |

# Lesson 37. The Multistore or Two-Process Theory of Memory

## Models of Memory

Is there a single thing we call a memory? How much does it hold? How long does it last? How is it organised? How does our memory "work"? Psychologists' investigations have led to a number of alternative suggestions about how memories work; the word "model" here can be replaced by the word "theory".

## 1. The Multistore Model of Memory (Atkinson and Shiffrin's Two-Process Theory)

Much of the detail of what we sense during our waking hours is not available for us in our memory (e.g. What colour was the third car you saw yesterday?) and although people do consider the possibility that we *may* store it all this seems highly inefficient and unlikely. Why carry around a lifetime's information when so little of it would be needed?

Atkinson and Shiffrin proposed a model of memory based on some concepts originally reported by James in 1890. The long term memory store and the short term store.

They also integrated these ideas with that of a Sensory Information Store; these are all explained further below. Atkinson and Shiffrin suggested a way in which these three stores work together and this is shown in Figure 1. The term "multistore" means "many stores" and stems from the ideas of the three stores in this model.

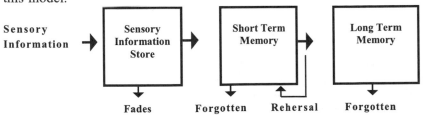

**Figure 1 Atkinson and Shiffrin's Multistore (Stage) Model of Memory**

The Short Term Memory (STM) is sometimes referred to as the Short Term Store (STS) and the Long Term Memory (LTM) as the Long Term Store (LTS). The word "store" may be more accurate but many texts refer to them as "memory". The model suggests that memory works as follows:

Sensory information is produced by all our sense organs; a word printed on a page produces an image on the eye's retina for example. In Atkinson and Shiffrin's model most of this information is lost very quickly through fading away, but a very small amount of it is taken into the short term memory where it may be further processed. So the vast majority of things you see will not even be considered for memory.

Some information is considered important enough to pay attention to and this is taken into short-term memory where it is held for between a few seconds to about 30 seconds. If the information is rehearsed (repeated usually more than once) it will pass into long term memory but if not, it will be forgotten. Everyday examples of this transfer from short to long term memory would be the "chanting" of times tables in school with the aim of learning them or repeating a song or lines from a poem or play.

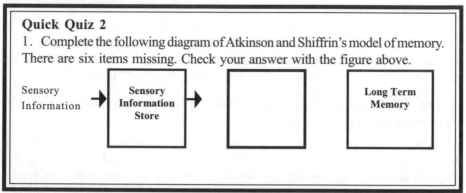

**Quick Quiz 2**
1. Complete the following diagram of Atkinson and Shiffrin's model of memory. There are six items missing. Check your answer with the figure above.

**Why is this model sometimes called the "Two-Process" Theory?**
Because there are two points at which the information is processed. First from the Sensory Information Store to the Short Term Memory; then from the Short Term Memory to the Long Term Memory.

**Short Term Memory – Coding**
Coding (or encoding) in STM seems to be mostly **acoustic**. We encode items to be remembered in the form of sounds. For example we remember a telephone number from the directory whilst we dial it by saying it to ourselves. Wicklegren asked participants to read a list of letters, then read a second list, and then recall the first. If the second list had similar sounding letters to the first then the participants made more mistakes recalling the first list. The fact that sound interferes with memory here suggests that sound is the medium in which the memory is encoded.

**Short Term Memory – Capacity**
Most people can comfortably remember about seven digits; you can test this hypothesis by reading six random digits to a participant and asking him or her to recall them; then increase the number of digits to seven, then eight, increasing the number until you find the participant unable to remember the full list. Miller found that most people would remember between five and nine digits so he referred to the "magic number 7, plus or minus 2".

Miller also pointed out the ability of people to "chunk" information into seven items; in this case it is possible for example to think of three numbers as one: 703 is thought of as one item, 201 another and so on for seven items. In this case, twenty one digits can be recalled if they can be chunked into seven items of three digits. The process is helped if the items are meaningful to the participant. For example, 747 is an aeroplane type, 999 is the emergency services number and so on.

**Short Term Memory – Duration**
Atkinson and Shiffrin suggested that items last for about 15 to 30 seconds in the STM. This is confirmed in studies like those of Peterson and Peterson in which participants were given items to remember then asked to perform tasks that took their attention and prevented rehearsal. When the participants were tested after periods of 10, 15, 20 and so on seconds, much of the information was forgotten after 20 seconds and all of it after 30 seconds.

**Short Term Memory – Organisation**
Information in short term memory seems to be stored in a simple sequence that corresponds to the order in which information is received. If the recognition method is used to test retrieval from STM people will take longer to recognise items that are received later in the sequence. We seem to search the list received item by item.

---

**Quick Quiz**
1. Cite one piece of evidence to support the idea that encoding is acoustic in the STM (1 mark)
2. What is "chunking" in terms of STM? (1 mark)
3. What do psychologists think is the duration of information in the STM? (1 mark)
4. State one word which describes the way in which information is organised in STM (1 mark)

---

**Long Term Memory – Coding**
In a 1966 study by Baddeley, participants looked at a list of words that were acoustically similar (e.g. cab, cap) and a list of words that were not (e.g. cab. men). They also looked at a list of words that had similar meanings (semantically similar) and words that did not. He found that when asked to recall the words immediately (testing STM) the participants made more mistakes with the acoustically similar words but fewer mistakes with the semantically similar words. This suggests that STM uses acoustic codes because the "sounds" of the words interfered with each other and supports the ideas that encoding in is acoustic.

When the participants were asked to recall the words after a delay, however, (testing LTM) the participants made mistakes with the words which had similar meanings (the semantically similar words) rather than with the words which has similar sounds which suggests that semantic coding is used in LTM because the similar meaning of the words interfered with each other at the encoding stage. You can probably think of long term memories which rely on visual codes (e.g. can you produce an image of your childhood best friend in your mind?) and ones, which rely on acoustic codes (e.g. can you "hear" your favourite piece of music from 10 years ago?). Whilst semantic codes are more important for LTM than for STM then, visual and acoustic codes are also likely to be used in LTM.

**Long Term Memory – Capacity**
There appears to be no real limit to the amount of information, which can be stored in the LTM. It would be difficult to conceive of a study, which tested the capacity of the LTM because we would first have to measure the amount of information in it and this would seem impossible. Most investigators seem to

accept then, that the LTM has unlimited capacity.

## Long Term Memory – Duration

Some items last for a few minutes (just falling within the definition of Long Term Memory), some for a few hours, days, months, years and some for a whole lifetime. Why the length of time differs for different items is probably best understood by referring to theories of forgetting and asking why the item has been forgotten rather than why some others have been remembered.

## Long Term Memory – Organisation

If we have to store lots of letters or notes on psychology or if we consider something practical like storing nails and screws, we do not just throw them into one big drawer with lots of other things. At least, screws go in one drawer, nails in another, books on a shelf, crockery in another place and so on. In the case of letters, when stored in the workplace we do not throw all letters into one drawer any old way. We file them in some sort of order – most commonly in alphabetical order of the addressee. Whatever method is chosen, some form of organisation is highly likely.

The same thing seems to happen with our memories and psychologists have found some fascinating evidence of how we do this.

## Organisation by Categories

i.   **At the encoding stage.** Bower asked one group to learn a list of 112 words which were already organised into categories (e.g., platinum, silver and gold under the heading of "rare metals") and another group was asked to learn the list of the same words arranged randomly. The category group remembered much more than the random group.

ii.  **At the recall stage.** Two groups were presented with randomly arranged words. Although the words could be arranged into categories they were not at this stage. One group was asked to use free recall (just remembering what they could whilst the other group was presented with the category headings of the words before being asked to recall. The group prompted with the category headings recalled more than the free recall group.

## Organisation by Hierarchies

Collins and Quillian found evidence that people probably organise the items in their memories not only by category but also by a sort of order of importance: a hierarchy. Figure 2, shows how memories about canaries are part of an overall memory about birds and that memories about birds are themselves part of memories about animals. Have a look at the diagram before reading the explanation that follows.

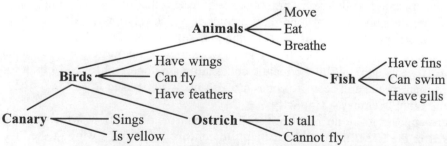

**Figure 2 An example of a hierarchy of memories adapted from Collins and Quillians' work.**

Collins and Quillian asked participants to press "true" or "false" buttons and measured very accurately the amount of time it took to respond. They found that participants took longer to respond to statements like "Canaries are animals" than it took them to respond to statements like "Canaries are yellow". They reasoned that the participants took longer to answer the first question because they had to start with their memories of canaries and work up through the network to memories about the general characteristics of canaries as animals. The first question can be answered quickly because knowledge about canaries is stored at the same "level" as the memory of canaries themselves, so the hierarchy does not need to be explored as much.

These two ideas of **Categories** and **Hierarchies** underlie the suggestion that memories are not just tossed into a giant "memory bin" like items into a drawer but are arranged in some sequence and order that makes sense to the person concerned. Memories are often *associated* too; a new item to be remembered will be linked to an item already in the memory so that stimulation of the associated item will often cause the memory to be recalled.

| **How much can you remember about STM and LTM? Fill in the table to summarise the findings of psychologists** (Answers in the Feedback section) | | |
|---|---|---|
| | **Short term memory** | **Long term memory** |
| **Coding** | | |
| **Capacity** | | |
| **Duration** | | |
| **Storage** | | |

### Long Term Memory and Elaboration

While Atkinson and Shiffrin claimed that merely rehearsing was sufficient to "lodge" items in Long Term Memory, Craik and Watkins found that items were not necessarily remembered more if they were rehearsed. Their studies showed that if they asked people to remember only words starting with a certain letter in a list, the participants would remember them more than words they rehearsed. Craik and Watkins therefore introduced the idea of "elaborative" rehearsal and "maintenance" rehearsal; suggesting that elaborating items by linking or associating them with other items in memory when they encoded them would improve the retention of the words. They also suggested that elaborating items by thinking about their meaning (which involves linking them with other items in memory) would improve their retention; they called this form of elaboration "semantic" elaboration.

### Long Term Memory and Context

When we encode an item for memory, we also seem to encode the context of the item. Context could be the physical surroundings of the item, music or other sounds we hear when we encode the item or anything else that occurs at the same time. Abernethy asked a group of participants to learn some items in one room then recall them in a different one. He asked another group to learn them in one room and recall them in the same room. The group who recalled in the same room as they learned were able to recall more than the other group. It is thought that this was because we encode all the sights, smells and other associations of the room at the same time as we encode the items. The contents of the room act as "cues" to help our memory when we have to recall.

## 2. Evaluation of the Multistore/Two-Process Model
### Evidence for the model

i.  **The primacy and recency effect** At the end of the previous lesson there was an exercise designed to collect some data on memory which you may have carried out. If you have not already done so you could still carry out the study but not on yourself – find a participant to complete the task because you have now read quite a bit about memory and it may bias your performance on the task.

    The data should consist of a list of words recalled from the original list. If you have not already done so, mark the list of recalled words so you know which ones are correctly recalled.

    Most of the words remembered were probably from the beginning and end of the list. Check this; of the 24 words, how many from the first 8 were recalled, how many from the second 8 (the middle of the list) and how many from the last 8? Put the answer in the table below.

| | No. of words remembered |
|---|---|
| First 8 | |
| Second 8 | |
| Last 8 | |

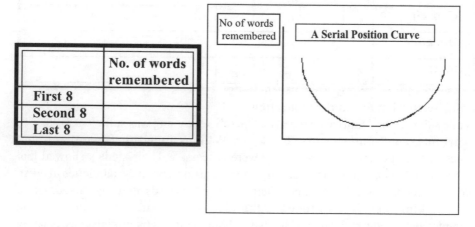

No of words remembered          A Serial Position Curve

Most studies that ask participants to learn lists of words find this effect, which is shown on the above Serial Position Curve. The words from the beginning of the list and the ones from the end of the list tend to be remembered. A study by Glanzer and Cunitz in 1966 found this for example. It is taken as support for the Atkinson and Shiffrin multistore model. The recall of items at the beginning of the list is known as the **primacy effect** and is taken to reflect the effect of the Long Term Memory; the first words have been rehearsed and passed into LTM. The recall of items at the end of the list is known as the **recency** effect because these are the items presented most recently to the memory. It is taken to show the effect of the STM because these recent items have only just been presented and so are still in Short Term Memory.

ii   **Rapid loss of items from STM** If participants are asked to learn a list of items but then given distraction tasks (like counting backwards in threes from 97) they forget the items rapidly. This was demonstrated by Peterson and Peterson who found that within 18 seconds, memory had fallen from 80% to 10 % of a list of three-letter "trigrams" or nonsense syllables. This is taken as evidence to support the idea that rehearsal is needed to move items to the LTM.

**Criticisms of the model**

i.   Rehearsal is not always needed to put items into LTM. There are many important events, people, experiences and ideas that people remember all their lives that are not necessarily rehearsed or repeated.

ii.  Some case studies have shown people with a damaged STM who are able to retain information in their LTM but the multistore model suggests that this is not possible because information has to be passed through STM first.

On the whole, then, the model does have support and seems at face value to be a reasonable way in which to explain some everyday findings about memory.

# Feedback

## Quick Quiz

1.  Either Wicklegren's study **or** the example of saying a telephone number over to oneself as we write it down or dial it would be appropriate. (1 mark)
2.  Putting items together to make them into one item, which has the effect of allowing more information storage in STM. (1 mark)
3.  About 15 to 30 seconds. (1 mark)
4.  e.g. Sequential, e.g. Linear. (1 mark)

**How much can you remember about STM and LTM? – Answers**

|          | Short term memory | Long term memory |
|----------|-------------------|------------------|
| **Coding** | Mostly Acoustic | Mostly Semantic |
| **Capacity** | 7 items plus or minus 2 Increased by Chunking | Unlimited |
| **Duration** | From moments to perhaps thirty seconds | From thirty seconds to a lifetime |
| **Storage** | Probably linear sequence (one memory after another) | Organised in categories and hierarchies |

Allow one mark for each correctly completed box: total marks available = 8

# Lesson 38
# Other Models of Memory

## 1. The Constructive (or Reconstructive) Model of Memory

A completely different approach to what memory is and to the way in which it works comes from the ideas of Bartlett. Up to now, we have viewed memory as we might view a tape recorder or a video camera – a machine for recording things; an attempt to make an accurate record of experiences. If you have covered the lessons on perception you may be familiar with the idea that instead of "seeing" what is in front of us we "create" a model of what may be there and then test the model against the data from our eyes. Seeing is not, therefore, an accurate record of what is in front of us.

Bartlett's work suggests that memory is not an accurate record of things that have happened but a version of past events that involves:

- **interpreting** events in the light of our hopes, fears and experiences
- **fitting** past experiences into our present frame of mind
- **striving** to make past events more logical and meaningful to us
- **inferring** or deducing what *should have* happened
- **constructing** and **reconstructing** our memories rather just "registering" them.

Bartlett came to this conclusion after asking his participants (his students) to re-tell stories in the way of a Chinese whisper in which one person tells the story to another and it is passed along from the first person to the last with participants only able to hear one version from the person before. Each participant remembered a different story from the person before and he felt that this reflected the way in which people construct memories that "fit in" with their circumstances. What is more, if he started the sequence off with a story that was outside the normal experience of the participant, he found that the participant would construct a memory of the story that was more in keeping with his own life.

For example, his best-known story is "The War of The Ghosts" which is based on native American groups travelling in canoes at night to fight other groups with bows and arrows; after the battle it becomes apparent that some of the antagonists were ghosts. Bartlett used this story with white north Americans some of whom even turned bows and arrows in canoes into guns in cars; they adapted the memories to fit their own culture.

### Evaluation of the Reconstructive Model

- This model explains many everyday aspects of our memory: few people have remarkable memories and the model does provide a picture of memory that includes all the "failing" aspects that we all experience.
- However, the model presents a view of memory that shows it to be so complicated that we are unable to make any accurate predictions about what

will be remembered and what will not. A good model should allow us to predict how people will behave.

**A comparison of the Multistore and Reconstructive memories**

- Far from being accurate records of events, then, memories verge on being figments of the imagination in the constructive model.

- Instead of taking a "mechanical", scientific approach similar to trying to work out how a car's engine works (the multistore model), Bartlett's ideas focus on the way in which memories represent our attempt to impose meaning and order on the world and tell us more about this process than they do about cause-effect processes in the mind.

> Imagine that you are a barrister defending a client in court who is accused of robbing a garage and is faced by a witness who has identified your client in a police identification parade as being the person he saw robbing the garage. Why would it be useful for you to know about Bartlett's ideas about reconstructive memory?

Because the witness's memory may be incorporating your client's image into the robbery whilst in reality, he was seen at a different time and place; you could explore this idea or similar "reconstructive" ideas in the court to undermine the witness's evidence.

## 4. The Levels of Processing Model of Memory

Some teachers put a lot of faith in the learning of times tables by repeating them often – asking children to "chant" them together in the classroom. Evidence about the success of this method is divided.

> Were you taught your times tables in this way?
> Did it work?

Many people found this to be a very successful method but others did not. Some psychologists' studies have found that this form of rehearsal does improve the retention of material in the long term memory but others have found that it does not. Craik and Watkins pointed out that some rehearsal does involve just repeating the material but some involves **elaboration** of the material while it is being rehearsed. **Elaboration** refers to the idea of linking the material with items already in the memory or extending its meaning in some other way. They claimed that elaboration tended to improve the retention of material in the LTM more than mere repetition (which they called "maintenance rehearsal").

This idea was taken further by Craik and Lockhart in 1972 . They asked groups of participants to look at a word then answer a question like one of the following:

(i)  Is the word written in capital letters?

(ii) Does the word rhyme with foot?

(iii) Does the word mean the same as "tall"?

The first question involves the participant thinking about the *structure* of the word:

what does it look like? The second involves thinking about the *sound* of the word and the third involves thinking about the *meaning* of the word. Craik and Lockhart described this as processing the words at different levels: the first level is the **structural** level, the second is the **acoustic** level and the third is the **semantic** level.

Groups were asked to do this a number of times with a number of words and a number of similar questions. The participants were then asked to recall the words they had answered questions about. They were not expecting to have to do this. Craik and Lockhart found the following results:

| Level of Processing | Amount Remembered |
| --- | --- |
| Structural | Least |
| Acoustic | Medium |
| Semantic | Most |

**Craik and Lockhart's findings**

This finding suggests that our memory of something depends on the way we think about it or, to put it Craik and Lockhart's way, the level at which we process the material. The **deeper** we process things the more we remember. If we only process something at a **shallow** level then we are less likely to remember it. These ideas support the findings about **elaboration** mentioned above; elaboration involves processing things at a deeper level than just repeating them.

These findings about memory lead to an even more radical picture of memory than the reconstructive model described above. The levels of processing approach suggests that there is no single thing we call memory. It is not a special mechanism in our mind designed to give us a store of items but simply a by-product of our normal, everyday thinking processes. If we have cause to think about something at one level (the semantic) then we are more likely to associate it with other items like ideas in our minds and it is more likely to be remembered. If we have cause to think about it at another level, however, (the structural) then we think about it so superficially that it is soon dealt with and we are unlikely to remember it. A consequence of this idea is that if we know there are some things we have to remember (like material for an exam) then we can manipulate the way we think about them to maximise the likelihood of us remembering them. This idea is taken up in a later lesson, Practical Applications.

**Evaluation of the Levels of Processing Model**

- Craik and Lockhart are not able to be sure that processing something at a semantic level really is any *deeper* than processing at a structural level. It "feels" right but there is no independent measure of how deeply something is being processed – it is an assumption more than anything else.
- The idea of "breadth" needs to be taken into account as well as the idea of depth. For example, look at the anagrams below:

  negdra                         gardne

  The solution is "garden" of course but the second one is easier to solve than the first (you could try it out on two groups of participants and time how long it takes each group to solve it; the first should take the longest to solve on average). From the view of the levels of processing model both anagrams are at the same level because both involve searching for the meaning of the letters and associating the letters with items in our minds.

- The model has useful practical applications.
- The idea that memory is a by-product of our everyday thinking is a useful one with the advantage of simplicity, which is always a sign of a good theory.

---

**Self-Assessment – Reconstructive Memory and Levels of Processing**

1  In the game Chinese Whispers, the story changes as it goes along the line; why is this similar to the idea of the reconstructive memory model?

2  What was the name of Bartlett's famous story used to illustrate this model?

3  Give one good point about the Reconstructive model of memory.

4  Give one negative point about the Reconstructive model of memory.

5  Give one difference between the Reconstructive model of memory and the Multistore model.

6  Name the three levels of processing investigated by Craik and Lockhart.

7  Which of the three levels named in question 6 is the deeper one?

8  Which model of memory implies that our memories are a by-product of our everyday thinking – the Multistore or the Levels of Processing Model?

9  Does the Levels of Processing model support the idea that elaboration is an effective way of moving items from the STM to the LTM?

10 Give one evaluative point about the Levels of Processing model.

As it requires some experience of marking to allocate marks to some of the answers to these questions it will be better not to attempt to give marks but instead to compare answers to those provided in the Feedback section

---

# Feedback

**Self-Assessment – Reconstructive Memory and Levels of Processing**

1  The story changes according to the characteristics of the person who is telling it; it is recreated within the context of the thoughts, experience, emotion and aspirations of the storyteller. The same happens with memories according to this model.

2  The War of the Ghosts.

3  It seems realistic; like real memories actually do work

4  We cannot use it to predict what people will remember.

5  The Multistore is very "mechanical" model of memory assuming a cause and effect for each memory for example; the reconstructive model takes more account of the "human" aspects of the person and allows things like emotions to affect memories.

6  Structural, acoustic and semantic

7  Semantic.

8  Levels of Processing

9  Yes

10 (e.g.) The model has useful practical applications.

# Lesson 39
# Eyewitness Testimony

## 1. Eyewitness testimony

Courts often require witnesses to describe what happened during an event. Psychology studies tell us that sometimes these accounts are very unreliable – i.e. the memories of the witnesses are inaccurate, but this is not always the case and does not mean to say that we should automatically ignore the testimony.

### The contributions of Loftus

Loftus asked participants to watch film of a car accident and later asked them questions about it. She found that the words used in the questions themselves could make a difference to what was reported by the witnesses and, presumably, to their memories.

- In one condition she asked, "About how fast were the cars going when they *hit*?" The mean estimate was 34 m.p.h.. In another she changed the word "hit" to *smashed* and the mean estimate was 40.8 m.p.h..

- In a similar way she asked one group "Did you see *a* broken headlight?" – 7 per cent said yes. The other group was asked, "Did you see *the* broken headlight?" – 15 per cent said yes.

This study implies that the **questions asked** in court can affect the reliability of eyewitness accounts though one criticism of the study is that it is not "real life" – it has little ecological validity. This is because the participants were watching a film and taking part in a study – which is not the same as seeing a real collision and testifying in court.

As this situation is likely to be associated with reconstructive memory it is likely that other factors could affect the testimony. The personality of the lawyers and witnesses, the courtroom setting, the recent other experiences of the witness and so on.

Not all studies of eyewitness testimony have shown them to be unreliable, however. The testimony of children has always been a contentious matter in courts but in cases of child abuse it is critical. As courts are aware of psychologists' findings about reconstructive memory and eyewitness testimony they are sensitive to any factors which could be cited as undermining the reliability of the evidence; consequently immediate counselling may be withheld from a child who has been abused because the defendant's lawyers may accuse the counsellors of altering the child's memory or "planting" memories. Withholding counselling can lead to continued distress for the child.

In 1989 Davies created a simulated medical inspection in which a "doctor"

- introduced himself to children between the ages of 6 and 11 years.
- interviewed them,
- noted their eye colour

- noted the condition of their teeth
- weighed and measured them, asking them to remove their shoes to do this
- touched each with his hand at some point in the procedure.

When interviewed a week later 52 per cent of the older children correctly remembered the stranger's name, 30 percent of the younger and 38 percent of the older children remembered correctly where and at what point they were touched and none of them were inaccurate when asked about whether they were asked to take their clothes off.

## 2. Practical Implication of studies of eyewitness testimony

### Improving Eyewitness Testimony – Police Reconstructions

One implication of Loftus's study is that eyewitness testimony is unreliable and so needs to be treated with care. However, eyewitness studies also show that there is a very positive role that eyewitnesses can play.

A person disappears on a Friday afternoon. The next Friday the police will ask someone of a similar stature to dress in similar clothes and re-enact the last known actions of the missing person – perhaps riding the same bicycle past the nearby shops. During the re-enactment the police stop passers-by to ask if they can remember anything about the person or about what other cars were parked in the area, who they saw walking along the pavement, who they recognised and who was unknown to them. A number of people will give details of their memories to the police that will be useful. You may have seen such a reconstruction on TV programmes like "Crimewatch". Why is this such an effective method of obtaining information?

By reconstructing the events at the same time of the week and place the police are likely to encounter people who were at the scene on the previous Friday. Those people are now in the same **context** they were at the time of the disappearance. Also, they are possibly in the same **state** – e.g. Friday may be payday and they are perhaps looking forward to the weekend. These are the conditions which best elicit **cue-dependent** memory: the context and the state are the same.

Other ways to improve testimony include **Hypnosis** and **Cognitive Interviewing**, in which eyewitnesses' personal and environmental states are recreated and they are asked to "talk through all their memories of the event" rather than asked specific questions.

---

**Complete the passage** (Answers in Feedback, below)
When Loftus asked, "How fast were the cars going when they *hit*?" participants gave a _____ estimate than when she asked, "How fast were the cars going when they *smashed*?". This suggests that the reliability of eyewitness accounts can be affected by _____ asked in court. This picture of eyewitness testimony is consistent with the _____ model of memory. However, if treated with care, eyewitness testimony can be useful. For example, the police will _____ incidents to "jog" the memories of possible eyewitnesses to crimes.

---

## Feedback

### Complete the passage

lower; questions; constructive (or reconstructive); reconstruct.

# Lesson 40
# Explanations of Forgetting

## Psychological Explanations of Forgetting
## 1. Context Dependent Forgetting

**Does this happen to you?**
- Do you ever find yourself at the top of the stairs wondering why you have come up?
- Do you go into a room and realise that you have forgotten why you came in?

Have you developed a strategy for resolving these situations? What do you do?

Godden and Baddeley asked a group of divers to learn a list of words underwater and another on the beach. They found that the divers recalled more of the list learnt underwater when they were tested underwater compared to being tested on the beach and vice versa. Earlier, the idea of encoding was introduced and it is likely that when we encode an item for memory some of the surrounding context is encoded too. Being put back in context will, therefore help us to remember because the context will give us cues to stimulate the memory. Researchers have also found that students will recall more when tested in the same room as that in which material was learnt.

If you get stuck with a blank mind at the top of the stairs or find yourself in the kitchen wondering why you are there, the problem can be quickly solved by returning to the spot where you decided to go up the stairs; or you may be successful by just imagining that you are back in the spot where you made the decision.

## 2. State Dependent Forgetting

This is very similar to Context Dependent forgetting and probably has the same causes. The "state" referred to is the state of mind or the emotional state of a person. Goodwin found that participants who learned material whilst under the influence of alcohol recalled more of it when put back under its influence than they did when free of it. Similarly, material learned when in an extreme emotional state like fear is recalled better if it is tested when in a similar emotional state. It may be that returning to the place where you decided to go upstairs (see 1. above) also helps to recreate the mental state you were in when you made the decision. **Context dependent and state dependent** forgetting are sometimes together referred to as **Cue dependent** forgetting because both failures to remember can be seen to some extent as resulting from a lack of cues that were encoded with the memory.

## 3. Interference

One memory item may interfere with another. The research in this area points to the idea that similar items may interfere with each other. If you were to be learning German vocabulary, for example, your memory of it could be weakened if you were to go straight into learning the Spanish for the same terms. At the same time, your ability to learn the Spanish vocabulary would be undermined by your recent learning of the corresponding German words.

When a new memory interferes with an old one it is referred to as **Retroactive Inhibition**. When an old memory interferes with a new one it is referred to as **Proactive Inhibition**.

> Name the type of inhibition illustrated in each of the following study procedures and results: (answers in Feedback section)
> Learn List A → Learn List B → Recall of List A is poor (Study 1)
> Learn List A → Learn List B → Recall of List B is poor (Study 2)

Studies that demonstrate Interference as a cause of forgetting have been criticised for being unrelated to real life memory situations. Laboratory studies such as these have little "ecological validity".

## 4. Displacement

A university professor once refused to learn the names of his students because he worried that for every student name he learned, he would forget the Latin name of a flower. He was probably wrong because, as you may remember, the capacity of the long-term memory is probably unlimited so he was unlikely to "knock out" old memories with new ones because there is plenty of room for all.

However, it is a different matter with short-term memory. We established earlier that the capacity of the STM is about 7 items plus or minus 2 (so 5 to 9 items), so the tenth item should knock out one of the others.

## 5. Motivated Forgetting

Freud was the first psychologist to draw considerable attention to the suggestion that our behaviour is largely determined by motives from our unconscious mind. We are not really aware of why we do most things. A fuller explanation of these ideas is given in the lesson on The Psychoanalytic Approach to Gender. To Freud, the reason we forget things is because we unconsciously **want** to forget them. We protect ourselves from disturbing, harmful thoughts or knowledge by keeping them out of our conscious mind. Missed the appointment at the dentist? It's because we are afraid of the pain. Forgot to keep a date with your boyfriend? It's because you don't really like him.

Of course, this is mere speculation when we put it this way but Freud's model of human beings is a more complex one than may appear at first sight. He wrote extensively on the idea of Defence Mechanisms, and the notion of motivated forgetting has to be related to his ideas of repression, suppression, projection and the other mechanisms, as well as to other elements of this model.

In a study by Bower, participants who were put into a good mood by the suggestion of the researcher tended to remember good things that had happened to them in the preceding week when put under hypnosis, and those put into a bad mood tended to remember the bad things. This supports the idea that they forgot the things they were motivated to forget.

### Evaluation of theories of forgetting

Freud's theory has the advantages of explaining some examples of forgetting that would be difficult to explain with the other theories. It also does have *some* empirical (i.e. "measurable") evidence to support it (see above). However, Freud's psychoanalytic theory in general comes in for a lot of criticism as being unscientific and difficult to verify empirically.

The other explanations of forgetting also have evidence to support them and they do fit the various models of memory explained in previous lessons. Also, it is wrong to look for a single explanation of forgetting as different explanations are more suitable for different situations; in this case, each of the above explanations is valid in its appropriate place.

---

**Self-Assessment**
**Which explanations of forgetting are represented by each of these statements?**
1. Putting further items into the memory will only cause some current ones to be lost
2. Now, why did I come in here?
3. The French word for "no"? It's "nein" isn't it?
4. Don't let him start drinking that whiskey; he'll only go on about the old days when he drank with the lads till dawn.
5. Now where did I put that bill?

---

# Feedback

### Name the type of interference

Study 1 is and example of Retroactive Inhibition. Study 2 is an example of Proactive Inhibition.

### Self-Assessment – answers

1. Displacement
2. Context dependent
3. Interference
4. State dependent
5. Motivated forgetting

# Lesson 41
# Practical Applications – Improving Your Memory

Mnemonics are devices for improving our memory of things. The first three, below, use imagery to aid memory. The next one uses our knowledge of organisation in memory.

## 1. Useful Mnemonics

(i) **Bizarre Images** Paivio asked participants to learn lists of words some of which were very easy to create an image of, like "house", "car" or "plant"; other words were more difficult to visualise, for example "hope", "fear" or "sense". He found a much higher recall of the concrete words (easy to image) compared to the abstract words (difficult to visualise). From this we learn that if we are able to increase the **distinctiveness** of an item by creating a bizarre image of it, for example, then it is much more likely that we will remember it. You need to remember that you met Patrick and Tracy at Rehana's party last week? Then imagine the pair dancing a jig (both names with Irish connections, so why not an Irish dance?) on the roof of Rehana's house being watched by others at the party.

(ii) **The Method of Loci** "Loci" means locations or places and this method involves imagining places or locations for items that you want to remember. It works best for things like shopping lists but most people would be happy writing down shopping lists so it may be more useful for memorising items for an exam. The method involves images so, again, it is better for concrete items though lists to be memorised for exams are often not concrete.

To remember the items you have to first use an image of a route you are familiar with. For example, you may imagine coming out of your back door, walking round the side of your house, up the front path, out of the gate, along the road to the corner and so on. As you go on the route you should mentally "deposit" the items to be remembered at particular points. For example, if your list includes a visit to the chemist to pick up a prescription you could imagine the paper bag for the prescription placed around an empty milk bottle outside the back door, letters you have to post could be imagined nailed to the back of the garden gate and so on. As with distinctiveness, it is better to make the images as bizarre as possible so letters nailed to your new car would probably be more effective. To recall the items, simply re-trace your route mentally.

This method makes use of the levels of processing model because you are processing the items for their meaning and there are elements of the multistore model because you are rehearsing them. It also capitalises on the impact that imagery has on memory.

**(iii) The Peg Word Method** This is another memory aid designed to help people remember lists of items. It is done in two stages:

* **Stage 1** You learn a rhyming list of numbers and associated images: these act as "pegs" on which the items to be remembered are "hung". For example:

  One is a bun

  Two is a shoe

  Three is a tree

  Four is a door

  and so on

**Stage 2** You then use bizarre images to link the items to be remembered with the rhyming list: for example, if one is a bun and the first item to be remembered is the prescription from the chemist you could use the green cross symbol displayed by chemists and imagine a green bun in the shape of a cross or a bun with an oversized drug capsule sticking out of the top. If the second item is the letter to post then it is simply a matter of linking the shoe (two is a shoe) with the letter so a simple letter sticking out of the shoe may suffice or a letter written on a shoe or a post office built into a shoe (like the Old Woman Who Lived in a Shoe illustrations from children's story books). This method uses levels of processing, imagery, rehearsal, elaboration and distinctiveness.

## 2. Applying Memory Models to Exam Revision and Study

**(i) Organised Notes and Cue Cards** The way in which information in the memory is organised in categories and hierarchies has been described in Lesson 2. Well-organised notes confirm that we are "in charge" of or "on top of" the material which has to be learned.

* Laying material out effectively in the first place can only be done if we have understood it so organised notes are "proof" of our understanding

* "Well organised" means that headings and subheadings are used along with numbers and lettering to divide parts of material – this page is a good example of well-organised notes.

* Organised notes can be reduced to cue cards that are easy to memorise (using the mnemonics in this lesson) for recall during exams. Cue cards can be written on postcard-sized cards. Here is an example of a cue card of this lesson up to now.

---

 **Practical Applications – exercise**
**1 Useful Mnemonics**
**(i)   Bizarre Images**
**(ii)  The Method of Loci**
**(iii) The Peg Word Method**
   * **Stage 1** (create peg words)
   * **Stage 2** (link peg words with items)
**2 Applying Memory Models to Exam Revision and Study**
**(i)   Organised Notes and cue Cards**

---

Whilst the card can be memorised, each item on the card will act as a **cue** to all the meanings of the items, which will be available for you to use in the exam.

Memorising the card can be achieved in a number of ways: **bizarre images** (picturing the word "mnemonics" made out of wooden letters of various sizes hung like tools in a workshop – for "Useful Mnemonics"?). **Acronyms** are also useful though they have not been mentioned so far; these are the first letters of keywords used to produce another word or some sort of phrase as when we learn **R**ichard **O**f **Y**ork **G**ave **B**attle **I**n **V**ain to denote ROYGBIV the colours of the spectrum – red, orange, yellow, green, blue, indigo and violet. So **UBBSSAO** (the first letters of the headings of the card, above) may turn out to be **U**ncle **B**radley's **B**ack**S**ide **S**its **A**stride **O**live (with a little cartoon image created to go with it).

## (ii) Revision techniques

- Many students use the technique of reading through their notes for revision. There is no doubt that this is useful but it can be improved upon greatly. It represents no more than **maintenance rehearsal** – repetition that does not necessarily move information from STM to LTM effectively.

- You can practise **elaboration** of the materials by ensuring that you **process them at a deeper level**. This can achieved by
  - Asking a friend to test you on your knowledge of them
  - Discussing them with another student
  - Practising answering past questions or other techniques.

- Increase the **distinctiveness** of the material by producing unusual versions of them – writing them on the bedroom wall in large letters (usually best achieved by attaching lining paper to the wall beforehand rather than writing directly on the permanent wallpaper by the way!), speaking them into a tape recorder or singing them.

---

Produce a cue card for revision techniques based on the suggestions above. An example of one is given in the Feedback section

---

## Feedback

---
**Revision Techniques**
- Read notes (maintenance rehearsal)
- Elaboration (deeper processing)
  - Examples
- Increase Distinctiveness
---

# AQA Exam Style Questions: Memory

- **Answer all questions**
- **There is no time limit to this assignment**
- **When completed you may compare your answers with the example answers at the end of the book**
- **If you have tutorial support you should send a copy of your answers to your tutor to receive further feedback, comments and guidance**

A mnemonist is a person who can display impressive performances of memory – sometimes a mnemonist may make a living from these displays. On a television chat show recently, a mnemonist said, "It is not just a question of being able to recall events well. To perform these feats you have to pay attention to all aspects of memory: encoding and storage can be just as important as retrieval".

(a) From your knowledge of the psychology of memory, state the meaning of "encoding". (2 marks)

(b) Describe **one** way in which remembered items may be organised in the memory (2 marks)

(c) Briefly describe **either** the Reconstructive model **or** the Levels of Processing model of memory. (4 marks)

(d) Describe **one** study of Eyewitness Testimony. (4 marks)

(e) Briefly evaluate the study you described in (d), above. (3 marks)

(f) Describe **one** explanation of Forgetting. (3 marks)

(g) Give **one** criticism of the explanation you described in (f), above. (2 marks)

**Total possible marks = 20**

When completed you should compare your answers with the example answers at the end of the book. If you have tutorial support you should send a copy of your answers to the tutor for feedback, comments and further guidance.

# OCR Exam Style Questions: Memory

- **Answer all questions**
- **There is no time limit to this assignment**
- **When completed you may compare your answers with the example answers at the end of the book**
- **If you have tutorial support you should send a copy of your answers to your tutor to receive further feedback, comments and guidance**

**Cognitive Psychology**
**Memory**

> As part of a television game show, Estelle had to memorise twenty objects that passed in front of her on a conveyer belt rather quickly. She succeeded in remembering all the objects and when asked by her friends afterwards how she managed to succeed Estelle said:
>
> "I just said the name of each item as it passed in front of me. I said it to myself loud and clear. Then when I had to recall them, I said each word and each one sort of reminded me of the next sound."

(a) **Encoding** refers to the form in which an item is represented in our memory. What type of encoding did Estelle use in her TV game task? (1 mark)

(b) Name one other type of encoding used by humans in memory. (1 mark)

(c) Describe a study that indicates that acoustic coding is used in the Short Term Memory. (3 marks)

(d) Outline Atkinson and Shiffrin's two-process theory of memory. (5 marks)

(e) Describe **one** piece of evidence that supports Atkinson and Shiffrin's theory. (3 marks)

(f) Briefly describe **two** theories of forgetting. (4 marks)

(g) Evaluate **one** of the theories you have described in (f) above. (3 marks)

**Total possible marks = 20**

When completed you should compare your answers with the example answers at the end of the book. If you have tutorial support you should send a copy of your answers to the tutor for feedback, comments and further guidance.

# Lesson 42
# The Structures and Functioning of the Eye

## 1. The Structures and Functioning of the Eye

### Figure I. A cross-section view of the eye

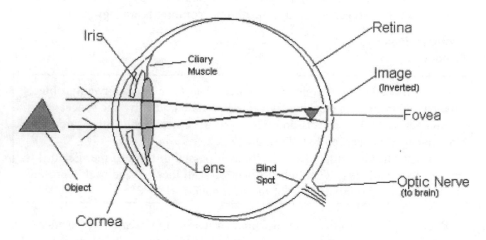

**How the eye works**

Figure I, above, shows how the image of a triangle is registered by an eye. Light from the sun or the electric lights around the triangle bounces off the triangle and some of it follows the route shown by the two arrowed lines. It passes through the transparent covering at the front of the eye, the cornea, and is "bent" by the lens so that is focused as a sharp image on the retina at the back of the eye. The eyeball is filled with a watery liquid so the light passes through it easily. The iris, at the front of the eye, forms a coloured disc with a "hole" in the middle; the disc is the part which gives a colour to the eye and the hole is the pupil which looks black if you look into someone's eyes. The iris can close in to form a smaller hole if the light is very bright or open up to let more light in if the light is low.

Find a friendly volunteer (this is where you find out who your friends really are!) and look closely into one eye. Can you see the iris and the pupil?

Now shine a torch into the volunteer's eye and watch the iris and pupil carefully. What happened to each one?

Turn the torch off. What happened to the pupil and iris? Be sure to tell the volunteer what you are going to do. The closer you can get, the better.

Using a good magnifying glass should make the effect easier to observe.

**Investigating The Eye**
Tick the box when the task is done
☐ Iris and pupil identified

What happened to the iris when the torch was turned on?

_____

_____

What happened to the pupil when the torch was turned off?

_____

_____

The image is focused on a small portion of the retina at the back of the eye; the small portion is the **fovea.** Some eyes cannot focus the image as sharply as necessary. The eye may be slightly misshapen (egg-shaped rather than round) so the image is focused before it lands on the retina and so is blurred when it eventually does reach the retina. Sometimes the muscles of the lens may become weaker as we get older and so they cannot "squash" and "stretch" the lens as much as they should to bend the light properly. In this case the image may hit the retina before it is properly focused and so, again, it appears blurred.

- **cornea** – helps the lens to bend the light
- **lens** – bends the light to focus it on the fovea which is an area of the retina
- **retina** – a covering of cells at the back of the eyeball which respond (fire electrical impulses) in response to stimulation from light
- **optic nerve** – carries the impulses from the retina to the brain

**Sensation: the eye produces sensory information (sensory data)**
The fovea is lined with cells which react to light like the rest of the retina. You may have a calculator which is powered by light; ôphotosensitiveö (light-sensitive) cells in a "solar powered" (sun-powered) calculator produce small amounts of electricity when light hits them. If you have such a calculator try to identify the light-sensitive cells which are clearly visible on the front of it. Cover the cells to stop the light from reaching them and then see how the figures fade and the calculator cannot work.

**Sensation and perception**
A strange thing about the image when it is projected onto the back of the eye is that it is upside-down. We do not see the world as upside-down, however, we see it as the right way up and this is a good example of the difference between the **sensations** we receive and the image we **perceive.** Our brain manages to turn the image the other way up but we are not aware of this process. This demonstrates how the brain is active in the process of perception; it does not just passively "receive" the image – it actively processes it.

Perception is not the same as "seeing". It involves taking the sensation we receive from the visual system but then interpreting and elaborating it to give it meaning like the way that our television picture is perceived as a whole picture rather than the series of dots on the screen from which it is composed. Another example of this is the way in which the picture at the cinema is perceived as moving, even though it is made up of a series of still pictures.

## 2. The Visual Pathways Leading to the Visual Cortex: the route of impulses from the eye to the brain

The electrical/chemical impulses travel along the cells of the optic nerve out of the eye and into the brain in the pathway shown in the following diagram.

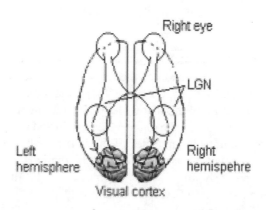

**Fig V The visual pathways leading from the eye to the visual cortex**

The above diagram is a cross section plan view of the brain (looking down on the brain and imagining what it looks like cut across). You can see what happens to the impulses from each side of each eye.

**Perception: understanding sensory information**

All impulses from the eyes pass through a structure inside the brain called the **lateral geniculate body** or nucleus **(LGB or LGN)** then eventually to the surface of the brain at the back – the visual cortex. It is the visual cortex which "recognises" or "understands" the image. What happens at the lateral geniculate body? Why does the optic nerve take the impulses to it? We are not sure. The LGB is part of the structure of nerves known as the **thalamus** and impulses from most of the senses pass through it (except impulses from the sensation of smelling). Information to the muscles from other parts of the brain pass through the same structure so it is likely that the eyes' impulses are somehow integrated with information about movement at this point.

Many other parts of the brain are linked to this structure – memory and emotions in particular are linked here. As you will read later, memories and emotions can affect the way we perceive an image and it is likely that the LGB is the place where this effect occurs.

The **visual cortex** turns sensation into perception. Here, for example, shape is detected: a line of light at a particular angle causes a particular combination of cells in the visual cortex to fire. Damage the visual cortex and you damage sight.

**Self-marked Assessment**
Answer the following questions. The answers will be found in the Feedback section at the end of this unit.
1. The fovea is the small part of the _____ at the back of the eye onto which the image is sharply focused.
2. If the image is not focused properly it may be because the eye is misshapen or because the ___ is not bending the light properly.
3. _____ falling on the retina causes a chemical/electrical impulse.
4. The impulse is carried by the _____ _____ out of the eye and into the brain.
5. The impulse finishes up at the _____ cortex at the back of the brain.
6. Of which structure in the brain is the lateral geniculate body a part?
7. What is the name of the point at which the optic nerves cross from one hemisphere to the other?

## Feedback

### Investigating The Eye

The Iris should have closed in to prevent too much light entering the eye so more of the iris should be visible.

The pupil should have enlarged as the torch was turned off because the iris opens up again

**Answers to the Self Marked Assessment**
1. retina
2. lens
3. light
4. optic nerve
5. visual
6. the thalamus
7. the optic chiasma

# Lesson 43
# Perception as an Active Process

## 1. Perception as an active process

We are not like cameras, i.e. merely registering on a film what is "out there". We strive to understand the information we get about the outside world and we try to integrate it with what we have experienced before and to make sense of it. As a result, we may change the information we receive.

> ## Pig farm is an
> ## an angler's paradise

> Above is a headline from my local newspaper. It contains a mistake but few readers (if any) would have noticed it. The editor failed to realise it was there even when I wrote to ask about it. Can you see the mistake? It illustrates an important point about perception.

In this example the word "an" is mistakenly repeated at the beginning of the second line – it had already appeared at the end of the first – but most people perceive the headline as having no mistake because in our previous experience headlines usually make sense. In this example there is a double helping of expectation based on previous experience because the word after "an" also begins with "an . . ." (angler's) so there is even more reason for us to expect and accept two "an"s

## 2. The difference between sensation and perception

The key idea is that **perception is not the same as sensation.** The information we get from the eyes (the sensation – the electrical/chemical signals passed from the eye to the brain) is changed by our thoughts, feelings, expectations and other factors so that what we eventually **perceive** is not necessarily what is really in front of us. In the rest of these lessons we turn to a deeper examination of what perception is. As you work through them you will see how we use a variety of active processes to construct our perceptions from the sensations we receive from the eyes.

Of course, we have the impression that what we perceive is "reality" – i.e. it is **really there.** It can be a rather strange feeling to realise that we may be making it all up – "in our head".

The way in which we turn our sensations into our perception in this way is one illustration of the idea that perception is an active process – we are not receiving a pre-set "picture" but we are constructing that picture through our active perceptual processing.

## 3. Visual Illusions

Visual illusions are "Figures which appear to be other than they really are", according to Stratton and Hayes (1993). When a machine breaks down it sometimes helps us to understand how it works – especially if we have to fix it. This is true of our perceptual processing. Visual illusions are, in a sense, examples of the visual processing system breaking down. The system produces outcomes we would not expect. If we examine these breakdowns we can learn something about how visual processing works.

### Types of Visual Illusions and Everyday Examples

Some illusions share certain **themes** and we can group them into four major categories. This does not mean that this is the only way to classify illusions, however. Also, some illusions could be put into more than one category.

1. **Ambiguity:** If something is ambiguous it has more than one meaning. Ambiguous figures have one set of sensory data with two possible interpretations. Consider the cube below: look at it for some time and you should find that it changes.

One moment we are looking at the front of the cube from slightly above it, the next we are looking at it from slightly below. It can be seen in two ways and one way is no better or worse than the other. Hence, this figure is ambiguous.

**Fig 1. Necker's Cube**

The Necker Cube is a good example of ambiguity. You may have come across it already. Another everyday example of ambiguity is Figure 2 below, Rubin's Vase; at one moment it is a vase, at the next, a pair of silhouetted faces looking at each other.

**Figure 2. Rubin's Vase**

2. **Distortions:** These are figures that are altered from what they really are – usually by their surroundings. Consider the two lines, (a) and (b) in the Muller-Lyer illusion below.

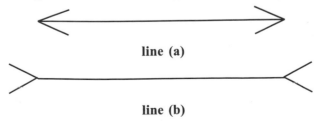

**line (a)**

**line (b)**

**Fig 3. The Muller-Lyer Illusion**

Line (b) appears longer than line (a) but in fact they are both the same length (try measuring them!). The fins at the end have distorted the length of the line.

The Muller-Lyer illusion is probably the best known and simplest distortion but the Ponzo illusion is a very good illustration of distortion too.

In the Ponzo illusion the top horizontal line looks longer than the bottom one. Tape measures out again! In fact, both lines are the same length.

Similarly, in the following example, it is difficult to believe that the two horizontal lines are not curved but place a straight edge against them and you can see that, in fact, they are both completely straight.

**Figure 4. The Ponzo**

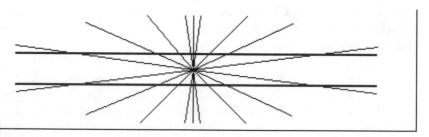

**Figure 5. The two horizontal lines are parallel but do they look it?**

3.  **Paradox:** A paradox is an idea that may appear absurd but is actually true, or it is something that contains contradictory ideas. For example, the Penrose triangle below can be drawn on paper but it cannot be made as a real object – so it can exist but, then again, it cannot (the paradox)

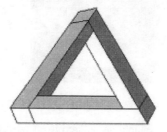

**Figure 6. The Penrose Triangle**

Another example of a paradox is shown below

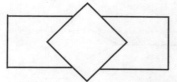 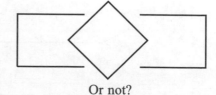

A square on top of a rectangle?                          Or not?

**Figure 7.** the rectangle appears to be continuous but it is not

4. **Fictions:** Fiction is falsehood, something that is not true. An example is the Kanizsa Triangle, below.

**Figure 8. The Kanizsa Triangle**

> **What do you see?**
> Spend a few minutes writing down a description of what you see in the Kanizsa Triangle, and then carry on reading.

Looking at the Kanizsa Triangle we have the impression that there are two triangles, one that is drawn with a black line and one that is white. The white one appears to be on top of the line one. There appear to be three circles, one partially covered by each corner of the white triangle.

In fact, none of the above statements is true. There are no triangles on the paper – only in your mind. There are no circles. The Kanizsa Triangle consists of three versions of a pair of shapes. Here is one shape, and here is the other:

We create the triangles in our minds. They are not really there. They are fictional.

This last type of illusion is a very good illustration of the way in which our perceptual system is an active one. We can see clearly how we are actively constructing the perception (strictly speaking, the thing we construct is called a percept whilst the object causing the image is called the proximal stimulus) and it seems sensible to assume that all our percepts are the result of active processing.

> **Quick Quiz**
> Try this quick quiz to summarise the lesson
> Which one of the following causes the sensation and which one results from the process of perception? (i) the percept (ii) the proximal stimulus (2 marks)
> What is the difference between sensation and perception? (2 marks)
> What are visual illusions? (1 mark)
> List four types of visual illusion (4 marks)
> List one example of each type of illusion (4 marks)
> How do visual illusions support the idea that perception is an active process? (2 marks)
> **Total 15 points possible**

## Feedback

### Answers to the Quick Quiz

1. The proximal stimulus causes sensation (1 mark) and the percept results from the process of perception (1 mark)
2. Sensation is the electrical/chemical signals produced by the eye and conveyed

to the brain; perception is the way the brain turns those signals into a percept – an understanding of the stimulus. (2 marks)

3. Figures that appear to be other than they really are. (1 mark)

4. Ambiguities (1 point)
   Distortions (1 point)
   Paradoxes (1 point)
   Fictions (1 point)

5. e.g.(Ambiguity) The Necker Cube: (Distortion) – The Muller-Lyer Illusion; (Paradoxes) – the Penrose Triangle; (Fictions) – The Kanizsa Triangle (1 mark for each)

6. We can see that visual illusions are not a "true picture" of the world outside; they are obviously constructed in our minds – suggesting that all our percepts are constructed in our minds. (2 marks)

## References

Stratton, P and Hayes, N (1993) *A Student's Dictionary of Psychology* (2nd ed) Edward Arnold

# Lesson 44
# Perception as a Modelling Process

## 1 Gregory's Theory of Cues and Hypotheses
### Hypothesis testing

Richard Gregory is a psychologist working in the area of perception. He has put forward a theory about how our brain understands the sensory information it receives from the eye. His theory is that when the brain receives impulses from the eye it makes sub-conscious suggestions about what the impulses represent – what the "picture" is. This suggestion is a hypothesis.

In general, a hypothesis is a statement to be tested. It is not necessarily a true statement, just a starting point. For example, I might put forward the hypothesis that the earth is round. To test the hypothesis I might set off and travel in one direction. If the earth truly **is** round then I should eventually arrive back in the same place from where I started. If I **do** come back to the same place, then I can accept the hypothesis that the earth is round. If I fall off the edge of the earth, then I have to reject the hypothesis that the earth is round – though hypotheses would be the last thing I would be thinking about under the circumstances.

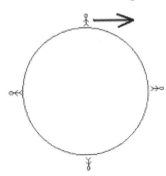

**If the Earth is round, we should end up where we started.**

Gregory suggests that the brain receives sensory data from the eye, we construct a hypothesis about what we can see, we test the hypothesis against the data, then we either accept or reject the hypothesis. For example, we look at a tree, we form the hypothesis "this is a tree", we test the hypothesis by asking about cues that tell us it is a tree – "Has it got a trunk? Has it got branches? Does it have leaves if it is summer?" And so on. If we answer yes to all those questions then we accept that we can see a tree. Of course, we can make mistakes. If we just go by the answers to the question above, we may be looking at a photograph of a tree but Gregory suggests that in most cases we make the most of the information we have and usually make a sound judgement.

> How do you know that this is a book you are looking at? Write down five tests you would make in a hypothesis to see if you are looking at a book. What cues would you use? There are some suggestions in the Feedback section.

You may be asking "Why go to all this trouble?" Why does Gregory not think we just "see" what is in front of us? Some psychologists suggest that Gregory has "gone over the top" and that his idea is unnecessary, but Gregory's ideas can help us to explain the occasions when we misperceive something or when we experience visual illusions.

## 2 Explanations of Visual Illusions: Gregory's ideas applied

Gregory's ideas about hypothesis testing can explain many illusions. This supports his theory because if we work on the other theory – that we just "see" what is there – then it is difficult to explain these occasions when the perceptual system fails and we are fooled by illusions.

We shall restrict ourselves to two examples of the use of Gregory's ideas to explain visual illusions.

**Fig I Rubin's Vase**

Firstly, consider Rubin's Vase:

If you look at the vase for a few moments then you should notice that it changes to the profile of two heads facing each other, then it changes back again.

To recap, Gregory's idea is that we are constantly making sub-conscious suggestions to ourselves about what it is that we can see. These suggestions are hypotheses – statements to be tested. We check our suggestions against the sensory data – the impulses from the eyes – and if the data matches the hypothesis we accept that this is what we can see.

> Can you already see how the idea of hypothesis testing could explain the Rubin's Vase illusion? Try writing it down: the answer follows this box.

In the case of Rubin's Vase, we make the hypothesis that there is an image of a vase in front of us; we test the hypothesis and accept it because the data fit it. For some reason we then make another hypothesis – that there is the image of two faces in front of us; again, we test the data and again we accept the hypothesis but this time it is the image of two faces that we see. All this happens sub-consciously of course; we are not aware that it is happening; we just perceive the end product. Then we change back to the first hypothesis and so on.

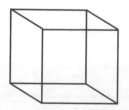

The same explanation can hold true for the Necker Cube.

First we hypothesise that we are looking at a cube from above, we accept this hypothesis then try another one – that we are looking at it from below. We check and accept the second hypothesis and the cube seems to change.

We shall see in a later lesson in this section that Gregory's ideas can be used to explain the Muller-Lyer illusion and there are further explanations of distortions of size, distance and movement.

So hypothesis testing is probably one of the mechanisms used by the perceptual system to construct a model of the outside world; we constantly make hypotheses about what is "out there", we test the hypothesis against the sensory data and if the data fit we accept the hypothesis. If the data do not fit, we reject the hypothesis and make another one. This idea of constructing, accepting or rejecting hypotheses is an important idea in conducting investigations and it plays an important part in the lessons on methods in psychology.

---

**Quick Quiz**

1. What is an hypothesis? (1 mark)
2. Complete the blanks in the following sentence: "Gregory suggests that the _____ receives sensory data from the ___, we construct a _____ about what we can see, we test the hypothesis against the ____, then we either accept or _____ the hypothesis." (5 marks)
3. Why does Gregory suggest that we cannot just accept the idea that we simply see what is there? (2 marks)
4. According the idea of hypothesis testing, why do we see a vase one moment then a pair of faces another moment in Rubin's Vase? (2 marks)

---

## Feedback

**Suggestions for cues to test the hypothesis "This is a book"**

- Does it have pages?
- Is there writing on the pages?
- Are there numbers on the pages?
- Is the writing printed?
- Are the pages bound in a spine?

**Quick Quiz**

6. A statement to be tested (1 mark)
7. Gregory suggests that the **brain** receives sensory data from the **eye**, we construct a **hypothesis** about what we can see, we test the hypothesis against the **data**, then we either accept or **reject** the hypothesis. (1 mark for each emboldened word = 5 marks total)
8. Because this would not explain visual illusions. (2 marks)
9. Because we test one hypothesis and accept it, then test the other hypothesis – and accept it too. (2 marks)

**Total marks = 10**

# Lesson 45
# Visual Constancies

## Why is vision not like an LSD trip?

If we use only our knowledge of the eye to explain how we "see" things, then we would expect to experience vision as though we were on an LSD "trip". Consider these ideas:

- Objects should look as though they get bigger as we approach them
- A chair should be unrecognisable if it is tipped over
- Our friends should change colour as we go outside
- People should look brighter as the sun comes out
- The world should swirl round as we move

All these ideas would be the world we experience if it were not for the processes of perception. We would be living in a permanent LSD "trip" of hallucinations and bizarre experiences compared to the stable experiences with which we are familiar. Here is why.

## 1. Size Constancy

- **objects should look as though they get bigger as we approach them**

The image of an object on the retina is large if the object is near and smaller if the object is further away. As a car approaches you the image of the car gets bigger and it is at its largest when the car is nearest. As the car recedes, so the image gets smaller again. If we only look at the mechanics of how the eye works, then, we should actually expect objects to appear this way. Passing cars and other objects should look as though they grow and shrink. As we pass objects and people the same should happen.

But this doesn't happen. We have the ability to recognise that the image of a car half the previous size is merely the image of the car further away. An elephant in the distance is not a miniature animal but a distant animal. This ability is referred to as **size constancy** – the ability to "keep" the object at its real (constant) size and realise that the small image means the object is at a distance.

## 2. Object Constancy

- **A chair should be unrecognisable if it is tipped over**

**Fig 1 What is this?**

As every school child knows, it's a giraffe passing a window! Seen from an unusual angle the object does not "make sense" – it is not perceived in its usual way but the object is its usual self and when we are "nudged" by being told what it is we can immediately perceive it correctly.

If we come across a chair we have never seen before that has been tipped over we are not lost for understanding. Instead we are able to extrapolate from the picture in front of us to the chair as it would look if it were standing upright.

Hence, we perceive it as a chair. We have the ability to keep the chair as a constant object and rotate it in our minds – hence object constancy.

## 3. Shape Constancy

Closely related to the idea of object constancy is the notion of **shape constancy**. A coin seen face on has a circle as its shape. But the circle turns to an oval shape if the coin is rotated a little. Carry on rotating it and it becomes a thin rectangle. This is illustrated below.

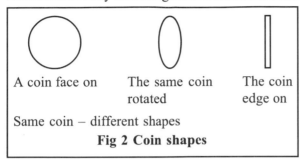

A coin face on    The same coin    The coin
                  rotated          edge on

Same coin – different shapes

**Fig 2 Coin shapes**

Yet when was the last time you failed to recognise a coin because it was the wrong shape? Our perceptual system has the ability to keep the shape of the coin constant and to accept that it is still round even though we are seeing a different shape. Imagine what the world would look like if we could see objects changing shape as their angle changed when we moved. Just paying for goods in a shop would be like a bad dream.

## 4. Colour Constancy

- **Our friends should change colour as we go outside**

> Do you remember learning at school how objects gain a colour? If so, jot down what you remember, then read on.

Sunlight is made up of the whole spectrum of colour (the rainbow). As the light hits an object, it absorbs some colours from the light but it reflects others. The light that is reflected is the colour of the object. A blue object, for example, absorbs all colours except blue – which is reflected.

However, different sources of light give off different amounts of each colour. The electric bulb in the living room gives off a different colour light from the fluorescent tube in the kitchen or the halogen lamp in the department store.

An object under an electric bulb, therefore, reflects a different light from the light it would reflect under the fluorescent tube. It **should** appear to be a different colour but we hardly ever notice the difference. You may see people in a shop taking clothing or material outside to see what colour it appears in sunlight but apart from these sorts of occasions it would not be usual to pay attention to the different colours.

And so, as you go outside with a friend, he or she changes colour – but you don't notice this. All objects change in this way. As we walk from the window to the opposite wall in a room our clothes change colour but we would find it difficult to cope if we saw the world as it really is – changing colour all the time. Instead, we keep colours constant even though they are not. This is colour constancy.

## 5. Brightness Constancy

Closely related to colour constancy is brightness constancy. Just as colour changes during movement, so brightness changes. The brightest source of light is sunlight.

As we go outside we become brighter and indeed sometimes we do notice this when the sun is particularly bright. Even when the light is on an "ordinary" day, however, the brightness changes constantly without us noticing. As we move from one room to another or from inside the house to outside, so the level of light changes and so we become brighter or duller – but we rarely notice.

This ability to perceive the world as though it has a constant brightness is **brightness constancy** and is an important element in our practice of keeping the visual world constant.

## 6. Location constancy
- The world should swirl round as we move

A number of pieces of information from our senses tell us that objects are moving. One of them is the way in which the light from the object passes over the retina at the back of the eyeball. Figure 3 shows how this happens.

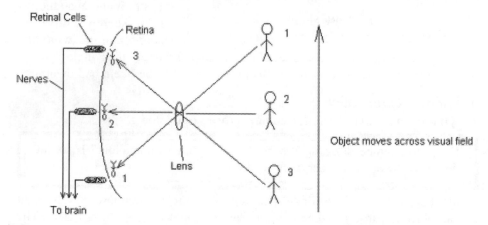

### Fig 3. Light from an object passes over the retina

In position 1 the light is reflected off the object (the stick person) and passes through the lens and onto the retina in the corresponding position 1, the lens inverts the image, of course. As the object moves to position 2 so the image moves to position 2 on the retina and the same with position 3. As the object moves, so does the image. At each position on the retina, the light falling on them activates cells and the resulting impulse is carried to the brain to register the position of the image. One of the ways in which the brain knows that an object is moving, then, is the information about the retinal cells firing.

But consider what happens when the person's head moves and the object remains stationary. This time the retina registers position 1 then it moves with the head and although the object is in the same place the image from the light from the object still moves to position 2 and as the head continues to move so the retina moves with it and the image falls in position 3. As far as the brain is concerned, the information is the same. Light has fallen on the same sequence of cells in the retina and so it has the impression that the object has moved.

But if we pass a person waiting at the bus stop we know that it is not the person at the bus stop who is moving but ourselves. How do we know? The brain must take information from other aspects of the body to be able to keep the stationary person constant. For example, if you move your head, then the muscle movements to move the head will register with the brain. Similarly, if walk past a person at the bus stop, then our brain can take information from our feet, legs and so on.

We can, therefore, keep the world constant instead of experiencing it as swirling around.

## 7. What good is constancy?

Why does our perceptual system operate in this way? Why do we keep this changing picture constant? In a way, we are fooling ourselves. Wouldn't it be better to perceive the world as it really is rather than gain an inaccurate picture?

We do benefit from these constancy processes in some ways. For example:

- It would be far too disorientating if the world were changing all the time. We wouldn't be sure about anything and couldn't predict what the world would look like next or what was going to happen to us.
- We would have to pay too much attention to minor aspects of our daily lives – so much so that we probably couldn't get on with anything because we are trying to work out what is happening to us.

By keeping the perceptual world constant we "free up" processing capacity in our thinking and can devote it to other things.

## 8. Summary

---

**Fill in the missing words**

Visual constancies are processes that allow us to keep our visual experiences of the world on an even keel. If we didn't have them, it would be like living in a permanent hallucination.

_____ constancy stops changes in light levels altering the way we see objects while _____ constancy keeps objects the same colour. We would not recognise familiar people from side views if it were not for _____ constancy. ____ constancy prevents objects appearing to get smaller

as they move away from you and ____ constancy allows us to recognise that a coin turned sideways will look like a rectangle but has not really changed its shape. Finally, the world would appear to swirl around if we did not use _____ constancy

---

## Feedback

Visual constancies are processes that allow us to keep our visual experiences of the world on an even keel. If we didn't have them, it would be like living in a permanent hallucination. Brightness constancy stops changes in light levels altering the way we see objects while colour constancy keeps objects the same colour. We would not recognise familiar people from side views if it were not for object constancy. Size constancy prevents objects appearing to get smaller as they move away from you and shape constancy allows us to recognise that a coin turned sideways will look like a rectangle but has not really changed its shape. Finally, the world would appear to swirl around if we did not use location constancy.

# Lesson 46
# Distance Perception and Depth Cues

## 1. Constructing three dimensions from two: 3D percepts from 2D images

The retina is two-dimensional; the image focused on the retina has height and width but it does not go back or stand out from the surface of the retina. If the image is two dimensional, how do we perceive this third dimension of depth? How do we create three-dimensional percepts?

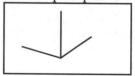

**Figure 2 Height, depth and width shown by three lines**

### Depth cues

The above illustration shows that we can perceive the third dimension, depth, even though an image may be only two-dimensional. How do we turn 2D into 3D? Part of the process involves picking up "cues" from the image or the sensory data which our brain receives from the eye. These cues act as clues for the brain to detect the third dimension.

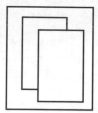

Look at the two rectangles in the box on the left. Which one appears closest? In reality neither is closer. They are both printed on the same piece of paper at the same distance from your eyes.

Can you suggest why one appears closer than the other?

One rectangle appears to be on top of the other. Actually, neither is on top. Now look at the enlargement of the points at which the rectangles seem to overlap:

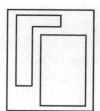

As you can see, one rectangle is not really a rectangle but a sort of inverted L shape and one is not on top of the other but simply next to it. The way that the rectangles are arranged, however gives the impression that one image is obscuring the other and in general if the image of one object obscures part of the image of another it is because it is in front of it and is therefore nearer.

Our perceptual system makes the assumption that one image has obscured the other and concludes that it is nearer. Usually, it would be correct of course.

This is an example of the way that the brain can make conclusions about depth when it only has information about the two other dimensions, width and height. It uses clues or "cues" from the two-dimensional image about the third dimension. Of course, we are not aware of this process consciously – we simply perceive the third dimension. This cue is referred to as **superposition** and occurs when one image appears to overlay or obscure a part of another image.

A second cue is **perspective.** Artists use this device to create the illusion of depth in pictures. Pictures are produced on two-dimensional surfaces like paper (height and width but no depth) so edges drawn in the picture can be made to appear as though they are all going towards the same focal point. This can be seen as a road goes into the distance or as a railway track disappears and is an important feature in the Ponzo illusion

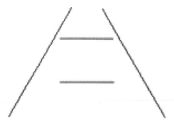

**Figure 3 The Ponzo Illusion**

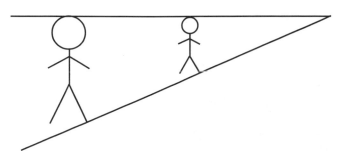

**Figure 4 Perspective gives the impression of depth**

**The smaller figure looks to be behind the larger one in both figure 3 and figure 4.**

A further depth cue is **retinal image size**. If you look at an elephant in the distance, the image that it casts upon your retina will be smaller than the image when the elephant is nearer. As the perceptual system expects elephants to be a more or less constant size, it translates the small image into the percept of a far-away elephant.

The brain picks up other cues from the sensory data supplied from the eye. Here are some questions to help you learn about the cues.

1. Compare the amount of detail you can see on the back of your hand to the amount of detail on the wall furthest from you. Where can you see the most detail? Can you see the hairs on the back of your hand? The pores of your skin? On the wall can you see the texture of the wallpaper or the paint? The weave of the fabric in the curtains?

2. Look straight ahead; do the things that are nearest to you tend to be in the top half of your visual field or the bottom half? Draw an imaginary line half way up your visual field then look at the cup and the paper, the book and the file, the window and the other objects far away. How about the things that are furthest away – which half of the visual field do they tend to be in? The top half or the bottom half?

3. Hold one finger as far away from you as you can. Focus on it then slowly bring the finger towards you until it touches your nose. What happened to your eyes as you kept the finger in focus?

4. Hold your finger up with your arm extended as far as it will go. Close one eye and line up the edge of the finger with a vertical line at a distance like the edge of the window or the corner of the room. Swap eyes quickly. What happened to the image of the finger? Swap back and forth a couple of times between eyes to see the effect again

Now try this again but this time keep your finger as near to your eye as you can. Can you see a difference in the effect with your finger near your eye compared to the effect with your finger at arm's length?

Make brief notes about what you observed

Here is what you have probably observed; the outcomes of your observations form the basis of more cues, which psychologists suggest are used by our perceptual system to detect the third dimension of depth or distance:

1. You will have seen more detail on the back of the hand and less on the wall at the other side of the room. Psychologists refer to this as the **gradient of texture** the level of detail seen increases as objects are nearer.

2. The things that are near to you are more likely to be in the bottom half of your visual field and the things further away are more likely to be in the top half. Psychologists refer to this as **height in the vertical plane.**

3. As your finger approached your eyes they needed to converge to focus on the finger. You will have gone cross-eyed if you brought your finger close enough. This is referred to simply as **convergence**.

4. As you switched eyes the finger would cease to be lined up with the vertical line you chose. You may have experienced the sensation of your finger jumping from one side to the other, especially if you repeated the action quickly. Comparing the experience with the finger close to your eye and at arms length you should be able to notice that the finger seems to jump much further when it is near. This experience of jumping fingers results from the fact that each eye has a slightly different picture of the scene and switching between eyes in this way gives a clear comparison of the two pictures. This difference in pictures is referred to as **retinal disparity** and the amount of retinal disparity

tells the brain how close or far the object is; large retinal disparity means the object is close, small retinal disparity means it is far.

Whilst the eyes take information about the scene to the brain then, the brain makes decisions about how far away things are by combining these cues (and others not mentioned here). It asks how much **detail** there is in the objects, how far up the **vertical plane** they are, how much the eyes have to **converge** to focus on the objects and how much **retinal disparity** there is for each object. Putting all these cues together allows it to make a decision about the distance of each object from the eye or about how much depth there is in an object. Of course, we do not experience any of these processes, we just perceive an object as nearer or further, shallow or deeper.

**Monocular Depth Cues and Binocular Depth Cues**

---

Two of the above four **depth cues** depend on the use of two eyes and will not work if a person only has the use of one eye. These cues are referred to as **binocular** (two eye) cues. The other two cues work even with one eye and are referred to as **monocular** (one eye) cues. Work out which is binocular and which is monocular. Correct answers are in the Feedback section. Check your answers against them now.

---

**A good illustration of the importance of binocular cues for you to try.** Close one eye, get up and carefully move around your house or other area well known to you. You should notice some difficulty in recognising the distance of objects from you as you move around. **We advise you to use only well known areas to avoid accidents.** Of course, if you only have the use of one eye normally, then you already know this point!

---

## 2. The contributions of Gibson

Gibson's work in the 1940s caused him to question the ideas that have been described up to now. He worked on films that trained pilots – early forms of the computer graphics used today. He found that pilots needed surprisingly little information to be able to land a plane successfully in the training equipment.

Eventually, Gibson came to the conclusion that we have no need to make the sorts of assumptions that Gregory's theory promotes. One of the principles of science is "parsimony" – the idea that explanations should be as simple as possible and should not contain any unnecessary concepts or details; if it **can** be left out, then it **should** be left out. Gibson's point was that in most everyday situation, the information we receive via our senses (vision for example) drives our perception and we have no need to call upon the "extra" processes of testing hypotheses which Gregory advocates.

According to Gibson the sensory data (e.g. visual information) is so rich that we form our percept directly from that information and we do not have to go beyond it to perceive what is in front of us. In particular, Gibson suggested we have three types of information from the data that cause us to perceive the stimulus accurately; they are the optic flow patterns, the texture gradient and the affordances.

- **Optic Flow Patterns** These are the patterns of visual information we get when we move. If you have ever played a computer game involving simulated movement (vehicles or people chasing or flying) it may have struck you that the object you are moving is actually kept in the centre of the screen and it is the rest of the picture that moves around the centre. Gibson pointed out that this is what the world really does look like. As we head towards an object we keep it in the centre of our visual field and use the rest of the visual information around it to direct us towards it.
- **Texture Gradients** You have already come across this idea earlier in the lesson. Closer objects give more details, further objects give less.
- **Affordances** This concept is debated by psychologists. Gibson suggested that the use of an object is generally obvious. A chair is obviously for sitting on, stairs are obviously for climbing and so on. These are the objects' affordances. Objects "contain" affordances and these "cause" us to understand their functions and so perceive them accurately.

---

**Affordances – What do You Think?**

If a desert nomad who had never seen a television were to come across a television and a remote control in the middle of the desert, do you think he or she would realise that you should point the remote at the set and press the buttons? Is the affordance of the remote control obvious?

---

Gibson argued that in normal, well lit, everyday environments we do not need to use any of the sophisticated mechanisms of perception that Gregory suggested, so depth is just "there" and we perceive something as distant because of the data we receive, not because of complex psychological process. He did agree that in some circumstances – like visual illusions or poor visual conditions – we might use the sorts of processes that Gregory outlined.

## Feedback
### Monocular Depth Cues and Binocular Depth Cues
The correct answers are:

| Monocular Cues | Binocular Cues |
| --- | --- |
| Superposition | Convergence |
| Perspective | Retinal Disparity |
| Retinal Image Size | |
| Gradient of Texture | |
| Height in the Vertical Plane | |

# Lesson 47
# The Factors Affecting Perception

## 1. Introduction

In previous lessons the perceptual system was seen to be an active process which translates sensory data into a model of the "outside" world in an organised way but which sometimes produces errors which we know as visual illusions and distortions.

In this final lesson on perception we shall see some of the factors which influence our perceptual system and which can explain why one person may perceive a stimulus one way whilst somebody else may perceive the same stimulus in a completely different way.

## 2. The factors affecting perception

**Motivation**

Motives are our reasons for doing something. They are not always obvious to us or to others. Psychologists study a range of things that can be seen as motives; sometimes, biological needs like hunger, thirst or sex are seen as motives.

In a study of people who had not eaten for some time, Gilchrist and Nesburg presented pictures and asked the participants to rate how bright they thought the photographs were. Some of the photographs were of food and some were of other items.

> Can you predict which photographs the participants consistently rated as brighter?

The photographs of food were rated as brighter than any other item. This suggests that the way that people perceive objects can be influenced by their motives. In this case the motivation was hunger. One of the most famous psychologists, Sigmund Freud, suggested that errors of speech can reveal our true motives sometimes; words like "organism" can often be misread as "orgasm" and our perception of the word in front of us may tell us more about our real motives than about our eyesight.

**Perceptual Set**

Perceptual Set refers to a predisposition to perceive images or objects one way rather than another. A variety of influences can give us a perceptual set. In a study in America in the late 1940s, Minturn and Bruner asked two groups of children to adjust a disc of light projected onto a screen until it was the same size as a specified coin. One group of children was from rich families: the other was from poor families.

All the children consistently set the disc bigger than real coins but the children from poor families always set the light bigger than the size set by rich children.

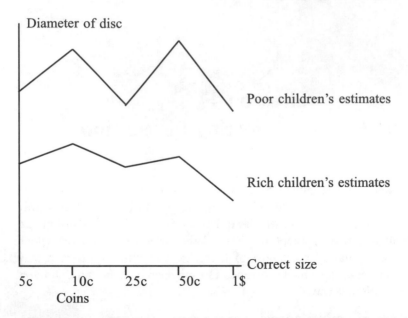

**The results of Minturn and Bruner's study of the size of coins as perceived by children from rich families and children from poor families**

There is more than one possible explanation of this finding. Minturn and Bruner argued that the children from poor homes placed more value on money than did the children from rich homes because it was more critical to their daily lives. They considered it to be more important and so exaggerated the size of the disc which represented it – they had a perceptual set which led them to perceive it this way.

It may be that the children from poor homes had less acquaintance with coins and so had not had as much opportunity to learn the correct size as the other children had.

### Emotion

Solley and Haigh asked children to draw a picture of Santa Claus on a number of occasions. As Christmas approached, the pictures got bigger, but after Christmas they got smaller.

It would appear that the excitement of the children caused them to perceive Santa as more important and that this was reflected in the fact that larger pictures were perceived as normal size.

### Previous experience

We expect images to make sense and be meaningful. This has been our previous experience. The distortion of an image caused by Ames's room illusion, described in Lesson 2 is a good example of the way that our perception is affected by our previous experience: in our experience rooms are regular shapes with horizontal floors, not irregular with different sized walls and "raked" floors.

A favourite illustration of the effect of previous experience is the "Paris in the spring" caption on the left. Can you spot the misprint?

> Paris
> in the
> the spring

Try showing the "Paris in the spring" caption to a friend. The answer is in the Feedback section at the end of the lesson

**Context**

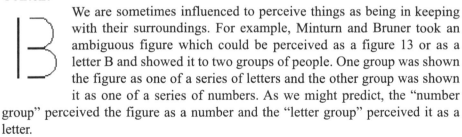
We are sometimes influenced to perceive things as being in keeping with their surroundings. For example, Minturn and Bruner took an ambiguous figure which could be perceived as a figure 13 or as a letter B and showed it to two groups of people. One group was shown the figure as one of a series of letters and the other group was shown it as one of a series of numbers. As we might predict, the "number group" perceived the figure as a number and the "letter group" perceived it as a letter.

**The ambiguous figure used by Minturn and Bruner**

Advertisements often make use of the context of a product to encourage consumers to form a desired perception of it sub-consciously. Cigarettes, for example, can be presented surrounded by images of open countryside, expensive cars or attractive people. Imagine the effect of presenting them within images of disease, stains and foul smells.

**Deprivation**

> Before reading the section below, see how many four-letter words you can list which start with the letters ME—

It may seem obvious that someone who has not eaten for longer than usual should perceive pictures of food as brighter, as in the Gilchrist and Nesburg study (under "Motivation" above), but food deprivation can have even more subtle effects on our perception of images. Sandford asked food-deprived participants to finish off four-letter words beginning with the letters ME— and found that these participants had a much higher use of words that were food related – like meal, menu, meat and mead.

> Find a friend who is on a diet – this is probably easy as about one adult in three is dieting at any given time, according to recent surveys. Try asking the friend to do the ME— word completion task, above, and then compare it with another friend who is not on a diet. Is there a difference in the use of food related words?

**Perceptual defence and perceptual sensitisation**

These phrases refer to the idea that we "defend" ourselves against perceiving things that we do not like or that can harm us in some way, and that we make ourselves more sensitive to things that we like.

Postman, Bruner and McGuiness presented "taboo" words for fractions of a second to participants on a screen. Taboo words are swear words or obscene ones: "forbidden" words. They found that participants had to have the taboo words exposed on the screen for longer than non-taboo words before they could recognise them and this was taken as evidence for the idea that the participants were "defending" themselves against the unpleasant experience of perceiving the taboo words. Of course, it could have been that the participants could perceive the taboo words just as fast as the other words but wanted to be sure that the word really was what they thought it was before reporting it. Also, they may have just been reluctant to tell the researchers what they saw because of their embarrassment.

Exposing people to taboo words in this way can and does shock people. It is not something that psychologists would accept as an ethical practice today and should not be done as part of a psychology study for GCSE or similar studies.

**Culture**

"Culture" refers to the different language, beliefs, attitudes, values, opinions and norms (accepted ways of behaving) which different groups of people have. Language differences between cultures are obvious but other differences can be less noticeable. For example, in France, it is obvious that somebody is speaking another language but perhaps not so obvious that you are expected to tip the person who shows you to your seat in the cinema (a norm).

To give an unusual example of how culture can affect perception consider a description by Turnbull in "The Forest People" published in 1961. He describes how his pygmy guide was leaving the forest for the first time in his life and saw some buffalo in the far distance. He had not seen a "far distance" before and asked what kind of insects the buffalo were. The guide had not been accustomed to making allowances in the size of an object for its distance away. He had never seen more than a few metres in front of him before because of the density of the forest. As far as he was concerned, a small image was just a small object – he had never had to cope with the possibility that a small image could be a large object at a large distance.

## 3. Evaluation of studies on factors affecting perception

**Criticisms**

- Most of the studies in this area are criticised for being artificial, laboratory-based investigations – not investigations of "real" life. They are, therefore, said to lack **ecological validity**. For example, we don't tend to spend time judging the brightness of images, drawing pictures of Santa Claus or altering the diameter of a spot of light.
- We may also be critical of the validity of some of the measures. In particular, does altering a spot of light really measure our values or reflect our culture? Does the size of the drawing really measure any emotional aspect of the children in Solley and Haigh's study? Did the speed with which participants reported taboo words measure their speed of recognising the words or was the speed affected by their embarrassment in saying them out loud to the investigator?

**Praise**

- Examples of perception being set by various factors often are found in real life, even if the studies were artificial. When people write, it is not uncommon for them to repeat a word at the beginning of a second line that finished the first. People often do make slips of the tongue that can be seen as being in line with their everyday concerns – whether it is sexual or not.
- The idea of perceptual set can be useful in understanding the behaviour of individuals and in understanding different cultures and resolving conflicts between either the cultures themselves or between people from different cultures. We can extend our ideas about visual perception to ideas like the perception of one person by

another. For example, we can understand that a person from the Middle East may perceive a European person as "cold" because of the way the European reacts to the death of a relative. At funerals in Europe it is common for people to be sombre and restrained and to sob quietly. In the Middle East people shriek with grief and wring their hands when at a funeral. It is easy to see how the person from the Middle East would perceive the European as "cold".

Similarly, a group of youths standing on a street corner may be seen as "threatening" by a middle aged or elderly person but in reality the youths are unlikely to be any threat at all and may simply be socialising in the only way open to them. This may be because they are too young to visit a public house and their homes are too small to accommodate such a group. The middle aged or elderly person has other ways of meeting groups of people (pubs, clubs etc.) and has not stood around on street corners for many years and so forgets how normal it can be for young people.

## Quick Quiz

**Try this quick quiz to summarise the lesson**
1. Is the following statement true or false?
"One person perceives an object the same way every time he or she comes across it; that person will also perceive it the same way as other people do" (1 mark)
2. Can you name 5 of the 8 factors affecting perception without looking back at the previous pages? (5 marks)
3. Many studies illustrate the effect of more than one factor affecting perception: which factor is Minturn and Bruner's ambiguous figure study used to illustrate in these materials? (1 mark)
4. Fill in the two missing words "Ames's Room Illusion is a good example of the way that our perception is affected by our_____ _____ " (2 marks)
5. Give a criticism of Postman, Bruner and McGuiness's "taboo word" study. (1 mark)

| Paris |
| in the |
| the spring |

## Feedback on the Factors Affecting Perception
**Did you spot the misprint?**

As you probably realised, the word "the" is repeated

**Quick Quiz Answers**
1  False (1 mark)
2  Motivation, Perceptual Set, Emotion, Previous Experience, Context, Deprivation, Perceptual Defence/Sensitisation and culture. (1 mark for each up to a maximum of 5 marks).
3  Context (1 mark)
4  Previous experience (1 mark per word; 2 marks)
5  It may have been embarrassment or uncertainty that caused the participants to need longer exposures of taboo than non-taboo words. (1 mark)
**Total possible marks = 10**

# Lesson 48
# The Development of Perception

## The Nature/Nurture Debate

Do we inherit our characteristics or do we learn them? Is it nurture (we learn the characteristics) or is it nature (we inherit them). This is a common debate among non-psychologists as well as psychologists. It is a particularly important topic when we consider intelligence and mental illness but we also need to consider it when we look at our perception abilities. In reality, the answer to the question is likely to be neither one nor the other but both. In this lesson we shall examine evidence that demonstrates that both factors influence perception.

## 1. The role of Nature in the development of perception

### Neonate studies

"Neonate" means "new-born". If an ability is inherited, then it should be present in newborn babies. It is not always easy to tell if an ability is present in a newborn, however, because it is unable to communicate well enough to tell us or answer our questions. Some ingenious ways of investigating the perceptual abilities of neonates have been devised, however.

(a) **Fantz's studies**. Fantz devised equipment that allowed psychologists to expose a pair of patterns to a baby and measure the amount of time the baby stared at each pattern in the pair. The patterns ranged from simple ones to more and more complex ones. For example, even babies as young as one week old showed differences in the time they looked at the pairs of patterns below in Fig 1:

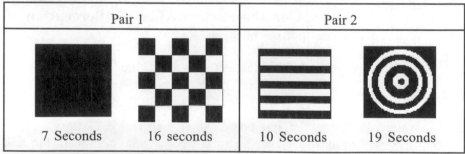

| Pair 1 | | Pair 2 | |
|---|---|---|---|
| 7 Seconds | 16 seconds | 10 Seconds | 19 Seconds |

**Fig 1 Time spent by babies looking at figures in Fantz's studies**

(b) **Gibson and Walk's Visual Cliff**

In a 1960 study of babies, Gibson and Walk devised a piece of equipment that consisted of a table covered with a chequered pattern and then covered with a piece of glass. The glass continued beyond the edge of the table and was supported at its far edge so that a baby could crawl across the piece of glass. The chequered pattern, however, dropped below the glass and onto the floor so it could be seen clearly that there was a drop under the glass. There is a diagram of the equipment in Fig 2.

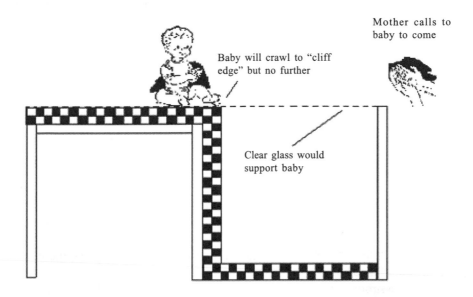

**Fig 2 Diagram of Gibson and Walk's Visual Cliff**

Babies tended not to cross the glass surface to their mothers. This was seen as evidence that the babies could recognise the drop and that they had a fear of falling to the floor below. Psychologists concluded that babies, therefore, had an inborn ability to perceive depth and this perceptual ability would have to be the influence of heredity.

Some researchers pointed out that the babies could not have been newborn because they could crawl; it is possible that babies have had plenty of opportunity to learn about depth by the time they are old enough to crawl (for example from rolling off a cushion onto the carpet).

## Human Deprivation Studies

**Cataracts** are growths that cover the eye and can produce blindness. Hebb studied reports of cases in which adults who had been blind from birth because of cataracts. In this case, the adults' eyes had been deprived of light stimulation since birth. They had undergone surgery to remove the cataracts and give them sight for the first time as adults. Some perceptual abilities seemed to be present from birth: patients could distinguish an object from its background and follow moving objects amongst other things. Some abilities, like recognising the faces of people they knew, only developed with time, however.

These cataract patient studies show some evidence that perceptual abilities are inherited but underline the idea that perception is unlikely to be either innate or learnt, but a combination of the two.

## 2. The role of nurture in the development of perception

### Animal Deprivation Studies

Some animal studies provide evidence that some perceptual abilities are leant. Of course, human beings are animals but they are not the same as the animals studied in the examples below. The human brain is different from that of a cat, for example. It may be argued that these studies cannot be applied to humans, therefore. Others argue that there are big similarities between the way a cat's brain works and the way a human's works. For this reason, they argue, we can learn a lot about the workings of a human's brain by studying cats.

These studies may seem cruel. They highlight some of the ethical problems faced by researchers when using animals:

- The studies could not be carried out on humans
- Is the information provided by the studies beneficial enough to "excuse" the treatment of the few animals involved?

### (a) Kittens raised in vertical or horizontal worlds

Blakemore and Cooper raised kittens in darkness but exposed them to light for five hours a day. During this period the kittens were only allowed to see either horizontal lines or vertical ones, not both. After five months, the researchers found that the kittens would only recognise the lines to which they had been exposed. They were "blind" to the other types of lines in the sense that they did not respond to them and acted as though they had not seen them.

The environment in which they had been raised had therefore, influenced the perceptual abilities of the kittens. This suggests that some perceptual abilities at least are the result of the influence of the environment.

### (b) Kittens with closed eyelids

Hubel sewed together the eyelids on one eye of newly born kittens so that they could not open it as they matured. Some kittens had this treatment to their left eye and some to the right. The part of the kitten's brain which corresponded to each eye was then investigated. Hubel found that the part of the brain corresponding to whichever eye had been sewn up at birth was underdeveloped. The part corresponding to the "open" eye was far more developed than normal.

This suggests that the part of the brain corresponding to vision develops with stimulation from the environment and "shrinks" without stimulation. In this way the environment can be seen to influence the development of perceptual abilities.

### Readjustment Studies

Studies of babies can be flawed because it is very difficult to be sure of what they are really experiencing, as opposed to adults, who can tell us what they perceive. In the following studies, adults have been shown to adjust their perceptual ability; this suggests that perception is a learnt ability.

### Inverting Goggles

A number of researchers have experimented by wearing goggles that inverted the visual image so they saw the world upside down and/or left to right. The first to record the results of such a study was Stratton in 1896. He wore a telescope that inverted the image in one eye, covering the other, for a period of eight days.

He reported seeing the world as upside down but not feeling that this was odd after three or four days. His perceptual processes were able to adjust to the point that he no longer experienced the inverted image as strange.

**Cross-Cultural Studies**

If different cultures perceive the same image differently, this would suggest that the members of each culture have learnt to perceive (since both cultures would have inherited the same visual equipment). A number of studies have shown such a difference. For example, the Muller-Lyer illusion was demonstrated earlier in this section.

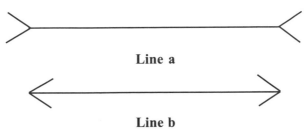

**Line a**

**Line b**

**Fig 3 The Muller-Lyer Illusion**

Line a and Line b are the same length but Line a seems longer to most Europeans. Segall showed this visual illusion to a range of cultures in the early 1960s and found that although Americans were "fooled" by it, South Africans of European descent and people in the Philippines were much less likely to see any difference in the length of the lines.

Other studies comparing African cultures with European and North American cultures show further differences in perception. In 1960, Hudson reported how he had shown a collection of line drawings to a variety of different cultures in Africa. The drawings were of hunters and animals in various positions. As an example, in one case, an elephant was depicted on a hill in the distance. Some participants in the study perceived the elephant as the American artist had intended it but some cultural groups described the elephant as being a tiny elephant on a mound of earth in the foreground rather than a normal size elephant in the distance.

Hudson realised that different cultures perceive three-dimensional information differently.

## 3. Summary

We have seen evidence from studies of neonates, animals and adults. Some of the studies demonstrate the influence of the environment on perception and some demonstrate the influence of heredity.

> To help you remember which studies support environmental influences and which ones support heredity, put the following terms into the following table: Gibson and Walk's Visual Cliff; Hubel's closed-eye kittens; Inverting goggles; Cataract Patients; Cross-cultural studies; Fantz's studies; Blakemore and Cooper's horizontal/vertical line kittens. The correct answer follows.

| Influence of Heredity | Influence of Environment |
|---|---|
|  |  |
|  |  |
|  |  |
|  |  |

## 4. Evaluation of research

Some evaluative points have been made about the research already but it is useful to consider the value of the research as a whole.

- The animal studies only tell us about non-human animals and although human visual structures and processing look to be very similar to other animals it does not mean to say that our development is the same as other animals.
- Some of the animal studies have ethical issues surrounding them. Should we really be carrying out studies that damage the visual system of animals?
- Children, and neonates in particular, cannot communicate fully with researchers and we can only infer what the child is experiencing.
- When is a neonate not a neonate? Some of the babies studied have been six months old and thus had the opportunity to develop learned perceptual processes – we are not studying the influence of "raw" nature, therefore.

## Feedback on the Development of Perception

| Influence of Heredity | Influence of Environment |
|---|---|
| Gibson and Walk's Visual Cliff | Hubel's closed-eye kittens |
| Cataract Patients | Inverting goggles |
| Fantz's Studies | Blakemore and Cooper's horizontal/ vertical line kittens |

# AQA Exam Style Questions: Perception

- **Answer all questions**
- **There is no time limit to this assignment**
- **When completed you may compare your answers with the example answers at the end of the book**
- **If you have tutorial support you should send a copy of your answers to your tutor to receive further feedback, comments and guidance**

Psychologists investigated people's reactions to the sketch shown below

Sketch 7

**Condition 1:**
30 participants were shown ten sketches of **young** women; sketch 7 is shown on the left

**Condition 2:**
30 participants were shown ten sketches of **elderly** women; sketch 7 is shown on the left

All participants were then asked to estimate the ages of the women shown in sketches three, seven and ten; their responses were then classified into age groups of "Old" and "Young". The responses to sketch seven are shown in Table 1.

Table 1: Number of people who classified sketch seven as Old or Young

|  | CONDITION 1 | CONDITION 2 |
|---|---|---|
| CLASSIFIED SKETCH 7 AS OLD | 1 | 29 |
| CLASSIFIED SKETCH 7 AS YOUNG | 28 | 2 |

(a) Describe the results of the study (2 marks)

(b) Explain how the results provide evidence for perception being an active process. (5 marks)

(c) It was discovered later that the two people in condition 2 who classified sketch 7 as young were a pair of elderly twin women who had featured in the tabloid newspapers that same week becoming famous for having "toy boy" companions in their early twenties.

(i) What does this tell us about how previous experience, motivation and emotion may influence perception? (3 marks)

(ii) Describe a study that investigates how perceptual defence may influence perception. (5 marks)

(d)

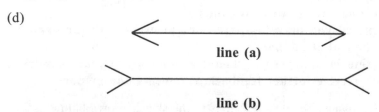

**line (a)**

**line (b)**

(i) The diagram above is the Muller-Lyer illusion. What type of illusion is it? (Tick the appropriate box)

    Distortion
    Ambiguous figure
    Texture Gradient

(1 mark)

(ii) Most people see line (b) as longer than line (a). Use your knowledge of psychology to explain this effect. (4 marks)

**Total possible marks = 20**

When completed you should compare your answers with the example answers at the end of the book. If you have tutorial support you should send a copy of your answers to the tutor for feedback, comments and further guidance.

# OCR Exam Style Questions: Perception

- **Answer all questions**
- **There is no time limit to this assignment**
- **When completed you may compare your answers with the example answers at the end of the book**
- **If you have tutorial support you should send a copy of your answers to your tutor to receive further feedback, comments and guidance**

Cognitive Psychology
Perception

---

## Perceptual Constancy

Perceptual constancy is the ability to keep our perception of an object constant even though the image of it on our eye is distorted from how we know it to be.

Turnbull studied a tribe of pygmies in the Congo in the 1960s. They had no experience of seeing for long distances as they lived in dense jungle and had never experienced seeing more than a short distance in front of them. When he took one of the tribe out of the forest and onto the plain the pygmy thought that buffalo in the distance were insects. This is because the image of the buffalo on the eye is about the same size as an insect close up. The pygmy had to be taken up to the buffalo and was confused as to how they had "grown" as he got closer.

---

1. According to source A, what is perceptual constancy? (1 mark)

2. What type of perceptual constancy had the pygmy in source A not acquired? (2 marks)

3. Name **one** type of perceptual constancy **other than the one in question 2** and give a brief explanation of what it is.
**(Name)** (1 mark)
**(Explanation)** (3 marks)

4. What is a "Depth Cue"? (2 marks)

5. Describe **one** depth cue with which you are familiar. (3 marks)

6. Describing and evaluating two psychological studies, outline the role of nature and nurture in the development of perception. (8 marks)

**Total possible marks = 20**
When completed you should compare your answers with the example answers at the end of the book. If you have tutorial support you should send a copy of your answers to the tutor for feedback, comments and further guidance.

# Lesson 49
# Stress

## 1. What is Stress?

The word "Stress" is used in two ways:

i.   The "force" or "pressure" on a person which causes psychological and physical problems (e.g. "I'm under a lot of stress at work at the moment"). In this use, the stress is the **cause** of the problem.

ii.  The response an individual has to events and conditions which are seen as dangerous or threatening. (e.g. "The doctor says I'm suffering from stress"). In this use, the stress is the **effect** of the problem.

This double use of the word can be confusing but each use is considered separately in this lesson.

## 2. Signs of Stress:

**The Physiological (biological) Signs of Stress: Seyle's General Adaptation Syndrome (GAS)**

**Stage 1 The Alarm Reaction**

When a person is subjected to a stressful experience the Fight or Flight response is triggered

**The Fight or flight response**

Have you ever had a "shock" experience like one of the following?

* You are walking along the street when a loud bang rings out – perhaps a car backfiring or something falling.
* You are dozing in a chair when someone drops something with a clang.

> Make a note of any such experience.

After experiences like these did you have any of the following symptoms?
(Tick the box for any you remember)

☐ Your heartbeat became fast and strong
☐ You started to breath more rapidly and noticeably
☐ You had a strange feeling in your stomach ("butterflies" in the stomach)
☐ You started to sweat

Did the symptoms persist for some time after the event? For example, a few minutes after you realised the loud bang was just someone dropping a ladder you still felt shaky?

Psychologists refer to this reaction to emergency situations as the Fight or Flight Response. It is common in these situations and can be mild or very strong. It can occur in extreme situations like riding the roller coaster, or in mild ones like receiving slightly offhand treatment from a shop assistant. It includes

**Heart rate:** increases (we feel our heart beating more strongly)
**Respiration:** increases (we start to pant)
**Digestion:** slowed down (we feel "butterflies" in the stomach)
**Pupils (eyes):** dilated (opened)
**Blood flow:** directed from the surface of the skin to the major muscles in the thighs and arms (we go pale)
**Sweating:** starts

The response is called the "Fight or Flight" reaction because it seems to prepare us to fight or to flee – the same physiological changes are necessary for both – e.g. we increase respiration to get more oxygen into the lungs and so on into the muscles which allows us to fight or to flee.

> Turn to the table summarising Seyle's GAS at the end of this section and write in the name of the first stage

### Stage 2 Resistance

The fight or flight reaction seems best suited to a quick, sharp shock but stress occurs when a person is subjected to harmful experiences over a period of time. Although the body is prepared for fighting or fleeing we do not, in reality either fight or flee. In this case, the second stage of the GAS comes into play. Nervous system activity falls and heartbeat, blood pressure etc. return to normal but the outer layer of the adrenal gland starts to secrete hormones like cortisone, which control the glucose in the blood so the body can cope with the continued stress. Selye called this stage "resistance" because the body is resisting the pressure put on it by the stress.

> Write this name into the second space of the summary table of Seyle's GAS

### Stage 3 Exhaustion

As the name implies, this stage occurs when the body's ability to produce the hormones for resistance fails. The resources needed to produce the hormones are depleted and blood glucose levels drop. **Psychosomatic** disorders like heart disease, high blood pressure, asthma and stomach ulcers may result. By this point the body's immune system has become damaged and so we are much more susceptible to viruses like flu or colds. Recent research suggests that ulcers may be due to bacteria rather than direct stress, but lack of a strong immune system will make us more susceptible to the effects of the bacteria. The name "exhaustion" again describes the situation at this third stage well.

> Write this name into the third space of the summary table of Seyle's GAS

| Summary Seyle's General Adaptation Syndrome (GAS) | |
|---|---|
| Stage | Name |
| 1 | |
| 2 | |
| 3 | |

**Physiological Ways of Measuring Stress**

There are medical devices that measure all the physiological indicators listed above but some of them are not convenient for people to use in day-to-day situations. However, readily available methods include:

- **Heart Rate**: heart rate can be measured easily via the pulse rate.
- **Sweating**: a simple hand-held device called the Galvanic Skin Response meter will pass a tiny current of electricity (from a torch battery) over the surface of the skin of the hand. When we sweat, the resistance to the current is decreased and the meter detects this. The meter can indicate the level of sweating by emitting a whistle, which becomes a lower tone as stress decreases or vice-versa. These meters are available to the public.

The **Polygraph** is a machine that can measure more than one of these indicators at once. It is better known as a "lie-detector" and uses the physiological changes to indicate the level of stress that the respondent is experiencing. The rationale behind this is that someone will experience more stress when they lie and this will be shown by the physiological measures.

## 3. Psychological Signs of Stress

Some signs are **cognitive** – they are to do with the mental aspects of the person, for example anxiety and anger. Other aspects are **behavioural** – they are to do with the way the person behaves, for example aggression and helplessness.

**Anxiety:** This is probably the most widely reported reaction to stressful pressures. The Section of these learning materials covering the topic of Obedience (Lesson 5 of the Section on Social Influence) describes Milgram's study in which participants are placed under a great pressure with some believing they have killed another person. The report of the study describes the participants as showing many of the symptoms of anxiety listed in part 1 of this lesson – "sweating, breathing problems, insomnia and crying." – "includes a feeling of worry or apprehension that something bad is going to happen – a foreboding."

**Anger and Aggression:** Aggression is an act which is designed to harm someone whilst anger is the emotion which accompanies it. Green and Berkowitz showed how someone who is under stress is more likely to respond with aggressive behaviour. They asked a group to solve a puzzle, which, in reality was unsolvable. The group could see a confederate (working secretly with the researcher) apparently solving his puzzle and the confederate insulted the participants, commenting on their stupidity.

When the participants were given the opportunity to punish "learners" by giving them electric shocks (so they thought) in a subsequent activity, it was found that the participants who had been insulted gave significantly more shocks than those who had not been insulted or who had been given a solvable puzzle at which they had succeeded.

**Depression:** Seligman suggested that when people are in stressful situations, which they think they are unable to control, then they learn to feel helpless and give up attempting to do anything about the stress. He first demonstrated this with dogs that were placed in boxes that delivered electric shocks to the paws. The dogs were unable to escape from the boxes. When the dogs were put into boxes from which they **could** escape they failed to try. Seligman referred to this as

**learned helplessness**. Similar studies with humans found the same thing. Klein et al gave their participants a motor task to complete which would supposedly terminate a noise when accomplished. The task could not be completed and when the participants were given a task that **could** be completed they failed to try. This illustrates the concept of learned helplessness but Seligman suggested that if people experience continued learned helplessness they will eventually develop **learned hopelessness** – a term which can be seen as depression.

### Psychological ways of measuring stress
### Performance

The psychological reactions generally lead to loss of performance. For example, cognitive tasks in which people have to concentrate are likely to be performed badly if they are subjected to too much stress. This could mean, perhaps that a student's work will receive lower marks than usual or a person's performance at work may become noticeably worse as they become distracted from the task. The relationship between stress and performance is not quite so straightforward, however, as a small amount of stress can **improve** performance – this is captured in the **Yerkes-Dodson Law.**

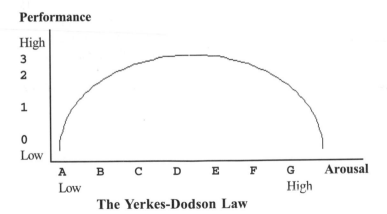

The Yerkes-Dodson Law

You will note that arousal is a good thing up to a point (point D on the graph above) because it causes an improvement of performance; any further arousal causes a fall in performance, however. Stress causes arousal so it too can be a good thing up to a point. Being stressed going into an exam is useful. The fight or flight reaction causes us to be alert and energetic, looking for success. These are all good qualities for exam candidates. If the stress is too much, however, the Yerkes-Dodson Law says that we go beyond an optimum point and our performance falls. This is when we need to do something about the stress.

### Compensatory Behaviour

People sometimes "make up" for the stress with behaviour that is out of the ordinary for them. For example, smoking more heavily or taking up smoking; changes in eating behaviour – either by increasing or decreasing; perhaps other forms might include becoming obsessive about something, becoming excessively tidy, for example.

### The Holmes-Rahe Social Readjustment Rating Scale

This is a list of events with "points" allocated to each event; it ranges from 100 for the death of a spouse to 11 points for a parking fine. Holmes and Rahe found a direct correlation between the number of points and the level of illness experienced by people. This scale can, therefore, be completed by people to assess their level of stress.

---

**Quick Quiz**
1. Name two **physiological** signs of stress
2. Name two **psychological** ways of measuring stress
Answers in the Feedback section below

---

**Check your reactions to stress**

Think back to a time when you have acted aggressively (an act designed to harm someone) or felt angry (the feeling which accompanies the act). Now, can you remember any surrounding circumstances that may have caused you to act in this way? Would you normally have not shown such aggression?

A problem with this sort of case-study evidence is that you cannot necessarily remember accurately the event or the circumstances. You may repress the memory or you may not have been aware at the time of the circumstances.

---

## Feedback

### Quick Quiz

1. Increased heart rate; ulcers
2. Performance changes; the Holmes-Rahae Social Readjustment Rating Scale

# Lesson 50
# Causes of Stress

## 1. Environmental Causes

**Noise:** Noise can be defined as "unwanted sound"; so what is good music to one set of ears can be noise to another. Glass et al played noise in two forms to two groups. The first group had noise that occurred at regular, predictable intervals. The second group had noise that occurred at random, unpredictable intervals. Both groups were asked to perform a task as the noise was played. Both groups were able to cope with the noise because the performance of both groups improved by the end of the session. The first group, with the predictable noise, performed better than the second group however. So whilst noise can cause stress, it can be overcome to some extent but it is more difficult to overcome unpredictable noise.

**Crowding:** Crowding occurs when people feel uncomfortable with the number of people surrounding them. This differs from person to person. Calhoun put rats in an enclosed space with sufficient food and water and adequate space. As the rats reproduced and multiplied in number he noted a deterioration in the social behaviour of the rats until they were carrying out large numbers of aggressive acts, the young were not being cared for, many young were dying and other unusual acts like withdrawal were observed. This suggests that stress levels increase with overcrowding, but of course these were rats, not humans and it may be a mistake to make direct comparisons between the two. Also, the measures of stress were indirect; can all these acts be interpreted as stress?

**Heat:** Baron and Ransberger looked back over the records of criminal proceedings for acts of violence and the records of air temperature in an area of the USA over a period of four years. They found a correlation between the two, which suggests that as air temperature increases, so does the incidence of violence. Again, we have to be sure that acts of violence really do reflect levels of stress. Even then, it is possible that the air temperature merely caused more people to come out of their houses and this would automatically mean more people on the streets and more opportunities for violence between people: it could even have been crowding that led to violence. Other laboratory studies carried out by Baron do show more aggressive acts with higher temperatures.

## 3. Life Events as a Cause of Stress

### The stress response to life events

Holmes and Rahe constructed a list of 43 events which they found had happened to patients in the few months just before their illnesses. All the events involved some form of adjustment to the way one lived, or some form of change, so they asked people to rank the events according to how much adjustment was needed.

This resulted in the Social Readjustment Rating Scale (SRRS) which assigns "scores" (mean values) to each event based on these rankings. A list of the events and their "scores" is given below, however the original was American and was constructed in 1967 so some small changes have been made to the list to make it more applicable to the present day United Kingdom.

| Mean Value (Score) | Event |
| --- | --- |
| 100 | Death of spouse |
| 73 | Divorce |
| 65 | Marital separation |
| 63 | Jail term |
| 63 | Death of close family member |
| 53 | Personal injury or illness |
| 50 | Marriage |
| 47 | Sacked from job |
| 45 | Marital reconciliation |
| 45 | Retirement |
| 44 | Change in health of family member |
| 40 | Pregnancy |
| 39 | Sex difficulties |
| 39 | Gain a new family member |
| 39 | Business readjustment |
| 38 | Change in financial state |
| 37 | Death a close friend |
| 36 | Change to different line of work |
| 35 | Change in number of arguments with spouse |
| 31 | Substantial mortgage |
| 30 | Foreclosure of mortgage or loan |
| 29 | Change in responsibilities at work |
| 29 | Son or daughter leaving home |
| 29 | Trouble with in-laws |
| 28 | Outstanding personal achievement |
| 26 | Wife begins or stops work |
| 26 | Begin or end school |
| 25 | Change in living conditions |
| 24 | Revision of personal habits |
| 23 | Trouble with boss |
| 20 | Change in work hours or conditions |
| 20 | Change in residence |
| 20 | Change in schools |
| 19 | Change in recreation |
| 19 | Change in church activities |
| 18 | Change in social activities |
| 17 | Smaller mortgage or loan |
| 16 | Change in sleeping habits |

| 15 | Change in family get-togethers |
| 15 | Change in eating habits |
| 13 | Holiday |
| 12 | Christmas |
| 11 | Minor violation of the law |

**Holmes and Rahe's Social Readjustment Rating Scale**
The Social Readjustment Rating scale was related to the late 1960s so it is likely that unmarried partners would suffer similar degrees of adjustment and stress if they separated nowadays as a married pair did in 1967.

Similarly, major religious festivals other than Christmas would probably result in similar levels of stress for members of that religion.

Conversely, it may be that mortgages and loans have become much more common today compared to 1967 so the stress caused by these factors may be less.

It may seem strange to think of holidays and Christmas as stressful events but positive correlations have been found between people's scores on the SRRS and the onset of illness – both physical and mental illness. Many people do report holidays as stressful and Christmas can be a time when people fall out more easily.

**Evaluation of Holmes and Rahe's SRRS**
- The scale has been shown by some researchers to predict illness and other disturbance through stress
- The scale is very easy to administer since participants only have to tick each item
- The categories are not necessarily applicable to today
- Smaller events may be more highly correlated with a person's stress level at the moment. For example, being late for work, receiving an annoying message, having a child off school with a cold – all of these could be causing high levels of stress for a person here and now but they would not show up on the SRRS questionnaire. This idea was investigated by Lazarus who found that there is indeed a relationship between what he called the "hassles and uplifts of everyday life" and stress.

---

**Check your adjustment rating**
Run through the Holmes Rahe SRRS ticking each item that applies to you; which of them has happened to you over a period of the last three months? Total the value of all the events that have happened to you. Holmes and Rahe found that totals of 300 or more were predictors of imminent ill health and high stress levels

---

## 2. Individual Differences
**Personality** Friedman and Rosenman suggested that there are two different types of personality, Type A and Type B. The former type is more likely to suffer stress. A long-term study by the Western Collaborative Group supported the findings
**Personality Type A**
- Middle Class
- Male

- American
- Chronic sense of time urgency
- Excessive competitive drive
- Very aggressive and hostile towards others
- Sets deadlines
- Does several things simultaneously
- Feels insecure
- Needs positive regard from others to support his self-esteem

**Personality Type B**

- Energetic
- Hard-working
- Relaxed and practical attitude to work
- Not worried about uncontrollable events
- Able to "shut off" from work at the end of the day

Type B people worked just as hard as Type A but they worked in a different way and achieved just as much. The Western Collaborative Group Study covered over 3000 men during an eight year longitudinal study and found Type A men were over twice as likely to develop heart diseases and over twice as likely to suffer heart attacks. This does indicate a positive relationship between personality and stress.

---

**Quick Quiz**

1. In Glass et al's study of noise, what was the difference between the noise situation where it caused stress and the situation where it did not? (1 mark)
2. Give one criticism of Calhoun's study of crowded rats as a cause of human stress. (1 mark)
3. What two variables did Baron correlate when he studied heat as a cause of stress? (2 marks)
4. How did Friedman and Rosenman measure stress in their study of personality types and stress?

---

## Feedback

**Quick Quiz Answers**

1. The predictability of the noise (1 mark)
2. Humans are not rats and do not necessarily behave like them. (1 mark)
3. Air temperature and recorded acts of violence. (2 marks)
4. Illnesses like heart diseases. (1 mark)

Total marks = 5

# OCR Exam Style Questions: Stress

- Answer all questions
- There is no time limit to this assignment
- When completed you may compare your answers with the example answers at the end of the book
- If you have tutorial support you should send a copy of your answers to your tutor to receive further feedback, comments and guidance

**Source Bio-psychology**
**Stress**

---

A note is circulated to all staff:

**Stress at Work**

As part of management's commitment to supporting staff in attaining the right Work/Life balance, the board of directors has arranged for Stress Limits Limited to visit the offices next month. Stress Limits Limited will help any staff who want to take advantage of their services by:

- Performing a complete individual Stress Audit
- Pinpointing the sources of stress in your life – both at work and at home
- Recommend suitable methods of stress control so staff can cope with the demands of work, family and other areas of life.

The service will be completely free and completely confidential. Any member of staff wishing to take advantage of this service should contact Personnel

---

1. According to the source, where may the sources of stress be? (1 mark)

2. Give a definition of stress (2 marks)

3. Outline the physiological signs of stress (4 marks)

4. Outline **one** behavioural sign of stress (4 marks)

5. Describe **one** physiological way of measuring stress (4 marks)

6. Describe research into **two** causes of stress, for example heat, noise, pollution, architecture, crowding or stressful life events. (5 marks)

**Total possible marks = 20**
When completed you should compare your answers with the example answers at the end of the book. If you have tutorial support you should send a copy of your answers to the tutor for feedback, comments and further guidance.

# Lesson 51
# Sex and Gender – Definitions

## 1. The distinction between Sex and Gender

**Sex**

**Sex** refers to physical and biological facts. Our sexes are "Female" and "Male"

| **Female** involves the physical facts of: | **Male** involves the physical facts of: |
|---|---|
| • two X chromosomes ovaries<br>• a womb<br>• a vagina<br>• a high level of the hormone oestrogen | • one X chromosome and one Y •<br>• chromosome<br>• testes<br>• sperm ducts<br>• a penis<br>• a high level of the hormone testosterone |

**Gender**

**"Gender"** refers to social and psychological characteristics attached to sex.

| **Female** gender is often seen as: | **Male** gender is often seen as: |
|---|---|
| • tender-minded<br>• "emotional"<br>• caring | • tough-minded<br>• unemotional<br>• uncaring<br>• "technical" |

Sex and gender tend to go together. People who are physically male tend to think of their gender as male too and vice versa. Sometimes, people who are one sex think of their gender as the opposite. "Camp drag queens" and male and female transvestites (people who dress in opposite-sex clothes) may be extreme examples of this opposite gender concept but more subtle versions exist in larger numbers. Many women will think of themselves as having characteristics often attributed to males. They may, for example think of themselves as "tough". Women often joke about men being "soft" at heart really. Some men may think of themselves as being "soft" and they may also feel uncomfortable about that idea. Also, a small number of people are born with mixtures of male and female physical characteristics – hermaphrodites.

**Sex typing**

**Sex typing** involves classifying things, people and behaviours into male or female categories. For example, children classify toys and games into male and female, playing football is commonly seen as a male behaviour and pink ribbons are seen as female objects. We sex type ourselves of course.

**Sex Identity**

**Sex Identity** refers to the way we see our biological make up. We have the physical characteristics of the female so we identify our body as a female biologically, and vice versa for males.

**Gender identity**

**Gender Identity** refers to the idea that we classify our self as either male or female in terms of the behaviours and characteristics that go with maleness or femaleness – we identify as a male or a female – hence the term gender identity. This is sometimes called gender concept because it is part of our self-concept (the picture we have of our self).

## 2. Androgyny

Androgyny refers to the existence of both male and female characteristics in one person. To an extent, everybody shows some male and some female characteristics so the term is usually reserved for people who show high levels of both types of characteristics.

Research by Bem suggests that people who are androgynous are mentally healthier than people who have strong, traditional expectations of male and female behaviour. She constructed a measure of maleness and femaleness – the Bem Sex Role Inventory – which measures the extent of male and female characteristics in a person. People who scored high in both male and female areas also scored high on measures of self-esteem and emotional well-being. This may be because high scorers would be more adaptable and have more choice of action in any given situation; they would not have to rely on always acting either like a male or a female.

## 3. Do Males and Females really behave differently?

What differences can we be sure exist in the behaviours of males and females? Are there **any** or do we just have **stereotypes,** mentally attaching certain behaviours to one gender and others to the other gender?

The surprising outcome of research is the lack of a significant number of differences. Maccoby and Jacklin's review of studies, summarised below, outlines the differences found, but it is likely that many more pieces of research discover **no difference.** Studies that find no difference are, perhaps, less likely to be published as they are thought of as "failing" to find anything rather than succeeding in finding nothing! So we tend to hear more about a few differences that are found than we hear about the "no differences" that are found.

**Maccoby and Jacklin's review**

This is still the best-known and most comprehensive study of sex differences even though it was published in 1974. The authors reviewed over 1,500 studies of differences in abilities and behaviours of children up to 12 years. They found:

- **Language differences:** girls were found to be superior at language skills. They had higher verbal abilities. Recent Australian research has suggested that language centres in the brain are 20% bigger in females than in males (fits with the stereotype of women talking more than men).
- **Visuo-spatial abilities:** This involves plans, maps, the ability to recognise shapes and rotate them in the mind, the ability to locate oneself in space. Boys

were found to be superior at this skill (fits with the stereotype of women getting lost with maps)

- **Arithmetic:** Boys were superior at arithmetic reasoning. It may be thought that girls' superior verbal abilities would help them lead in arithmetic too but this was not the case
- **Aggression:** Consistently, boys were shown as more aggressive than girls. This finding has been echoed by later studies of adults which consistently show males as more aggressive than females. The studies involved children as young as 2 years showing this difference.
- **Intelligence:** Girls scored higher on tests of intelligence. (until recently, in Northern Ireland, boys could "pass" the 11 plus and gain a grammar school place with a lower score than girls because the education authority wanted to "even out" the number of boys and girls in grammar schools and girls, on average, scored higher).

Although these differences were found, they were not the large and extensive differences you might expect from the stereotypes of males and females, that are prevalent. They **did,** amusingly confirm comedians' jokes about teenage girls and women spending lots of time on the phone whilst boys want to be train drivers, but the support for even this was very weak.

## 4. Sexual Orientation

Finally, in this lesson on definitions, the term **Sexual Orientation** refers to the way in which people are attracted to (and would prefer sex with) a male or a female.

**Heterosexual** refers to somebody who is sexually attracted to the opposite sex (**hetero** means **opposite**).

**Homosexual** refers to somebody who is sexually attracted to members of the same sex (**homo** means **the same**).

**Bi-sexual** people are attracted to members of both sexes and may be male or female.

---

**Summary Exercise**
(answers below in the Feedback section)
1. What is the difference between sex and gender? (1 mark)
2. State two ways in which male and female behaviour differs according to Maccoby and Jacklin's study (2 marks)
3. Androgyny refers to being extremely male or extremely female – true or false? (1 mark)
4. What is gender identity? (1 mark)

---

## Feedback

1. Sex refers to biological facts, gender refers to the psychological characteristics attributed to each sex
2. e.g. Verbal ability (girls superior) and visuo-spatial ability (boys superior)
3. False. It refers to demonstrating a high level of both male and female characteristics
4. The idea that we define ourselves as one gender or the other.

# Lessson 52
# Becoming Male or Female:
# The Influence of Biology

## 1. Introduction

Look again at the title of this lesson, "Becoming male or female. . .". Surely one simply **is** male or female? It may seem strange to suggest that being male or female results from "The Influence of Biology": surely, being male or female is simply the **result** of biology and nothing else? What else **could** influence it?

Being male or female consists of much more than having the appropriate sex organs. For example, try answering the following questions:

1. What sort of umbrellas do men carry in Brazil?
2. Would men normally walk down the street holding hands with their male friends in India?
3. Would women drive to work in Saudi Arabia?
4. Would a French woman wait on a table in a Paris restaurant?

Here are the answers:

1. None, only girls and women carry umbrellas in Brazil; it's considered unmanly.
2. Yes, they are also likely to have their arms round each other's shoulders if they are young (say, under 25 years).
3. Don't be silly. It is illegal for women to drive cars in Saudi Arabia
4. Usually men wait on tables in Paris restaurants though things are changing – just like men are starting to iron their wives' blouses in Britain!

Being male or female involves all sorts of accepted behaviours, which differ from society to society. The same processes, which are involved in learning the ways of those around us, are involved in learning to be what is accepted as male or female.

The non-biological aspects of being male or female are referred to as "gender" and it is these aspects that we take on through the process of socialisation. These will be dealt with in the next lesson. In this lesson, the biological aspects of sex are covered.

## 2. Genes and heredity

Cells are basic building blocks of the body. Each organ, limb, strand of hair or other part of the body is made from cells. Cells specialise: some specialise in being fingernail cells, some in being stomach-lining cells, some in being brain cells, some in being surface-of-the-tongue cells and so on. In a sense, cells are just a collection of chemicals. Some cells can be seen easily under the microscope.

All cells have common features like membranes on the surface, that act like a sort of "skin" around the cell, and cytoplasm which forms the bulk of the cell and in which hundreds of chemical reactions take place. Each cell also has a nucleus at its centre which controls the things that are going on in the cell: cells die if the nucleus is removed.

### Chromosomes and Genes

Each nucleus contains a number of thread-like bodies called **chromosomes**. In fact, in most human beings each nucleus contains 23 pairs of chromosomes. There are hundreds of **genes** arranged along each chromosome and genes control the way we develop, making us have certain characteristics like a particular eye colour, hair colour, length of tongue, fingerprint, size of nose, colour of skin and so on.

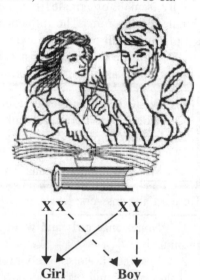

One pair of chromosomes is responsible for the sex of the person. One of the pair is longer than the other; this is called the **X chromosome**. The shorter one is the **Y chromosome**. Men's cells contain one of each, an X and a Y. Women's cells contain two X chromosomes. Each sperm contains only one chromosome so it could be an X or a Y. Women's eggs, however, contain only X chromosomes.

When the egg is fertilised at conception, it could be fertilised by an X sperm or a Y sperm. This means the new child could start off with two X cells or one X and one Y. Two X cells cause the child to be female. One X and one Y cause the child to be male. The diagram opposite shows this process.

X X                   X Y

Girl        Boy

### Hormones

Hormones are chemicals put into the bloodstream by glands inside the body. Some of them are very short-term and have an effect that lasts for as little as a few minutes, but some have an effect lasting for a lifetime. At about twelve to fourteen years of age a set of hormones triggers some important changes in the body which are important for the biological elements of being male or female. This period is known as **puberty**.

The testes (testicles) in the male start to produce the hormone **testosterone** and the female's ovaries produce **oestrogen.** These hormones affect the body's sex organs and give the person the physical characteristics we normally associate with maleness and femaleness.

Testosterone causes the boy's penis to get larger, the voice to break, and hair to start growing on the legs, chest, face and genital area. In girls, oestrogen causes the breasts to develop and fat is laid down in the thighs. Pubic hair starts to grow in the genital area in girls too. These changes are known as secondary sexual characteristics and here again, maleness and femaleness is directly related to biological processes. During this period, interest in sexual activity is likely to increase.

These hormonal differences continue throughout life and so they continue to exert their influences on male and female bodies to give them their relative "rough" and "soft" characteristics respectively. The system of glands and hormones is called the **endocrine system** and can become faulty in some people. In this case, hormone replacement therapy (HRT) can replace the missing hormones to maintain the right balance. Some people think of themselves as being in the wrong body: a man may think of himself as a woman "trapped" in a man's body and vice-versa. Surgery may be used to alter the person's genitals and breasts but hormones need to be introduced through lifetime drug therapy to maintain the secondary sexual characteristics of the "adopted" sex.

## 3. Distinguishing between Sex Identity and Gender Identity

As mentioned in the previous lesson, "sex" refers to biological facts, "gender" refers to psychological or social facts.

### Sex Identity

In general we identify our sex according to our sexual organs. Not everybody has clear sex organs. Some people are born with organs that are not fully formed and surgery can by used to construct a penis or a vagina and breasts later on in life. To do this, however, the decision must be made about whether the child is a boy or a girl. Modern chromosome tests can confirm whether a child has two Xs or one X and one Y chromosome, so it is possible to determine the biological sex without sex organs.

### Gender Identity

It is not always possible to construct male sex organs. There have been cases of boys who have been raised as girls because of this difficulty. Surgeons have constructed a vagina because the boy's penis was severed during circumcision (a procedure to remove the foreskin commonly practised by some religions and sometimes used for medical reasons). Until recently, it was thought that the children had not experienced any difficulty as a result of this. They thought of themselves as girls. Only the parents and a few other people would have known the truth. They adopted female behaviours and attitudes and this is the key to **gender identity.** Recent reports of these cases during adolescence question whether the "conversion" has been successful, however. The girls who were born as boys did feel they were really boys and had to be informed of the truth. If these children and later adults had a female gender identity then this would suggest that gender identity can be more powerful than sex identity.

Some adults experience a conflict between their sex identity and their gender identity. Most reports of these conflicts seem to be men (by sex identity) who think of themselves as women (gender identity) "trapped inside a man's body". This feeling can be strong enough for the person concerned to seek surgery to transform their sex identity and have their penis removed and replaced with female sex organs. The opposite also occurs and some women seek surgery to construct a penis. Life-long hormone treatment is needed in these cases.

## 4. Evaluation of the Biological Explanation

There is no doubt that a biological approach explains the physical facts of our sex. We have the physical characteristics of a male or a female because of physical causes but does this explain our gender?

Is our gender the result of biological processes? Are "feminine" women and "masculine" men the result of hormone and brain processes?

**Criticism**

- Many people would reject the notion that our biological processes determine our behaviour and feelings. This seems to put us "at the mercy" of our biology and take away from us the power to decide how we behave and the ability to understand why we feel the way we do.

- The biological approach ignores the influence of other people on the way we behave – this is covered in more detail in the next lesson.

**Praise**

As support for the biological approach, consider this case reported by Money in 1974.

---

## A Circumcision Accident

Money reports the case of a boy whose penis was so badly damaged during a circumcision operation that it had to be removed altogether. The decision was taken to fully castrate the boy (remove his testicles) and bring him up as a girl. The castration would prevent testosterone being produced in adulthood. Until recently this case was quoted in textbooks as a success but when the child went into adolescence she became so confused by her feelings of maleness (e.g. wanting to do "boy" things and hating girl's clothes) that she had to be told the truth – she had been born a boy.

This case supports the notion that maleness and femaleness are biologically based and that biological forces may be too strong to override. The boy elected to grow up as a male when told the truth.

---

Whilst this study gives support to the role of biology it is probably more sensible to see biology as **one** of the factors that influences our behaviour. We do not have to choose between biology and social factors influencing us. Both of them could play their part with, perhaps, biology setting the "ceiling" on our gender. In this perspective, our potential for being very feminine (for example) is set by our biology but whether or not we actually are very feminine is set by circumstances. For example, a woman born into a poor background having to work manually in difficult circumstances, might behave in a more masculine way than a woman with the same biological characteristics born into a life of physical ease.

---

**Try this Quick Quiz to check your understanding**
**See if you can answer without looking back at the material each time**
1. Being male or female depends only on your physical attributes. True or False? (1 mark)
2. —— are the basic building blocks of the body. (1 mark)
3. The nucleus of each cell contains 23 pairs of ————. (1 mark)
4. Hundreds of —— are strung out along each chromosome. (1 mark)
5. Men's cells contain two Y-chromosomes. True or false? (1 mark)

6. Women's cells contain two Y-chromosomes: true or false? (1 mark)
7. For a child to be a boy, the sperm cell needs to be a Y: true or false? (1 mark)
8. ――――――― is a hormone that promotes "maleness". (1 mark)
9. A person's sex identity is determined by what? (1 mark)
10. What does gender identity refer to? (1 mark)

## Feedback on The Influence of Biology

**Answers to the Quick Quiz on the influence of biology**

1. False. There are many accepted ways of behaving which tend to be seen as appropriate for males and females. (1 mark)
2. Cells. (1 mark)
3. Chromosomes (1 mark)
4. Genes (1 mark)
5. False. Men's cells contain one Y and one X. (1 mark)
6. False. Women's cells contain two X chromosomes. (1 mark)
7. True. Boys are one X, one Y; only the male's sperm cell can supply the Y. (1 mark)
8. Testosterone. (1 mark)
9. His or her sex organs. (1 mark)
10. The behaviours, attitudes and feelings of a person; whether they think of them selves as male or female. (1 mark)

**Total marks = 10**

# Lesson 53
# The Social Learning Theory
# Approach to Gender

## 1. Introduction

The previous lesson pointed out the way in which **Gender Identity** differs from **Sex Identity**. Whilst sex identity is determined by biological factors (the sex organs, chromosomes and hormones for example), gender identity is the result of our feelings about ourselves, behaviours and attitudes. Also, if **Socialisation** refers to adopting the accepted behaviours of the society into which we are born, then we need to understand the way in which our gender identity may result from socialisation.

These learning materials will look at two very different ways in which psychologists have explained the process. In this lesson the idea of Social Learning Theory is explored. In the next lesson, the psychoanalytical approach, created by Sigmund Freud will be introduced.

The principles of Social Learning Theory are described in a lesson of that name in the Learning section. They could be used in an attempt to explain **all** behaviours, not just gender identity. Put in its simplest form, they suggest that behaviour is learned, so we learn the behaviours associated with our gender identity. There are two important processes involved in Social Learning Theory: **Imitation** and **Identification**. A third process, **Vicarious Learning** may also play a part.

## 2. The Social Learning Theory Approach

**Imitation**

Imitation occurs when a child copies the behaviour of someone else. This is also referred to as **Observational Learning**. Adults may also copy behaviour. This does not mean that the learner makes a conscious effort to learn, nor that the model (the person whose behaviour is copied) makes the conscious effort to teach; the learner simply observes and copies "automatically".

Studies have shown that certain features of the model affect the likelihood of the behaviour being copied and this could give clues to how gender identity is acquired.

- **Similarity** If the model is similar in some way to the child then the child is more likely to imitate. This was shown in a study carried out by one of the best-known researchers in this area, Albert Bandura. He showed how boys were more likely to copy the aggressive behaviour of men than the aggressive behaviour of women and he concluded that the similarity of sex was a feature of this imitation.

- **Appropriateness** In the same study it was found that girls as well as boys were more likely to copy the aggressive behaviour of a man rather than the aggressive behaviour of a woman and Bandura concluded that aggression was seen as more appropriate in men and so was more likely to be copied.

> Take one of these two features above and say how it may explain the way in which gender identity is acquired. A suggestion follows

If a child copies the behaviour of similar models then it is more likely to copy that of its own sex as long as it perceives sex identity as an important characteristic of similarity. Attitudes are also a part of gender identity and a child can observe and imitate the behaviour component of attitudes and so take on board the attitudes of its gender in this way.

If particular behaviours are seen as appropriate to one sex then the child is more likely to copy and adopt those behaviours. If it is seen as more appropriate for women to express their emotions than for men, then girls are more likely to imitate this characteristic if they see women crying than if they see men crying. Boys are also more likely to copy this behaviour, however; it is the fact that it is seen as appropriate which makes it more "copiable". In this case, the increased likelihood of the adoption of this behaviour by boys is offset by the lack of similarity between the boy and the woman; the similarity between the girl and the woman is likely to increase the likelihood of its adoption for girls.

> **Predict the outcome!**
> A boy and a girl watch another girl practising on a skateboard in the street. Taking into account the idea of similarity and appropriateness:
> **What is the girl observer likely to do and why?**
> **What is the boy likely to do and why?**
> (Suggested answers are in the Feedback section at the end of the lesson)

## Identification

Identification is a psychological process that takes us one step further than imitation in a way. It is a method of acquiring behaviours which involves putting ourselves in the shoes of someone else and acting as though we were that person. Children imagine that they are the person they are identifying with and behave as they would expect that person to behave in those circumstances. Playing school is a good example of an obvious case of identification: the child acts like a teacher and produces behaviours which could be shown by a teacher – telling pupils what to do, scolding and praising as teachers might and giving instructions in a subject. All of these may be behaviours that the child imagines a teacher would perform.

Clearly, this idea would be useful in explaining the way that children develop their gender identity. Boys would act like their fathers or similar males who have supplied some form of positive experience and girls would identify with their mothers or other females who have rewarded them. Children's knowledge of their gender models would allow them to put into action all the attitudes, opinions and general approach to life that the models have previously displayed.

---

**Short Exercise 1**

Read back over the section "Identification" then try to answer the following questions without looking back. Look back if you cannot complete the exercise. Suggested answers are in the Feedback section.

1. How does identification work?
2. Give one advantage of the process of identification over the process of imitation
3. How does identification explain the development of gender identity?

---

### Vicarious Reinforcement (Vicarious Learning)

Vicarious reinforcement refers to a situation in which a person observes someone else's behaviour being rewarded and then copies the behaviour. The principles of learning theory (conditioning) suggest that seeing someone being rewarded for a piece of behaviour should make it more likely that we would reproduce that behaviour. In one of the most famous studies of imitation, however, Bandura found that this idea was not supported.

In the mid 1960s Bandura carried out a number of studies in which children observed actors attacking "Bobo" dolls. These are large dolls, shaped with a rounded base and weighted in such a way that, when knocked over, they stand up again. In one study, one group of children watched an adult attack a doll. Another group watched the adult attack the doll and then saw another actor entering the room and praising the attacker for his behaviour, rewarding him with sweets and a drink. A third group watched the actor attack the doll then receive a telling-off from another actor for being so rough with the doll.

The principle of Vicarious Learning would suggest that the second group would imitate the actor the most as they had seen the actor being rewarded and it was thought that this would "spill over" into the experience of reward for the learner. The children who observed the actor being rewarded did not imitate the actor any more than the other children, however, so this undermines the validity of the idea of Vicarious Learning.

---

**Short Exercise 2**

If vicarious learning is a valid idea then we should expect it to contribute towards the socialisation of gender identity. Explain how this would happen. There is a suggested answer in the Feedback section.

---

## 3. The evidence for the Social Learning Theory approach

### Bandura's studies

Two of Bandura's studies have already been mentioned in this lesson. In the first, it was noted that he found that both boys and girls are more likely to copy aggression displayed by women than by men. It is thought that this is because aggression is seen as more appropriate to males in the western world.

In the second study, children who had seen actors rewarded for aggressive behaviour were shown to be no more likely to display the aggressive behaviour than children who had observed the behaviour of the adult but who had not seen the adult rewarded. This leads us to doubt the notion of Vicarious Learning. In a similar study, however, Bandura did establish evidence that children imitated behaviour. He set up four groups of children:

- **Group 1** watched an adult behaving aggressively towards a bobo doll.
- **Group 2** watched the same thing but the adult was on a film
- **Group 3** watched the same thing but in the form of a cartoon
- **Group 4** saw no aggressive behaviour.

Bandura found that when the children were allowed to play with toys which included the bobo doll the ones who had watched the cartoon produced the most acts of aggression towards the bobo doll. Next came the children who had watched the filmed aggression, then the ones who had watched the "real" actor. The children who watched no aggression displayed the least aggression towards the dolls.

As the "no aggression" group displayed the least aggression it seems valid to conclude that exposure to aggression had provided the children with a model to imitate and that they tended to do so. Is this evidence useful for our study of gender identity? It does provide evidence that children copy behaviour but there are some reservations.

- The studies are in very artificial settings; like most laboratory studies they are not the same as "real life". In real life, the children would perhaps have some form of interaction with their models – perhaps talking about what they were doing. The child may be able to change the model's behaviour too.
- Aggression is a specific behaviour but gender identity involves all sorts of attitudes, feelings, and assumptions. It may be that this one limited aspect of behaviour is not representative of the sort of psychological processes involved in gender identity.

**Fagot's study**

A number of studies have been carried out into the way in which different behaviours are encouraged in boys and girls. A good example of these is the one by Beverley Fagot. She observed the interactions of twenty four sets of parents with their young children and found that boys were encouraged to explore "male" toys (like building blocks and toy lorries) and to manipulate these toys and be active. Girls, on the other hand, were encouraged to play with "female" toys like dolls, to dance and to appreciate clothes. They were also encouraged to stay close to their parents. Both sexes were actively discouraged from playing with "opposite-sex" toys but boys were more heavily discouraged from this than were girls – perhaps "tomboys" are more acceptable than "cissies"!

Studies like these form a good basis for coming to conclusions about the effects of learning on our gender identity:

- The studies are made on behaviour which is true to life – the parents and children studied by Fagot may have been influenced by her presence to some extent but the situations are far more realistic than laboratory settings.
- Studies such as these do consistently come up with the conclusion that gender appropriate play is commonly encouraged by the family and this coincides with most people's personal experience.

## 4. Implications of this evidence

Faggot's study and Bandura's study imply that our behaviour is shaped by those around us. It also implies that differences between the behaviours of girls and the behaviours of boys is caused not by natural factors but by the different models and rewards they are exposed to. In terms of equal opportunities, therefore, we need to be careful that we present children with models of behaviour and with rewards that encourage both boys and girls to achieve and succeed in all aspects of life. This implies that toys, books, games, the media and the school curriculum should be examined carefully to ensure that males and females are depicted equally across all activities.

---

**Quick Quiz the evidence for the Social Learning Theory Approach**
1.  In the bobo doll study reported in the evidence section, which group of children copied the actor the most? (1 mark)
2.  Can you suggest why this group should copy the most? (2 marks)
3.  Give one criticism of Bandura's bobo doll studies. (2 marks)
4.  In Fagot's study, give one of the behaviours encouraged by parents in girls. (1 marks)
5.  Which group was more heavily discouraged from displaying "cross-gender" behaviour? (1 mark)
6.  Give one advantage of Fagot's study over Bandura's (1 mark)
7.  Give one criticism of Fagot's study. (1 mark)
8.  State one implication of the evidence from this approach (1 mark)

---

## 5. An evaluation of the Social Learning theory approach
### Praise
Social Learning Theory is not **just** about repeating rewarded behaviour, however; it does take account of the idea that thinking processes are involved and this is reflected in the way in which gender identity is influenced by such factors as the appropriateness of the behaviour to the model and the similarity of the model to the child copying the behaviour. The idea of learning gender identity does fit very neatly with the Social Learning theory.
### Criticism
Against this approach are the ideas that:
* it does not take account of the physiological influences like hormones and chromosome differences – there seems to be little reason why girls should not adopt male gender identity far more often than they do and vice versa, and,
* it is difficult to explain why some males do adopt female gender identity and some females adopt male gender identity using this model. If all males are subjected to similar influences of families, the media and school, why do some grow up identifying with different genders from the others?

## 6. Practical issues raised by the Social Learning Approach
* **Single parent and non-traditional forms of family.** This is an issue with both this approach and with the psychoanalytical approach. Most single parent families consist of a mother with children. Who will be the male role model for boys in such a household? The evidence suggests that there is no problem with children's gender identity in this style of family but some writers question the quality of male role model behaviour available to boys in these circumstances.

- **Male aggression in gender models.** Studies comparing male and female aggression levels consistently show males displaying higher levels of aggression than females. Is this because boys are exposed to aggressive gender models? Could we and should we attempt to manipulate levels of aggression in males by ensuring that boys are exposed to non-aggressive male gender models? We could do this by reducing television, film and other media portrayals of male violence.

## Feedback

### Predict the outcome: suggested answers

1. The behaviour is not seen as appropriate for the girl on the skateboard by other children (debatable of course! but how often does one see girls on skateboards compared to boys?) so this reduces the likelihood of **either** child observer copying the behaviour.
2. The girl observer is similar to the girl skateboarder so this increases the likelihood of her copying the behaviour. The boy observer is different from the girl skateboarder and this makes it less likely that he will copy her. Notice, however, that it is only possible to talk in terms of "likely": in reality, it is not possible to be sure what either child will do.

### Short Exercise 1: suggested answers

1. The child takes on the role of the model and puts himself or herself in the shoes of the model, acting as though he or she were the model.
2. It allows for more flexibility of behaviour so the child has more chance of knowing how to act in a given situation.
3. Children will identify as male or female and take on the behaviour, attitudes, values and opinions of the chosen sex model.

### Short Exercise 2: Vicarious Learning

If vicarious learning is a valid concept then we should expect children to see others rewarded for adopting a gender identity which matches their sex identity. They would see boys rewarded for "boy's" behaviour and girls rewarded for "girl's" behaviour and so be more likely to adopt that behaviour themselves. This would be maintained during adulthood when we continue to see others rewarded in this way.

### Quick Quiz: the evidence for the Social Learning Theory approach, Answers

1. The ones watching the cartoon
2. Some psychologists suggest that evidence shows how children can differentiate between fantasy and "real" aggression; it may be that the children recognise the aggression in the cartoon as "pure fantasy" and so see no reason why they should not copy it in the context of hitting a bobo doll which feels no pain. It may be that your suggested answer to this question is different but just as acceptable. (2 marks)
3. The bobo doll studies are not like "real life"– they are laboratory studies. (1 mark) You may have a different but equally acceptable answer.
4. Interest in clothes, playing with female toys, staying close to parents. (1 mark)
5. The boys (1 mark)
6. It is more lifelike (1 mark)
7. The people may have changed their behaviour for the observation (1 mark)
8. (e.g.) We should represent males and females equally in the media (1 mark)

# Lesson 54
# The Psychoanalytic Approach to Gender

## 1. Introduction
In the previous lesson we examined one way of explaining how we acquire gender identity; the Social Learning Theory was explained and then related to the way in which gender identity is formed. In this lesson we examine an alternative explanation – the psychoanalytic approach. This approach was suggested by one of the most famous psychologists ever, Sigmund Freud. He outlined a theory that was controversial when it was first published (covering a period from about 1900 to Freud's death in 1939) and which remains so today. The ideas in the theory have influenced thought outside psychology and affected literature and art in many areas of the western world. Once again, the theory will be explained then related to gender identity.

## 2. Freud's Psychoanalytic Theory
Freud suggested that there are three parts to our personality. These three parts are in constant interaction with each other and are constantly moving against each other – which is why it is also referred to as **psycho** (self) **dynamic** (energy and motion). They are described below.

### (i) The Id
This is the first part of the personality to come into existence and consists of a very animal-like element which is focused on ensuring that its desires and needs are satisfied; these needs are biological ones of food, warmth, comfort and sex.

### (ii) The Ego
As we grow, so we come to realise subconsciously that demanding things and satisfying our needs instantly (instant gratification) may not be the best thing to do. We need to satisfy our needs but it has to be done within a social setting. We cannot just expect to eat what and when we want. We have wait until it is convenient for others to make the food and to eat with us. We have to arrange to pay for our food, not just take what we see in front of us.

The Ego develops to deal with these social constraints and ensures that the Id's wishes are fulfilled but within society's rules.

### (iii) The Superego
Eventually, our personality develops a third element: the Superego. This part acts as a conscience and questions whether the things done by the Ego are acceptable. It checks the excesses and imposes feelings of guilt for acts and thoughts which it considers to be wrong or bad; it rewards us with a feeling of self-esteem when we do something it considers to be right – you may recall such a feeling when you have donated to charity or helped someone in difficulty. In doing so, it is helping the Ego to keep the Id in check.

**Name the Parts.** Put the correct name of the part of Freud's model in the box on the right. The correct answer is in the Feedback section.

| Name of Part | Description of Part |
|---|---|
| | This part acts as a conscience and questions whether the things done by the Ego are acceptable |
| | This part of the personality consists of a very animal-like element, focused on ensuring that its desires and needs are satisfied |
| | This part develops to deal with social constraints and ensures that the Id's wishes are fulfilled but within society's rules. |

### The unconscious mind

Most of our thoughts, wishes and other mental processes happen at an **unconscious** level, which means that we are unaware that they are there and we need special techniques to gain access to them; Freud used hypnosis, dream interpretation, slips of the tongue ("Freudian slips" like saying "orgasm" when we mean to say "organism") and free association to gain access to these unconscious thoughts. Free association involves talking about whatever is "on your mind" at the moment you are talking.

## The Importance of the Unconscious Mind

Everything that Freud said about the psychodynamic personality and about stages of psychosexual development, described below, depends on the notion of the unconscious mind. His ideas are based on the assumption that we are not usually aware of the true (i.e. unconscious) reasons for our doing things.

### Psychosexual Development

Freud made the controversial claim for Victorian times that sexual feelings are present from birth, not from adulthood as many people believed at that time. We now know from scans of baby boys in the womb that their penises are sometimes erect and being manipulated by their hands so it would appear that sexual feelings start even before birth.

He suggested that we mature naturally through five stages of development, each of which is centred on a particular part of the body. Failure to pass successfully through any stage produces **fixation** at the stage and leads to neurotic behaviour of a particular type later on in life and this contributes to the whole personality of a person.

### The Oral Stage (first year of life)

When a baby is born, one of the things at which it quickly becomes adept is sucking. Not only does it suck at the breast or bottle but also it will suck virtually anything placed in its mouth. At this age, it will also explore any objects given to it by putting them in its mouth. The baby is gaining pleasure from the mouth at this stage.

**The Anal Stage (1 to 3 years old)**

Potty training is **the** big event for many two to three year olds (or certainly for their parents). At this stage the child is learning to control its bowels and bladder and eventually to understand that defecation and urination are supposed to fit conveniently into the daily routine. Physical pleasure is experienced when bowel motions and urination occur.

**The Phallic Stage (3 to 5 years old)**

This is the important stage of development for Freud's theory from the point of view of gender development. The genitals become the most important source of pleasure and this is achieved through masturbation. Boys' feelings for their mothers become intense and passionate – Freud said these feeling were sexual too. But this means that they are rivals with their fathers for their mother's love. Boys are afraid that if their fathers find out about their love the fathers will castrate them and so their fear makes them repress the love and identify with the father to ward off his anger. **In identifying with the father the boy takes on the male characteristics and this is the source of gender identity in this theory.**

There is a parallel process with girls but it is not quite a "mirror image" of the boy's process. Freud referred to the female Oedipus complex in girls but Carl Jung, a colleague of Freud's, referred to it as the Electra complex in girls. Both names are taken from Greek myths – Oedipus unwittingly murdered his father and married his mother.

Girls fall in love with their fathers but instead of fearing that their mother will be angry if they find out, girls instead worry about losing the love of their mothers. In order to keep their mother's love, girls become more like their mothers. They do this for two reasons: firstly, they hope that the mother will be flattered by the daughter's attempts to copy her and secondly, the daughter herself "becomes" the mother and so the mother will always be there. **At this point, the girl identifies with the mother and takes on her characteristics – thus gaining her gender identity**.

Freud suggested that boys have more to lose than girls (their penises!) and therefore identify more strongly, and so we may perhaps expect them to have "stricter" gender identity. He also said that failure to pass through this stage successfully can lead to a variety of adult personality disorders, including homosexuality.

---

**The Case of Little Hans – one of Freud's most famous studies**

Little Hans's father consulted Freud with the problem that Hans was afraid of being bitten by horses, especially white ones wearing blinkers and with black colouring around the mouth. Bearing in mind that horses were common in the streets at the time (1909) this would have caused some inconvenience to Hans and his family as well as seeming irrational. Freud believed that the horse symbolised Hans' father and the real fear that Hans had was of him, not horses. Freud said that Hans was passing through his Oedipus stage and was afraid that his father would castrate him (symbolised in Hans's mind by the fear that the horse would bite him).

Hans's father had a moustache and wore spectacles and Freud said these were symbolised by the colouring round the mouth and the blinkers of the horse.

The remaining two stages of development described in Freud's theory are not as important for gender identity but they are:

**The Latency Period (5 years old to puberty)**
The child represses its sexual thoughts at this stage and turns its attention to other pursuits.

**The Genital Stage (Adolescence and adulthood)**
The genitals again become the part of the body through which pleasure is derived and the personality is driven to enter heterosexual relationships to achieve the fulfilment of this pleasure.

---

**Complete these sentences**

1. There are _____ stages in Freud's theory of psychosexual development
2. In the first stage, the Oral stage, the _____ is the most important part of the body
3. The Anal stage is one in which children of about _____ years focus on the anus.
4. The important part of the sequence of stages from the point of view of gender development is the phallic stage. Freud said boys and girls fall in love with ___ _____ ___ _____ and wish to posses them sexually.
5. The remaining two stages, Latency and Genital, are not as important for the development of _____ _____.

---

## 3. The evidence for the Psychoanalytic Approach

Freud constructed his theory from case studies – studies of individuals. He was a practising expert in the nervous system and started his long psychology career when faced with a patient who was unable to move her arm but who had no physical problem with the nerves. He concluded that the patient's problem was in the mind and went on to investigate problems of the mind. The study of Little Hans, above, is an example of one of his case studies.

## 4 Implications of this evidence

One implication of this evidence is that our behaviour, thoughts and emotions are usually beyond our control. We are constantly driven by thoughts of which we are not aware and they are often "murky", dark, unpleasant ones.

In terms of equal opportunities Freud also outlined a number of ideas that portray females as inferior to males:

- Girls experience Penis Envy – an unconscious wish that they had a penis and an unconscious thought that they used to have one but were punished in the past by castration. It is likely of course that many girls at the phallic stage in Freud's times had never seen a penis and had no basis for such envy. Quite apart from this, the idea does imply that a penis is superior to a vagina and that, therefore, males are superior to females.

- Freud suggested that girls do not internalise their same-sex parent as much as do boys so they are less moral because they have not internalised their parent's morals fully. This is clearly another negative assumption about girls.

## 5. Evaluation of the Psychoanalytic Approach

**Criticism**

- Freud's theory itself has been criticised for using case studies as evidence; these cannot be generalised to the rest of the population
- Women are pictured as inferior in this theory – girls have "penis envy" and weaker moral development because they do not internalise their gender as deeply as boys do.

**Praise**

- Freud's model of personality is highly internally consistent – all the intricate parts of his complex theory fit together – and some people feel it is intuitively correct
- Case studies are considered by some researchers to be as valid as classic experiments.

## 6. Practical issues arising from the Psychoanalytic Approach

- **Single parent and non-traditional forms of family.** Freud wrote at a time when single-parent families were uncommon. Today, single parents are more common, with most single parent families being mothers with children. If he was right, then today we should expect boys brought up by their lone mothers to be unable to resolve their Oedipus complex and hence have problems with gender identity. In fact, studies like one undertaken by Green in 1978 show that there are no gender identity problems when children are brought up by single mothers, single fathers, lesbian couples or transsexual parents.

## Feedback

| Name of Part | Description of Part |
|---|---|
| Superego | This part acts as a conscience and questions whether the things done by the Ego are acceptable |
| Id | This part of the personality consists of a very animal-like element, focused on ensuring that its desires and needs are satisfied |
| Ego | This part develops to deal with social constraints and ensures that the Id's wishes are fulfilled but within society's rules. |

**Complete these sentences**

1. There are **five** stages in Freud's theory of psychosexual development
2. In the first stage, the Oral stage, the **mouth** is the most important part of the body
3. The Anal stage is one in which children of about **two** years focus on the anus.
4. The important part of the sequence of stages from the point of view of gender development is the phallic stage. Freud said boys and girls fall in love with **the opposite sex parent** and wish to posses them sexually.
5. The remaining two stages, Latency and Genital, are not as important for the development of **gender identity**.

# Lesson 55
# The Cognitive Approach to Gender Identity

## 1. Kohlberg's Cognitive Approach to Explaining Gender Identity

Kohlberg suggested that there might be three stages in the development of our gender identity:

(i) **Gender Labelling:** This is more or less a stage at which children learn that gender exists – that some children are boys and some are girls, some people are women, some men. It is the equivalent to learning that there is a red group and a blue group at nursery and that he or she is in the red group.

(ii) **Gender Stability:** It may seem odd to think that children do not necessarily assume that they will remain a girl or a boy all their life but this is the case up to the age of about 3 years. Until this stage children may assume that a girl can become a boy by dressing like one and playing with the other boys. At about the age of 3 years, however, the child comes to believe that she or he will stay a girl or boy forever but that changing external appearance can change gender.

(iii)**Gender Constancy:** Children eventually come to understand that even though people may change their external appearance, they will not change gender. Somewhere between the ages of 5 to 7 years children will understand that their sex is generally fixed for life.

---

**What age is Tasneem?**

Tasneem is playing with Lesley in the home corner. They dress up in long, flowing dresses and high-heeled shoes. Tasneem says
"I am going to be a mummy when I grow up" but Lesley says
"Boys can't be mummies. You will be a daddy when you grow up". Tasneem says
"That's alright, I'll borrow mummy's dress".
What does this tell us about the ages of Tasneem and Lesley according to Kohlberg's ideas? (the answer follows this box)

---

When Lesley says, "Boys can't be mummies. You will be a daddy when you grow up" this leads us to believe that Tasneem is a boy and has made a mistake in stating that he will grow up to be a female. He probably recognises that genders exist as he is referring to "mummy" but he does not recognise that he won't change sex and probably assumes that by dressing as a female he could become a female. He suggests that he could achieve this with his mother's dress. This would be characteristic of children at the Gender labelling stage so he is probably three or younger. Lesley understands that Tasneem will not change sex by dressing in opposite sex clothes so she is probably over 5 years.

This theory turns social learning theory on its head. In social learning theory, a person is seen as a "blank sheet" that is "moulded" into becoming male or female by the rewards received for copying the behaviours of others. In the cognitive theory of Kohlberg, however, we decide **first** whether we are male or female and **then** copy the behaviour of the gender we have decided we are, feeling rewarded by the extent to which we are successful in doing this.

## 2. An evaluation of the theory

### Support from studies

There is some support from a study by Slaby and Frey. They divided children into two groups. One group was "high gender constancy" – that is, they were clear that we stay one sex all our lives. The other group was "low gender constancy" – that is, they were not clear that people stay the same sex. The children then watched films of adults performing simple tasks and it was found that the high constancy group spent more time watching their own sex actors whilst the low constancy group did not show this behaviour. This suggests that the high constancy group were giving themselves the opportunity to look for behaviour appropriate to their sex – they had already decided what sex they were and were looking for behaviour to model.

### Criticism

Studies such as one by Macoby have found that children learn gender stereotypes well before the age at which Slaby and Frey investigated gender constancy. They already show these preferences before the age that Slaby and Frey say they are attended to same-sex models. If Kohlberg's cognitive approach were correct, children would also be giving more attention to same-sex models at the earlier age.

---

**Revision Exercise**

Read through the lesson first then complete the following paragraph without referring back to it. If you are unable to complete a blank after some thought, then refer back to the lesson

There are _____ stages in Kohlberg's cognitive theory of gender identity. At the _____ _____ stage, children learn that gender exists while in the gender stability stage they think that _____

_____. At the **gender constancy** stage we come to understand that gender stays constant for people throughout life.

---

## Feedback

### Revision Exercise

There are **three** stages in Kohlberg's cognitive theory of gender identity. At the **gender labelling** stage, children learn that gender exists while in the gender stability stage they think that **we stay the same sex unless we decide to change it by changing our clothes or altering our hair**. At the **gender constancy** stage we come to understand that gender stays constant for people throughout life.

# Lesson 56
# Cultural Differences in Gender Role Development

## 1. Studies of different cultures

Gender roles differ from culture to culture: as children grow up exposed to different models and being rewarded for different behaviours they adopt roles that are not the ones we would necessarily recognise in the West.

### Margaret Mead's Studies

Margaret Mead studied a variety of different gender roles in different cultures from New Guinea in the 1930s. She found a variety of differences in roles, summarised in the table below

| Temperament and Gender Roles of Three New Guinea Tribes (after Mead, 1935) | | |
|---|---|---|
| Tribe | Male | Female |
| Arapesh | Gentle, loving co-operative | Gentle, loving co-operative |
| Mundugumor | Self-assertive, arrogant, fierce, quarrelsome | Self-assertive, arrogant, fierce, quarrelsome |
| Tchambuli | Discouraged from economic roles. Sentimental, emotional not decision-makers. Gossiped, "preened" themselves | Encouraged to take an economic role – trading and food gathering |

The Arapesh not only had similar roles for both genders but also seemed to have roles traditionally associated with females in Western societies. The Mundugumors had similar roles too but these were associated with males in Western societies. The Tchambuli had different roles but these were the reverse of the ones normally associated with Western cultures.

Margaret Mead's studies were heavily criticised in the 1980s. Freeman was able to interview elderly women who had acted as teenage participants in one of her earlier studies (*Coming of Age in Samoa*, published in 1928) and it seems likely that Mead's accounts were very subjective; it may be that her role descriptions were inaccurate.

### Multi-gender cultures

Some studies have found cultures that do not restrict themselves to two genders. For example a Native American group, the Mohave, have four genders. Apart

from the "traditional" male and female types familiar in the West, they also have:
- Alyha – biological males who live as females, marrying and taking female roles,
- Hwame – biological females who live as males, marrying and taking male roles

Whilst some males in the West choose to adopt these lifestyles it is difficult to argue that they are accepted as a "real" gender. At best, they are tolerated or humoured by most other people. The Mohave, however, accept these roles as a normal part of their society.

## 2. Multicultural Societies

It is increasingly common to find multicultural societies in the West. Subtle differences may be observed between cultures living side-by-side – perhaps not as obvious as the Arapesh and Hwame described in the section above. One of the most obvious contrasts between male and female gender roles might be thought to be the role of Moslem women in the West who are often depicted as "protected" and "passive". In contrast to Western women who are coming to be accepted as career orientated and potential high status role occupants, Moslem women are sometimes seen as being bound to the home and therefore powerless. This view can be very much mistaken. Some Moslem women exert a high degree of power within their society and lead families and communities.

---

**Quick Quiz**
1. Who studied different cultures in New Guinea in the 1930s?
2. In which tribes did that researcher find little difference between the male and female roles?
3. What were Mundugumor female roles like?
4. Give one criticism of that research
5. How many gender roles do the Mohave Native Americans have?
Answers in the Feedback section below

---

## Feedback

1. Margaret Mead
2. Arapesh and Mundugumor
3. Self-assertive, arrogant, fierce, quarrelsome
4. Because she was not a member of the culture, Mead may have misunderstood the roles and not described them accurately
5. Four

# Lesson 57
# Sex and Gender:
# Putting Theory into Practice

## 1. Promoting and Reinforcing Gender Differences and Stereotypes

Do you know this poem?

> What are little girls made of?
> Sugar and spice and all things nice
> That's what little girls are made of
>
> What are little boys made of?
> Slugs and snails and puppy dogs' tails
> That's what little boys are made of.

What picture does this paint of girls? Sweet and nice? What does it say about boys? Gooey and active. What does it say about the person next to you?

### Stereotypes

A stereotype is

"A belief about a class of people which is then applied to individual members of the class to provide expectations about the person in the absence of specific knowledge" according to *A Student's Dictionary of Psychology* (Stratton and Hayes, 1993). So we might believe *Americans are "brash", our new professor is American, so our new professor will be brash.*

Stereotypes usually have a negative aspect to them – Americans are brash, women can't drive, men are uncaring. Few positive stereotypes seem to exist. Do people generally hold these stereotypes of girls and boys? If they do hold them, does it matter? Have equal opportunities, laws and the progress of time erased these ideas from people's minds? We shall now briefly examine these questions.

## 2. Studies of gender stereotypes

A number of studies have been carried out into the way in which stereotyped behaviours are encouraged in boys and girls.

### Fagot's study – the influence of the family

A good example is the one by Beverley Fagot.

She observed the interactions of twenty-four sets of parents with their young children and found that boys were encouraged to explore "male" toys (like building blocks and toy lorries) and to manipulate these toys and be active. Girls, on the other hand, were encouraged to play with "female" toys like dolls, to dance and to appreciate clothes. They were also encouraged to stay close to their parents. Both sexes were actively discouraged from playing with "opposite-sex" toys but boys were more heavily discouraged from this than were girls – perhaps "tomboys" are more acceptable than "cissies"!

Studies like these form a good basis for coming to conclusions about the effects of learning on our gender identity:

- The studies are made on behaviour that is true to life – the parents and children studied by Fagot may have been influenced by her presence to some extent but the situations are far more realistic than laboratory settings.
- Studies such as these do consistently come up with the conclusion that gender appropriate play is commonly encouraged by the family and this coincides with most people's personal experience.

### Smith and Lloyd's study – more family influence

This is, perhaps, the best known of the gender stereotype studies – sometimes known as the "Baby X" study – and one that has a clear message.

Babies were dressed in the "traditional" colours for boys (blue) or girls (pink) but their clothes did not always match their real sex: they were given names appropriate to the sex of their clothes. Mothers were asked to play with them so the children's play could be observed. In fact, Smith and Lloyd observed the mothers' behaviour, not the babies'. When the babies were dressed as boys, the adult would typically encourage them to play with the "boys' toys" (e.g. a toy hammer) and when dressed as girls they were encouraged to play with the "girls' toys" (e.g. a doll). "Boys" were also encouraged to move around more than "girls".

### Studies of the media and gender stereotypes

Some psychologists suggest that gender stereotypes are continually presented in the characters in the media. For example, females on television are shown using washing powder while male voices – over give technical details. There is some evidence to support the notion that **sex-role stereotypes and television viewing** go together.

- Gunter and McAleer demonstrated that children who were heavy viewers of television also had the strongest sex stereotyped beliefs; it could be that cause and effect is confused here, however. The children may have he stereotypes from another cause and may chose to watch television more. Also, the type of television programme watched is not reported, only the amount of television watched. The content of the programme should be significant.
- A study by Williams monitored what happened to children's behaviour when television was introduced into a remote town in Canada (the town was called "Notel" for the sake of anonymity). It showed an increase in sex-stereotyped behaviour amongst the children. These children were compared with those in a town that already had television.

---

**Your Own Study**

You could carry out your own short study of the way that girls and boys are depicted in children's books. Set up a table like the one shown below, then take some children's books (e.g. from the library) and look at every picture of a child in the book.

---

Look at each character in the picture and decide if the character is performing one of the behaviours in the lists in the table. If so, put a tick in the table for that behaviour – one in the male column if a male is performing it or one in the female column if a female is performing it.

By totalling the ticks you may find that a pattern emerges showing males performing the stereotypical male behaviours (the left-hand-list), and females performing the stereotypical female behaviours (the right-hand list).

| Behaviour | Male | Female | Behaviour | Male | Female |
|---|---|---|---|---|---|
| Active | | | Passive | | |
| Doing | | | Watching Others | | |
| Mechanical or Practical Activity | | | Domestic Activity | | |
| Related to Work | | | Related to Home | | |
| Concerned with Own Appearance | | | Unconcerned with Own Appearance | | |
| Aggressive Behaviour | | | Peace-Inducing Behaviour | | |
| **Total** | | | | | |

## 3. Implications of these studies

The implications of these studies are important. The studies imply that children develop "fixed" and often limited pictures of males and females. Their expectations of males and females are often negative – girls and women are seen as passive, shy, retiring, lacking in practical skills and in leadership, unconcerned about careers and pre-occupied with domestic and family matters. Boys are shown as insensitive, more involved with "things" rather than people and unable to express emotions but with, perhaps more positive characteristics – dominant, exploring, robust, active, adventurous and career orientated.

Until recently, these stereotypes coincided with the different educational and career achievements of males and females. Females achieved better at school up to age 11 but then boys overtook them so that by age 16 boys were achieving higher examination passes than girls in most subjects. The situation is different now.

- Girls out – perform boys in exam attainment at age 16 now and a slightly higher proportion of girls than boys goes on to university.

This is probably because attention has been paid to stereotypes of girls and boys at school and concerted efforts have been made to improve educational performance of girls.

- Teachers have become aware of the problems presented by stereotypes in books and there have been active attempts to rectify the images and impressions.
- Equal opportunities has appeared as an issue in the daily life of school students – ranging from girls' rights to wear trousers as part of school uniforms, to

equal access to the curriculum (girls and boys following the same National Curriculum so that girls **and** boys study food technology and play football). This situation has not become perfectly equal, however. Children still play with toys that are within their stereotype – though in the year 2000, clothes topped the list of preferred boys' Christmas presents for the first time ever. Girls can still not take part in FA league football teams after age 12 or so, and child care courses at Key Stage 3 are virtually all girl entries.

However, the issue of underachieving boys has now arisen and the spotlight has turned to the "lad culture" that stereotypes boys as unconcerned about school achievement, noisy, mischievous and "out for a laugh", instead of being serious students.

In later careers, men still out-perform women significantly in terms of earnings, promotion, security of contract (permanent employee or temporary employee) and in terms of being a part-time or full-time worker.

Although more complex than it used to be, then, gender stereotypes still do leave boys and men in a more favourable position than girls and women.

## Feedback
### Quick Quiz
1 True, 2 False, 3 True, 4 False, 5 True.
### References
Stratton, P and Hayes, N (1993) (2nd ed.) *A Student's Dictionary of Psychology* London, Edward Arnold

# AQA Exam Style Questions: Sex and Gender

- **Answer all questions**
- **There is no time limit to this assignment**
- **When completed you may compare your answers with the example answers at the end of the book**
- **If you have tutorial support you should send a copy of your answers to your tutor to receive further feedback, comments and guidance**

(a) Males and females have different combinations of chromosomes. Put the correct answers in the boxes below using the terms *male* and *female*

| | |
|---|---|
| Two X chromosomes | |
| One X and one Y chromosome | |

(2 marks)

(b) Psychologists distinguish between *sex identity* and *gender identity*. Amir was born with the outward appearance of a boy but later in life he asked for operations to change him into a female.
(i) What is Amir's sex identity? (1 mark)
(ii) What is Amir's gender identity? (1 mark)

(c) Describe the social learning approach explanation of how gender is acquired. (5 marks)

(d) Give **two** criticisms of this approach
(1 mark for each)

(e) Use your knowledge of psychology to outline how the family **or** the media may promote and reinforce gender stereotypes. (5 marks)

(f) Outline **one** equal opportunities issue raised by either the social learning or the psychoanalytical approach to gender development. (4 marks)

**Total possible marks = 20**

When completed you should compare your answers with the example answers at the end of the book. If you have tutorial support you should send a copy of your answers to the tutor for feedback, comments and further guidance.

# OCR Exam Style Questions: Sex and Gender

- **Answer all questions**
- **There is no time limit to this assignment**
- **When completed you may compare your answers with the example answers at the end of the book**
- **If you have tutorial support you should send a copy of your answers to your tutor to receive further feedback, comments and guidance**

**Source A Bio-Psychology**
**Sex and Gender**

| | |
|---|---|
| Tourist 1 | "Wow! Look at that guy in a skirt! Hey London sure has some strange people walking around. You wouldn't see a man in a skirt back home." |
| Tourist 2 | (Wife of Tourist 1) "But Henry…" |
| Tourist 1 | "How can he stand there like that with a skirt on? How come nobody says anything?" |
| Tourist 2 | "But Henry…" |
| Tourist 1 | "Men shouldn't walk around like that. Back home the guys would give him such a hard time he couldn't stand it. Men should be hiking in the woods or fishing or something. He should be drafted into the army. That would soon change the way he dressed!" |
| Tourist 2 | "Oh for goodness's sake, Henry, he's a Scots Guardsman on duty wearing a kilt – it's part of his uniform!" |

1. According to source A, what does Tourist 1 think the Guardsman is doing wrong? (1 mark)

2. The phrase "Cultural differences in gender development" refers to the idea that different cultures are brought up to believe that different things are appropriate behaviours for males and females. What is the cultural difference in gender development between Tourist 1 and the Guardsman in Source A? (1 mark)

3 Psychologists distinguish between *sex identity* and *gender identity*. Amir was born with the outward appearance of a boy but later in life he asked for operations to change him into a female.
(i) What is Amir's sex identity? (1 mark)
(ii) What is Amir's gender identity? (1 mark)

4  What is androgyny? (2 marks)

5   Male sperm cells contain one X chromosome and one Y chromosome. What chromosomes do female ovum cells contain? (1 mark)

6  Describe **one** piece of evidence that supports the notion that gender behaviour is influenced by our biology. (4 marks)

7  Describe and evaluate the social learning approach explanation of how gender is acquired. (9 marks)

**Total possible marks = 20**

When completed you should compare your answers with the example answers at the end of the book. If you have tutorial support you should send a copy of your answers to the tutor for feedback, comments and further guidance.

# Lesson 58
# What is an experiment?

You are no doubt familiar with the word "experiment" but you may not realise that it has a precise meaning. It is important to use it correctly; after this lesson always check that you really mean "experiment" when you say (or write) it.

## 1. Smoke gets in your eyes

Imagine for a moment that you have invented a new form of therapy designed to help people stop smoking. Let's say it consists of a series of breathing exercises coupled with the silent repetition of a number of phrases like "I am very happy to be a non-smoker". You have had some success with this method. A number of clients have tried it and confirmed that they feel it was the thing that stopped them smoking. You start to advertise your services but the Advertising Standards Authority contact you and say that a complaint has been made; you are claiming to stop people smoking but it is doubted that your claim is true. The Authority want to know if you have any proof that your method works!

> How might you find out **whether or not** your method **does** stop people smoking? (Notice that you haven't been asked how you can **prove** your method works)

Does your answer go along the lines of take a group of people, give them the treatment and see if they tend to stop smoking? If so, then we are not really showing that your method has had an effect because there could be many coincidental reasons why the group stopped at the same time they had your treatment.

> Can you think of any coincidental reasons why the group tended to give up at the same time as receiving your treatment?

The tax on cigarettes could have been increased, making them more difficult to afford. There could have been a national advertising campaign built around National No Smoking Day during the period of your treatment. A nationally known figure could have died from a smoking related disease. The list is endless and although some people may argue "but you cannot show that these other things caused the group to cease smoking" it is also true that we cannot in this way show that it was the treatment either.

> If your previous suggestion had been like the one described above, then have another go at suggesting how we could establish if your treatment works.

To be more certain about the effectiveness of the treatment we really need to compare the "treatment" group with another group who are not going through your treatment. If the treatment group tend to give up while the no-treatment group do not, then we can feel more certain because all the other coincidental reasons would have happened to both groups. Both groups would experience National No Smoking Day and if only your group stops then it was not the No Smoking Day that caused them to because both groups were subject to it.

The important thing about the experiment is the idea of a similar group that is compared to the group we are interested in. The group we are experimenting on is referred to as the **Experimental Group**. The one we are comparing it to is referred to as the **Control Group**. The experimental group is put in the **Experimental Condition**; the control group is put in the **Control Condition**. Beware of imitations. If the study that is being suggested does not have a control group and an experimental group then **it is not an experiment** but some other sort of study. From now on, only use the word "experiment" when you are sure that it has both groups.

## 2. All things being equal

> What would you think if all the people in the group receiving treatment (the experimental group) were women and all the people in the "no treatment" group (the control group) were men?

> Depending on your opinion you may think that one group will find it easier to give up because of their sex. Whatever opinion you hold, one thing is clear – we cannot say that the group gave up smoking because of your new treatment: it could have been the group's sex that caused the change. How would you overcome this problem?

Yes of course. We would have to ensure that the people in the experimental group were the same sex as the people in the control group. You may have suggested that we have equal numbers of males and females in both groups
or we ensure that both groups are the same sex

> Whichever way we do it, we need to ensure that both groups are equal. Can you think of anything else that needs to be equalised between the two groups?

You may have suggested:
- the personalities of the people (if one group is composed of "strong-willed" people they will be more likely to give up)
- the ages of the people (perhaps younger people find it easier to give it up because they have not become as addicted?)
- the social class of the people

The aim, then, would be to ensure that both groups of smokers are equal and that **the only difference between the groups** is that one group receives the treatment and the other does not. Another way to put this is to say that only one thing should vary between the two groups, all the other things that **could** vary have to be kept constant.

## 3. Independent and Dependent Variables

> Things that could or do vary and that could affect the outcome of the experiment are called **variables**. See if you can list all the variables that have been mentioned in these materials up to now in our smoking therapy study.

Up to now we have mentioned:
- the treatment
- National No Smoking Day
- the sex of the smokers
- the personality of the smokers
- the age of the smokers
- the social class of the smokers

> In the above list only one thing should be allowed to vary, the others have to be kept constant. Which one should vary between the two groups?

The answer is that **the treatment** should vary. The treatment should be given to one group but not to the other. The treatment is the variable that the experimenter has deliberately altered to find out what the effect will be. When the variable is deliberately altered in this way it is known as the **Independent Variable** (or **IV**).

> What may alter as a result of the experimenter deliberately altering the independent variable in our smoking study?

If the treatment works, the smoking behaviour of the treatment group will change. The variable that changes as a result of the independent variable being altered is called the **Dependent Variable** (or **DV**) – its state **depends** on what we have done to the other variable.

**So What is an experiment?** Two important characteristics of an experiment are:
i.   It has a **control group** and an **experimental group**
ii.  It is a study in which an **Independent Variable** is **manipulated** or **altered** to cause a change in the **Dependent Variable**.

> **Recap: the experiment**
> Read the following account of an experiment and answer the questions that follow to help you learn about this method of research.
>
> It has been suggested that adults see smiling babies as more rewarding than ones who are not smiling. A study was therefore devised in which a group of parents was asked to take part in a survey of baby clothes. They were shown photographs of babies. Half the group were shown photographs of babies who were smiling, the other half were shown photographs of babies who were not smiling.

No attention was drawn to the fact that the babies were smiling or not smiling. The parents were simply asked to rate the attractiveness of the clothes on a scale from 1 (poor design) to 10 (very good design). The outcome is shown below:

Average rating of clothes worn by smiling babies:          7.4
Average rating of clothes worn by non-smiling babies:      3.2

1.  What is the independent variable in this study?
2.  What is the dependent variable in this study?
3.  Is this study an experiment? Say why
4.  State one variable concerned with the babies that would have to be controlled.
5.  State one variable concerned with something other than the babies that would have to be controlled.
Answers are in the Feedback section

## 4. Confound them variables!

In section 3, above we listed a number of variables that could affect the outcome of the experiment. They were:

- the treatment
- National No Smoking Day
- the sex of the smokers
- the personality of the smokers
- the age of the smokers
- the social class of the smokers

We wanted to ensure that only the treatment varied between the two groups. All the other variables have to be controlled to ensure that they are either removed or that they apply equally to both conditions. Other variables that can affect the independent variable are regarded as **extraneous variables**. If we do not control the extraneous variables they **confound** (confuse) the situation, so they are sometimes called **confounding variables**.

## Feedback

### Recap: the experiment

1.  The facial expression of the babies (smiling or not smiling)
2.  The rating given to the babies' clothes
3.  Yes, because it has two groups, one of which can be considered an experimental group (the smiling babies) and the other which can be considered the control group (the non-smiling babies) – though on this occasion either group could be control and either could be experimental. It also has an independent and dependent variable.
4.  Examples would include:
    - the race of the babies (if all black babies were in one group and all white in another we would not be sure if race or smiling had caused

any difference in rating),
- the attractiveness of the babies or
- the age of the babies.

5. Examples would include
- the clothes (these would have to be equally attractive for the smiling and non-smiling babies) or
- the photograph quality (clear, well photographed pictures in one group and unfocused, dull photos in another would obviously not be equal).

# Lesson 59
# Carrying Out Experiments

You need to read the previous lesson before studying this one.

## 1. Who are we talking about?  The Population

If we conduct an experiment and come to some conclusion, we have to be careful about the scope of our claims. Different groups of people behave in different ways. People in the north of England buy different products from those bought by people in the south. People from one social class have different leisure habits from people in another social class. Different ethnic groups have different attitudes, values and beliefs. Men and women sometimes behave in different ways.

Researchers refer to different groups as different **populations**. You have probably been used to using the word "population" to mean "everybody" – probably everybody in the UK. In research, the word is used slightly differently and refers to the group of people to whom our conclusions are meant to apply. A population could mean all smokers, all the people who live in one particular area, all children between the ages of 5 and 10 who attend public schools, and so on.

It is usually impossible to study all the members of a population because it contains such a large number of people, so we have to take a sample which represents the population. If the sample is truly representative of the population then anything that we find out about the sample is true of the population too. We can **generalize** from the sample to the population.

If the smoking therapy experiment shows that the therapy group have given up smoking then we can conclude that the therapy works. If the experimental group is a true sample of the population then we can conclude that the therapy would work on the population of smokers.

## 2. Obtaining the sample

Clearly, we cannot get our sample of smokers from our own local pub. We have to obtain a sample of participants who represent all shades of opinion of smokers: we need a sample of people that represent the **target population**. The **target population** is the group of people to whom our study's conclusions are meant to apply. There are different ways of obtaining samples. For example:

- **Random samples**. These are obtained by identifying a target population (e.g. all the people who live in a particular area of a town), finding a list of the population (known as the **sampling frame**, e.g. the electoral register for that part of town), then choosing a sample (say one in a hundred) making sure that each person on the sampling frame **has an equal chance of being selected** (e.g. by putting all the names into a hat and picking out the right number – of course, you may need an extra large hat!)

- **Quota samples**. If you know that half the smoker population is male and half is female then you set a quota of, say, twenty males and twenty females so that the male to female ratio of the sample is proportionate to the population.
- **Opportunity samples**. This is probably the most widely used sample by students, because it is the most convenient to organise. You simply ask people you come across to take part in the study. You take the "opportunity" to ask those around you. This method often gives a sample that is very restricted. If a researcher goes into the local pub to ask for volunteers probably the only thing the sample represents is users of that pub who have a "volunteer personality".

## 3. Work it out for yourself!

Imagine that you have received the letter from the Advertising Standards Authority mentioned in Lesson 1 about your stop smoking therapy. You will need to provide some form of evidence about the effectiveness of the therapy.

Write down in the box below some idea of how you would go about setting up the experiment in practice. Bear in mind that you would need to achieve the following factors:

- a control group
- an experimental group
- a control condition
- an experimental condition
- an independent variable
- a dependent variable
- control experimental variables to make sure they do not become confounding variables.

> You may like to start your plan with something like "I would advertise in a range of national newspapers for smokers who want to give up. . . ." It does not have to be completely realistic at this stage but it should be reasonably practical. When you have finished, compare your suggestion with the notes that follow and see if you can identify your study

## 4. Experimental Design

There are different ways of achieving the control of variables and the groups required.

### i. Independent Measures

This is also referred to as **Independent Groups** or **Independent Participants.**

In this design of experiment we take the group of participants (the people who are to be investigated) and we put some of them into the control condition – making them the control group – and we put the rest into the experimental condition – making them the experimental group.

We need to ensure that the participants in the control group are the same as the participants in the experimental group in important characteristics.

Sometimes, it is not possible to be sure what the characteristics are that may make a difference and the independent measures group is just right for this situation. We allocate people to groups by purely **random chance**. You can put all the people's names into a hat and pull out the first ten and put them in the experimental group, for example. This method ensures that **every participant has an equal chance of being chosen for either group**. If there arc important characteristics of the participants that could be confounding variables (e.g. the strength of will of the person) then chance will usually (though not always) put them into each group evenly (e.g. some strong-willed people will go in the experimental group and some into the control group).

ii. **Matched Groups**

This is also sometimes called **Matched Pairs**. In this design we choose extraneous variables and try to make sure that they appear evenly in both the experimental and control group to stop them confounding the situation. We are matching the groups in this way. We can do it by "averaging" – for example checking the ages of the participants and making sure that the average age of the experimental group is the same as the average age of the control group (remember that an average is calculated by adding together all the ages and dividing by the number of people). Alternatively, we can match one person in one group with a person in the other (e.g. putting a 28 year old in one group and a 28 year old in the other); this latter method is the matched pairs design. Identical twins are sometimes used for matched pairs.

iii. **Repeated Measures**

In this design the people who go in the experimental group also go in the control group. That way, we know that the participants' variables in one group are exactly the same as the participants' variables in the other group – they must be because they are the same people! For example, if we want to investigate the effect of drinking coffee on memory we could take a group of people, give them a memory test (control condition – without coffee), give them a cup of coffee and give them another memory test (experimental condition – with coffee).

---

**Can you see any drawbacks to the design of the coffee experiment?**

---

You may have suggested that the second test result would be better than the first not because of the coffee but because the participants have had practice in the first condition. On the other hand you may have thought that one test is enough for anybody in a day and that the performance on the second test would be worse because the participants are fed up with tests. Either of these could be the case. They are referred to as **order effects**. One order effect is practice, the other is fatigue.

To overcome order effects we use **counterbalancing**. Half the group go in the experimental condition first then the control second. The other half go in the control condition first then the experimental second. If there is an order effect (e.g. an improvement because of practice) then it will be cancelled out. For example if scores increase by 20% because of practice then going from control to experimental will increase scores by 20% and going from experimental to control will increase scores by 20% so if there is no effect of the coffee then the two sets of scores will be the same, but if the coffee has an effect then scores after drinking coffee (the experimental condition) will be higher than 20% and this higher score will still represent the effects of coffee.

> Can you see the problem with the experimental-to-control group here?

How can you go from a coffee condition to a no-coffee condition? If you drink some coffee (experimental condition) then you cannot go in the no-coffee condition without waiting for it to pass through the body! We could wait of course and in the case of coffee it would not be impossible to do this but there are times when it is impossible for participants to be put in both conditions – for example if the task is to solve a problem then once you have seen the solution you cannot "unsee" it again. So it is not always possible to use the repeated measures design.

> Which design was your suggestion (on page 1) most like?
> Can we use the repeated measures design with our treatment study?

Here are some advantages and disadvantages of the different designs. Complete the table by filling in the blank spaces. Answers are in the Feedback section

| Design | Advantage | Disadvantage |
|--------|-----------|--------------|
|  | There are no order effects – fatigue or practice – caused by this method. groups. | Unnoticed participant variables may occur more often in one of the two |
| Repeated Measures |  | Cannot always be used |
|  | We can ensure important extraneous variables are the same in both groups effect on the DV | Sometimes impossible to predict which extraneous variables may have an |

## 5. Finishing touches

### i. Standardised Procedures

Whatever we do to the control group we must do to the experimental group – except for the independent variable of course. This means that we cannot ask our treatment group to be tested during a period in the winter whilst we ask our non-treatment group to be tested during the summer; the time of year may have an effect on people's smoking and winter, for example, could make it less likely that treatment would work. Noise, temperature, time of day sequence of testing and other variables relating to the situation of the measurements have to be carefully equalised for the two groups.

### iii. Standardised Instructions

The instructions given to one group must be the same as the instructions given to the other, except for the altered independent variable. Not only must they be the same but they must be delivered in the same way. An experimenter may put more emphasis on an instruction to one group than to the other (for example "Do your best to remember as many words as possible" may be said with more conviction to the experimental group than to the control group). Sometimes researchers hand out written instructions or play a recording to the participants to overcome this.

## iv.  Objectivity in Measurement

"Objective" means something that does not depend on someone's personal feelings or opinions. If we really want to know how long a piece of wood is we take a ruler and measure it; we don't say "It's 50cm" just because we believe it to be. If we are saying that people have given up smoking as a result of our treatment, for example, then we have to say what we mean by "given up". For how long must someone go without a cigarette to be classified as "given up"? One month? Six? Twelve? We also need someone who has no vested interested in the outcome of the study to decide whether or not the person matches the criterion for "given up".

---

Why would it be a bad idea for the person who carried out the stop-smoking therapy to be the one who decided whether or not the participant had given up? (the answer follows)

---

It would be a great advantage to the therapist if all the smokers who had undertaken the treatment could be classified as having "given up" because this would allow the therapist to claim that the treatment was a success. This means there is temptation to lie, perhaps to ignore the odd cigarette smoked, or to err towards the side of "given up" if there is any doubt about the participant's behaviour. We need someone who does not stand to gain anything to be the one who decides whether or not the participant has given up.

## 6. Types of Experiment

**Laboratory experiments** are carried out in places specifically set aside for the study. The "laboratory" is not of the sort that you did your chemistry experiments in at school, rather, it may have special equipment of some sort or just be set aside for the study.

### Field experiments

These are carried out in situations where the behaviour under study actually tends to happen. For example, a researcher may want to see if a new reading scheme is better than an old one so he or she may ask a school to introduce the scheme and compare it with a similar school that uses the old scheme – measuring the reading progress of the children to see if one is better than the other.

### Natural experiments

These are similar to Field Experiments in as much as they carried out in "the field" – the place where the behaviour usually does occur. In these, however, the researcher does not manipulate the variables, they are manipulated by someone else "naturally" and the experimenter merely observes and measures the outcome. For example, a school itself may decide to introduce a new reading scheme and the researcher merely measures the progress of the children in the school and compares it with a similar school using the old scheme.

## 7. Advantages and Disadvantages of Experiments

- Experiments can let us establish cause and effect; we can be reasonably confident that the independent variable has caused the change in the dependent variable. This is not the case with other research methods.
- The researcher has a lot of **control** over the variables and situation, experiments can always be replicated so everyone can be sure that what you have said happens, really does happen.
- **Laboratory experiments** have the additional advantage that the researcher has complete control over the variables but the disadvantage that they are not observing real behaviour in real situations, so we cannot be sure the findings can be applied to real behaviour in real life.
- **Field experiments** have the additional advantage that they are measuring real behaviour but the disadvantage that the researcher does not have as much control.
- **Natural experiments** have the advantage that they are coming to conclusions about real behaviour but the disadvantage that the researcher has virtually no control over the situation.

## Feedback

**Can we use the repeated measures design with our treatment study?**
No. For example, we could not put smokers in the treatment group and then turn them into non-treatment people.

| Design | Advantage | Disadvantage |
|---|---|---|
| **Independent Measures** | There are no order effects – fatigue or practice – caused by this method. | Unnoticed participant variables may occur more often in one of the two groups. |
| Repeated Measures | **Participant variables are identical in the control and experimental groups** | Cannot always be used |
| **Matched Groups or Matched Pairs** | We can ensure important extraneous variables are the same in both groups | Sometimes impossible to predict which extraneous variables may have an effect on the DV |

# Lesson 60
# The Correlation

## 1. What is it?

A correlation is **a measure of the extent to which two variables change together**. For example, take tooth decay and sweet-eating behaviour. As sweet-eating behaviour increases so does tooth decay. There is a correlation between these two variables (sweet eating being one variable, tooth decay being a second). We could also consider fat intake and heart disorders. As fat intake increases, so does heart disorder.

Because we know a lot about tooth decay and the action of sweets on teeth we can also say that the sweet eating behaviour causes the tooth decay but we cannot say that from the correlation alone. **Just because there is a correlation between two variables does not mean to say that one causes the other**. For example, there has been an increase in the use of telephones over the last thirty years and an increase in the consumption of wine in the UK, but using the telephone has not caused an increase in the consumption of wine nor vice-versa. Sometimes a third factor causes changes in both variables – here, we could suppose that an increase in spending power has had an effect on both telephone use and wine drinking.

Whilst a correlation may give us cause for thought, it cannot establish cause and effect like an experiment can. An interesting example of this is the way in which we still cannot establish that smoking causes lung cancer. We do not know the biological mechanism that links smoking to cancer in the way that we know the biological mechanism that links sugar to tooth decay. As a result, we can only say that as smoking increases so does the risk of lung cancer. Indeed some cigarette manufacturers have claimed in the past that personality type causes both smoking and lung cancer; there is a correlation between an anxious type of personality and smoking (as anxiety increases so does smoking) and there is a correlation between anxiety and some forms of cancer (doctors have found that certain types of personality are more likely to be able to combat incidents of cancer). In this case, it can be argued that smoking does not cause lung cancer but personality causes both.

---

**Can you think of any variables that may correlate with the following ones?**
1. Age
2. Family size
3. Outgoing-ness (a scale from shy to outgoing)
4. Driving mileage in a week
5. Weekly hours worked

**There are some suggestions in the Feedback section**

## 2. Types of Correlation: positive and negative

Some variables go in the opposite direction from each other. For example, as alcohol consumption increases, driving ability decreases. As age increases hours spent dreaming decrease. When this happens, there is still a relationship between two variables, they still change together but it is a negative relationship, so these are **negative correlations**. The other sort of correlations, when one variable increases the other increases, are known as **positive correlations**

## 3. Representing Correlations

Correlations can be shown as diagrams or as numbers. As diagrams they are called Scattergrams. As numbers they are known as Correlation Coefficients.

### i. Scattergrams

Let's say that general knowledge increases with age. We could measure general knowledge with a quiz score and age, obviously, in years. Notice, incidentally that it is not age alone that has "caused" the increase in general knowledge. We could grow older without finding out anything more if we were not exposed to the outside world. This reinforces the point about correlations not establishing cause and effect. The following table may represent the results of the two variables.

| Age | General Knowledge Quiz Score |
|-----|------------------------------|
| 10  | 5                            |
| 15  | 15                           |
| 20  | 26                           |
| 25  | 34                           |
| 30  | 44                           |
| 35  | 57                           |
| 40  | 65                           |
| 45  | 77                           |
| 50  | 84                           |
| 55  | 95                           |

We could turn the results into a form of graph known as a **scattergram** by putting age on one axis and quiz score on the other. Try this. Simply label one axis "Age" and the other "Quiz Score" then put a small cross where the two readings coincide. The first cross has been put on for you. Put the rest of the crosses on but don't join them.

A completed version is shown on the next page.

Your version should look like the one below. Notice that the crosses are not joined with a line. You can still see a pattern, however. The crosses almost form a straight line – though not quite. Looking at the figures in the results table we can see that as age increases by five years, quiz score increases by *roughly* ten marks but not exactly – sometimes it is a little more, sometimes a little less. If it had been exactly ten every time then we would have had a straight line.

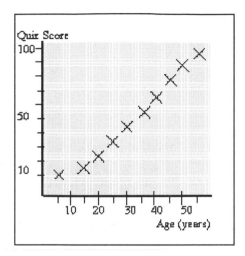

**Completed version of the scattergram to show how Quiz Score correlates with Age**

This is the scattergram for a **positive correlation**. The crosses go upwards from left to right. If a scattergram is produced for a negative correlation the pattern is different, however. You may be able to visualise what it would look like. Here are some figures that show a **negative correlation**. They show the scores from a computerised driving accuracy test alongside the corresponding amount of alcohol consumed. Alcohol is measured in "units": put the crosses on the scattergram below.

| Alcohol Consumed (units) | Driving Accuracy (%) |
|---|---|
| 1 | 96 |
| 2 | 90 |
| 3 | 82 |
| 4 | 72 |
| 5 | 64 |
| 6 | 60 |
| 7 | 56 |
| 8 | 40 |
| 9 | 39 |
| 10 | 39 |

**Plot the results on the graph paper**

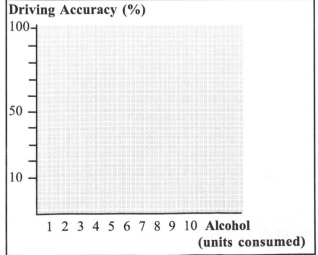

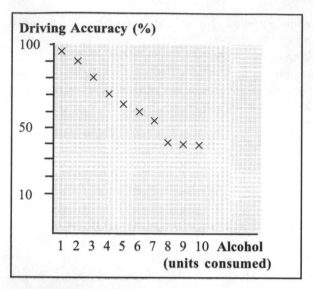

**Scattergram to show the correlation between alcohol consumption and driving accuracy.**

Your scattergram should look something like this. Notice the changed pattern. As the alcohol consumed increases, so the driving accuracy falls. As the line goes from left to right, so the line falls.

What if there is no correlation at all between two variables? Take outgoing personality and reading ability, for example. We would not particularly expect a more outgoing personality to have a higher or lower reading ability than a less outgoing person. If we had a measure of outgoingness from 1 (not at all outgoing) to 10 (very outgoing) and a scale of reading ability from 1 (just literate) to 10 (highly developed reading skills) then we might get results like this:

| Partici-pant | Out-goingness | Reading Ability |
|---|---|---|
| 1 | 3 | 6 |
| 2 | 6 | 3 |
| 3 | 1 | 7 |
| 4 | 8 | 9 |
| 5 | 6 | 6 |
| 6 | 9 | 3 |
| 7 | 3 | 1 |
| 8 | 5 | 5 |
| 9 | 7 | 0 |
| 10 | 2 | 5 |

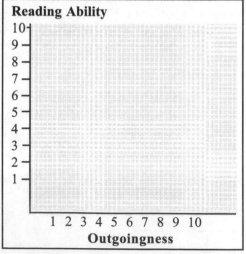

Use the graph paper next to the table of results (or another piece of graph paper if you prefer) and plot the scattergram. There is a completed one on the next page.

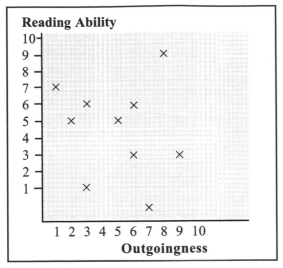

**Scattergram to show the relationship between outgoingness and reading ability.**

As can be seen, there is no particular pattern to the crosses. It is not possible to predict what a reading age will be if we are given the outgoingness score and vice-versa.

**ii. Correlation Coefficients**

A number known as the correlation coefficient can give the closeness of a relationship between two variables. We can use the coefficient to measure this closeness.

If there is no correlation the coefficient is 0. If there is a perfect correlation (one variable increases by one unit when the other variable increases by one unit) then the correlation is 1. If the correlation is perfect but negative (one variable decreases by one unit as the other **in**creases by one unit) then the coefficient is -1 (minus one). Coefficients can be anywhere between these numbers from -1, through 0 to +1.

A correlation of -0.11 suggests that two variables have a negative correlation but it is not very strong (it is close to 0). A correlation of +0.87 suggests the correlation is positive and very strong (quite close to 1)

## 4. Advantages and Disadvantages

Whilst correlations can indicate the general pattern of relationships between two variables, they have the frustrating disadvantage of not being able to establish cause and effect – however tempting it is to conclude that smoking causes cancer, we can only establish that the two things go together.

## Feedback

Can you think of any variables that may correlate with the following ones?

**Suggestions**

1. Age/Reaction time (as age increases, so does reaction time)
2. Family size/Food bill
3. Outgoing-ness/Party-going! (the more outgoing, the more party-going!)
4. Driving mileage in a week/Tiredness
5. Weekly hours worked/Income

# Lesson 61
# The Observation

Many methods involve observing behaviour, but the observation can also be its own type of approach with its own rules. Observations of people's behaviour can be taken in "natural" settings (i.e. where the behaviour would normally occur – in the home, at work, on the bus etc.) and these would be referred to as **naturalistic observations** but they may also take place in "laboratory" settings (i.e. in a space set aside especially for the observation and usually with some aspect of the situation altered or controlled by the observer).

## 1. Types of Observation
### i. Unstructured Observations
Sometimes psychologists simply want to understand how other people see the world. The **unstructured observation** is a good method for achieving this. It involves simply entering the world of the people to be understood and observing whatever is there. In this case, the psychologist may, for example, sit in the bar of a local pub and watch and listen. The "observation" in this case may come from listening to what people are discussing rather than looking at what they are doing but it results in a picture of what the observed people are concerned about.

> Suggest a real-life group of people you could investigate in this way. Be as realistic as possible.

It is a good method for triggering ideas for further study but critics of it would argue that psychologists cannot really see things through other people's eyes, they only see through their own eyes. So in the example of the pub the researchers will only pay attention to the things the others say that interest them in the first place.

### ii. Structured observations
These involve deciding beforehand what is to be observed and making strenuous attempts to ensure that objective records are made of what is observed. For example, we may want to record the behaviour of a mother and her baby to investigate the notion that babies take part in "conversations" with adults using smiling, eye contact, and "baby noises". It has been suggested that babies lead conversations consisting of these actions; the baby smiles and the adult responds, not, as we may think, the other way around.

When we decide beforehand what is to be observed we construct a record sheet of the observations; this is often called an **observation schedule**. The following is an example of an observation schedule that could be used in the case of the baby observations to see if "conversations" take place.

| Observation Number | Baby | | | Adult | | |
|---|---|---|---|---|---|---|
| | Smiling at adult | Looking at adult | Baby noise | Smiling at baby | Looking at baby | Baby noise |
| 1 | | | | | | |
| 2 | | | | | | |
| 3 | | | | | | |
| 4 | | | | | | |
| 5 | | | | | | |
| 6 | | | | | | |

**Observation Schedule to Investigate Adult-Child "Conversations"**

An observer would make a series of observations looking first at one of the pair and then at the other. If we wanted to be completely accurate the adult and child could be recorded on video and an index number put onto the screen so that an observation of, say, the child is taken and then the tape rewound to find the same place so that the adult's behaviour could be recorded at the same moment. The "record" would simply be ticks on the schedule to indicate the type of behaviour observed.

> What pattern of ticks would you expect to see on the above schedule if there really were "conversations" as psychologists would predict?

The ticks should appear as pairs in the same row: when the baby is smiling the adult should be smiling too.

This use of a schedule makes the observation more **objective**. It relies less on the opinions and attitudes of the observer. To make it even more objective we could use **Time Sampling**. It could be a coincidence that we have observed the parent and child at times when they accidentally happened to be looking at each other. To reduce the chances of this coincidence, we could take a more representative sample of occasions when the parent and child are together. To achieve this we could make the sample **random** – for example, choose an hour in the day by writing them all on pieces of paper (1pm to 2pm, 2pm to 3pm etc.) and drawing one out of the hat. We could then decide we want, say, twenty observations and put the numbers 1 to 60 in the hat and pull out 20. Each number could represent the minutes past the hour we had chosen earlier. If we see the pattern emerge by taking observations at these times we could be more confident that the pattern really exists.

Sometimes, researchers take time sampling observations every, say, fifth minute but although it is a reasonable procedure and very practical, it is not strictly speaking, random.

> Can you see why this is not a truly random method of time sampling?

It may be that there is some pattern of activity that happens every five minutes which affects the behaviour of the observed people. For example, a clock may make a particular noise and movement every five minutes (especially a nursery clock with play animals or other figures and visible moving parts); this could distract the baby and the observations would show no interactions at all.

As well as being a good representation of the usual interactions between parent and baby our observations must be accurate, of course. To help make sure that they are, we can use a technique called **inter-observer reliability** (sometimes also known as inter-rater reliability). In this technique, two people make observations of the same event independently but later compare their observations to ensure that they have both of the records are the same. In our example, two people would fill in an observation schedule like the one above then they would calculate the extent to which their observations were the same. A simple percentage could be calculated. If 80% or more of the observations were the same, then it could be accepted that the observations were reliable.

## 2. Participant and Non-Participant Observers

Sometimes it is possible and preferable for the observer to be a part of the group he or she is observing. In the case of observing the people in the pub a psychologist wanting to be a participant observer could join in the conversation and/or be a regular member of the group. It may be possible to take a job behind the bar and observe as a different sort of participant in the social proceedings or find some other arrangement to be part of the group.

Can you see any problems with this approach? Some suggested problems follow.

Problems with this method include:
- If the other members of the group know that you are observing them they may change their behaviour
- If you do not tell the group that you are observing them you may be accused of an unethical practice – would you like to think that someone is observing everything you say or do without your knowledge and agreement?
- Being part of the group interferes with your ability to see what is happening – even in practical terms it makes it difficult to make a record of what is happening

Can you see any advantage to this approach?

An advantage is that the observer is able to understand what it is like to be a member of that group and is therefore in a better position to understand the behaviour.

**Quick Quiz**
Give a definition of each of these terms:
i. Non-participant observer
ii. Participant observer
iii. Inter-observer reliability

> iv. Random
> v. Time sampling
> vi. Objective
> vii. Observation schedule
> viii. Structured observations
> ix. Unstructured observations
> x. Naturalistic observations

Suggested answers to this quiz are in the Feedback section. The materials do not necessarily give a definition of all these terms though they are all described. You may have to provide your own ideas of definitions, therefore, before comparing them with the answers.

## 3. Advantages and Disadvantages

You are more likely to record "natural" behaviour and less likely to make people change their behaviour than you would if you conducted an experiment (this method has high "ecological validity so the observations will be valid and your conclusions can be applied to real life. On the other hand, observations cannot be replicated so they cannot be checked by others, the researcher has no control over the situation, observers can be biased and only see what they want to see, participants may suspect what you are doing and alter their behaviour and there are ethical aspects to be taken into account – particularly if you are doing an observation without telling the observed people.

## Feedback

i.   Non-participant observer: observer who is not part of the observed group
ii.  Participant observer: observer who is a member of the observed group
iii. Inter-observer reliability: checking one observer's records with another to ensure they match
iv.  Random: no pattern; each event (or person) has an equal chance of being chosen
v.   Time sampling: making an agreed number of observations in a given time
vi.  Objective: not subjective; not affected by the feelings, opinions or attitudes of the researcher
vii. Observation schedule: pre-determined scheme of observation records
viii. Structured observations: pre-determined scheme of objective observations
ix.  Unstructured observations: taken without any preconception of what to look for
x.   Naturalistic observations: ones taken in settings where the behaviour would usually occur.

# Lesson 62
# Other Research Methods

## 1. The Survey

Surveys are "snapshots" of the behaviour, opinions or attitudes of people, usually taken of large numbers of people. The information is usually gathered by asking questions of the people concerned. The questions can be asked by meeting the people face to face or by sending them questions through the post or via another convenient point where people are likely to volunteer a response. In some cases telephone interviews can be carried out but these tend to be for market research or political opinions rather than psychological research. It is likely that you have taken part in some form of survey about goods or services either in your home or in the street.

As surveys are usually meant to tell us about the population in general then it is important that the sample of people interviewed is representative of the population of which they are meant to be a snapshot. Ideas about sampling are discussed in the lesson on carrying out experiments. It would be worth re-reading it now to refresh your memory. Apart from this, good surveys depend on good interviews or questionnaires.

**Advantages** – we can gather information that we could not otherwise obtain. For example, we cannot know people's attitudes merely by observing their behaviour; to be sure, we have to ask them.

**Disadvantages** – people may not be willing to reveal the truth about what they think or, indeed, they may not actually know. People do not necessarily behave in the way they say they would in a survey.

## 2. The Interview

Like observations, interviews can be structured, unstructured or somewhere in between these extremes.

i.  **Unstructured Interviews**. In this type, the psychologist has an idea of what questions to ask and what topics to cover but the questions are not rigidly pre-set and can be altered or even created according to what the respondent (the person being interviewed) is saying. It is often used in "clinical" settings – when people are exploring their innermost feelings and thoughts or when participants are being asked why they reacted in a particular way in a study.

When Asch carried out his studies into conformity (see the Social Influence lessons) he interviewed the participants afterwards to explore their thoughts about why they had conformed or not conformed. This type of interview is very much like a guided conversation.

> Do you feel that you could "open up" your thoughts on a personal matter to an interviewer? Imagine you are being interviewed and that you are comfortable with the situation; what does the interviewer look like in your mind? Make a mental note of the image for a moment.

**Advantages** – the unstructured interview allows the respondent to go into depth about their thoughts and feelings and the interviewer can explore any avenue or topic thought to be relevant, from what the respondent is saying.

**Disadvantages** – the interview is a social situation and both the interviewer and respondent react to each other like any human beings. Labov studied the effect of black boys from Harlem being interviewed by white interviewers, and black interviewers, and concluded that the boys responded differently. The setting (in a formal office behind a desk or in an informal room on the carpet) also affected responses. There is more chance in this type of interview that the researcher could use a tone of voice or gesture that created **demand characteristics** – that is, encourage the respondent to answer one way rather than another. This is true of structured interviews too. The way in which the questions are asked need to be **standardised**, just like the instructions in an experiment.

> Return to the question asked above; was the mental image of a person who was the same sex and race as you? Do you think it would make a difference to what you said if the interviewer was quite different from your mental image?

ii.  **Structured Interviews** These involve using pre-set questions, often written down but read out to the respondent by the interviewer. Answers can be in one of two forms:

- **Open Ended** – the respondents can say what they like and their answers are recorded on paper or by some other means
- **Closed** – the respondents are given a number of answers to choose from – a sort of multiple choice response

> 1.  If you were being interviewed, would you prefer to be asked open-ended questions or closed questions?
> 2.  Would you define this question as an open-ended **or closed one?**

The answer to question 2 is that it is an open-ended one because if you wanted you could say "It has elements of both" or "Neither open nor closed"; you are not restricted to any pre-set answers.

The answer to question 1 is a matter of opinion of course but you might like to consider the advantages and disadvantages.

**Open-ended:**

**Advantages** – the respondents can express their complete answer to a question and say what they really believe. Closed questions restrict answers to pre-set choices and none of them may be the ones the respondent wants to give. Instead of being forced to choose between "always" and "never", the respondent can say "sometimes" if it is true. Interviewers can also help the respondents to go further in their answers and give more information.

**Disadvantages** – it is difficult to classify the answers when they are open-ended questions. This makes it difficult to compare or collect together answers from many respondents. It is much easier to turn "Yes" and "No" into "57% yes, 43% no" than it is to turn answers like "Sometimes 'yes', sometimes 'no'" into an overall finding.

**Closed:**

**Advantages** – it is easy to tabulate (turn into tables) large quantities of information. They can be put into computers and analysed statistically and the results can be counted. "72% of respondents had experienced . . . ." conveys a lot of "hard" information. Also, the interviews are standardised and so less likely to be affected by confounding variables like the mood of the respondent.

**Disadvantages** – as mentioned above, the "true" answer may not always be listed as a choice for the respondent and the interviewer cannot explore a response any further.

---

**Memory Aid**
To help you remember some of the advantages and disadvantages, summarise one of each for an open question and one of each for a closed question.

---

## 3. The Questionnaire

If a postal questionnaire is used then there is no way of explaining the questions to the respondents or answering any questions they may want to ask for clarification. Because of this, the questions have to be right first time and this means:

- **unambiguous questions** – there must be only one meaning to the question. "Do you like gay parties?" has two meanings nowadays, for example, (it was originally in a 1956 version of a well-known personality measure when the word "gay" had one less meaning). Even if we settle on one agreed meaning we still have to agree what we mean by the word "like" – like enough to go to parties every weekend or once in a while?

- **questions which do not lead** – "Do you agree with most young people that parties are good ways of meeting others?" would have a built in bias of telling respondents that young people tend to favour parties and this is likely to encourage a positive response in young people and a negative one in older people.

- **adequate answers for all respondents** – if we are looking for attitudes and opinions of respondents then we need to allow them to express their true belief but there are times when we may want to force a respondent into choosing one response or the other (the same personality measure mentioned above only allows yes/no answers because ones in between allow the respondents to "sit on the fence" and not reveal their inclination towards a particular type of personality)

- **careful administration** – a correctly chosen sample must be used. The questionnaire must not be so long that it becomes off-putting. If an interviewer completes the questionnaire, then the respondent must feel confident in her or him. If the questionnaire is postal then it must be as convenient as possible for the respondent to return it – a pre-paid envelope or easily accessible drop off point should be used.

## 4. Pilot Studies

It is rarely possible to get all these factors right first time. A question may seem unambiguous to the person who writes it but the respondent may still have difficulty with it. The purpose of the pilot study is to ensure that there are no impediments to the real study being carried out. This allows the researcher to find questions that are difficult to understand or, perhaps, ones that embarrass the respondent and which need to be dropped.

## 5. The Case Study

Probably the most famous psychologist, Sigmund Freud, created one of the longest-lasting theories of human behaviour ever suggested. He used the **case study,** which consists of an in-depth study of a single individual or sometimes a single group. It may contain details of the person's life history, interests, experiences and so on, much of it gained from in-depth interviews with the person.

**Advantages** – we can gain a wealth of detailed information about the single person or group or event, as did Freud.

**Disadvantages** – the information depends on the person in question remembering details and these memories may be inaccurate. Also, the person compiling the case study is unlikely to be objective; to an extent what is recorded will depend upon the researcher's likes, interests and attitudes.

## 6. The longitudinal study

This involves studying a person or group over a considerable period of time (even their whole life) to see how they change. The National Child Development Study is one such study that follows the educational, social and health progress of a cohort of children over decades.

**Advantages** – some questions can only be answered using this sort of study. For example, does intelligence decline with age? We cannot decide the answer to this by comparing groups of 20 year olds, 30 year olds and so on, because these groups will have had very different experiences and so the experiences may have been the causes of differences in intelligence. To be sure about this, we need to follow a single group over the course of their lives.

**Disadvantages** – one of the biggest disadvantages is that people drop out of the study or are difficult to trace over years and get "lost". Also, researchers change and funding is difficult to secure for a study over an unlimited time.

## 7. The cross-cultural study

This is used to compare behaviour and life between two or more cultures in an attempt to reach conclusions about all human behaviour. For example, child-rearing practices or teenage attitudes to sex are compared in some studies.

**Advantages** – can give insights into behaviour that cannot be obtained otherwise. For example, comparing sexual behaviours and attitudes to sex among teenagers from Holland and Britain may give us insights into why the teenage pregnancy rate is much higher in Britain than in Holland.

**Disadvantages** – it is often very difficult for a researcher from one culture to understand fully another culture. Often language difficulties make full understanding difficult. It is also difficult to be sure that the sample of the culture observed by the researcher is truly representative f the culture.

## 8. Content analysis

A psychologist may examine television programmes for levels of violence, or children's books for the gender roles they depict. This involves analysing the content of these media. Similarly, conversations may be recorded and analysed for their attitude content or for other elements. These are content analyses.

**Advantages** – the things that are analysed can reveal ideas, attitudes or beliefs of the writer or speaker that would otherwise be "hidden", since the person concerned may deny holding them. Also, they are "real" artefacts that are being examined and so reveal the true working of the mind of the speaker or writer.

**Disadvantages** – the things being studied may not be a representative sample of the writer's "mind" and the people analysing the artefact will apply their own subjective view of it.

# Lesson 63
# The Hypothesis

## 1. Is the moon made of green cheese?

Like all other research, psychology research sets out to find out about something. When we carry out a piece of research we are not setting out to **prove** anything; rather, we are setting out to find out if something is true **or not**. We should not be hoping that we find one thing rather than another; instead, we should be just as happy to find out that one thing is true as another.

This means that research is **always successful!** We are never disappointed. If we go to the moon to find out what it is made of we should be just as happy to find out that it **is not** made of green cheese as we would be to find out that it **is** made of green cheese. This is because we have found out **something** and increased the total knowledge about the moon.

Similarly, if we find out from our experiment into a treatment for smoking (introduced in the first lesson on research methods "The Experiment") that it does not work then, as psychologists we should be happy because we have increased our knowledge of how the human mind works – i.e. this type of therapy has no effect. Of course, there is some disappointment in this finding because we are not able to help people to give up by using our therapy but we have moved one step closer to helping them because we can at least say that it is not worthwhile for smokers to try this method.

In reality, researchers often are disappointed at the outcome of their research because in reality they **do** hope they can do things like invent therapies for smoking. But in research terms we are only setting out to find out what is there, not to prove that one particular thing is there.

To achieve this, all research should start with a hypothesis. **A hypothesis is a statement to be tested.** The statement for the moon exploration, mentioned above, would be "The moon is made of green cheese". We should set up this hypothesis, go to the moon, collect information about the moon's composition, then either **accept the hypothesis** or **reject the hypothesis** on the basis of the evidence. Some textbooks describe the hypothesis as a prediction. This is not a good idea. It is a prediction in a sense and it may help you to understand it if you think of it as one but it is not a prediction in the sense that the researcher should not be investing "belief" in the hypothesis. It is merely a statement to be tested. Often, hypotheses (the plural of hypothesis) **are** based on a "hunch" and though we may suspect that our hypothesis is true, in terms of research methods hypotheses are neutral, not a statement of belief.

A hypothesis is a statement to be tested. Can you suggest a hypothesis for the experiment on smoking therapy outlined in the first Research Methods lesson – "The Experiment"? A suggested answer follows

A statement like "People who use this smoking therapy will give up smoking" is a good start. As we are looking at an experiment and experiments always have two conditions – the experimental and the control – we could become a bit more precise and say

"The experimental group is more likely to give up smoking than the control group" or

"The group undergoing therapy is more likely to give up smoking than the group not undergoing therapy".

All we have to do then is count the number of each group giving up smoking and see if we can accept our hypothesis or if we have to reject it. As you may realise, we would have to be careful about how we measured giving up smoking. Perhaps we could ask the members of each group six months later whether or not they are still smoking, or perhaps there is a better definition of "giving up". Also, we have to be clear about whether we would expect the *whole* group to give up. However we decide we could collect the result and accept or reject the hypothesis.

Try creating some hypotheses for the following experiments
Suggested ones follow.
1. We want to see if men play with their children in a different way from the way women do.
2. One group of participants is asked to remember a list of words by repeating it twenty times, another group is asked to create mental images of each word. Will the "repeating" group remember more than the "image" group?
3. A psychologist investigates whether people tend to notice swear words faster than non-swear words

These hypotheses could be:
1.  Men will play with their children in a different way from the way women do.
2.  The group asked to repeat the list will remember more than the group asked to create an image of each item.
3.  People will notice swear words faster than non-swear words.

As you know, we do not always use experiments in our studies so our hypotheses do not always refer to differences between two groups. Here are some examples of hypotheses from other methods: can you suggest what type of method was used for each? Choose from **Observation, Interview, Questionnaire, and Correlation.** Answers follow.
1.  – There will be a positive correlation between a viewer's blood pressure and strength of emotion when watching a romantic film.

> 2. Children under 3 years who are separated from their parents for more than one week will behave in a detached manner.
> **3.** People with strict upbringing as children will express more prejudice than those brought up less strictly.
> 4. People who have experienced many life changes in a one-year period will tend to suffer from poorer health than those who have experienced few.

1. Correlation
2. Observation or possibly an interview with the parents or child's carers.
3. Interview or Questionnaire
4. Questionnaire or Interview

## 2. The null hypothesis

Every hypothesis should have a null hypothesis. It is not quite the opposite of the hypothesis but it is not far off. As an example, consider the hypothesis "The moon is made of green cheese" again. What is the opposite of that?

"The moon is made of *blue* cheese"?

"The moon is made of chocolate pudding"?

"The moon in *not* made of green cheese"?

A null hypothesis **negates** the hypothesis – a bit like saying it "cancels it out". In this case, the null hypothesis would be "The moon is *not* made of green cheese". It is not always easy or clear to construct the null hypothesis but a little practice can help.

> Construct a null hypothesis based on the following:
> (Suggested answers follow)
> 1. There will be a positive correlation between a viewer's blood pressure and strength of emotion when watching a romantic film
> 2. Children under 3 years who are separated from their parents for more than one week will behave in a detached manner.
> 3. People with strict upbringing as children will express more prejudice than those brought up less strictly.
> 4. People who have experienced many life changes in a one-year period will tend to suffer from poorer health than those who have experienced few.

1. There will be **no relationship** between a viewer's blood pressure and strength of emotion when watching a romantic film
2. Children under 3 years who are separated from their parents for more than one week will **not behave** in a detached manner
3. People with strict upbringing as children will express **no more** prejudice than those brought up less strictly
4. People who have experienced many life changes in a one-year period **will have the same health** as those who have experienced few.

**What is it for?**

The null hypothesis is accepted if the hypothesis is rejected. The null hypothesis is rejected if the other one is accepted. In the end, all studies accept one and reject the other.

**If the null is called "the null", what is "the other one" called?**

That depends:

If the study is an **experiment**, then the other hypothesis is called **the experimental hypothesis**.

If the study uses some other method then the other hypothesis is called **the alternative hypothesis** (because it is an alternative to the null!)

# Lesson 64
# Ethics

## 1. The Need for Ethics
**"Ethics: a consideration of what is acceptable or right behaviour. . . ."**
(Cardwell, 1996)

Psychologists can be in very powerful positions. People sometimes put their complete trust and confidence in professional, practising psychologists to help them recover from a variety of mental disorders or to develop their lives to the full. If they were inclined to do so, psychologists may be able to take advantage of these vulnerable people and manipulate them to their own advantage, creating clients who would hand over their possessions and life at the psychologist's request. You may have read of accusations of "False Memory Syndrome" in which psychologists have been accused of planting false memories of childhood abuse in the minds of clients under hypnosis.

One way of curtailing this sort of behaviour is to have a set of rules which psychologists must follow and which would protect clients and the public from unscrupulous psychologists. A set of rules does exist. It is published as a guideline for psychologists by the **British Psychological Society**, the psychologists' professional body. If the Society is presented with evidence that a psychologist has not followed the "acceptable or right" behaviour mentioned in the opening lines to this section then that psychologist is removed from the Society and the ability to practise is damaged though not, as yet, forbidden by law.

Not only do psychologists have to follow rules when they practise their profession but also they have to follow rules when they carry out research. Anyone who carries out psychological research adheres to these rules for at least two reasons:

- it is only right and proper that psychologists, who are there to improve the quality of life of others, should behave in an acceptable way towards others
- acting in an improper way gives psychology a bad name and the public are less likely to trust what psychologists say, or to seek their help when it is required.

Students who are carrying out psychological research must also follow these rules for the same reasons and this includes people studying for any level of qualification or for their own knowledge. GCSE students are no exception to this rule. If their research does not comply with the rules, the exam board is unable to accept the work submitted and the student loses the marks.

## 2. What are the guidelines or rules that should be followed?
For our purposes the British Psychological Society's rules have been "translated"

by the Association for the Teaching of Psychology into a set that can be used by all students. To help us consider the rules, here is a reprint of the account given in another lesson, of the study carried out by Milgram when he researched obedience.

---

## Milgram's Studies

These are probably some of the most often quoted studies in psychology. In 1963 Milgram advertised in a local newspaper for male participants in a study at Yale University (one of America's most famous and prestigious) and offered a small payment (which is quite normal). The people who responded to the advertisement were told that the study was looking at the effectiveness of punishment on learning and they were to work with another participant. The other participant was really a confederate of the researchers so he knew what was really happening.

At the beginning the pair drew lots to see who would be the "learner" and who would be the "teacher" in the study. Actually, the lottery was fixed so that the real participant always became the teacher. The participant watched as the learner was strapped into a machine, which appeared to give electric shocks, and then the learner was placed in another area, partitioned from the teacher, at a control box which appeared to deliver the shocks.

The teacher was instructed to deliver shocks every time the learner gave a wrong answer to a question. The control box was designed so that the switches were marked from low voltages (15 volts) to high ones (450 volts). At 350v the switches were clearly marked "danger, severe shock". The shocks had to start off at low levels and increase by 15v every time the learner made a mistake. As the shocks increased the learner (really a confederate who was not really receiving any shocks at all) acted appropriately – calling out a little at first, shouting louder as the voltage increased, asking to stop later, crying out in pain and mentioning that he had a weak heart, screaming, then eventually falling silent to feign death.

---

If you have already covered that lesson then you will have tackled the question
1.  How do you feel Milgram treated his participants? Note any ways you consider that he mistreated them.
and considered some of the implications of such a study. Milgram's study was carried out in the USA so his conduct would have been covered by the American Psychological Association.

As you read through the "rules" devised by psychologists, see if you can complete the boxes to apply them to Milgram's study.

**Competence**

Researchers should not do any research that is beyond their level of ability

---

Do you think that Milgram was able to run this study competently?

---

It cannot be denied that some of Milgram's participants could have suffered badly and it was reported that one, at least, suffered "a seizure", but perhaps this could not have been predicted and you may think that Milgram would have been quite competent to have dealt with an emergency like that by calling for medical help.

## Consent

Participants should give **informed consent,** which means that they should agree to be in the study and they should know what it is they are agreeing to before they do so.

> Did Milgram's participants give their informed consent?

The participants were deceived – lied to – about the true purpose of the study so although they gave their consent to take part in what they thought was the study (a study of learning) they were, in reality, not giving their consent to the true study. The rules do allow psychologists to carry on without informed consent if, for example:

- it is not possible to carry out the study any other way: in Milgram's case the participants could not be allowed to know the true purpose of the study or it would completely change their behaviour. Deliberate deception should always be kept to a minimum, however.
- the participant is told as soon as possible after the research what the true nature of it was: Milgram did do this.
- participants are told that they can withdraw their results whenever they want.

These last two points are covered in the idea of the **debrief**. The debrief should be given for all studies no matter what type of research method is used and it is an explanation to the participant of the study and information on the participant's results. If it is thought that the participant will be distressed or annoyed by the results then they should not be given.

The idea of consent is also taken to mean that participants can *withdraw from the study whenever they want*. Not only were Milgram's participants not given this choice but also they were led to believe exactly the opposite – they were told that they must continue (with the "pretend" study) when they protested about the learner's condition.

Milgram's participants were all adults but if children are used in studies it is assumed that they are unable to give their consent; it is still normal practice to ask children but their parents or legal guardians must also be asked. In school situations, headteachers would also be expected to write to parents or guardians to ask permission as well as giving their own permission for the study to be carried out at the school.

People with learning difficulties and other special needs and the elderly are also assumed to be unable to give their own consent and the guardians of these people should also be consulted.

If people are being observed in public places and if they cannot be identified as individuals in the report of the study, then it is usual to accept that neither their consent nor a debrief is required.

## Confidentiality

It should not be possible for other people to identify individuals from your study nor should they be able to identify anyone's results. If individual participants have to be identified in the report (e.g. "One participant scored less than 2 in the memory test") then it is normal practice to use a number or initials to refer to that person.

> Did Milgram observe the Confidentiality rule?

There are no reports that Milgram revealed the identity of his participants.

**Conduct**

You should not claim to be an expert in psychology. People may approach you knowing that you are a psychology student and ask you for psychological advice; you should always point out that you are not a qualified, trained psychologist though there is no reason to withhold your opinion.

You should always consider the welfare of the participants; work safely, do not involve the participants in embarrassing, dangerous, painful or illegal tasks; there should be no physical or psychological risk and people's personal privacy must not be invaded.

You should never:

- insult, offend or anger participants
- make participants believe that they have harmed or upset someone else
- break the law or encourage others to do so
- contravene the Data Protection Act
- illegally copy tests or materials
- make up data
- copy other people's work
- claim that somebody else's wording is your own

> How does Milgram fare on this one? Notice any broken rules?

Lots of them seem to have been broken here. Some of Milgram's participants believed they had killed! They stand a good chance of being embarrassed at the extent of their own obedience; they were, arguably, exposed to psychological risk and some of them to physical risk if they were suffering from heart conditions.

If you are worried about these features of your own study you should ask your tutor for advice.

**Research with non-human animals**

In general, these should only be carried out by students if they involve observing the natural behaviour of animals in their usual environment. Animals should not be used for experiments at GCSE level.

If animals are to be observed, care should be taken not to disturb them or distress them.

Milgram clearly did not use non-human animals in his study.

**Choosing the best method of study**

Psychology studies should be chosen with care. You should always consult an experienced person before carrying one out. For GCSE students this will normally be the tutor.

The actual Guidelines for students produced by the Association for the Teaching of Psychology are reproduced in an appendix to these learning materials

Can you remember the six key words that lead each rule of the ethical principles without looking back at the materials? (Hint, they all start with the letter "C" except one)

1.

2.

3.

4.

5.

6.

You can check the answers by looking back in the materials.

**References:** Cardwell, M, 1996, *The Complete A-Z Psychology Handbook* Hodder and Stoughton.

# Lesson 65
# Handling Data

When we carry out a piece of research we collect data (information). The next job is to do something with it so that we can reach a conclusion. This lesson covers how we manipulate the numbers to tell us something

It is easier to explain and to understand the ideas presented in this lesson if we use a practical example, so we shall imagine that we have carried out a study to see if one way of trying to remember something is better than another. In this case, we shall imagine that one group of participants has been asked to spend five minutes creating mental images of twenty items on a shopping list. Another group of participants has been asked to spend five minutes repeating the same shopping list silently to themselves. As this is an experiment, all the other variables are kept constant and the usual standardised procedures and instructions are observed.

## 1. Tables of raw data

"Data" means information and "raw" means that these are the results as recorded; the data have not been processed in any way. Incidentally, "data" is plural so we should really say, "the data have not been processed" rather than "the data **has** not been processed; the singular is "datum" so "The datum has not been used" means that a single result has not been used.

The hypothesis for this study might be "The repeating group will remember more items than the image group"

The null hypothesis might be "There will be no difference in the scores of the image and repeating groups"

| Participant No. "Image" Group | No. of items remembered |
|---|---|
| 1 | 14 |
| 2 | 16 |
| 3 | 18 |
| 4 | 15 |
| 5 | 18 |
| 6 | 19 |
| 7 | 20 |
| 8 | 16 |
| 9 | 17 |
| "Repeating" Group | |
| 10 | 20 |
| 11 | 12 |

| 12 | 10 |
|----|----|
| 13 | 7 |
| 14 | 15 |
| 15 | 1 |
| 16 | 2 |
| 17 | 15 |
| 18 | 2 |

Just looking at the raw data might give us some idea of how the study has turned out. Here the image group seems to contain more high scores and the repeating group seems to contain more low scores so a first glance suggests that the image group has performed best.

It is not always so obvious that one group has scored higher, however.

## 2. Measures of central tendency

One way of deciding if one group is better than the other is to ask where the centre of the scores tends to be. If the centre of one group of scores tends to be higher than the other group's then it would be fair to conclude that the higher group has done better.

To find the centre of the data, there are three methods we could use. You will be familiar with the word "average" and will probably know how to calculate it but there are three types of average that we could consider.

### i The mean

This is the average that most people are familiar with. It is calculated by adding up all the figures and dividing by the number of figures. Try adding up the scores for the "image" group and dividing by the number of scores. Then do the same for the "repeating" group. Do this before looking at the answer, which is shown in the table below.

| Image Group | Repeat Group |
|-------------|--------------|
| 14 | 20 |
| 16 | 12 |
| 18 | 10 |
| 15 | 7 |
| 18 | 15 |
| 19 | 1 |
| 20 | 2 |
| 16 | 15 |
| 17 | 2 |
| Total = 153 | Total = 84 |
| No of scores 9 | No of scores 9 |
| Mean = 153÷9 = 17 | Mean = 84÷9 = 9.3 |

Our impression of these two groups is confirmed by the mean. The centre of the Image group (mean 17) is higher than the centre of the Repeating group (mean 9.3). There are two other measures of central tendency to consider, however.

---

## The Mean

**Advantage**

The mean uses all the scores and is considered to be a good measure of central tendency because of this.

**Disadvantage**

It can be badly influenced by very high or low scores as can be seen from this example:

**4,6,2,1,5,3,98.**

With the high score (98) the mean is 17. Without the high score the mean is 3. 17 does not seem to be typical of either the low scores or the high ones but 3 seems representative of the low scores at least.

---

### ii. The median

This is the middle number in a set of numbers when they are placed in order of size.

---

**Put the scores from the table of raw data in order of size onto each line**

Image Group_____

Repeat Group_____

    What is the middle number of the Image group? ___

    What is the middle number of the Repeat group? ___

The answers are shown below

---

Image group 14 15 16 16 **17** 18 18 19 20 The middle number is 17 (there are four numbers on either side of the 17)

Repeat group 1 2 2 7 **10** 12 15 15 20    The middle number is 10

This measure of central tendency also suggests that the Image group's scores are better than the Repeat group's.

Notice that some numbers appear more than once but they are still listed. There are nine scores in each group so the fifth is the middle one but what if there happened to be ten scores? What would be the middle one then? As there is no middle score when there are even numbers of scores we take the mid-point between the two in the middle. For example, ten scores of

    14 15 16 17 **18 19** 20 20 20 22

The middle two are the fifth and sixth (there are four scores on each side of them) so they are 18 and 19. The mid point between 18 and 19 is:

$$\frac{18+19}{2} = 18.5$$

---

**What is the median of the following series?**

    21 23 23 23 25 25 26 27 27 28 28 31

**The answer is below (no peeping!)**

---

**Advantage of the Median:** it is not as badly affected by extreme scores

**Disadvantage of the Median:** it does not really use every score in the series

(The answer to the above question is 25.5)

**iii. The mode**

This is the most frequently occurring score. Consider the series in the box above. The score of 23 occurs most frequently (three times) so it is the mode.

**Advantage of the mode:** if the scores are bunched together around the centre then the mode can be a reasonable measure of where the centre lies.

**Disadvantage of the mode:** if they are widely dispersed with many on one side and few on the other then they are not really representative of the whole group.

Modes can be very useful in shoe shops! If the shopkeeper wants to know which shoe size to stock most of it is no good calculating the mean: nobody actually wears a size 5.29 shoe; the most frequently sold size will be the mode and this is the one to stock.

# 3. Measures of Dispersion

While measures of central tendency tell us about where the centre of a group of data lies, measures of dispersion tell us about how spread out a group of scores is.

We shall just consider one measure of how to gauge how spread out a group of data is:

**The range:**

Consider the scores from the Image and Repeat memory groups:

Image group 14 15 16 17 18 18 19 20

Repeat group 1 2 2 7 10 12 15 15 20

The range is easy to calculate. We just take the lowest number from the highest. The range of the Image group, then is $20 - 14 = 6$

The range of the Repeat group is $20 - 1 = 19$

What does this tell us? The Repeat group's scores are much more widely spread out than the Image group's. The scores of the Image group are more closely gathered round the mean so it can be argued that the mean is more representative of the scores in this group.

A disadvantage of the range is that it too can be badly affected by any extreme scores. If we add a score of 40 to a series like the Image group then a range of 6 suddenly becomes a range of 26 (40-14) just because of one score.

# Lesson 66
# Presenting Data in Tables

The purpose of this lesson is to understand some basic techniques of presenting data in the form of tables.

## 1. Raw data into tables

Here are some results from a study of perception. Participants were asked to press a button when they recognised the word that appeared on a computer screen. The computer measured, in hundredths of a second, how long it took for the participant to press the button. A simple table of results might look like this:

**Table 1 Group 1 Time taken to recognise words presented on a computer screen**

| Participant No. | Time (hundredths of a second.) |
|:---:|:---:|
| 1 | 8 |
| 2 | 13 |
| 3 | 21 |
| 4 | 37 |
| 5 | 42 |
| 6 | 25 |
| 7 | 23 |
| 8 | 14 |
| 9 | 21 |
| 10 | 8 |
| 11 | 45 |
| 12 | 12 |
| 13 | 22 |
| 14 | 12 |
| 15 | 17 |
| 16 | 18 |
| 17 | 20 |
| 18 | 14 |
| 19 | 27 |
| 20 | 15 |

Although this is a "simple" table it is not easy to see what conclusions could be drawn from the data, mostly because there is a lot of data

**Notice that the table has the following:**
*   **A title** (Table 1 Group 1 Time taken to recognise words presented on a computer screen)

> - **Headings for each column and row** (e.g. Participant No. and Time )
> - **Units of measurement** (e.g. hundredths of a second.)

## 2. The frequency distribution

One thing we could do is ask how frequently each score occurs. The next table shows each "score" (hundredths of a second) and the number of times it occurs

**Table 2 Frequency table of time taken for Group 1**

| Time | Frequency |
|------|-----------|
| 8    | 2         |
| 12   | 2         |
| 13   | 1         |
| 14   | 2         |
| 15   | 1         |
| 17   | 1         |
| 18   | 1         |
| 20   | 1         |
| 21   | 2         |
| 22   | 1         |
| 23   | 1         |
| 25   | 1         |
| 27   | 1         |
| 37   | 1         |
| 42   | 1         |
| 45   | 1         |

Columns go downwards. Rows go across.

The column marked "Time" shows the time it took participants to press the button. Nobody took less than 8 hundredths so we have not included times less than 8. Nobody took longer than 45 hundredths so 46 to 50 are not shown. Some of the other possible times between 8 and 45 were not represented either so they are not shown either (e.g. 31).

The number of times (frequency) each score occurs has been inserted. For example, two participants scored 8 so the figure 2 is placed next to 8.

One thing to notice is that no score occurs more than twice. This leaves a picture that is still not very clear compared to how it could be.

> Construct a frequency table like the one above from the data in the following table

**Table 3 Group 2 Time taken to recognise words presented on a computer screen**

| Participant No. | Time |
|-----------------|------|
| 21              | 12   |
| 22              | 21   |
| 23              | 32   |
| 24              | 43   |
| 25              | 47   |
| 26              | 39   |
| 27              | 47   |
| 28              | 33   |
| 29              | 48   |

| | |
|---|---|
| 30 | 29 |
| 31 | 16 |
| 32 | 34 |
| 33 | 44 |
| 34 | 23 |
| 35 | 22 |
| 36 | 35 |
| 37 | 44 |
| 38 | 36 |
| 39 | 30 |
| 40 | 47 |

**Table 4. Frequency table of time taken for Group 2**

| Time (1/100th sec) | Frequency |
|---|---|
| 12 | 1 |
| 16 | 1 |
| 21 | 1 |
| 22 | 1 |
| 23 | 1 |
| 29 | 1 |
| 30 | 1 |
| 32 | 1 |
| 33 | 1 |
| 34 | 1 |
| 35 | 1 |
| 36 | 1 |
| 39 | 1 |
| 43 | 1 |
| 44 | 2 |
| 47 | 3 |
| 48 | 1 |

This is what the table should look like. Again, no frequency is higher than 2 and it is not easy to get much more of a picture out of the table.

## 3. Grouped frequency distribution

We can rearrange the data to produce a table that often shows us more. The grouped frequency distribution shows how frequently scores in a particular group occur. How many scores are there in the 0 to 10 hundredths group? How many in the 11 to 20 group and so on? A look at the above table shows that there are no scores in the 0 to 10 group (the lowest is 12), two in the 11 to 20 group (a score of 12 and a score of 16), five in the 21 to 30 group (21,22,23,29 and 30), seven in the 31 to 40 group (32,33,34,35,36,39) and seven in the 41 to 50 group (43, 44, 44, – there are two of them – 47,47,47, – there are three of them and 48).

These figures are much easier to understand in a table form, of course: it would look like the following one. The phrase **Class Interval** is used instead of "group".

**Table 5. Grouped Frequency Distribution of Time to Recognise Words – Group**

| Time (1/100ths of sec.) | Frequency |
|---|---|
| 0-10 | 0 |
| 11-20 | 2 |
| 21-30 | 5 |
| 31-40 | 7 |
| 41-50 | 7 |

You have to be careful when constructing class intervals. It is no good having an interval of 10 to 20 and the next one of 20 to 30. If someone scores 20, which group do we put it in? To avoid this, start the second interval with 21, not 20.

Does this make the data any easier to understand? From the grouped frequency table you can quickly see that most of the scores (7+7) fall in the higher times of 31 to 40 and 41 to 50; very few fall in the lower time groups.

Try constructing a grouped frequency distribution table from the following data; it is the first data from page 2. Use the same class intervals as the table above.

**Table 6 Group 2 Time taken to recognise words presented on screen**

| Time 1/100ths of secs. | Frequency |
|---|---|
| 8 | 2 |
| 12 | 2 |
| 13 | 1 |
| 14 | 2 |
| 15 | 1 |
| 17 | 1 |
| 18 | 1 |
| 20 | 1 |
| 21 | 2 |
| 22 | 1 |
| 23 | 1 |
| 25 | 1 |
| 27 | 1 |
| 37 | 1 |
| 42 | 1 |
| 45 | 1 |

What conclusions would you draw from your table?

**Table 7. Group 2. Grouped Frequency Distribution of Time to Recognise Words**

| Time (1/100ths of sec.) | Frequency |
|:---:|:---:|
| 0-10 | 2 |
| 11-20 | 9 |
| 21-30 | 6 |
| 31-40 | 1 |
| 41-50 | 2 |

Your table should look like this. This time most of the data fall in the 11 to 30 groups. Compared to the previous set of data, most of these participants took less time to recognise the words.

Remember that tables should always have a title to say what they represent; the columns should be labelled and the units that the numbers represent should always be stated.

From the mass of data we started with, we now have a comprehensible picture.

# Lesson 67
# Charts, Graphs, Histograms
# and Scattergrams

Pictures can sometimes speak louder than words. It is not always necessary to turn numbers into graphs and it is sometimes worth asking if data should be left in number form rather than turning it into graphs or charts just for the sake of it. The purpose of this lesson is to outline some of the basic techniques for using graphs and charts.

## 1. Bar Charts and Histograms

Bar charts can be constructed for simple data like the performance of two or more groups, as in the following example. This is sometimes done better on graph paper.

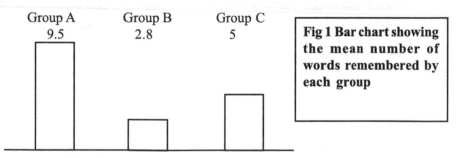

Fig 1 Bar chart showing the mean number of words remembered by each group

Here, the results of memorising words under different conditions are shown. The size of each performance is represented by the height of each bar. There is no real need to label either the horizontal axis (the x axis) or vertical axis (the y axis) as long as each group is clearly labelled and the performance of each is shown in some way; here, it is written above each bar. **Remember to add a title** so the purpose of the chart is clear.

More complex data can also be shown in bar charts and sometimes this helps to simplify the picture that is formed by the data, making it clearer. For example, here is the last grouped frequency distribution from the lesson "Presenting Data in Tables" (Table 7) presented as a bar chart.

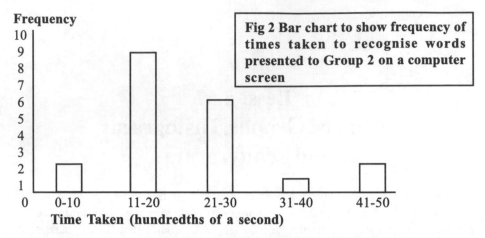

Fig 2 Bar chart to show frequency of times taken to recognise words presented to Group 2 on a computer screen

In this example, the axes have been labelled, the units of measurement are shown (hundredths of a second) and the chart is also labelled. It is easy to see that most people took 11 to 20 hundredths, closely followed by 21 to 30.

Try constructing a bar chart from the data given in Table 5 of the lesson on Presenting Data in Tables, the Grouped Frequency Distribution of Time Taken to Recognise Words Group 1

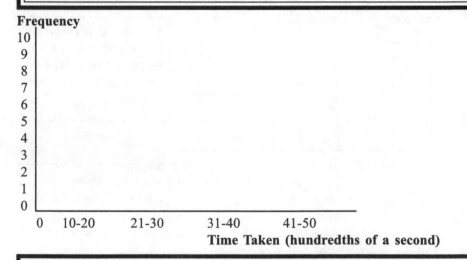

Use the axes above to draw a bar chart of Table 5 from Lesson 8: Grouped Frequency Distribution of Time to Recognise Words – Group 1

An answer follows.

**Frequency**

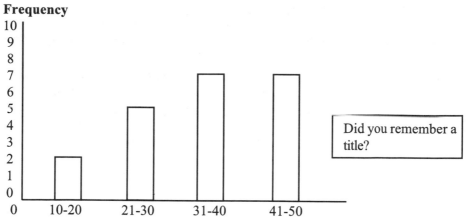

**Fig 3 Bar chart to show grouped frequency distribution of time to recognise words Group 1**

Comparing the bar chart for Group 1 with the bar chart for Group 2, we can see that most of the data in Group 1 is concentrated at the higher end whilst most of the data for Group 2 is concentrated at the lower end of the times. This suggests that Group 1 tends to take more time to recognise the words than Group 2.

**Histograms** are, strictly speaking, different from bar charts. The sides of the bars in a histogram touch and this has a particular meaning mathematically but for our purposes this difference is not important and we shall deal with both as though they were the same thing.

## 2. Line Graphs

These are used when we want to plot two variables that change continuously like reaction time (which can change from 0 seconds to any number of seconds) and alcohol (which can change from 0 milligrams in a litre of blood to any amount of milligrams in a litre of blood). Here is an example.

**Number of correctly solved maths problems**

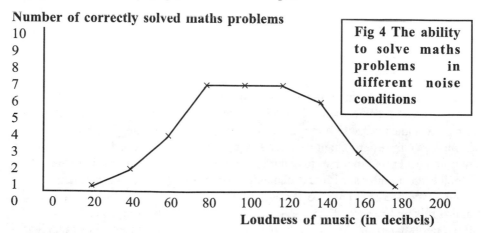

In the above example, researchers investigated students' claims that they can work better if they listen to loud music while working. They were maths students so researchers gave them pages of similar maths problems to solve and played their favourite music over headphones at different levels of loudness. 200 decibels is dangerously loud so please note that this is only a theoretical example. The number of problems solved per minute was counted.

As can be seen from the graph, at 20 decibels (quite soft) the students solved only one problem per minute. At 40 decibels the number solved doubled to four per minute and this increase continued till 80 decibels per minute was reached. Further volume increases did not lead to increases in performance but they did not lead to decreases either; performance remained constant until the sound level reached 140 decibels (very loud) when it fell from 7 problems per minute to 6. This decrease continued till it returned to 1 per minute at 180 decibels.

Notice that both axes represent things that can change in number from 0 to any other number and that they represent **real** increases in the sense that 8 problems are twice as many as 4 problems; 200 decibels can be thought of as twice as loud as 100 decibels.

Because the numbers are like this we can join up the crosses on the graph with a line and this implies that the points between the crosses represent values too. For example, at 70 decibels we would expect 6 problems per minute to be solved; even though there is no data for 70 decibels the line shows that 70 corresponds to 6 so we are making predictions.

**When Not To Use a Line Graph**

A common mistake is to draw a line graph using one variable that is **not** a continuous one or not **real**. For example, many people are tempted to draw a line graph of the performance of individual participants like this:

**Number of
words recalled**

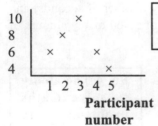

Fig 5 The number of words recalled by participants in a memory test

**Participant
number**

Joining the crosses with a line on the above display is a bad idea because it gives the impression that as we move from participant number 1 to participant number 5 we are somehow getting bigger or better. But participant number 5 is no greater in any way than participant number 1. He or she just happened to be labelled as number 5. The number is just another way of naming him or her. We could replace the numbers with the names of the participants if we wanted to. The person we have called number 1 could just as easily have been called number four and if this had happened the "graph" would be a completely different shape. The lines and shapes of the "graph" therefore would not represent any meaningful relationship between the two variables, unlike the sound/maths problems graph above.

In general, it is usually not worth changing individual participants' scores into any form of graphical display other than a bar chart and this is often not worth doing as it can be just as easy to understand the performance as a number in a table.

**Starting a Graph**

Graphs are usually best drawn on graph paper. They often look better if they occupy most of the space on the graph paper too. Sometimes it is difficult to know which way round to have the paper – horizontal (landscape view) or vertical (portrait view). To solve both these problems it is often a good idea to calculate the range of both variables first. For example, in the maths/music volume graph above, the maximum decibel variable ranges from 180 to 20 so we have a range of 160 with 20-decibel steps so we need 8 points on one axis.

The other variable is "problems solved" and these range from 7 to 1 so we need 6 steps on the other axis. With 8 on one and 6 on the other we could probably use 10 steps on each axis to give room to go down to 0 and leave a little space at the end so the graph does not go right to the edge of the paper.

Remember that, like tables, graphs should have **a title**, **axes labelled** and **units of measurement** stated on each axis.

# 3. Scattergrams

Scattergrams show where two coordinates meet on a chart. We have already seen examples of them when we studied Correlations in a previous lesson. Here is one of the scattergrams from the lesson:

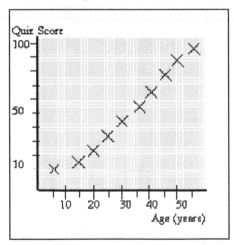

**Scattergram to show how Quiz Score correlates with Age**

Like a graph, we plot the point at which two variables coincide – for example, 30 year olds score 44 points in the quiz score. Unlike a graph, however, it is normal practice to **not** join the points. We can see how coordinates are scattered over the graph.

---

As this is the last lesson in the Methods section you should now turn to the Exam-Style Assessment on Methods, complete it and show it to your tutor.

# Assessment: Methods of Investigation

- **Answer all questions**
- **There is no time limit to this assignment**
- **When completed you may compare your answers with the example answers at the end of the book**
- **If you have tutorial support you should send a copy of your answers to your tutor to receive further feedback, comments and guidance**

PLEASE NOTE THAT NEITHER OF THE EXAMINATION BOARDS SETS QUESTIONS ON RESEARCH METHODS IN A SEPARATE SECTION. RATHER, THE SECTION IS EXAMINED THROUGH QUESTIONS ASKED IN THE OTHER SECTIONS OF THE EXAM PAPER. WE HAVE SET THESE SEPARATE QUESTIONS, HOWEVER, SO THAT STUDENTS MAY TEST THEIR UNDERSTANDING OF THE METHODS CONTENT – IT IS NOT MEANT TO REPRESENT AN EXAM QUESTION

**A1** An experiment was carried out to find out how group norms affect the way we conform. The experiment was carried out as follows.

A random sample of 20 students aged 16 to 19 was obtained from a college population of 300 students

The 20 students were assigned to either group A or B, 10 in each group. Each group had a further 50 members who were confederates of the experimenters so each group contained 10 true participants and 50 confederates. The confederates in group A were of a **similar age** to the participants. The confederates in group B were **much older** than the participants

| **Group B (different age)** | **Group A (same age)** |
|---|---|
| The members were asked to estimate the number of beans in a jar. Each of the confederates was asked to give an estimate out loud then each participant did the same. | The members were asked to estimate the number of beans in a jar. Each of the confederates was asked to give an estimate out loud then each participant did the same. |

The estimates given by each group of participants were compared

a) State the independent variable (1 mark)

b)  State the dependent variable (1 mark)

c)  What experimental design was used? (1 mark)

d)  State **one** reason for using this design (1 mark)

c)  What is meant by the term *random sample*? (1 mark)

f)  How would you have obtained a random sample for this experiment (2 marks)

g)  Identify **one** extraneous variable that should have been controlled in the experiment. (1 mark)

h)  Why should the variable you have identified in g) have been controlled? (2 marks)

i)   The results of the experiment are given in Table 1, below. Use the information given in Table 1 to complete Table 2 below.

*Table 1* The number of beans estimated by each student.

| Group A | | Group B | |
|---|---|---|---|
| **Participant** | **Estimate** | **Participant** | **Estimate** |
| 1 | 340 | 11 | 350 |
| 2 | 285 | 12 | 500 |
| 3 | 266 | 13 | 450 |
| 4 | 301 | 14 | 505 |
| 5 | 240 | 15 | 100 |
| 6 | 325 | 16 | 535 |
| 7 | 335 | 17 | 640 |
| 8 | 390 | 18 | 770 |
| 9 | 355 | 19 | 600 |
| 10 | 400 | 20 | 750 |

*Table 2* Mean, median and range scores for group A and group B

|  | Group A | Group B |
|---|---|---|
| **Mean** |  | 423 |
| **Median** | 330 |  |
| **Range** |  | 680 |

(3 marks)

j)   Use the data in Table 1 to construct a frequency distribution using the class intervals shown in Table 3. Put your answer in Table 3. The Group A frequencies have been done for you.

*Table 3* Frequency Distribution of estimates of beans for groups A and B

| Estimate | Group A Frequency | Group B Frequency |
|---|---|---|
| 100 – 149 | | |
| 150 – 199 | | |
| 200 – 249 | 1 | |
| 250 – 299 | 2 | |
| 300 – 349 | 4 | |
| 350 – 399 | 2 | |
| 400 – 449 | 1 | |
| 450 – 499 | | |
| 500 – 549 | | |
| 550 – 599 | | |
| 600 – 649 | | |
| 650 – 699 | | |
| 700 – 749 | | |
| 750 – 799 | | |
| 800 – 849 | | |

(2 marks)

k) Use the squared paper below to display a bar chart of the results shown in Table 3. Provide a suitable heading and label the chart appropriately

Title ........................................................................................................
(1 mark)

(4 marks)

l) Using your knowledge of psychology, explain the different ranges of scores found between group A and group B. (3 marks)

m) Suggest **one** way in which you could improve this experiment (2 marks)

**Total marks possible = 25**
When completed you should compare your answers with the example answers at the end of the book. If you have tutorial support you should send a copy of your answers to the tutor for feedback, comments and further guidance.

# Lesson 68
# Introduction to Coursework

## Do I have to do coursework?

If you want to gain a GCSE you should also submit work completed during your studies. If you do not submit the work then you cannot gain the marks for it and these constitute 20% of the GCSE mark. Although you can still sit the exam and gain a GCSE, the grade of the GCSE would be greatly reduced without the coursework.

## What is the purpose of the coursework?

The purpose of this study is to demonstrate skills that can only be shown by carrying out your own work and writing a report of what happened. The report is all that the tutor has to go on to award marks for the coursework so it is important that you put everything you can into it.

## When should I do the coursework?

- You have to pass it to the exam board early in May of the year you intend to sit the exam and your tutor will give you an opinion on the mark you are likely to get. You should **agree a hand-in date with your tutor** that will allow time for marking, so you should probably be thinking in terms of early to mid-April.
- The coursework has to be based on the content of the psychology specification so you should have studied some of the topics before you start the coursework
- The coursework involves putting into practice some aspects of the Research Methods lessons so you are advised to complete them before you start the coursework
- You should also have submitted pieces of work for assessment (i.e. assignments) and received feedback from your tutor before starting your research so that you know your strengths and weaknesses.

In general, many students will start the research about December or January before the June exam.

## How long should I take over it?

Agree a timetable for the coursework assignments with your tutor. Make sure your study can be carried out in this period. The Board will not accept late marks so it is out of your tutor's hands if your report is late. Check as you go along that you are keeping up with the time limits.

## What do I have to do?

You have to design and carry out a piece of research that involves collecting data on people, analyse the data and write a report describing what you have done and the conclusion you have reached. To help you do this, a series of assignments follows this Introduction, one for each of the two specifications.

## Can I do any research I want?

The research must comply with the ethical guidelines explained in the lessons of the Research Methods section. It must also be relevant to the syllabus – so it must relate to something covered by the learning materials. Other than that, you may carry out any research you want. You must consult your tutor about your plans before you start the coursework.

## Which research method do I use?

Whichever one you think is the most appropriate for your subject of study. You could also take practical considerations into account. Have you the time and resources to organise an experiment involving gathering groups of people together? Can you get permission to observe children's behaviour in school? Could you recruit enough people to interview on a particular topic?

## Are there examples of studies?

OCR gives examples of appropriate studies in their specification. They include an observation of gender differences in playground behaviour; a survey of stressful events which involves asking people to rank stressful events then analysing the answers according to sex or age or professional groups; and a content analysis of the number of violent events in popular television programmes. Examples of studies can also be found in these lessons along with some suggestions from time to time.

## How will my work be marked?

Each specification has a marking scheme for the coursework, which is summarised, in the section on writing up your report, in the assignments that follow this Introduction. Full details of the marks and the marking scheme are given in each specification. Addresses of the boards are in "How To Use This Book". We recommend that you obtain a copy of the specification and refer to the marking scheme as you do your coursework and write up your report.

## Where do I start?

The lesson after this one gives guidance on the AQA coursework and the one after that gives guidance on the OCR coursework. When you know which board's exam you will be taking, turn to the appropriate lesson and start to work through it. There is a substantial overlap between the two Boards' coursework and the reports produced by students at the end of the processes will be very similar but the boards use different marking schemes so it is important that you follow the right one.

# Lesson 69
# Coursework Assignments

## Six Steps to Full Marks
## Step 1 – Preparation
Before proceeding with your study you should:
- Complete the Research Methods lessons in the course
- Complete at least one of the other sections in the course; we recommend at least four.

## Step 2 – Preliminary Assignment
The purpose of this assignment is to produce the design of the study and have the tutor agree that you can carry it out. You should not go any further than this assignment until the tutor has seen it and agreed that it is relevant to the specification, ethical and practical.
- Your original idea. This may come from the course materials, a textbook, an idea you have always had at the back of your mind, a suggestion by a friend, a suggestion from the lessons or some other source.
- Start by jotting down a rough, short account of what you intend to do. If you have more than one idea then jot them all down. Look at the ethical guidelines and check each one of them to make sure your idea complies with them. **State the aim of the study and a hypothesis at this point.**
- If you are satisfied with the study and have chosen one from the suggestions you started with, decide on what method it is. Is it an experiment, a correlation, a survey, or an observation? We recommend you avoid case studies because at GCSE level it is very difficult to overcome ethical drawbacks and the data collected is difficult to analyse.
- Finally, write out a concise, clear outline of what you intend to do, including **the aim**, the **hypothesis**, what **type of design** it is and what **procedure** you will use (what you will actually do). Show this to your tutor. Wait for your tutor's agreement before going any further.

## Step 3 – The Full Design
When your tutor has agreed a course of study then elaborate the outline so that it becomes a full account of the design. Expand your preliminary outline to now include:
- The aim
- The hypothesis
- The design and why this is a good one for the study
- The IV and DV (if it is an experiment)

- The other variables that may affect the dependent variable and how they will be controlled
- The sample type and sampling method
- Details of the materials and apparatus and why you have chosen them (you may want to put an example of things like a questionnaire in the appendix later)
- Why you think each ethical guideline has been met.

## Step 4 – Carrying Out the Study

1. Now you should prepare:
- equipment,
- materials,
- instructions to participants,
- apparatus,
- observation schedules,
- your debriefing,
- other items you will need.
2. Make sure you are ready to record any data you collect. You may think it is worthwhile to try a small pilot study to make sure you are fully prepared.
3. Collect your data. Remember to observe the ethical guidelines as you deal with participants. Make good records of what happened as well as the data collected.
4. Analyse your data. Review the Research Methods lessons on Handling Data, Presenting Data and Charts etc. and choose your tables, charts and graphs carefully to give the best display of your data. The way you analyse your data needs to be related to your hypothesis (e.g. if your hypothesis says that one group will score higher than another group, then you need to calculate the mean scores of each group and compare them).

## Step 5 – Writing Up your Report

### 1. Length

There is no fixed length but the board recommends that the maximum should be 1000 (AQA) to 1500 (OCR) words; this is about four to six sides of A4 paper for most handwriting. Reports may exceed this length if necessary but should not be much longer.

### 2. Style

It should be formal. Use the third person and avoid "I" if possible ("The participants were divided into two groups" rather than "I divided the participants into two groups"). You should check the spelling, punctuation and grammar before handing it in.

- Use lined A4 paper or a word processor.
- If handwriting, it can be helpful to start each section on a new page; if you make a mistake it is easier to remove and correct a small section rather than correct a large part of the report.
- Avoid repeating yourself and irrelevant details or ideas.
- Write clearly and present charts and graphs clearly.

### 3. Contents – Format of the Report

The following is based on the format required by the Boards and so it is important to make sure that everything mentioned below is included. Use these subheadings for your own report.

**Title**. Should be short but give a good idea of what the study is about. An example could be "Children's views of the opposite sex", for example. It is often not worth starting off with phrases like "An investigation into . . . (children's views of the opposite sex) . . ." as they do not really add anything to the meaning.

**Introduction**. Your study has been prompted by some of the psychology you have read about. The Introduction should begin by telling the reader about the psychology that is relevant to the study. For example, in the case of an observation study on males being shown as authoritative in television advertisements, compared to females, you could write about stereotyping, sex-role stereotyping, socialisation and gender identity.

The Introduction should then go on to say clearly what the aim of your study was **and end with a statement of the hypothesis and the null hypothesis** based on the psychological ideas in the Introduction. If you use an experimental design, you should also sate the independent variable and the dependent variable.

**Method**. This is sub-divided into four parts

i.  **Design**. State the design your study used. If it is an experimental design, say which sort. Say why you chose this design (e.g. It was not possible to set up an experiment in which the content of television programmes could be manipulated but an observation of male and female behaviour in current television programmes was possible). Say what the independent and the dependent variables were (if there were any). Say what the confounding variables might have been and how you controlled them if it was practicable. State the variables in a correlation or observation.

ii. **Participants.** Say how you chose the participants – why did you ask the people you did ask? Say how you asked the participants to take part. Say what sort of sample they were (very often students use an opportunity sample). Go through each point in the ethical guidelines in the Research Methods lessons and state how your study relates to it and what you did about it (e.g. "In terms of informed consent, I was observing in a public bus station so there was no need to inform the users of the station that I was carrying out an observation" or "In terms of informed consent, each participant was asked for permission to carry out the experiment once he or she knew what was going to happen".)

iii. **Apparatus**. State any equipment or materials used. Examples of questionnaires, observations schedules, lists of items in a test, diagrams or illustrations shown to the participants, or any other such items, should be put in an appendix at the end of the report.

iv. **Procedure**. Describe the sequence of events you managed. What did you ask the participants to do? (Give the standardised instructions either here or in an appendix) How was the design achieved (e.g. if you stated in the Design section that you used an independent measures design say how you allocated participants to groups randomly – was it by picking numbers out of a hat or did you use a different method?) Say how you recorded the data.

**The method section should give enough detail of what you did to allow someone else to replicate the study if they so wish.**

**Results**. Use summary tables, charts or graphs to record and analyse your data. If you have a large table of raw data, put it in an appendix at the back of the report. Remember to add titles, label axes and column headings and insert units on axes (see the Research Methods lessons). Make the best use of graph paper and draw charts and graphs of an appropriate size. Say why you used this form of presentation – e.g. "A bar chart shows the differences between the two groups' scores at a glance".

State in this section whether you are going to accept or reject the hypothesis (see the lesson on the hypothesis in the Research Methods chapter). Summarise with a sub-heading "Main Findings". Link these to the aim of the study (e.g. the hypothesis was accepted and so the results show that women and men are not portrayed with equal authority in television advertisements).

**Discussion and Conclusions.** Refer to the following:

- Say what patterns were in the data (e.g. this group scored higher than the other or both groups scored the same).
- Relate the results to the aim of the study – if the aim of the study was to investigate a particular psychological idea, what have the results told you about that idea? Refer to the work you mentioned in the Introduction.
- Relate the results to the theories and psychological concepts outlined in the Introduction – do they support, contradict or supplement the theories?
- State shortcomings of your study – e.g. how limited the data were (any uncertainties there may be about the measurements or perhaps the fact that only 20 people have been observed and this is not a representative sample of the whole of the country); refer to any flaws in the study you can think of – in the way the participants may have had suspicions about the purpose of the study, which could have affected their responses, or perhaps you made mistakes in the procedure.
- Say how you would overcome these shortcomings if you were to carry out the study again.
- Say what else you would do if you were to do research in this area again (e.g. teenage magazines could be investigated as well as television).
- Say what conclusions you would draw from the data – e.g. words can be remembered more easily if they can be turned into an image. Be as detailed as possible.

## Step 6 – Check your language!

Marks are awarded for the quality of language used in the report so check that:
- spelling, punctuation and grammar are accurate
- psychological and other specialist terms (e.g. in data analysis and presentation) are accurate
- ideas are expressed clearly
- the style of language is a formal, scientific one – not expressed as though you are chatting to a friend.

## Step 7 – Submit your report

Submit your report to your tutor. Although your tutor may tell you the mark he or she has given the work, tutors' marks are moderated (checked) by the exam Board who may alter them up to the point when the GCSE results are announced. Your tutor may ask you to do some additional work to improve the report.

## Notes for AQA students

**Step 2**: This assignment itself may be used as part of the basis for the marks for Aim and Design later on.

**Step 4**, point 4: and **Step 5**, point 3, sub-heading Results:
full marks are only given if you do at least two calculations, for example the means and ranges or other indicators like these: say why you chose to do these particular calculations.

## Notes for OCR students

**Step 2**: you may also use the Content Analysis method

**Step 5**, Point 3, sub-heading Introduction: You should refer to psychological concepts and theories that are relevant to your study and use relevant terminology clearly

**Step 5**, Point 3, sub-heading Method, (i) Design: Also state the variables in a content analysis

# Example Answers to AQA Exam-Style Questions: Social Influence

A small town in England is well known for its glass products. At one of the factories, tourists are encouraged to visit and watch the glass blowers make their jugs, vases, and other glassware. Coach tours bring the tourists who walk round the factory in groups, four or five times per day accompanied by a factory guide. After the tour, the tourists may buy glassware in the factory shop.

The production manager counts the number of products made every hour as part of the normal collection of information, but one day a comparison is made between production per hour and the presence of tourists. The data are shown in Table 1.

| Time | 10:00 a.m. | 11:00 a.m. | 12:00 a.m. | 2:00 p.m. | 3:00 p.m. | 4:00 p.m. | 5:00 p.m. |
|---|---|---|---|---|---|---|---|
| No of glassware items produced | 493 | 568 | 544 | 571 | 523 | 502 | 489 |
| Tourists present? | ✗ | ✔ | ✔ | ✔ | ✔ | ✗ | ✗ |

**Table 1**

**Key**

✔ = tourists present

✗ = no tourists present

**a)** Describe the results of the study.
*When tourists are present the number of glassware items produced is always higher than when no tourists are present. The figures are 568, 544,571 and 523 when the tourists are present. These figures are all higher than 493, 502 and 489 shown when the tourists are not present.*
(2 marks)

**b)** The figures show one of the effects of the presence of others. What do psychologists call the effect shown in the results of this particular study?
*The audience effect*
(1 mark)

**c)** As well as the presence of tourists, other factors could have caused the effects shown in the data. State **one** other factor that could have caused the effect shown.

*Time of day*

(1 mark)

**d)** You are walking through the town centre when you notice a young man flat on the pavement on the other side of the road. Nobody is stopping to help the young man. Using your knowledge of psychology, say what is likely to happen unless you take action yourself.

*Nothing may happen. It may be that nobody stops to help the young man at all. It could be that nobody stops to help for quite some time.*

(1 mark)

**e)** What is **deindividuation**?

*The idea that when we are in a group we lose our sense of self and are more likely to behave in uncharacteristic ways*

(1 mark)

**f)** Describe a study that has investigated **deindividuation**

*(e.g.) In a study by Zimbardo, female participants were asked to give shocks to learners when they made mistakes. In reality, the shock machines were not connected but the participants thought that they were. The first group were dressed in their own clothes and in a well lit room. The second group were dressed in hoods and gowns in a dimly lit room. The first group gave higher levels of shocks than the second. This was thought to be because the women in the gowns had lost their sense of self.*

(3 marks)

**g)** Make one criticism of the study you described in f) above.

*The study was not true to real life. It lacked ecological validity*

(1 mark)

**h)** What do psychologists mean by the term "obedience"?

*They mean that people will do as they are told.*

(1 mark)

**i)** Identify a factor that has been shown to affect obedience. Use evidence from a psychological study to support your answer.

*One factor is the presence of an authority figure. When Milgram carried out his study of obedience he found that the participants would be more obedient if he wore a laboratory coat than if he did not wear this coat. He also found that people would obey more when the experimenter was in the room rather than when he was giving orders from another room over the telephone. These finding suggest that people are more likely to obey if there is a figure of authority present.*

(4 marks)

**j)** Identify **one** source of social influence and explain how it can have an effect on our behaviour

**Source**      *One source of social influence is the group norm.*
(1 mark)

**Explanation**

*This is an accepted way of behaving within the group. For example, it may be a group norm among elderly men in a social club that they stand up when a woman joins them at a table (this used to be a common practice among some groups of men). This would be an example of normative influence of the group norm; we look for guidance about how to behave in an unfamiliar situation. Men joining this situation would observe other men standing and would copy them. Women would observe that the men stood and understand that the men saw this as a form of politeness.*
(4 marks)

These answers are only examples. Your answers may be different yet still attract full marks. For feedback and comments on your answers you should consult a tutor. If you already have tutorial support you should send a copy of your answers to the tutor.

# Example Answers to AQA Exam-Style Questions: Learning

**A1** Read the following letter and answer the questions that follow.

---

## Problem Page

Dear Masie,

When I was two months pregnant with my first child I had some days when I felt I was going to be sick all day. My doctor told me that it was perfectly normal during early pregnancy. Usually, I didn't eat at all on those days because I was scared I would bring it all back up; I couldn't even cook because I felt sure I would be sick. On one of those days my mother in law came round and prepared a meal for my husband; it was smoked haddock. She asked me to try some and I didn't want to seem ungrateful so I tried to eat it. After the first taste of the stuff I vomited all over the place and caused an awful mess. I was so embarrassed.

Now, two years later, I still cannot face smoked haddock. Every time I so much as see it I feel sick! The thought of it makes me sweat and the smell of it makes me retch. What is the matter with me and can I do anything about it?

Yours sincerely,
A fish lover.

---

(a) The following diagram can be used to explain how "A fish lover" was conditioned. Fill in the empty spaces inside the square brackets choosing from the terms in the box that follows.

|  |  |  |  |
|---|---|---|---|
|  | Pregnancy Sickness ( UCS ) | $\longrightarrow$ | Vomiting ( UCR ) |
| [Smoked Haddock] + ( CS ) | Pregnancy Sickness ( UCS ) | $\longrightarrow$ | Vomiting [_UCR____] |
|  | Smoked Haddock [___CS__] | $\longrightarrow$ | Vomiting [_CR____] |

---

**Choose from these terms**

Smoked Haddock, Pregnancy Sickness, Vomiting,
Unconditional Stimulus (UCS), Conditioned Stimulus (CS),
Unconditioned Response (UCR), Conditioned Response (CR)

---

(4 marks)

(b) The writer does not feel sick when she has cod or tuna or other fish. Use your knowledge of classical conditioning to explain why this is.

*The conditioning process has caused the letter writer to be conditioned to the stimulus of the smoked haddock but not the other fish. Psychologists call this process discrimination. She has only learned to associate the reflex reaction to the specific stimulus, not something similar.*

(3 marks)

(c) In her letter, "A fish lover" asks if there is anything she can do about her reaction to smoked haddock. Using your knowledge of conditioning, outline how a psychologist may remove her reaction.

*The association between the stimulus (smoked haddock) and the reaction (vomiting) has to be extinguished. We can do this by continually presenting the conditional stimulus (the fish) without the unconditional stimulus (pregnancy!). So the psychologists would simply encourage the writer to keep on eating fish.*

(2 marks)

(d) State one similarity between classical and operant conditioning

*Both involve reinforcing behaviour – associating a stimulus with a response.*

(1 mark)

(e) State one difference between classical and operant conditioning

*Classical Conditioning involves reinforcing reflex behaviours whereas Operant Conditioning involves reinforcing voluntary behaviour.*

(1 mark)

**2** Choose one attempt to apply conditioning procedures to human behaviour.

(a) Name the procedure

*(e.g.) Behaviour modification*

(1 mark)

(b) Describe the procedure.

*This procedure involves either removing an unwanted (maladaptive) behaviour or encouraging a new, wanted (adaptive) behaviour or a combination of these two processes. To remove a maladaptive behaviour the psychologist first works out what is reinforcing it. For example, it may be that attention is reinforcing the disruptive behaviour of a child in the classroom. The reward is then identified and removed; for example the child is ignored when behaving badly (perhaps removed from the room and left alone). To encourage the development of adaptive behaviours the psychologist decides what the behaviour is that is required; for example, it may be that the child sits quietly and reads. At the first sign of the child being quiet a reward is introduced to reinforce the behaviour – for example the child may be praised by the teacher for sitting quietly. Behaviour can be shaped from simple ones that are approximations of the eventually required behaviour, and rewards are withdrawn until the child produces behaviour that is closer to that required. Most schools operate systems of rewards involving tokens like merit marks, commendations or similar rewards.*

(5 marks)

(c) Evaluate the procedure

*There are ethical problems with this procedure. For example, who decides which behaviour is adaptive and which is maladaptive? Should we only encourage behaviours that the "patient" agrees with and what if the patient disagrees? In terms of practical considerations, we may only be treating the symptoms and not the underlying causes of maladaptive behaviours. The process also pays no attention to the motives, feelings or conscious thoughts of the patient and so may not be an adequate method of changing behaviour properly.*

*On the positive side, behaviour modification has been very successful. It is used as the major form of treatment in most National Health Service provision for mental illness and is an efficient form of treatment for behavioural disorders that would be prohibitively expensive to treat in any other way.*

(3 marks)

These answers are only examples. Your answers may be different yet still attract full marks. For feedback and comments on your answers you should consult a tutor. If you already have tutorial support you should send a copy of your answers to the tutor.

# Example Answers to AQA Exam-Style Questions: Anti-Social Behaviour

---

## Aggression Spills Over at World Cup

City shoppers took to their heals yesterday when fans attacked each other at the world cup final. Shop windows and street furniture were badly damaged in the City's main shopping district when rival fans left the bars in which they had been drinking all day and confronted each other, responding to taunts from the opposite side by throwing bricks from a city centre construction site. A total of about eighty men were arrested as police in riot gear fought the fans for two hours.

---

(a) What is "aggression"?
*An attempt to harm another being*
(1 mark)

(b) The ethological approach is based on the idea that aggression is instinctive. Objects or events called "sign stimuli" trigger fixed action patterns. Give an example of an aggressive fixed action pattern with which you are familiar.
*The male stickleback displays a red spot on his belly in spring and other male sticklebacks will attack another male in a fixed, zigzag pattern when they see the red spot.*
(2 marks)

(c) Appeasement gestures may be used to terminate aggression. Give an example of an appeasement gesture in human behaviour.
*Humans may hold their hands above their heads and say, "I give in".*
(2 marks)

(d) Give one criticism of the ethological approach to explaining human aggression.
*We may not be able to use evidence from other animals to explain human behaviour.*
(1 mark)

(e) Aggression may be the result of biological factors in a person. Name one brain structure that has been implicated as a cause of aggression
*The Limbic System*
(1 mark)

(f) Some psychologists have found that hormones may affect levels of aggression. Name one hormone that has been implicated as a cause of aggression
*Testosterone*
(1 mark)

(g) Give one criticism of the biological explanation of aggression

*Biological explanations do not account for cultural differences in levels of aggression.*
(2 marks)

(h) Using the idea of the life instinct and the death instinct, explain why we show aggressive behaviour according to Freud.

*Freud suggested that a part of our unconscious mind, the Id, is driven by the energy of the Libido. The Libido takes the form of two drives, the life instinct, Eros and the death instinct, Thanatos. The death instinct is behind aggression since it is the death instinct that puts us in a position whereby we have to display aggression. This may take the form of signing up for the armed services for example. The life instinct and the death instinct are in conflict – sometimes one is dominant and sometimes the other. If a person commits suicide it is because the death instinct has overcome the life instinct.*
(3 marks)

(i) Using your knowledge of psychology, outline the social learning theory of aggression

*According to the Social Learning Theory, aggression is behaviour that has been imitated. Bandura showed in his Bobo doll studies how, from childhood we observe and imitate the behaviour of other people, known as models. We tend to imitate models who are similar, appropriate and/or relevant. For this reason, boys are more likely to imitate men and as men display more aggression than women, they are more likely to imitate aggression than are girls. We also tend to imitate behaviour that is rewarded or reinforced – either in the model or in ourselves. The media not only portray a lot of violence but also often portray people who use violence as being rewarded. Television police, for example, may be portrayed as succeeding through violence.*

*Social Learning theory may explain why differences exist in the levels of violence to be found in different cultures – because people grow up observing and imitating the models they see around them and some cultures display more violence to imitate. Parents, peers and teachers are particularly important as models of behaviour for children but modelling goes on throughout life as folk heroes act as models for adults.*
(5 marks)

(j) Outline one method of reducing aggression according to the social learning theory approach.

*Teaching prisoners to use alternative behaviours to deal with their aggression has been successful in helping them to reduce their aggression. In this method, prisoners (or anybody who is willing to learn) are taught to use strategies that help them to identify situations when they are likely to use aggression (for example when they visit a particular pub), to avoid those situations and to behave in a different way when faced with an aggression-provoking situation.*
(2 marks)

These answers are only examples. Your answers may be different yet still attract full marks. For feedback and comments on your answers you should consult a tutor. If you already have tutorial support you should send a copy of your answers to the tutor.

# Example Answers to AQA Exam-Style Questions: Pro-Social Behaviour

Read the following transcript of a conversation between a new arrival in the town and a long established resident:

**Resident:** "What do you think of the town then?"
**New arrival:** "Well the shopping centre is just like the one I left but the bus service is good round here and I like the market. I haven't seen much of the social life yet though so I don't know about that".
**Resident:** "And what about the people?"
**New arrival:** "I've only met a couple of people including you but I can tell that people are really helpful".
**Resident:** "How do you reckon that?"
**New arrival:** "You can tell by the way that people do things like look round to see if there's anyone behind them then hold the door open when you're going into a shop, for example".

(a) What is "Pro-social behaviour"?
*Behaviour that benefits other people in some way*
(1 mark)

(b) Give an example of "Empathy"
*When a disaster like an earthquake occurs in one country and people feel so sorry for the victims they raise money to send towards rebuilding*
(2 marks)

(c) Outline Hoffman's four stages of Empathy
*The first stage of Hoffman's theory applies to children under 1 year old and is called "Global Empathy". Children in this sage will demonstrate some gross indications that they can empathise since they will cry if other children cry but they will not reflect the more sophisticated feelings that older children and adults will experience.*

*In the second stage, Egocentric Empathy, children will notice when the feelings of others are different from their own feelings and will try to alter them to be like their own but again this will only apply to gross behaviours and feelings. For example, a child in this stage may give a distressed child something to make it happy. This applies to children from about 1 to 2 years old.*

*From about 3 to 6 years old the child's understanding of feelings becomes more sophisticated – which reflects its language development. He or she starts to express more sophisticated empathetic behaviour. This is the stage of Empathy for Another.*

*The last stage, Empathy for Another's Life Condition, involves mature empathy*

*behaviours and includes empathy for more abstract victims like "the poor" who the child may not actually come into contact with or be able to see. This stage applies to children from about 7 years old.*
(6 marks)

(d) Pro-social behaviour can be affected by a variety of factors including socialisation and social norms. Take one of these factors and describe how it can affect pro-social behaviour.

*Social Norms are the accepted ways of behaving in a given situation. For example, in the conversation reported at the beginning of this paper, the social norm in this town appears to involve looking behind to see if anyone is following you through the door and holding it open if they are.*

*Norms like accepted levels of privacy will affect pro-social behaviour. If privacy is highly valued then people may be more reluctant to help others in case it breaches the privacy of the other person. If equal opportunity is an important social norm then it is likely that there will be agencies to promote pro-social behaviour towards this direction.*
(4 marks)

(e) Give a critical analysis of the factor you have described in question (d).

*Social norms may be overridden by individual characteristics and personalities. For example, any given individual may ignore the convention of holding open a door for others. This does not mean to say that social norms do not play some part in pro-social behaviour, however; even the "rudest" person may be affected by social norms.*
(2 marks)

(f) Outline and evaluate one study of bystander behaviour.

*Latané and Darley set up a situation in which groups of people were required to sit in a room together in the belief that they were to be interviewed. "Smoke" (in reality steam) was introduced into the room and the researchers measured how long it took for the participants to report the smoke. They found that the participants took longer if there were more people in the room compared to if they were alone. They concluded that this demonstrated the need for people to define a situation as an emergency before they intervene. The fact that nobody else took action suggested that the situation was not an emergency.*
(5 marks)

These answers are only examples. Your answers may be different yet still attract full marks. For feedback and comments on your answers you should consult a tutor. If you already have tutorial support you should send a copy of your answers to the tutor.

# Example Answers to AQA Exam-Style Questions: Attachment and Separation

Read the description of a child's behaviour, below, and then answer the questions that follow.

## Hospital Visit

Baby X was brought into the hospital waiting room by her mother who pointed out the toys to the child. The mother attempted to encourage the child to look at and play with the toys but the child was clinging to the mother and would not allow himself to be put down. The assistant entered the room and the child ignored her. The mother put the child on the floor and the child cried bitterly. The mother left the room to go for her x-ray and the child continued to cry. The assistant tried to comfort the child but the child ignored the assistant and continued to cry. The mother returned from her x-ray and picked up the child who continued to cry. The child would not stop crying for quite some time despite the mother's attempts to comfort him.

(a) How did the baby behave when the mother showed him the toys?
*The baby clung to the mother and would not allow himself to be put down.*
(1 mark)

(b) What type of attachment does the child's behaviour reflect? Tick the correct box.

☐   Securely attached

✔   Insecurely attached

☐   Anxious avoidant

(1 mark)

(c) Using your knowledge of psychology, give one practical application of the study of attachment.
*Attachment study shows that the quality of attachment is important. We can teach parents how to form secure attachments with their child and improve the quality of the attachment and the lives of parents and children.*
(2 marks)

(d) Describe Bowlby's work relating to Maternal Deprivation
*In his theory of attachment Bowlby suggested that mother love in infancy is as*

*important as vitamins and proteins. He proposed the idea of monotropy – i.e. the idea that babies will instinctively form an attachment to one person – usually the mother – and that this attachment is fundamental to the well being of the child. The mother will also have an instinct to form this attachment. Bowlby's idea stems from his psychoanalytical background.*

*If this attachment is broken, Bowlby said that there would be serious consequences. This was his theory of Maternal Deprivation. The consequences included affectionless psychopathy and intellectual retardation (as well as dwarfism – i.e. a failure to grow physically.*

*In a study of 44 juvenile thieves Bowlby claimed evidence to support his ideas. His study showed that the ones who were affectionless tended to be the ones who had been separated from their mothers.*
(6 marks)

(e) Give two criticisms of Bowlby's work on Maternal Deprivation
*One criticism is that Bowlby failed to differentiate between Deprivation and Privation. Deprivation is the situation in which children form bonds which are later broken when the child and mother are separated. Privation occurs when children do not have the opportunity to form the attachment in the first place.*

*A second criticism is that Bowlby's idea of Maternal Deprivation fits too closely with the policy of western governments at the time the theory was published – that it was a convenient way of getting women back to the kitchen so that men could retake their positions at work on their return from the second world war.*
(4 marks)

(f) Using your knowledge of psychology, outline the reaction we might expect from a young child if it has to be taken into hospital for a period of three weeks.
*Bowlby observed, and the work of the Robertsons confirmed, that children seem to pass through three stages under these circumstances. Firstly the child will protest at the separation – it will cry and try to pursue its parent at the point the parent departs. After some time it will go through a period of despair when it will be calm but apathetic and sad; it cannot be consoled during this phase. Finally, it will go through a phase of detachment when it will seem distant. It may even ignore the mother upon her return.*
(3 marks)

(g) Describe what Rutter found about the long-term effects of breaking attachment bonds
*Rutter found that separation from the mother was not in itself necessarily the cause of behavioural difficulties for the child. He studied a group of children on the Isle of Wight who had been taken into care for a variety of reasons. Some of the boys had maladjusted behaviour (behaviour problems) others were well adjusted. If separation causes behaviour problems, how could it be that some of the separated children were not maladjusted? Rutter found that the boys who were maladjusted were the ones who had experienced conflict and discord whilst the*

*well-adjusted boys had been taken into care because of housing problems or the hospitalisation of the mother.*

*In this sense, Rutter found that good attachment bonds could withstand separation but poor attachment was associated with maladjusted behaviour.*
(3 marks)

These answers are only examples. Your answers may be different yet still attract full marks. For feedback and comments on your answers you should consult a tutor. If you already have tutorial support you should send a copy of your answers to the tutor.

# Example Answers to AQA Exam-Style Questions:
# Cognitive Development

- **Answer all questions**
- **There is no time limit to this assignment**
- **When completed you may compare your answers with the example answers at the end of the book**
- **If you have tutorial support you should send a copy of your answers to your tutor to receive further feedback, comments and guidance**

Read the description of the study below.

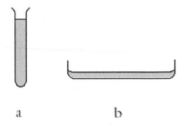

a                    b

A student was describing the work that she did in her chemistry class at school to her four year old sister. She had some equipment from a chemistry set and she demonstrated a test tube (a in the diagram) and a wide, shallow glass dish (b in the diagram). She put some water in the test tube to show her sister how they used them at school then poured it into the wide glass dish. During their conversation the older sister asked the younger one if the two containers had the same amount of water in. Even though the younger one had seen the older sister pour the same water from a to b, she still said she thought there was more water in the test tube than in the dish. The older sister was surprised.

(a) In Piaget's theory of intellectual development, what did he mean by a schema?
*A store of information about things and how to do things*
(1 mark)

(b) In the following table, match the definitions to the terms by drawing a line between the boxes. One of them has been done for you.

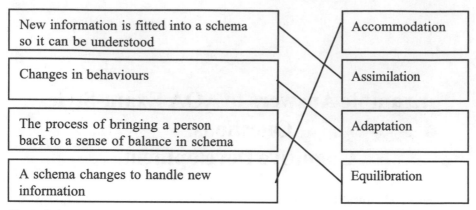

| | |
|---|---|
| New information is fitted into a schema so it can be understood | Accommodation |
| Changes in behaviours | Assimilation |
| The process of bringing a person back to a sense of balance in schema | Adaptation |
| A schema changes to handle new information | Equilibration |

(3 marks)

(c) Piaget suggested that the concept of object permanence did not exist at the sensory-motor stage. Outline what Piaget meant by "object permanence".

*By object permanence, Piaget was referring to the idea that we understand that objects continue to exist when we do not actually perceive them. So, for example, when we left the house and came to college this morning, we assumed that the house continued to exist while we were at college, even though we are not able to see the house. While this seems obvious to us adults, it appears that babies do not assume that things continue to exist while they cannot perceive them; they seem to work on the basis that the objects cease to exist.*
(3 marks)

(d) Outline the Concrete Operational stage of Piaget's four stages of development.

*The Concrete Operational stage is based on the idea that we can think about the world as long as we have concrete examples or representations from which to work. It seems to exist from about age 7 years to about age 11 years. Children develop the ability to conserve during this stage. So they are able to understand that changing the shape of a piece of clay from a sausage to a ball does not change the amount of clay concerned. They develop the ability to decentre; thus they can see things from the point of view of others – for example, they can see how someone would be insulted by a remark that questions their ability, and they can see what a scene looks like from where someone else is standing. Reversibility is also achieved at this stage, so the child can understand that while passing an electrical current through a coil of wire causes the wire to heat up, heating a coil of wire will also cause a current of electricity to pass through it. , The child will still* very much benefit, however, from carrying out a demonstration in which a coil of wire is actually heated and the current measured.
(5 marks)

(e) Outline one piece of evidence that suggests Piaget's theory may be inadequate to explain all aspects of cognitive development.

*McGarrigle and Donaldson replicated Piaget's conservation study using their counters. For their replication, however, they made a change to the routine in which, instead of simply spreading out the counters, they used a hand puppet –*

*Naughty Teddy – who came along and "messed up" the row. When they used this method, the children were much more likely to say that the two rows still had the same number of counters in them and that Naughty Teddy had simply spread them out a little.*
(4 marks)

(f) Piaget's work has been applied to various aspects of working with children. Describe one such application.

*The principle of matching the child's stage of reasoning with toys and equipment to encourage it to learn and develop, is applied at all stages of formal education. For example, language development is a very important characteristic of the nursery-age child and so this is encouraged with the use of nursery rhymes and songs. Nurseries will devote specific periods in the day to these activities and to extending language skills through story-telling and discussion*
(4 marks)

These answers are only examples. Your answers may be different yet still attract full marks. For feedback and comments on your answers you should consult a tutor. If you already have tutorial support you should send a copy of your answers to the tutor.

# Example Answers to AQA Exam-Style Questions: The Development of Moral Behaviour

*The Unlikely Daily News*

---

## Cabinet Minister in lie shock!

A cabinet minister's career lay in ruins today as his daughter revealed that he had lied to her as a child. Minister X's daughter, Little Miss X said to a packed press conference:

"My father told me that my Christmas presents were delivered by a man in a red suit with white fur round it and black boots. In fact, I now know that he and mother bought the presents and placed them at the foot of the bed themselves!"

---

Is it right to lie to children under some circumstances? We often face problems in deciding whether our behaviour is **Moral** or not.

1.  Give a definition of Moral behaviour
*Moral behaviour is behaviour that is seen as right or good.*
(1 mark)

2.  The **Cognitive** approach to explaining moral development involves stages. Piaget's theory suggested that we pass from a **Heteronomous** stage to an **Autonomous** stage.

(a) At approximately what age do we pass from the heteronomous stage to the autonomous?
*At approximately eight years.*
(1 mark)

(b) Give a definition of each term heteronomous and autonomous
**Heteronomous**
*Heteronomous means that others are in charge*
(1 mark)
**Autonomous**
*Autonomous means we set our own rules.*
(1 mark)

(c) Briefly describe a study that illustrates Piaget's cognitive theory of moral development.

*In one study that illustrates Piaget's theory he used moral dilemmas. He described a situation in which a child damaged large amounts of crockery by accident and another in which a child damaged a single piece on purpose. When asked "Who was the naughtiest?" younger children tended to say the child who damaged large amounts, even though he had not intended to do the damage. Older children tended to say that the child who damaged the small amount on purpose was the naughtiest. Piaget concluded the idea of taking intention into account is a more mature approach and reflects the autonomous stage in which we are in control of our own behaviour. It also reflected the use of moral relativism where the consequences of the behaviour are not the most important point about behaviour when it comes to judging its morality.*

(3 marks)

(d) Give **two** criticisms of the Piaget's cognitive approach to explaining moral development.

### Criticism 1

*Piaget used children in his studies and this can raise problems about whether they fully understand what is being asked of them. Children's language is not as fully developed as an adults and their attention spans are not as great, so they may not be giving a full answer to the question and this may mean they are not fully revealing what they think.*

### Criticism 2

*The theory says that there are only two stages of moral development – heteronomous and autonomous – but this seems inadequate. It does not seem to take account of the fine differences we might expect across human development. For example, if we switch from heteronomous to autonomous reasoning at about age eight this means that a fourteen year old should have the same answer to a moral dilemma as a forty year old but in reality these two age groups often differ in what they see as right or wrong.*

(4 marks)

3. Describe **one** other theory of moral development

### Name of theory

*The Psychoanalytic Theory*

### Description

*Sigmund Freud suggested that our moral development was a process that occurred in the unconscious mind through two main routes, firstly through the Superego and secondly through a process of Internalisation.*

*The unconscious mind develops through the same stages in all of us according to this theory. The first element to develop is the Id which drives us to satisfy our biological needs; the second stage is the Ego which directs us to satisfy our Id's needs in a socially acceptable way. The last part to develop is the Superego – the conscience of the unconscious mind which causes us to ask whether what we are doing is morally acceptable and can punish us with guilt if we do something it decides is not morally correct or can reward us with feelings of high self-esteem if we do something that is morally good.*

*At about the age of five years children fall in love with opposite sex parents*

*according to Freud. This is known as the Oedipus Complex. Freud suggested that children actually desire the parent sexually and are worried that the other parent will realise their true feelings. They resolve the problem by trying to become like the same sex parent. This is known as Internalising the same sex parent. As part of this Internalisation, children also take on the moral code, belief and behaviours of the parent and this is also part of the development of the child's moral outlook.*
(6 marks)

4.  Describe Gilligan's contribution to the evaluation of theories of moral development.

*Gilligan noted that Freud's theory suggested that males developed stronger morals than females – they put more energy into internalising the father because they believed he would castrate them if he found out they desired the mother sexually. Also, she noted that another well-known theory by Kohlberg continually placed women below men in stages of moral development.*

*Gilligan, therefore, interviewed both men and women about morals and found that there is indeed a difference in the way that men and women develop morally. When men think about what is morally correct they tend to focus on justice (what is right is what is just) whereas when women think about what is morally correct they tend to think about minimising suffering and maximising caring (what is morally correct is what is best for people). Gilligan pointed out that psychologists who had written about morals previously were men who saw morals from a man's point of view.*
(3 marks)

These answers are only examples. Your answers may be different yet still attract full marks. For feedback and comments on your answers you should consult a tutor. If you already have tutorial support you should send a copy of your answers to the tutor.

# Example Answers to AQA Exam-Style Questions: Prejudice and Discrimination

Read the following conversation

---

**Welcome to the club!**

"Hi Asif, welcome to the club"

"Huh; hi"

"You look down Asif, what's the matter?"

"Its nothing, just the bus journey over here"

"What about it?"

"Well, I travelled all the way from town and the bus filled up and I was the only non-white on it."

"So what?"

"So there was one empty seat and it was next to me but nobody took it, that's what. Two elderly people even stood at the front rather than sit next to me. I felt like rubbish"

"What, no-one at all sat on it?"

"Well there was a bloke who sat on it just before I got off – but he looked gay!"

---

(a) What do psychologists mean by the term prejudice?

*Prejudice means judging someone before you know anything about the individual. The judgement is usually negative and is often based on the assumption that the person belongs to a group and that all members of the group are like that.*
(2 marks)

(b) What do psychologists mean by the term discrimination?

*Discrimination means that a person treats someone unfairly compared to other groups. Discriminating against a person or group is likely to be based on a prejudice against that group.*
(2 marks)

(c) Adorno explained prejudice in terms of the Authoritarian Personality. Describe one characteristic of the Authoritarian Personality according to Adorno.

*Conservatism: wanting to keep everything the same and disliking change and difference*
(2 marks)

(d) Outline **one** criticism of Adorno's explanation of prejudice.

*It cannot explain why a whole nation would be prejudiced – for example why the majority of Germany supported anti-Semitism during the Second World War.*
(2 marks)

(e) Outline **one** other psychological explanation of prejudice

*Inter-group conflict can sometimes be a cause of prejudice. If two groups compete for the same goal then prejudice by members of one group against members of the other group may follow. Sherif showed that two teams of boys competing for a prize developed very obvious prejudices; even boys who had been friends before the rivalry developed prejudices against the friend during it.*

(3 marks)

(f) Give **one** criticism of the explanation you have outlined in (e) above.

*There are examples of people making friends across the divide of two rivals groups – for example, individual members of Catholic and Protestant communities in Northern Ireland do form friendships across the political divide.*

(2 marks)

(g) Describe one psychological study in which the reduction of discrimination was investigated. Indicate in your answer the method used, the results obtained and the conclusions drawn

**Method**

*Sherif ran an American summer camp in which he arranged for the two rival groups to be put in a situation in which they had to co-operate to achieve a common goal – for example the boys had to work together to mend the water supply, which Sherif had arranged to break down.*

**Results**

*The measures of prejudice that Sherif used (involving interviewing the boys on their views of the other group) showed that prejudiced attitudes had reduced dramatically.*

**Conclusion**

*Prejudice can be reduced by arranging for the holders of the prejudice to work towards a common goal with the object of the prejudice.*

(4 marks)

(h) Assess the likely success of the technique of prejudice reduction which follows from the study you outlined in (g)

*Whilst the method worked for Sherif in a manipulated observation this does not mean to say that it will work in all situations of conflict. Whilst there are many examples of joint enterprises being set up in Northern Ireland, for example, which result in the people who have been involved reducing their prejudice, this has not stopped all prejudice in the conflict.*

(3 marks)

These answers are only examples. Your answers may be different yet still attract full marks. For feedback and comments on your answers you should consult a tutor. If you already have tutorial support you should send a copy of your answers to the tutor.

# Example Answers to AQA Exam-Style Questions: Memory

A mnemonist is a person who can display impressive performances of memory – sometimes a mnemonist may make a living from these displays. On a television chat show recently, a mnemonist said, "It is not just a question of being able to recall events well. To perform these feats you have to pay attention to all aspects of memory: encoding and storage can be just as important as retrieval".

(a) From your knowledge of the psychology of memory, state the meaning of "encoding".
*Encoding is the process by which an item is represented in memory – often in the form of a sound, a "picture" or a meaning. These are referred to as "acoustic", "visual" and "semantic" codes.*
(2 marks)

(b) Describe one way in which remembered items may be organised in the memory
*Items may be organised in Categories. This involves storing items according to what type of thing they are. For example, we may store all types of car under one heading, trees under another and houses under another. Bower showed how participants could remember items presented in categories better than they remembered items presented randomly.*
(2 marks)

(c) Briefly describe either the Reconstructive model or the Levels of Processing model of memory.
Name of Model __*Levels of Processing*__       _____
*The Levels of Processing model is based on the idea that memory is a by-product of our ordinary thinking rather than a separate system in itself. It includes the notion that the deeper we think about something, the more likely we are to remember it. This model is consistent with the findings that we remember more about something is we are allowed to "elaborate" on it rather than just rehearse it.*

*Craik and Lockhart asked participants questions about some items. The first set of questions was designed to make the participants think about the items at a very short level so they included questions like "Is the item written in capitals?" Another set of questions was designed to make the participants think at a much deeper level about the items – so this included questions like "Can you cook with this?" To answer the last question, the participants would have to think about what the word in front of them meant. The researchers found that the participants remembered more of the deeply processed words than the ones that were processed at a shallow level.*
(4 marks)

(d) Describe one study of Eyewitness Testimony.

*Loftus asked two groups of participants to watch a film of two cars crashing. After the film, she asked the first group to estimate the speed the cars were travelling when they "hit". She asked the second group to estimate the speed the cars were travelling when they "smashed". She found that the group who were exposed to the question with the word "smashed" estimated a much higher speed than the group who were exposed to the word "hit".*
(4 marks)

(e) Briefly evaluate the study you described in (d), above.

*There is no doubt that this study, and further similar ones with similar results, provide a good illustration of the way the participants' reports of speed could be affected by the language of the question but the study lacks ecological validity – it is not "true to life". Eyewitnesses see a real crash and know when they are questioned that their testimony makes a real difference. Participants have only seen a film and know they are in a study so this may affect their responses.*
(3 marks)

(f) Describe one explanation of Forgetting

*Freud suggested that we forget because the item we want to remember is somehow painful to us; forgetting is a defence mechanism that protects us from the trauma we would suffer if we remembered the item. We forget the appointment with the dentist because we are afraid of the pain that may result from the appointment. We forget early experiences of our lives because they are painful to us. This is an unconscious process and of course we are not aware of the reason we forget. The approach was part of Freud's overall Psychoanalytic Theory and is called "Motivated Forgetting".*
(3 marks)

(g) Give one criticism of the explanation you described in (f), above

*It is not usually possible to verify Freud's theory by collecting empirical evidence because the ideas in the theory are based on processes that Freud says are unconscious.*
(2 marks)

These answers are only examples. Your answers may be different yet still attract full marks. For feedback and comments on your answers you should consult a tutor. If you already have tutorial support you should send a copy of your answers to the tutor.

# Example Answers to AQA Exam-Style Questions: Perception

Psychologists investigated people's reactions to sketch A, shown below

**Sketch A**

**Condition 1:**
30 participants were shown ten sketches of young women; sketch A was shown as the seventh sketch
**Condition 2:**
30 participants were shown ten sketches of elderly women; sketch A was shown as the seventh sketch

All participants were then asked to estimate the ages of the women shown in sketches three, seven and ten; their responses were then classified into age groups of "Old" and "Young". The responses to sketch seven are shown in Table 1

*Table 1 Number of people who classified sketch seven as Old or Young*

|  | CONDITION 1 | CONDITION 2 |
|---|---|---|
| CLASSIFIED SKETCH 7 AS OLD | 1 | 29 |
| CLASSIFIED SKETCH 7 AS YOUNG | 28 | 2 |

(a) Describe the results of the study
*The perception of the image has been affected by the other pictures shown. The people who were shown pictures of young women have perceived the ambiguous figure as a young woman and the ones who were shown an old woman have perceived an old one.*
(2 marks)

(b) Using your knowledge of psychology, explain how the results provide evidence for perception being an active process.
*The participants have not really seen the image that is in front of them, instead, they have turned their sensory data into a percept that is based on their previous experience. This is one of the main points about the psychologists' findings on perception; we do not just register what is in front of us like a camera registers a picture. The participants have used their previous experience (which in this case*

*was just a few moments ago) to construct a percept and this is an active process,
not just passively "receiving" a picture.*
(5 marks)

(c) It was discovered later that the two people in condition 2 who classified
sketch 7 as young were a pair of elderly twin women who had featured in the
tabloid newspapers that same week becoming famous for having "toy boy"
companions in their early twenties.

   (i) What does this tell us about how previous experience, motivation
      and emotion may influence perception?

*Somehow these two women have "overridden" the effect of the pictures that were
shown of elderly people. Their previous experience of their "toyboy" partners has
been more influential, as has their motivation (to "find" younger people, perhaps,
or to be more open to young images) and their emotional involvement with younger
people. All have influenced their perception.*
(3 marks)

   (ii) Describe a study that investigates how perceptual defence may
      influence perception.

*McGuiness flashed images of words to participants who were asked to say
when they recognised the words. Some of the words were taboo ones. The researchers
found that participants took significantly longer to identify the taboo words than
to identify the non-taboo ones. McGuiness concluded that the participants wanted
to subconsciously defend themselves from the emotions around the taboo words
and so failed to perceive the words normally.*
(5 marks)

(d)

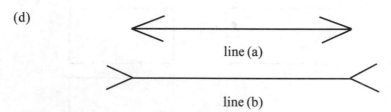

line (a)

line (b)

   (i) The diagram above is the Muller-Lyer illusion. What type of illusion
     is it?
(Tick the appropriate box)

✔ Distortion

☐ Ambiguous figure

☐ Texture Gradient

(1 mark)

   (ii) Most people see line (b) as longer than line (a). Use your knowledge
     of psychology to explain this effect.

*Gregory suggested that we use cues and hypotheses to construct perceptions. In the case of this illusion, we use the cues of two images we have seen before, the inside corner of a room (line b) and the outside corner of a building (line a). The retinal images of both lines are the same but the rules of size constancy say that for this to be true of the corners the actual line (b) must be longer and so we perceive it as longer.*

(4 marks)

**Total possible marks = 20**

These answers are only examples. Your answers may be different yet still attract full marks. For feedback and comments on your answers you should consult a tutor. If you already have tutorial support you should send a copy of your answers to the tutor.

# Example Answers to AQA Exam-Style Questions: Sex and Gender

(a) Males and females have different combinations of chromosomes. Put the correct answers in the boxes below using the terms male and female

| Two X chromosomes | *Female* |
|---|---|
| One X and one Y chromosome | *Male* |

(2 marks)

(b) Psychologists distinguish between sex identity and gender identity. Amir was born with the outward appearance of a boy but later in life he asked for operations to change him into a female.
  (i)  What is Amir's sex identity?      *Male*      (1 mark)
  (ii) What is Amir's gender identity?    *Female*    (1 mark)

(c) Describe the social learning approach explanation of how gender is acquired.
*Children imitate the behaviour of models they see as relevant and similar. Bandura's research generally supports this idea. Girls will see other females as relevant and boys will see other males as relevant so gender behaviour will develop by this process of modelling behaviour. Apart from this, they will be encouraged to copy such behaviour by direct rewards and punishments given by others. For example, boys may be told they are "strong like daddy" or girls may be told they are "good girls for helping in the kitchen like mummy" so their gender behaviour will be reinforced by these rewards. Children will also be punished for displaying cross-gender behaviour. Faggot found, for example, that boys are more heavily criticised for displaying female behaviour than were girls for displaying male behaviour. Children will also imitate behaviour which they see others being rewarded for – this is known as vicarious reinforcement.*

*As well as imitating behaviour, children come to identify – this occurs when we "put ourselves in the shoes" of the model and act **as though we were** the model.*
(5 marks)

(d) Give **two** criticisms of this approach
1 *This explanation does not take account of biological factors like hormones and chromosomes that may be the basis of gender differences.*
(1 mark)
2 *This theory doesn't explain why some people adopt cross-gender behaviour.*
(1 mark)

(e) Use your knowledge of psychology to outline how the family or the media may promote and reinforce gender stereotypes.

*Fagot showed how parents may encourage different behaviours in boys and girls. She observed 24 sets of parents and recorded how boys were encouraged to play with "male toys like building blocks and girls were encouraged to play with "female" toys like dolls. Both sets of children were discouraged from playing with "opposite sex" toys. The work of Bandura also showed how children will imitate the behaviour of models. In the home, parents will act as models and also are in the most powerful position to give rewards for behaviour they favour. Finally, Smith and Lloyd's study of "Baby X" showed how a baby presented as the opposite sex to its true sex would be encouraged to play in the way that is appropriate to its presented sex so, again, parents seem to be in the habit of encouraging gender-appropriate behaviour.*

(5 marks)

(f) Outline **one** equal opportunities issue raised by either the social learning or the psychoanalytical approach to gender development.

*If we accept the social learning approach is correct and children copy behaviour then we should be careful about presenting them with models behaving in a way we do not want children to behave. For example, if we constantly show children that girls behave in a passive, timid and deferential way and that boys explore, command and take the lead then we would expect these behaviours to be repeated in adult life and this would limit the achievement and success of women as well as burden men unfairly with lead roles.*

*We would need, for example, to think carefully about the images of males and females presented in children's textbooks and in other forms of the media. We need to ensure that these images do not give the impression that girls do not take lead roles or act in "brave" ways.*

(4 marks)

These answers are only examples. Your answers may be different yet still attract full marks. For feedback and comments on your answers you should consult a tutor. If you already have tutorial support you should send a copy of your answers to the tutor.

# Example Answers to OCR Exam-Style Questions: Social Influence and Environment and Behaviour

**Source A Social Psychology**
**Social Influence Environment and Behaviour**

> One of the best-known studies in social psychology is the conformity study carried out by Asch. A "stooge" participant was asked to join a group of other students (who all knew what was going to happen and that the stooge was really the only person being studied). They all gave the wrong answers to questions about the length of some lines and the stooge tended to give the same wrong answers in many cases. The researchers concluded that the stooge had conformed to an expected way of behaving. Some critics were concerned about the ethics of humiliating the stooge.

1. According to the source, what did the researchers conclude?
*That the stooge had conformed to an expected way of behaving.*
(1 mark)

2. Suggest **two** reasons why people might think that Asch's study of conformity was unethical.
1. *Because he studied a participant without obtaining his permission.*
2. *Because the participant was put under stress.*
(4 marks)

3. When Asch interviewed the participants later, he built up a short list of reasons given by the participants for why they had conformed. State two of these reasons.
*One reason given was that the participant did not want to upset the experiment. Another reason was that the participant did not want to appear to be the odd one out.*
(2 marks)

4. Give a definition of conformity.
*Conformity is yielding to group pressure.*
(2 marks)

5. Psychologists suggest that there are different **types** of conformity: **Compliance, Normative Conformity** and **Informational Conformity**. Choose **one** of these types and describe it.
**Type** (e.g.) *Compliance*

**Explanation** *Compliance involves doing something that you know others want you to do but not changing the private thought that you would not have done this if it had not been for the others.*
(3 marks)

6. Outline **two** factors that have been shown to affect conformity.
A. *Conformity is affected by the existence of an ally. This means that if only one other person acts the way you would have preferred to have acted then you are very likely to join the other person. Asch found this when he asked one of his confederates to not conform. He found that the participant was much more likely to give the correct answers to the questions on line length.*
B. *A second factor that can affect conformity is the size of the majority. If the participant is faced with only one confederate then conformity is very low and if there are two then conformity increases. This increase in conformity continues with three confederates but after this conformity does not increase very much. It looks, then as though we will conform to three people as much as to ten. Again, Asch found this out be varying the number of confederates in the groups.*
(4 marks)

7. Suggest how an individual might establish his or her own territory in daily life.
*Territory is an area that a person claims ownership of – even though it may be like rented accommodation and the person may not be the legal owner but merely have responsibility for it. In this case, we can see that the "individual touches" that a person puts on his or her property are ways of establishing territory. The fence or hedge around the garden and the garden gates are the most obvious symbols of "This is my territory". Further outside decoration – the colour a house is painted, the style of the garden and so on can also be ways in which an individual may establish territory.*

*Inside the house too, people may mark their territory out from the rest of the family's territory. A son or daughter may wish to decorate a bedroom in a particular style or just put up posters. At work, people may want to personalise their office to make it their "territory" – even the plants people bring to work can act as symbols of territory.*
(4 marks)

**Total possible marks = 20**

These answers are only examples. Your answers may be different yet still attract full marks. For feedback and comments on your answers you should consult a tutor. If you already have tutorial support you should send a copy of your answers to the tutor.

# Example Answers to OCR Exam-Style Questions: Phobias

Source A Behavioural Psychology
Phobias

---

## Little Albert's Phobia

Two psychologists, Watson and Rayner, caused a small child, Albert, to be afraid of white, furry objects. They put a number of play objects in front of Albert. One of the objects was a white rat. Albert played happily with all the objects, including the rat. After some time Watson and Rayner banged a metal bar with a hammer every time he moved towards the rat and this caused Albert to cry in a fear response. They did this a number of times, waiting on each occasion until Albert started to play with the white rat before banging the metal bar.

After a number of trials, Albert was seen to cry when the rat was brought into his view, without the metal bar being banged. He had been given a fear of white rats. It was also noted that Albert would cry at the sight of other white, furry objects like cotton wool, a white rabbit and a white beard.

To rid Albert of the phobia, the experimenters let him see and then play with the rat many times without banging the metal bar. Albert lost his fear of other white, furry objects too.

---

1. Draw a line between the psychological term and the correct event or object

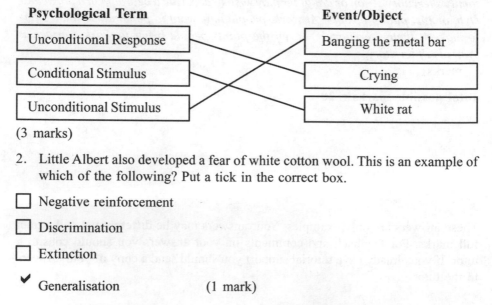

| Psychological Term | Event/Object |
| --- | --- |
| Unconditional Response | Banging the metal bar |
| Conditional Stimulus | Crying |
| Unconditional Stimulus | White rat |

(3 marks)

2. Little Albert also developed a fear of white cotton wool. This is an example of which of the following? Put a tick in the correct box.

☐ Negative reinforcement

☐ Discrimination

☐ Extinction

✔ Generalisation          (1 mark)

3. (a) Give a definition of "phobia"
*An irrational fear of an object, event or person that poses no real threat*
(1 mark)

(b) Name and describe a common phobia. Name: *Agoraphobia* (1 mark)
Description
*Agoraphobia is a fear of open spaces. This can include just ordinary spaces outside the house – the garden, street or other ordinary place, not necessarily a wide open desert or grand beach. The fear is not just a slight discomfort but can even be strong enough to cause the sufferer to vomit just at the thought of the outside world.*
(2 marks)

4.  In the past, some psychologists have argued that all human behaviour can be explained using conditioning theory. State one limitation to explaining human behaviour in terms of classical or operant conditioning.
*This approach dehumanises us; it takes no account of our motivation, wishes, aspirations, hopes or conscious understanding of our selves.*
(1 mark)

5.  Phobias can be explained in alternative ways to conditioning theory. Briefly describe one such alternative.
*Sigmund Freud suggested that phobias were the result of unconscious mental processes – often produced by guilt or the failure to resolve a complex like the Oedipus complex.*
(3 marks)

6.  Social Learning Theory uses conditioning principles along with other concepts. Outline the basic principles of Social Learning Theory using evidence from psychological studies.
*An important idea in Social Learning Theory is Imitation. This theory suggests that we tend to imitate the behaviour of others. Bandura carried out a study in which a group of children were made to observe an actor* behaving aggressively towards a bobo doll – a doll that stands back up again if you knock it down. After watching the actor a group of children were left alone with the doll and were observed to imitate the acts of violence. Children who did not observe an actor in this way did not perform the violent acts towards the doll when they were left to play with it.

*Social Leaning Theory also involves Vicarious Learning. This is the idea that if we see someone being rewarded for a behaviour then we are likely to perform the behaviour ourselves. It is similar to the idea of Conditioning where, as Thorndike's Law of Effect says, behaviours that are rewarded are likely to be repeated. Bandura's study did not support this, however. Children who saw an actor being rewarded for acting aggressively towards a bobo doll were not more likely to act aggressively towards the doll than children who did not see the actor rewarded.*

*Another important aspect of this theory is that people are more likely to imitate the model (the person who is copied) if certain features of the model and the situation are present. For example, if the model is similar to the person, then the person is more likely to imitate the model (e.g. if the model and person are both from the same ethnic group). If the behaviour is relevant to the person (e.g. the person is a boy and the model is an adult male so the boy sees adult male behaviour as relevant to him) or if the behaviour is appropriate (e.g. the person is a girl and the behaviour is about a sex-appropriate thing like make-up) then the person is more likely to imitate the model.*

*Sometimes, the person goes beyond imitating the model and instead "identifies" with the model. The person puts him or her self in the shoes of the model and acts "as if" he or she were the model. This allows the person to adopt behaviours that have not been seen but that would probably be displayed in those circumstances by the model.*

*Although the basic principles of Social Learning Theory are based on conditioning principles and suffer from the same drawbacks – e.g. they assume we are not in control of our behaviour but are at the mercy of the rewards of society – the theory does allow us some control in the way that we choose to imitate some models but not others.*

(8 marks)

These answers are only examples. Your answers may be different yet still attract full marks. For feedback and comments on your answers you should consult a tutor. If you already have tutorial support you should send a copy of your answers to the tutor.

# Example Answers to OCR Exam-Style Questions: Aggression

**Source A Behavioural Psychology**
**Aggression**

Researchers asked parents to list all the programmes a child watched in a week then, using this information, added up all the hours the child spent watching programmes considered to be aggressive. The researchers also asked the child's peers to rate how aggressive they thought the child was on a scale from 1 to 10 where 1 is "not aggressive" and 10 is "very aggressive". The results are displayed in the following scattergram.

Hours per week
Watching Aggressive
TV Programmes

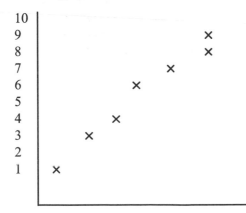

Scattergram to show the relationship between the time a child spends watching aggressive programmes on the television and a rating of aggressiveness in the child, supplied by the child's peers.

Peer rating of Aggressiveness

(a) What is the peer rating of aggressiveness for a child who watches 1 hour of aggressive television programmes per week?

*1*

(1 mark)

(b) What do the results show is the relationship between television watching and aggression in the children?

*The more time spent watching aggressive programmes, the higher the peer rating of aggressiveness (or vice-versa).*

(2 marks)

(c) Why can we not say from the above results that watching aggressive television programmes causes children to be aggressive?
*Because it could have been that children who were naturally more aggressive tended to watch more aggression on television, which would mean that cause-effect was the other way round.*
(1 mark)

(d) What is meant by "cultural differences in the levels of aggression"?
*"Cultural differences" refers to the idea that societies or groups of people have different ideas about what is an acceptable level of aggression.*
(2 marks)

(e) Outline the findings of a study of cultural differences in levels of aggression
*Margaret Mead studied three tribes in the South Pacific and found aggression levels were different. There were low levels of aggression in the Arapesh, high levels in the Mundugamor and a reversal of Western gender roles in the Tchambuli who had aggressive females and passive males.*
(3 marks)

(f) Most studies investigating gender differences in aggression find that males show more aggressive behaviours than females. How would the social learning theory explain this?
*People imitate examples of others. Boys are presented with models of males who are more aggressive than females. Bandura showed that people imitate models who are relevant, appropriate and similar, so boys will imitate men's behaviour rather than women's. They are also presented with media images of aggressive males being rewarded with success so this acts as vicarious reinforcement. Parents also reward boys for being aggressive and discourage girls from being aggressive.*
(3 marks)

(g) Give one criticism of the social learning theory explanation of aggression
*Most of the evidence for this theory is based on artificial, laboratory studies.*
(2 marks)

(h) Outline and evaluate the psychoanalytical approach to aggression
*Freud's idea was that when we are born we act instinctively and think unconsciously. The part of our mind that we are born with is the Id which is a biologically based mechanism driven by the Libido. The energy of the Libido consists of two competing instincts: one to live (Eros the life instinct) and one to die (Thanatos, the death instinct).*

*Whilst it may seem illogical to suggest that we are driven by an instinct to die, Freud cited the fact of suicide as a manifestation of this instinct as well as the fact that millions of people went to war in the knowledge that they stood a good chance of dying during the two world wars.*

*Thanatos drives us to put ourselves in positions where we may die and these are also the situations in which we express aggression – fights, battles and so on. To Freud, then, aggression is unavoidable; it builds up until it is released and the best way to deal with it is to accept it and channel it into harmless or even useful*

*directions like competitive sports. This will allow it to be dissipated in socially acceptable circumstances.*
(6 marks)

These answers are only examples. Your answers may be different yet still attract full marks. For feedback and comments on your answers you should consult a tutor. If you already have tutorial support you should send a copy of your answers to the tu

# Example Answers to OCR Exam-Style Questions: Attachment

Source A Developmental Psychology
Attachment

---

## Hospital Visit

Baby X was brought into the hospital waiting room by her mother who pointed out the toys to the child. The mother attempted to encourage the child to look at and play with the toys but the child was clinging to the mother and would not allow himself to be put down. The assistant entered the room and the child ignored her. The mother put the child on the floor and the child cried bitterly. The mother left the room to go for her x-ray and the child continued to cry. The assistant tried to comfort the child but the child ignored the assistant and continued to cry. The mother returned from her x-ray and picked up the child who continued to cry. The child would not stop crying for quite some time despite the mother's attempts to comfort him.

---

(a) How did the baby behave when the mother showed him the toys?
*The baby clung to the mother and would not allow himself to be put down.*
(1 mark)

(b) What type of attachment does the child's behaviour reflect? Tick the correct box.

☐ Securely attached   ✔ Insecurely attached   ☐ Anxious avoidant (1 mark)

(c) Describe Bowlby's work relating to Maternal Deprivation
*In his theory of attachment Bowlby suggested that mother love in infancy is as important as vitamins and proteins. He proposed the idea of monotropy – i.e. the idea that babies will instinctively form an attachment to one person – usually the mother – and that this attachment is fundamental to the well being of the child. The mother will also have an instinct to form this attachment. Bowlby's idea stems from his psychoanalytical background.*

*If this attachment is broken, Bowlby said that there would be serious consequences. This was his theory of Maternal Deprivation. The consequences included **affectionless psychopathy and intellectual retardation (as well as dwarfism – i.e. a failure to grow physically.)***

*In a study of 44 juvenile thieves Bowlby claimed evidence to support his ideas. His study showed that the ones who were affectionless tended to be the ones who had been separated from their mothers.*
(6 marks)

(d) Give **two** criticisms of Bowlby's work on Maternal Deprivation
*One criticism is that Bowlby failed to differentiate between **Deprivation and Privation**. Deprivation is the situation in which children form bonds which are later broken when the child and mother are separated. Privation occurs when children do not have the opportunity to form the attachment in the first place.*
*A second criticism is that Bowlby's idea of Maternal Deprivation fits too closely with the policy of western governments at the time the theory was published – that it was a convenient way of getting women back to the kitchen so that men could retake their positions at work on their return from the second world war.*
(4 marks)

(e) Describe **one** study of the long-term effects of breaking attachment bonds
*(e.g.) Rutter studied a group of boys on the Isle of Wight who had been taken into care for a variety of reasons. The behaviour of the boys was observed and rated by the staff as **well-adjusted** or **maladjusted** (behaviour problems). If separation causes behavioural problems, how could it be that some of the separated children were not maladjusted? Rutter found that the boys who were maladjusted were the ones who had experienced conflict and discord whilst the well-adjusted boys had been taken into care because of housing problems or the hospitalisation of the mother. Separation from the mother was not in itself the cause of behavioural difficulties for the child.*
   *In this sense, Rutter found that good attachment bonds could withstand separation but poor attachment was associated with maladjusted behaviour.*
(3 marks)

(f) State the difference between deprivation and privation
*Deprivation refers to the situation in which a child has developed an attachment bond with an adult but then been separated from the adult. Privation refers to the situation in which a child does not have the opportunity to form an attachment bond in the first place.*
(2 marks)

(g) Using your knowledge of psychology, outline an example of a cultural variation in childcare practices
*It is common practice within the Shona people of Zimbabwe, for a mother and a child to undergo an extended period of separation. At about the age of 2 years the child goes to live with its grandparents. Grandfathers take responsibility for boys and grandmothers take responsibility for girls. The child stays with its grandparents for about five years then goes back to live with the mother and completes its childhood with her. This is quite different from Western society where it more common for children to stay with their parents for the whole period of childhood and adolescence.*
(3 marks)

These answers are only examples. Your answers may be different yet still attract full marks. For feedback and comments on your answers you should consult a tutor. If you already have tutorial support you should send a copy of your answers to the tutor.

# Example Answers to OCR Exam-Style Questions: Cognitive Development

> Egocentrism is the tendency to see the world only from our own point of view. Piaget's theory of how our thinking develops as we get older suggests that up to the age of 7 years, children can only see the world from their own point of view. He discovered this by making a model of mountains and placing various objects on the model to represent buildings for example. He asked children to look at the model from one point of view and choose a photograph that corresponded to how the scene would look from a different point of view. In general, children up to age 7 could not do this and tended to choose the picture of the scene as they saw it themselves at that moment. After the age of about 7, however, children could perform this task successfully.

(a) According to the source, what does egocentrism mean?
*The tendency to see the world from our own point of view.*
(1 mark)

(b) In Piaget's test what would a child of 12 years usually do if asked to pick correctly a photograph showing the scene from a different point of view?
*The 12-year-old child would be able to carry out the task correctly.*
(1 mark)

(c) What is the name of the stage at which children become able to decentre?
*The Concrete Operational Stage*
(1 mark)

(d) Describe **one** other feature of this stage of cognitive development.
*Children become able to conserve. That is, the child can understand that the shape of a piece of plasticine can be changed whilst the **amount** of plasticine remains the same (is conserved).*
(2 marks)

(e) Piaget also carried out studies that led him to propose the idea of **conservation**. Describe **one** such study.
*Piaget lined up a row of about six counters and asked a child to watch while he placed an identical row below it, matching the rows counter-for-counter. He asked the child to say whether or not the two rows had the same amount of counters in and the child confirmed they did. He then spread out the counters in one row and*

*asked the child which row had the most counters. Children below about 7 years tended to say the row that had been spread out had the most counters. Above this age, they tended to say the rows still had the same number of counters.*
(3 marks)

(f) Outline **one** criticism of the study you described in (e) above.
*One criticism of this study is that the child may be misled by comments from the investigator like "Are you sure?" which may have led the child to alter the answer on the assumption that the investigator would not have asked "Are you sure?" if there was not something wrong with the first answer.*
(2 marks)

(g) Piaget suggested that cognitive development occurs through the processes of **assimilation** and **accommodation**. State what each of these concepts means.

**Assimilation**

*Assimilation refers to the way in which a schema for one situation can deal with another which is very similar. For example, the schema for grasping a bowl can cope with grasping a toy. The toy is assimilated into the schema for grasping.*
(2 marks)

**Accommodation**

*Accommodation refers to the way in which a schema for one situation cannot cope with another situation and has to change (to accommodate itself to the new situation). For example, the schema for grasping a bowl may have to change to allow for a new schema for grasping the handle of a toy hammer.*
(2 marks)

(h) Outline **one** study that produced findings that questioned Piaget's theory
*McGarrigle and Donaldson replicated Piaget's conservation study using the counters. For their replication, however, they made a change to the routine in which, instead of simply spreading out the counters, they used a hand puppet – Naughty Teddy – who came along and "messed up" the row. When they used this method, the children were much more likely to say that the two rows still had the same number of counters and that Naughty Teddy had simply spread them out a little.*
(4 marks)

(i) Give **one** criticism of Piaget's theory other than the existence of contrary findings from other studies.
*The idea that people suddenly "jump" from one stage to another in all aspects of their cognitive abilities seems too simple. People may be at different stages for different aspects of their thinking and it may be that the process from one stage to another is much more complex than waking up one morning having moved from pre-operational to concrete operations.*
(2 marks)

These answers are only examples. Your answers may be different yet still attract full marks. For feedback and comments on your answers you should consult a tutor. If you already have tutorial support you should send a copy of your answers to the tutor.

# Example Answers to OCR Exam-Style Questions: Aspects of Morality

Source A: Moral Development Individual Differentiation
Aspects of Morality

---

## Androcles and the Lion

*In this famous fable, a slave, Androcles, helps a lion and is rewarded.*

Androcles was fleeing from the Romans when he hid in cave. As he went further into the cave he saw a lion and was overcome with fear as the lion suddenly let out a tremendous roar. Androcles thought the lion would kill him but he noticed that it was holding its paw strangely so instead of escaping he looked carefully and saw a thorn in the paw. He removed the splinter and the lion's roaring stopped. Androcles then ran from the cave but fell straight into the arms of the Romans.

About a year later the Romans took Androcles to fight as a gladiator in the great Coliseum. He was full of fear as he was pushed into the arena and the gates locked behind him. In front of him a huge lion paced around the arena then ran towards him roaring for blood. But the lion suddenly stopped. It was the same lion that Androcles had helped in the cave. The lion licked and caressed Androcles instead of eating him. The crowd was so amazed at the lion's behaviour that they thought Androcles must posses some special qualities and the Emperor released him.

---

1. What did Androcles do to help the lion?
*He pulled a thorn out of the lion's paw.*
(1 mark)

2. What reward did Androcles receive for helping the lion?
*The lion did not attack him in the arena. (and/or) The lion licked and caressed him.*
(1 mark)

3. An important principle in the Social Learning theory of moral development is "imitation". How might this principle play a part in children's moral development if they are told the story of Androcles?
*Children may imitate Androcles's behaviour and be kind to animals and they may extend this to being kind to people.*
(2 marks)

4. From your knowledge of psychology, give an example of a study that supports the principle that people imitate morally good behaviour.
*Bryan and Test found that motorists were more likely to stop and offer to help a*

*woman whose car tyre was flat if she was already receiving help from another passing motorist. The first helper acted as a model for other motorists to imitate.*
(4 marks)

5. Piaget considered that moral development occurred through fixed stages. In the table below, enter the information about his theory in the blank spaces. One space has already been completed.

| **Stage of Moral Development** | *Heteronomous* | Autonomous |
|---|---|---|
| **Approximate Age** | *Up to 8 years* | *8 years and over* |

(3 marks)

6. Give **one advantage** and **one disadvantage** of Piaget's theory

**Advantage**

*Piaget's theory fits the evidence he collected and his theory of cognitive development.*
(2 marks)

**Disadvantage**

*Two stages do not seem sufficient to account for the different moral decisions and behaviour we would expect from people. For example, Piaget's theory would predict that teenagers and older people would share the same moral decisions but this often does not seem to be the case.*
(2 marks)

7. Outline possible methodological and gender biases in research into moral development.

*The clearest criticism of gender bias came from Milligan who pointed out that women seemed to be shown as inferior in morals compared to men according to the major theorists who were all male. Kohlberg's studies put women at lower levels of the development stages than men and Freud's theory suggested that men were motivated to achieve higher moral levels than women.*

*An important part of Piaget's studies were based on questions related to games of marbles and boys usually play this, so the studies are really of boys 'ideas, not girls'. Also, the dilemmas posed as part of the investigations were mostly centred on the notion of what is "just". Gilligan argued that women's ideas about what is right centre around ideas of caring for others rather than justice, so the theories of Piaget and Kohlberg are based on men's ideas.*

*Bias also occurred in the methods used by Piaget when he used his own relatives as participants in his studies – this meant the children would be biased towards giving Piaget the answers they thought would please him and the answers would be coloured by their knowledge of what Piaget was like.*
(5 marks)

These answers are only examples. Your answers may be different yet still attract full marks. For feedback and comments on your answers you should consult a tutor. If you already have tutorial support you should send a copy of your answers to the tutor.

# Example Answers to OCR Exam-Style Questions: Attitudes of Prejudice

**Source A Individual Differentiation**
**Attitudes of Prejudice**

---

### Welcome to the club!

"Hi Asif, welcome to the club"

"Huh; hi"

"You look down Asif, what's the matter?"

"Its nothing, just the bus journey over here"

"What about it?"

"Well, I travelled all the way from town and the bus filled up and I was the only non-white on it."

"So what?"

"So there was one empty seat and it was next to me but nobody took it, that's what. Two elderly people even stood at the front rather than sit next to me. I felt like rubbish"

"What, no-one at all sat on it?"

"Well there was a bloke who sat on it just before I got off – but he looked gay!"

---

(a) Why did Asif feel that other passengers were prejudiced against him?
*Because none of them sat next to him on the bus: he felt this was because he was not white.*
(1 mark)

(b) What do psychologists mean by the term *prejudice*?
*Prejudice means judging someone before you know anything about the individual. The judgement is usually negative and is often based on the assumption that the person belongs to a group and that all members of the group are like that.*
(2 marks)

(c) Each of the terms in the following list corresponds to one of the words in the left hand box below describing the components of prejudice. Put the correct term from the list in the right hand box. **List**: discrimination, stereotyping, dislike

| Affective component | *dislike* |
|---|---|
| Behavioural component | *discriminating* |
| Cognitive component | *stereotyping* |

(3 marks)

(d) Ethnocentrism involves seeing the world only from your own cultural point of view. Give an example of ethnocentrism that you have studied.

*In Japan it has been traditional to "slurp" as you eat noodles or other food, as a compliment to the cook; the more you slurp, the bigger the compliment. In the west, such a noise would be considered rude – but this would be seeing slurping through western eyes. The younger generation in Japan is beginning to adopt the western view, much to the dismay of the older generation.*

(2 marks)

(e) What do psychologists mean by *stereotyping*?

*Stereotyping involves simplistic beliefs about what a particular group of people is like. An example of this would be the idea that all French people like eating frogs' legs and snails. Any individual we meet who is from the group is seen as having those characteristics.*

(2 marks)

(f) Describe and evaluate **one** psychological theory of prejudice with which you are familiar.

*Adorno suggested that prejudice comes from having an authoritarian personality. People with such a personality are ethnocentric, Fascist, conservative and anti-Semitic. This sort of person, then, thinks that other cultures are inferior and cannot understand that other societies have different beliefs, values and ways of behaving that are just as valid as his or her own. Authoritarian personalities don't like change and are upset when things do change; they dislike Jews and tend to have other extreme Right Wing political views. Adorno suggested that this type of personality develops from a strict upbringing. He based his beliefs on a statistical analysis of personality questionnaires.*

*Evaluation: Being prejudiced does seem to fit this personality type as the inflexibility it suggests would be "protected" by such prejudiced beliefs. Whilst it may explain the prejudice of some people, it is difficult to see how it can be an explanation for situations like the hatred of Jews in Germany during the 1930s; not all Germans could have had authoritarian personalities and strict upbringings.*

(7 marks)

(g) Describe **one** means of reducing prejudice according to psychologists

*Reducing conflict between groups may be one possible way of reducing prejudice. Sherif showed how a group of boys who were made to compete for prizes would develop prejudices about the opposition group. He also showed that removing the competition and replacing it with the need to co-operate and work towards a common goal would reduce the prejudice. In real life, this can take the form of, for example, people in a mixed-race residential area working together to achieve better facilities for the whole area.*

(3 marks)

These answers are only examples. Your answers may be different yet still attract full marks. For feedback and comments on your answers you should consult a tutor. If you already have tutorial support you should send a copy of your answers to the tutor.

# Example Answers to OCR Exam-Style Questions: Memory

**Source A Cognitive Psychology**
**Memory**

> As part of a television game show, Estelle had to memorise twenty objects that passed in front of her on a conveyer belt rather quickly. She succeeded in remembering all the objects and when asked by her friends afterwards how she managed to succeed Estelle said:
>
> "I just said the name of each item as it passed in front of me. I said it to myself loud and clear. Then when I had to recall them, I said each word and each one sort of reminded me of the next sound."

(a) **Encoding** refers to the form in which an item is represented in our memory. What type of encoding did Estelle use in her TV game task?
*Acoustic*
(1 mark)

(b) Name one other type of encoding used by humans in memory.
*Visual*
(1 mark)

(c) Describe a study that indicates that acoustic coding is used in the Short Term Memory.
*Wicklegren asked participants to read and remember a list of words; he then asked them to do the same with a second list. Finally, he asked the participants to recall the first list. One group of participants had similar sounding words in the first and second list. Another group had no similar sounding words. The groups with similar sounding words made most mistakes so Wicklegren argued that the sounds in the second list must have interfered with the sounds in the first. This meant that the memories must have been encoded in sound – acoustic coding.*
(3 marks)

(d) Outline Atkinson and Shiffrin's two-process theory of memory.
*There are three stages in this model. The first stage is the Sensory Information Store. Sensory information comes into this store and is held for up to about one second; the majority of it is forgotten. Some, however, is attended to by the person (e.g. the person's own name is very likely to be attended to whilst other names will not). This allows the information to be passed to the Short Term Memory Store. Information in this short-term store may last for a few minutes to, perhaps, a few*

*hours. Much of this information is also discarded but if it is repeated (rehearsed) in short term memory then it may be passed to the Long Term Memory Store. For example, we may have put our times tables into long term memory by repeating them often in the classroom. Information may last in the long-term memory for up to a lifetime.*

*This model is called a "Two Process" model because the information is processed twice; once from Sensory Information Store to Short Term Memory and a second time from Short Term Memory to Long Term Memory.*
(5 marks)

(e) Describe **one** piece of evidence that supports Atkinson and Shiffrin's theory.
*The Primacy and Recency Effects are often seen as evidence for this theory. If participants are asked to memorise a list of about 20 words in two minutes they are likely to recall words towards the beginning and end of the list rather than those in the middle. Remembering the words at the beginning of the list is known as the Primacy Effect and remembering those at the end is known as the Recency Effect. This is consistent with the multistore model because the memory has had time to rehearse the words that appeared at the beginning of the list and put them into Long Term memory. The words at the end of the list were presented recently so they are still in Short Term Memory.*
(3 marks)

(f) Briefly describe **two** theories of forgetting.
***Motivated Forgetting****: Freud suggested that we forget because the item we want to remember is somehow painful to us; forgetting is a defence mechanism that protects us from the trauma we would suffer if we remembered the item. We forget the appointment with the dentist because we are afraid of the pain that may result from the appointment.*

***Interference****: According to this theory, new memories may interfere with old memories and vice versa. We forget because one memory has affected another. When old memories interfere with new ones we refer to it as "Pro-active Inhibition". When new memories interfere with old ones we call it "Retro-Active Inhibition".*
(4 marks)

(g) Evaluate **one** of the theories you have described in (f) above.
*It is not usually possible to verify Freud's theory by collecting empirical evidence because the ideas in the theory are based on processes that Freud says are unconscious. Freud's ideas are often criticised for being unscientific because they rely on case studies. However, sometimes, empirical evidence can be collected on these ideas and some psychologists argue that case studies are just as scientific as experiments.*
(3 marks)

These answers are only examples. Your answers may be different yet still attract full marks. For feedback and comments on your answers you should consult a tutor. If you already have tutorial support you should send a copy of your answers to the tutor.

# Example Answers to OCR Exam-Style Questions: Perception

---

## Perceptual Constancy

Perceptual constancy is the ability to keep our perception of an object constant even though the image of it on our eye is distorted from how we know it to be.

Turnbull studied a tribe of pygmies in the Congo in the 1960s. They had no experience of seeing for long distances as they lived in dense jungle and had never experienced seeing more than a short distance in front of them. When he took one of the tribe out of the forest and onto the plain the pygmy thought that buffalo in the distance were insects. This is because the image of the buffalo on the eye is about the same size as an insect close up. The pygmy had to be taken up to the buffalo and was confused as to how they had "grown" as he got closer.

---

1. According to source A, what is perceptual constancy?
*The ability to keep our perception of an object constant even though the image of it on our eye is distorted from how we know it to be.*
(1 mark)

2. What type of perceptual constancy had the pygmy in source A not acquired?
*Size constancy*
(2 marks)

3. Name **one** type of perceptual constancy **other than the one in question 2** and give a brief explanation of what it is.
(**Name**) (e.g.) *Brightness constancy*
(1 mark)
(**Explanation**) *We sometimes move from a bright light to a duller light but we fail to notice that we have become duller and so have any objects we are carrying. As we move back into a brighter light we become lighter and so do the objects but as far as we are concerned our level of brightness has remained constant.*
(3 marks)

4. What is a "Depth Cue"?
*Anything that causes us to understand how far away from us an object is.*
(2 marks)

5.  Describe **one** depth cue with which you are familiar.

(e.g.) *Gradient of texture is a depth cue. When an object is close we can see a lot of detail of its surface. We can see individual stitches in the sleeve of a shirt we are wearing, for example. When an object is further away we see less detail. We see a smooth surface of the sleeve of the shirt worn by somebody at the other side f the room for example. The level of detail – or texture – of an object guides us towards knowing how far away it is.*

(3 marks)

6.  Describing and evaluating two psychological studies, outline the role of nature and nurture in the development of perception.

*Both nature and nurture play a part in the development of perception. Gibson and Walk conducted a study that seems to provide evidence that nature plays a part in perception. They constructed apparatus on which a baby could be placed on a surface covered in Perspex and allowed to crawl. The baby was never in any danger but the apparatus gave the appearance that half-way across there was a drop – the "visual cliff" – though the Perspex continued across this "drop". When Gibson and Walk put the baby on the "secure" side it started to crawl towards its mother on the other side of the apparatus. However, when the baby reached the point at which the surface under the Perspex fell away it stopped and refused to continue, even though the baby's mother encouraged it to carry on.*

*At first sight this study supports the idea that babies are born with the ability to perceive the drop – which implies that they can perceive depth. However, one of the flaws with the study is that if the babies can crawl they must be some months old and we are not really examining neonates (newborn) but infants who have had the opportunity to learn about depth – even if it is only by rolling off a changing mat. We cannot rule out this evidence, however, and it does give some support to the notion that some of our perceptual abilities are the result of nature.*

*On the nurture side, Hubel sowed together the eyelids of a newborn kitten and allowed it to grow to maturity. This immediately seems a very cruel thing to do to an animal and the ethics of this are very questionable but experimenters argue that it certainly could not be done with humans and so is a good way of gathering evidence. When the cat reached maturity it had poor perceptual abilities compared to normal cats, suggesting that perceptual abilities are learned as a result of interaction with the environment. This is very strong evidence for a role for nurture. Some people argue that cats are not human so we cannot conclude anything from studying cats, but cats have visual equipment and neural pathways that are very similar to humans so the evidence may be more use than thought.*

*The evidence suggests that both nature and nurture processes play a part in the development of human perceptual abilities.*

(8 marks)

These answers are only examples. Your answers may be different yet still attract full marks. For feedback and comments on your answers you should consult a tutor. If you already have tutorial support you should send a copy of your answers to the tutor.

# Example Answers to OCR Exam-Style Questions: Stress

**Source A Bio-psychology**
**Stress**

---

A note is circulated to all staff:

## Stress at Work

As part of management's commitment to supporting staff in attaining the right Work/Life balance, the board of directors has arranged for Stress Limits Limited to visit the offices next month. Stress Limits Limited will help any staff who want to take advantage of their services by:

- Performing a complete individual Stress Audit
- Pinpointing the sources of stress in your life – both at work and at home
- Recommend suitable methods of stress control so staff can cope with the demands of work, family and other areas of life.

The service will be completely free and completely confidential. Any member of staff wishing to take advantage of this service should contact Personnel.

---

1. According to the source, where may the sources of stress be?
*At work and at home*
(1 mark)

2. Give a definition of stress
*Pressure on a person that causes psychological or physical damage*
(2 marks)

3. Outline the physiological signs of stress
*Seyle noticed a syndrome of physiological reaction that he divided into three stages. In the first stage was an alarm reaction. This was what many psychologists refer to as the Fight or Flight response. In this stage the body prepares itself for action as heart rate increases, respiration increases and other bodily changes take place designed to make the body ready to fight or flee.*

*In the second stage, which Seyle called the resistance stage, the alarm reaction dies down but the system of hormones, the endocrine system, continues to produce hormones that protect the body from the continued stress. The third stage is the exhaustion stage and this is when the continuous production of hormones has caused the depletion of the body's resources and the body can no longer fight back. Psychosomatic illnesses are more likely during this stage as the body can no longer protect itself – its immune system is too weak. Symptoms like ulcers, heart*

*disorders or other serious physiological signs are shown.*
(4 marks)

4.  Outline **one** behavioural sign of stress
*Learned helplessness is one behavioural sign of stress. This is a situation researched by Seligman, in which a person under stress reacts to it by "giving up". This does not necessarily mean that the person gives up all aspects of life but starts to exhibit behaviour in which any difficulties are not tackled.*

*Seligman showed how people who are put in situations with problems that are literally impossible to solve (designed to be impossible by the researcher – although the participant is not aware of this) "learn" this reaction and display it when put in a situation with a problem that is resolvable. Seligman suggested that this could develop into "hopelessness" in which the person displays behaviour much akin to depression.*
(4 marks)

5.  Describe **one** physiological way of measuring stress
*A common method involves the Galvanic Skin Response Meter. This is simple device that can be bought by the public. It sends a very small current of electricity – only the strength of a torch battery – over the surface of the skin. As we sweat (a physiological reaction to stress) the resistance of the skin is less and so the current passes more easily and the meter detects this. It can emit a whistle or hum or other noise that changes its pitch to indicate increase or decrease in sweating. This, then, is indicating increases or decreases in stress.*
(4 marks)

6.  Describe research into **two** causes of stress, for example heat, noise, pollution, architecture, crowding or stressful life events.
*Holmes and Rahe asked ill people to list all the important life events that had happened to them in the three months before their illness. They found that there was a correlation between the seriousness of the illness and the level of life events involving change that had happened to them. They assigned points to the events and compiled a "Social Readjustment Rating Scale" which would predict whether or not a person was likely to become ill according to the life events they had experienced.*

*Calhoun put rats into a closed system of "rooms" with enough food and water. The rats reproduced but had to share the same amount of space. As the rats became more crowded so the amount of aggressive behaviour rose. As well as increases in aggression, Calhoun noted that the rat behaviour was deteriorating in other directions. For example, the young rats were not being looked after and some were being eaten. The anti-social behaviour was taken as a measure of stress and so Calhoun concluded that overcrowding could cause stress.*
(5 marks)

**(Total possible marks = 20)**
These answers are only examples. Your answers may be different yet still attract full marks. For feedback and comments on your answers you should consult a tutor. If you already have tutorial support you should send a copy of your answers to the tutor.

# Example Answers to OCR Exam-Style Questions: Sex and Gender

**Source A Bio-Psychology**
**Sex and Gender**

> Tourist 1   "Wow! Look at that guy in a skirt! Hey London sure has
>     some strange people walking around. You wouldn't see a
> man in a skirt back home."
> Tourist 2   (Wife of Tourist 1) "But Henry…"
> Tourist 1   "How can he stand there like that with a skirt on? How
>     come nobody says anything?"
> Tourist 2   "But Henry…"
> Tourist 1   "Men shouldn't walk around like that. Back home the guys
>     would give him such a hard time he couldn't stand it. Men
> should be hiking in the woods or fishing or something. He
> should be drafted into the army. That would soon change the
> way he dressed!"
> Tourist 2   "Oh for goodness's sake, Henry, he's a Scots Guardsman on
>     duty wearing a kilt – it's part of his uniform!"

1.  According to source A, what does Tourist 1 think the Guardsman is doing
    wrong?
*Wearing a skirt*
(1 mark)

2.  The phrase "Cultural differences in gender development" refers to the idea
    that different cultures are brought up to believe that different things are
    appropriate behaviours for males and females. What is the cultural difference
    in gender development between Tourist 1 and the Guardsman in Source A?
*The guardsman has been brought up to believe that men can wear kilts but the
Tourist hasn't*
(1 mark)

3   Psychologists distinguish between *sex identity* and *gender identity*. Amir was
    born with the outward appearance of a boy but later in life he asked for
    operations to change him into a female.
        (i)    What is Amir's sex identity?       *Male*    (1 mark)
        (ii)   What is Amir's gender identity?   *Female*   (1 mark)

4   What is androgyny?

*The existence of both male and female characteristics in one person*
(2 marks)

5    Male sperm cells contain one X chromosome and one Y chromosome. What chromosomes do female ovum cells contain?
*Two X chromosomes*
(1 mark)

6    Describe **one** piece of evidence that supports the notion that gender behaviour is influenced by our biology.
*Money came across the case of a boy who had the victim of an accident during his circumcision. His penis had been so badly damaged that it was decided to remove the remainder of it. Money encouraged the parents to bring the child up as a girl. A vagina was formed through surgery and hormone implants were used to simulate those of a female. The child was treated as though he were a girl and did seem to assume he was a girl for a while, displaying "typical" female behaviours. Eventually, however, the child grew confused by the female role and suffered to the extent that his parents decided to tell him the truth about his accident and upbringing. He opted to continue his development as a male.*

*This suggests that the biological forces were strong enough to overcome the attempts to reverse the child's gender and sex.*
(4 marks)

7    Describe and evaluate the social learning approach explanation of how gender is acquired.
*Children imitate the behaviour of models they see as relevant and similar. Bandura's research generally supports this idea. Girls will see other females as relevant and boys will see other males as relevant, so gender behaviour will develop by this process of modelling behaviour. Apart from this, they will be encouraged to copy such behaviour by direct rewards and punishments given by others. For example, boys may be told they are "strong like daddy" or girls may be told they are "good girls for helping in the kitchen like mummy" so their gender behaviour will be reinforced by these rewards. Children will also be punished for displaying cross-gender behaviour. Faggot found, for example, that boys are more heavily criticised for displaying female behaviour than were girls for displaying male behaviour. Children will also imitate behaviour that they see others being rewarded for – this is known as vicarious reinforcement. For example, boys will see detectives on television using force to overcome the criminals – the police will be rewarded for this behaviour by achieving success. However much girls enjoy football they will not see female football matches at the centre of media sports attention – as they will male football matches.*

*As well as imitating behaviour, children come to identify – this occurs when we "put ourselves in the shoes" of the model and act **as though we were** the model. This is taking gender identity to its fullest extent; we "become" the male or female when we do this.*

*There is considerable evidence to support the social learning explanation of gender identity. Apart from the Bandura and Faggot studies mentioned above,*

*Smith and Lloyd observed the behaviour of adults who were presented with a baby that was sometimes dressed and named in the opposite sex to its real sex. They reported how adults would encourage the babies to adopt stereotypical gender behaviours. Also, the general theory of conditioned behaviour that underpins social learning theory has a lot of evidence to support it.*

*In criticism of this approach we can cite the importance of biological influences as shown in the failure of Money's attempt to change the sex of the child victim of a circumcision accident. Also, the theory doesn't explain why some people display less stereotyped gender behaviour than others and why some people completely cross their gender.*
(9 marks)

These answers are only examples. Your answers may be different yet still attract full marks. For feedback and comments on your answers you should consult a tutor. If you already have tutorial support you should send a copy of your answers to the tutor.

# Example Answers to Methods of Investigation

**A1** An experiment was carried out to find out how group norms affect the way we conform. The experiment was carried out as follows.

A random sample of 20 students aged 16 to 19 was obtained from a college population of 300 students

The 20 students were allocated to one of two groups A or B, 10 in each group. Each group had a further 50 members who were confederates of the experimenters so each group contained 10 true participants and 50 confederates. The confederates in group A were of a **similar age** to the participants. The confederates in group B were **much older** than the participants

**Group A (same age)**
The members were asked to estimate the number of beans in a jar. Each of the confederates was asked to give an estimate out loud then each participant did the same

**Group B (different age)**
The members were asked to estimate the number of beans in a jar. Each of the confederates was asked to give an estimate out loud then each participant did the same.

The estimates given by each group of participants were compared

a) State the independent variable
*The age of the confederates*
(1 mark)

b) State the dependent variable
*The estimates given by each group of participants*
(1 mark)

c)  What experimental design was used?
*Independent measures*
(1 mark)

d)  State **one** reason for using this design
*It gives a good chance that the participant variables in both control and experimental groups will be similar*
(1 mark)

e)  What is meant by the term *random sample*?
*A random sample is a way of selecting items in such a way that each item has the same chance of being selected.*
(1 mark)

f)  How would you have obtained a random sample for this experiment
*We could go to the College registry and, with the college's permission, obtain a list of all the students enrolled at the college, put each name into a box individually and pull out 20 at random without looking at them. We could then ask the college to send our letter to the 20 students inviting them to take part in the study.*
(2 marks)

g)  Identify **one** extraneous variable that should have been controlled in the experiment.
*Gender.*
(1 mark)

h)  Why should the variable you have identified in g) have been controlled?
*Males or females may be more susceptible to the opinions of others and if all the participants in one group were one sex and the other were the other sex and there was a difference between the scores of the groups we would not know if it was the sex or the age of the confederates that had caused the difference.*
(2 marks)

i)  The results of the experiment are given in Table 1, below. Use the information given in Table 1 to complete Table 2 below.

*Table 1* The number of beans estimated by each student.

| Group A | | Group B | |
| --- | --- | --- | --- |
| Participant | Estimate | Participant | Estimate |
| 1 | 340 | 11 | 350 |
| 2 | 285 | 12 | 500 |
| 3 | 266 | 13 | 450 |
| 4 | 301 | 14 | 505 |
| 5 | 240 | 15 | 100 |
| 6 | 325 | 16 | 535 |
| 7 | 335 | 17 | 640 |
| 8 | 390 | 18 | 770 |
| 9 | 355 | 19 | 600 |
| 10 | 400 | 20 | 750 |

*Table 2* Mean, median and range scores for group A and group B

|        | Group A | Group B |
|--------|---------|---------|
| Mean   | 323     | 520     |
| Median | 330     | 400     |
| Range  | 160     | 670     |

(3 marks)

j)  Use the data in Table 1 to construct a frequency distribution using the class intervals shown in Table 3. Put your answer in Table 3. The Group A frequencies have been done for you.

*Table 3* Frequency Distribution of estimates of beans for groups A and B

| Estimate   | Group A Frequency | Group B Frequency |
|------------|-------------------|-------------------|
| 100 – 149  |                   | 1                 |
| 150 – 199  |                   |                   |
| 200 – 249  | 1                 |                   |
| 250 – 299  | 2                 |                   |
| 300 – 349  | 4                 |                   |
| 350 – 399  | 2                 | 1                 |
| 400 – 449  | 1                 |                   |
| 450 – 499  |                   | 1                 |
| 500 – 549  |                   | 3                 |
| 550 – 599  |                   |                   |
| 600 – 649  |                   | 2                 |
| 650 – 699  |                   |                   |
| 700 – 749  |                   |                   |
| 750 – 799  |                   | 2                 |
| 800 – 849  |                   |                   |

(2 marks)

k)  Use the squared paper below to display a bar chart of the results shown in Table 3. Provide a suitable heading and label the chart appropriately

Title: *Bar Chart to show frequency distribution of estimates of beans*
(1 mark)

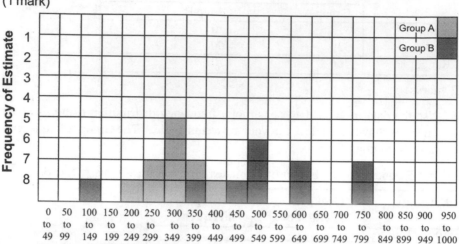

Number of Beans Estimated

(4 marks)

l) Using your knowledge of psychology, explain the different ranges of scores found between group A and group B.

*Group A was exposed to the opinions of confederates who were of a similar age. The range of their answers is much more narrow than the range of the group that was exposed to confederates who were older, indicating that they all gave similar answers. A number of studies have shown that different factors can affect levels of conformity. It is likely that participants will conform to the behaviour of people who are similar and this is reflected in the tendency to give estimates that are similar.*
(3 marks)

m) Suggest **one** way in which you could improve this experiment
*The sample could be improved by increasing its size from ten, which is a rather small number of people on whom to base conclusions.*
(2 marks)

These answers are only examples. Your answers may be different yet still attract full marks. For feedback and comments on your answers you should consult a tutor. If you already have tutorial support you should send a copy of your answers to the tutor.

# Indices

## AQA INDEX

**Major topics /sub-topics from the specification are shown in bold**

# Index for OCR

**Major topics /sub-topics from the specification are shown in bold**